Crime and Victimization of the Elderly

E.A. Fattah   V.F. Sacco

Crime and Victimization of the Elderly

Springer-Verlag
New York Berlin Heidelberg
London Paris Tokyo

Ezzat A. Fattah
School of Criminology
Simon Fraser University
Burnaby, British Columbia
Canada V5A 1S6

Vincent F. Sacco
Department of Sociology
Queen's University
Kingston, Ontario
Canada K7L 3N6

Library of Congress Cataloging-in-Publication Data
Fattah, Ezzat A., 1929–
    Crime and victimization of the elderly / E.A. Fattah, V. Sacco.
    p. cm.
    Bibliography: p.
    1. Aged offenders—North America.   2. Aged—North America—Crimes
against.   3. Crime and age.   I. Sacco, Vincent.   II. Title.
HV6791.F37   1989
364.3′0880564—dc19   89-5903
                                                                        CIP

Printed on acid-free paper.

Camera-ready copy prepared by the authors.
Printed and bound by Edwards Brothers, Ann Arbor, Michigan.
Printed in the United States of America.

9 8 7 6 5 4 3 2 1

ISBN 0-387-96973-X Springer-Verlag New York Berlin Heidelberg
ISBN 3-540-96973-X Springer-Verlag Berlin Heidelberg New York

TO OUR WIVES

PREFACE

The unprecedented and continuing growth of the North American elderly population means that increasing numbers of older citizens will come into contact with the criminal justice system in one capacity or another: as offenders, victims, complainants, witnesses and so on. In the presence of these changes, we are slowly learning about the crime problems of older persons. We are discovering that elderly offenders are different in many ways from younger ones; that patterns of victimization of the elderly are not identical to those of other adults; and that the level of fear of crime among the elderly is not only higher than it is among other age groups but that it is also disproportionate to the volume of actual victimization suffered by senior citizens. The force of social and demographic change and the fragmentary nature of much of our knowledge points to the need to study the problems of elderly offenders and elderly victims.

To this end, we offer in the chapters that follow a "state of the art" review of the available literature on crime and the elderly. Because criminology and social gerontology are both interdisciplinary areas of study, the relevant research literature is not the exclusive domain of any one behavioral science. Instead, it cuts across a wide array of disciplines including sociology, psychology, nursing, economics, psychiatry, social work and policy studies, among others. Our intention is not merely to organize and summarize this knowledge but also to subject it to critical assessment.

We are guided by the belief that social scientific knowledge about crime and the elderly is essential for the development of policies, programs and strategies aimed at preventing crimes by or against older persons. We also believe that understanding deviant behavior that occurs in later life, as well as the exploitation and abuse of the elderly can lead to a better understanding of many of those aspects of the lives and behavior of senior citizens that lie beyond the realities of crime and crime control.

Throughout our discussion we have tried to remain faithful to Nils Christie's definition of the role of the criminologist as a problem-raiser rather than problem solver. Our interest centers around asking the pertinent questions without necessarily providing the answers; defining the issues but not always offering their resolution.

We hope that this material will be of interest and of value to the student of criminology or gerontology and to the social service professional who works with older persons. We have tried to organize the book in a way that anticipates the needs of the user. For this reason, we include an introductory chapter that details the demographic and social dimensions of the elderly population of North America. The remaining chapters are divided into two major sections; the first deals with the elderly offender and the second concerns elderly victims of crime. Because of the relatively low degree of overlap, we have kept separate the bibliographic references associated with each section. This, we hope, will facilitate access to these materials.

We wish to express our sincere appreciation to the many people who assisted in the completion of this project. We are grateful to Karlene Faith of the School of Criminology, Simon Fraser University, who oversaw the preparation of the distance education course out of which this book emerged. We would also like to thank Colin Yerbury and the staff of the Centre for Distance Education at Simon Fraser University for their technical assistance and patience in the early stages of our collaboration. We are also grateful to Robert F. Kidd of Springer-Verlag for his enthusiastic response to our initial proposal. A debt of gratitude is owed to Chris Walmsley and Fiona Kay for their editorial assistance in the preparation of the manuscript; and to Elia Zureik for helping, in very practical ways, to move this book along. The support staffs of the School of Criminology at Simon Fraser University and the Department of Sociology at Queen's University also provided help in numerous and varied situations. We are also very grateful to the Faculty of Arts and Science and the School of Graduate Studies and Research at Queen's University for making available the financial support which allowed the manuscript to be brought to fruition.

Finally, we wish to thank our families for their understanding and tolerance, without which this book would still be in the planning stages.

CONTENTS

PART I

CRIME AND THE ELDERLY

WHO ARE THE ELDERLY?

INTRODUCTION

At what age should a person, male or female, be considered old? When does "middle age" cease and "old age" begin? There is no satisfactory or universal answer to these questions. Aging is a process and there is no agreed cut-off age between these two phases of life. The selection of age 65 as the demarcation between middle and old age is, therefore, an arbitrary one. The choice of this age, as Butler and Lewis (1982:5) point out, has been made for social purposes, as a means for determining the point of retirement or the point of eligibility for various services available to older persons. In their book on Canada's older population, Stone and Fletcher (1980) address the question "Who is a senior citizen?". They write:

> There is no simple and completely defensible answer to this question. Chronological age alone is a poor basis for classifying people according to their social, health, and economic needs and capabilities. An arbitrary line drawn at ages 65 or 55 is even less acceptable in principle. Yet we are forced to adopt such arbitrary lines as they are the ones used in almost all of the available statistics. In adopting these arbitrary boundary lines, we hasten to acknowledge that the older population is a "statistical grouping" of highly heterogeneous individuals and families. The needs, problems, and assets of these families vary greatly. Statistics for the whole group necessarily obscure such variations, while portraying an "average or group situation" that may have no concrete reality from the perspective of an individual family. (1980:1-2)

This view is echoed by Butler and Lewis (1982), who note that age 65 has limited relevance in describing other aspects of functioning such as general health, mental capacity, psychological or physical endurance, or creativity, and for our purposes we can add criminality. Moreover, the 65 and over age group lends itself to further categorization. Several gerontologists divide the over-65 into two subgroups: early old age comprising those aged 65 to 74 and advanced old age including those who are 75 or older (ibid.). Others distinguish between the "old" (that is 65 to 74), the "very old" (that is 75 to 84) and the "old old" (that is 85 and over).

From a criminological viewpoint, that is, for examining crimes committed by or against the elderly, the designation of elderly status only from age 65 might not be quite appropriate. To differentiate between victims of crime who are under or over 65 years old may make some sense. However, age 65 is much too advanced for a consideration of criminality of old age. In almost every society for which statistics are available, arrest data consistently indicate a sharp drop in the proportion of arrestees in the 55 to 59 age category with a leveling off of the curve for the 60-64 and the 65 and over age groups (see Shichor & Kobrin, 1987). For studying criminality in old age, age 55 may, therefore, be a more appropriate cut-off point. A breakdown by age, for criminological purposes, may thus be:

Under 14 15-24 25-34 35-44 45-54 55 and over

The elderly (whether defined as those 65 and over or 55 and over) do not constitute a homogeneous group. The rates of crime committed by, and against, the elderly are likely to vary among the various sub-groups. Crime and victimization differentials are likely to be found not only among age sub-categories but also among health sub-categories (the healthy /the sick; the able/the disabled; those suffering from mental deficiency or mental disorder and those who are not; those who have an alcohol problem and those who have not; and so on). Variations are likely to exist among residence sub-categories (those placed in some sort of institutional care; those living on their own, alone; those living with spouses, mates, friends or relatives of the same generation; those living with younger family members; those living in high crime areas and those living in low crime areas; those living in age-segregated housing projects and those living in age-integrated housing projects and so on). Differences may also be found between different income groups (those who are financially independent and those who are financially dependent on others; those who are financially well-off and those who live on a low income, and so on).

Some gerontologists have criticized chronological age as the criterion for distinguishing between the elderly and other age groups. They point out that other ages, such as the "functional age" which relates to the ability to perform a job, may be more appropriate for such distinctions. Hahn (1976) offers a distinction between the strict chronological age and three others:

1. personal age: that is, how old a person seems to himself/herself;

2. interpersonal age: that is, how old the same person seems to others who know him/her;

3. consensual age: that is, the degree of agreement between the personal age and the interpersonal age.

If age is supposedly one of the criteria criminals take into account when choosing their victims, then it is not the chronological age but the interpersonal age that is of importance. Unless the chronological age of the prospective victim is known to the attacker (as in cases where the two are related) the assess-

3

ment of the victim's vulnerability will be made on the basis of how old he/she appears to the offender.

THE AGING OF THE NORTH AMERICAN POPULATION

In recent years a major shift in age structure of the population in North America has taken place. A decrease in the number of births coupled with increased longevity has led to a disproportionate increase in the size of the upper age groups in the general population.

In 1900, there were approximately three million persons 65 years and over in the USA, that is one person in every 25. By 1980, the number has swollen to 24 million, or one person in every 9. By the turn of the twenty- first century, there will be 30 to 33 million elderly citizens or one in every 8 persons. More broadly, in the USA today, there are six times as many 55 year olds, eight times as many 65 year olds, and ten times as many 75 year olds as in 1900. In contrast, the total population of the USA has barely tripled in this time, (see Butler and Lewis, 1982).

Both the absolute and relative numbers of the 65 and over age group are increasing rapidly. Butler and Lewis (1982:5) report that at the end of 1981 there were an estimated 25.6 million elderly persons 65 years and over in the USA. In mid-1979 most older people were under 75 (61.9%); over half were under 73; more than a third (35.2%) were under 79; and about 9% (2.3 million) were over 85 years of age.

In 1851, in Canada, 2.7% of the population was over 65; by 1901 the same age group constituted 5% of the total population. The percentage rose to 6.7 by 1951 and 9 in 1980 (Myles, 1981;35).

In 1971, there were 1.7 million Canadians aged 65 and over. But population projections (Statistics Canada, 1984; Romaniuc, 1974) indicate that we can expect the number of senior citizens in Canada to increase to 3.3 million by the end of the century, and to 8 million by the year 2031 when approximately 20% of the Canadian population will be aged 65 and over. Another report "One in Three: Pensions for Canadians to 2030" published by the Economic Council of Canada (1979) projects that by the year 2030 one out of every three Canadians over the age of 21 will be over 65 and, therefore, dependent on the working population between 21 and 64 to support them.

According to Statistics Canada (1984), the 65 and over age group is the fastest growing component of the population. It is predicted that if present trends continue, Canada will have unprecedented numbers of older people, particularly in what has been termed the "old-old" category (i.e., 85 years and over). In the year 2031, the more than 400,000 Canadians 85 years or older will represent a 300% increase from the 137,000 in this age category in 1971.[1]

The marked change in the age structure of the North American population and the unprecedented growth in the numbers and percentage of the upper age groups can be traced to several factors:

1. Great improvements in life conditions: hygiene, nutrition, health care, physical fitness, and so on. The North American population is much more health conscious now than it used to be. Working conditions are con-

4

tinually improving and there is an enhanced awareness of health hazards associated with the work place or with certain types of occupations. More and more people are ceasing to smoke. Exercise has become a very popular pastime. People are constantly trying to improve their health and physical fitness through changes in their lifestyle and dietary habits.

2. Great progress in medicine resulting in vast advancements in the diagnosis, treatment and prevention of many diseases, in particular killer diseases such as strokes, heart attacks and other cardiovascular diseases, especially high blood pressure (the silent killer). In recent years, techniques for the detection and early treatment of certain types of cancer have vastly improved. The discovery of antibiotics and anti-viral substances has dramatically increased the recovery rate from various diseases that used to claim a large number of lives. The result of all this has been a significant increase in longevity and an enhanced life expectancy. The current life expectancy at birth in Canada is 69 years for males and 77 years for females. Moreover, among those 60 years old today, women can expect to live another 22 years to age 82, men another 17 years to age 77. At age 65 life expectancy is 18 years for women and 13.5 years for men; and at 80, about 8 and 6 years respectively (see Havens, 1982). In the United States, the average life expectancy in 1900 was 47 years and only 4% of the population was 65 years and older. In 1979, the average life expectancy at birth was nearly 73 years and over 10% of the population was 65 and older.

3. A marked decline in the birth rate in the last twenty- five years or so brought about by affluence, urbanization, better education, modern technology, and new methods of birth control as well as an apparent increase in abortions. While people are living longer, fewer babies are born. The net result is a general aging of the population, a phenomenon which has been called "the greying of America"; the upper age groups are swelling, the lower age groups are shrinking.

4. Migration; the early waves of migration to Canada brought to the country large numbers of adult single males. These immigrants reach the upper age groups faster than children born in the country, thus inflating the size of these groups in relation to others. They also contribute to a higher mean or median age for the total population. Bringing in parents or other aging relatives under the sponsored immigrant system also adds numbers to the older groups.

GENDER AND MARITAL STATUS OF THE ELDERLY POPULATION

In all western societies, elderly females out-number elderly males. Women, on average, live longer than men. Besides having lower death rates at all age levels, females are not afflicted so much as men by the two main killers in our later years, namely cancer and heart disease.

The demographic changes in Canada in recent years, together with the changing age structure of the Canadian population, have been responsible for a substantial and growing imbalance in numbers between females and males. According to Stone and Fletcher (1980), in the first half of this century males outnumbered females slightly in all of six selected age groups of the population 55 years and over, excepting that of 80 years and over. Since 1961, females have been predominant in the population aged 65 and over. They add that Canadian society has never experienced imbalances between older males and females of the order that are now being projected for the next two decades and beyond (1980:3).

Because of the discrepancy in life expectancy at birth and in longevity between the two sexes, there is usually a larger number of widowed females. This is accentuated by the fact that men tend to be older than their spouses.

A majority of elderly women 65 years and over are widowed, while the majority of elderly men are married. In Canada, almost 75% of all men aged 65 and over are married and only 15% are widowed. But among the women, approximately 40% are married and almost 59% are widowed (Havens, 1982). Canada's sex ratio at the present time is 77 males to 100 females aged 65 and over, which is higher than that of the USA and that of many of the developed nations. The higher sex ratio is the result of a large, predominantly male immigrant wave in the early decades of this century (ibid.,p.13).

The marital condition of the elderly population south of the border is not much different. For example, in 1975, 53% of older women were widowed compared to 39% who were married. On the other hand, nearly 79% of older men were married and only 13.6% were widowers. For every man over 65 who is unmarried, there are four older women who are unmarried.

The living arrangements and residential patterns of the elderly population reflect to a large extent the male/female differences in marital status. The percentage of elderly women living alone is much higher than the percentage among men and the gap tends to widen with advancing age.

In Canada, Stone and Fletcher (1980) found that the popular image of most older persons being abandoned to lives of destitution in institutions by negligent relatives is not supported by available data. They affirm that only a small fraction of the older population (about 8%) resides outside private households. The authors do predict, however, that by 2001, nearly 67% of females aged 65 and over will be living without a spouse.

Another trend noted by Stone and Fletcher (1980) is the growing metropolitanization of the elderly population. They point out that, like the total Canadian population, the aged have increasingly become metropolitanized and this trend is expected to continue:

In 1976, over one million of Canada's two million older people lived in Census Metropolitan Areas (CMAs). The projections indicate a rising proportion of Canada's older population living in CMAs, from about 53 percent in 1976 to about 58 percent by 2021. In 1976, the three largest CMAs (Toronto, Montreal and Vancouver) together contained 28.6 percent of the Canadian population age 65 and over... In all three CMAs, the senior citizen population is projected to grow by more than 75 percent from 1976 to 2001. (1980:22,26)

This trend has important criminological and victimological implications since the rates of crime and of criminal victimization are much higher in urban centres than they are in rural areas.

THE PLIGHT OF OLDER PEOPLE IN WESTERN SOCIETY

In rural, agricultural societies where the extended family is still the dominant pattern of social grouping, the elderly are better integrated than in western, industrialized societies where the dominant pattern is the nuclear family. Moreover, in less developed societies, old people do not suffer the same loss in status and power that retired people suffer in western societies. In agrarian societies, old people continue to perform useful, productive tasks unless hindered by sickness or disability. They also possess much needed knowledge and coveted secrets and enjoy the status and power that go with such knowledge. In societies with limited formal education, and few professionals, knowledge and expertise are acquired from experience; those with the most experiences are the most knowledgeable. The elderly are the living reservoirs of knowledge and the young have no choice but to seek their wisdom, help and advice. This means that elders have to be treated with dignity, respect and veneration.

The situation of the elderly in western societies is quite different. Those in their middle age dread growing old because of all the losses they have to endure in the autumn of their lives.

Dr. Eric Pheiffer (1971) described old age as a "season of loss", meaning that old age for most people means a series of age-related losses: income, status, the loss of one's spouse and companions, and the decline of one's physical and mental powers. For many elderly people these interrelated factors produce what may be viewed as a vicious cycle: crisis of old age may lead older people to isolate themselves, yet isolation often leads to increased loneliness and anxiety or depression. There is also the vicious circle of isolation and fear: fear leads to, and is aggravated by, isolation. When people are afraid they isolate themselves and when they are isolated their fear increases.

Physical Decline

Aging is a process leading to physical weakness and a decline in bodily strength. Even when the old person is not suffering from disease, is not afflicted by any handicap and is enjoying relatively good health, his or her physical strength is bound to decline with age. In addition, old age is usually accompanied by the weakening (or even the loss) of some of the senses, particularly hearing and eyesight. The criminological importance of this decline is that it increases vulnerability to victimization and makes the elderly easier targets than younger age groups. On the other hand, the decline in hearing and eyesight may render the elderly more suspicious thus instigating them to take certain measures to protect themselves and their property.

Mental Decline

According to Roth (1968), the organic psychoses of the aged are the commonest form of cerebral disease seen in the psychiatric hospital and clinic. Many elderly persons, in particular the very old, i.e., those over 75, suffer from severe and progressive cerebral damage, the end result of which is the syndrome of dementia. Dementia is a state of deficient and disorganized intellectual and personality functioning, the main features of which are impairment of memory and orientation, failure of grasp, failure of concentration and capacity for conceptual thought, loss of emotional control leading ultimately to blunting of affect, and disturbances of consciousness which may in the early stages be variable and thus associated with striking fluctuations of mental state (Roth,1986:35).

The effects of cerebral damage are not confined to deficits in mental functioning. They include schizophrenia-like states, depression and other affective disorders, hallucinoses, neurotic syndromes and personality change (ibid. p.35).

Such mental decline and those symptoms brought about by old age can have forensic, medico-legal, and criminological implications and are quite important for understanding and dealing with criminal behavior in old age. (See Chapters Three, Four, Five and Six).

Financial Decline

Old age is generally accompanied by a decline in economic and financial strength resulting from:

- lower income: since pensions are invariably lower than salaries, retirement means a lower income for most people.

- fixed income: the majority of old people live on fixed income. The plight of those living on fixed income in an inflationary age is too well known to need much elaboration. Suffice it to point out that even where pensions are indexed to inflation, indexing is usually limited to the small portion of income that comes from the government, that is old age pension. The net result is a sharp decline in purchasing power.

- growing financial and economic dependency: many elderly people have to rely on younger family members or on the state for subsistence and survival.

Butler and Lewis (1982) note that poverty, like substandard housing, is typically associated with old age. People who were poor all their lives can expect to become poorer in old age. But they are joined by a multitude of people who become poor only after becoming old. They point out that in the USA, in 1978, about 14% (3.2 million) of older people were below the official poverty level (measured by an annual income of $3,116 for a single person and $3,917 for a couple). According to Butler and Lewis, a more realistic poverty line would put the percentage at 25%.

The same authors report that older persons receive half the income of younger persons. In 1978, in the USA, half of the families headed by an older person had incomes of less than $10,141, as compared with $19,310 for families with heads under 65. The median income for an older person living alone or with non-relatives was $4,303, compared with $8,530 for those under 65.

In Canada, the National Council of Welfare (an advisory group to the federal health minister) reported in 1984 that one of every four people over the age of 65 is still living in poverty, though the poverty rate has fallen sharply in the last 15 years. In a report summarized by Canadian Press (The Sun, Vancouver, Feb. 9, 1984) the Council attributes the improvement to government-run programs such as the federal old-age security pension and guaranteed income supplement as well as the Canada and Quebec pension plans. As a result, the percentage of old people (65 years and over) living below the poverty line went down from 41.4% in 1969 to an estimated 11.7% in 1982. Among people over 65 living alone or with non-relatives, the decline was less dramatic, to an estimated 57.7% below the poverty line in 1982 from 69.1% in 1969.

Despite those overall trends, the report says that more than 600,000 of Canada's 2.5 million people over 65 are poor, and slightly more than two-thirds of them are women. The report also points out that the poorest of the elderly poor have little or no outside income other than from governments, and they qualify for the maximum federal guaranteed income supplement as well as the federal old-age pension paid to all persons 65 and older. A single person with income from only those sources received a total of $6,147 in 1983 when the poverty line for single people ranged from $7,052 in rural areas to $9,538 in the largest cities. A couple with the old-age pension and maximum supplement got $10,883 in 1983, and the poverty line for a family of two ranged from $9,218 to $12,583.

The report shows striking differences in the percentage of elderly people living below the poverty line in different parts of the country. In 1981, for example, the percentage of families headed by people over 65 who were living in poverty ranged from a low of 10.1% in B.C. to a high of 22.2% in Quebec. The provinces with the lowest rates - B.C., Alberta, and Ontario - were those with the most generous provincial supplements.

The criminological importance of the financial decline in old age cannot be overestimated. As will be seen later on, many elderly people are forced to live in the poorer districts of town with characteristically high rates of street crime. Their mobility is reduced and they have to use public transportation such as the bus or the metro where the chances of being victimized are high. The poor financial situation of the elderly also means that the consequences of criminal victimization, whether personal or property victimization, are usually more dramatic and traumatic.

It would be incorrect, however, to speak of old age only in terms of negation, decline, physiological, psychological and economical regression, involution, or diminishing values and abilities, or to look upon it as an essentially pathological stage of life (see Pollak, 1941). It would also be inaccurate to define old age, *per se*, as a stage of pathological changes. As Pollak (1941) points out, old age, like every other age, has a psychology of its own which, for this stage of development, is normal. What is essential is to distinguish between the normal characteristics of ald age and those traits which are truly pathological. Nor should one forget that alongside the somewhat undesirable psychological traits usually associated with old age (such as slowness, dissatisfaction, lack of humor, dependence, conceit, reminiscence, stubbornness, over-criticism, suspicion, depression, and so on) there is a large number of positive traits. These include experience, wisdom, ability to keep perspective, power of organization and conservation, serenity, unselfishness, tolerance and dignity (ibid.,p.215). Nevertheless, negative attitudes toward old age are quite prevalent in western societies.

Society's Negative Attitudes to the Elderly

In western society, where the emphasis is on work, activity and productivity, negative attitudes abound toward weak, inactive and unproductive groups (such as the old, the disabled, the handicapped, the mentally retarded, the unemployed, etc.). Not only are they made to feel inferior, burdensome and unwanted, but many of them are also dumped in institutions or special homes to keep them out of sight and out of mind.

These prevalent negative social attitudes generate specific feelings among senior citizens, feelings that have become associated with age. The following list is not meant to be exhaustive and it should be stressed that although these feelings are common in old age, many old people, because of their own make-up or environment, do not suffer from them or their consequences:

- feelings of helplessness and of lack of control over one's environment;

- feelings of being prisoner of one's own weakness, of being restricted and confined as a result of physical inability, incompetence, physiological ailments, or simply as a result of reduced mobility;

- feelings of resignation, sometimes bordering on despair;

- feelings of being rejected, unwanted, discarded and unloved;

- growing sense of futility, purposelessness, unproductiveness, combined with feelings of superfluity and failure, feeling of being burdensome or troublesome;

- growing sense of vulnerability and defenselessness accompanied by feelings of insecurity and fear, of distrust and mistrust, as well as mounting suspiciousness. These feelings may lead to withdrawal, isolation and consequently increasing loneliness and solitude.

For some elderly persons, the effects of the feelings listed above may be quite positive through submergence into intense religiosity, or charitable, benevolent activities aimed at helping others and alleviating the sufferings and misery of some unfortunate, handicapped or underprivileged groups. For others, these negative feelings may lead to situational stress, depression, neurosis, functional psychosis, alcoholism, dependence on drugs, criminality or suicide.

10

NOTES

1. These projections are similar to the ones cited by Stone and Fletcher (1980). The authors note that in 1921, only five out of every one hundred Canadians were aged 65 and over. This proportion rose gradually until the 1950s, when the post-war baby boom reversed the trend until the 1970s. It recommenced in the 1970s, and by 1976 9% of the national population was aged 65 and over. According to Stone and Fletcher, unless there is an upsurge in birth rates in the near future, about one percentage point will be added to the proportion aged 65 and over every ten years up to the turn of the century. By the year 2006, the "leading" edge of the baby boom generation will enter the ranks of senior citizens, and population aging could then escalate rapidly for twenty-five years. Without another upsurge in birth rates, some 18% of Canadians will be age 65 and over in 2031, when the aging process will again slacken its pace markedly. Stone and Fletcher (1980) also point out that in 1901, there were eight persons aged 65 and over to every one hundred aged 15-64. This percentage will double near the end of the century. By 2021, it may reach about 24%, and rise still further to about 29% by 2031.

CHAPTER ONE: RECOMMENDED READINGS

Bengston, V.L. and D.A. Haber.
1975. Sociological Approaches to Aging. In D.S. Woodruff and J.E. Birren (Eds.) Aging. New York: Van Nostrand.

Butler, R.N. and M.E. Lewis
1982 Aging and Mental Health. 3rd edition, Toronto: The C.V. Mosby Co. (Chapter One: Who are the elderly? pp.3-22.)

Statistics Canada
1984 The Elderly in Canada. Ottawa: Minister of Supply and Service. Catalogue 99-932.

Stone, L.O. and S. Fletcher
1980 A Profile of Canada's Older Population. Montreal: Institute for Research on Public Policy. (Chapter One: Introduction, and Chapter Two: Population Aging in Canada. pp. 1-27.)

CHAPTER TWO

AGE AS A CRIMINOLOGICAL VARIABLE

INTRODUCTION

Since the dawn of scientific criminology, age has been identified as the most important criminological variable. On the basis of their statistical studies of criminality, Guerry and Quetelet declared that age is the factor that has the greatest impact on crime. In 1839 Quetelet wrote:

of all the causes which influence the development of propensity to crime, or which diminish that propensity, age is unquestionably the most energetic.

He also reported that with advancing age cunning replaces force and trickery replaces violence in the commission of crime. Subsequent criminological research on the relationship between age and crime confirmed the findings of Guerry, Quetelet and their followers.

Hirschi and Gottfredson (1983) point out one basic and persistent fact constantly revealed by available data, namely that the age- crime relation is invariant across sex, race and culture. Victimization surveys conducted in the last two decades revealed that age is not only an important correlate of criminality but also of victimization. There is a linear negative relationship between age and crime as well as between age and victimization. Older individuals are much less likely to commit crimes and much less likely to be criminally victimized than more youthful individuals. Both of the negative relationships seem to be universal. Everywhere, the young tend to prey upon the young. Other factors being equal, it is safe to say that cities with aging populations have less crime than cities with youthful populations.

The influence of age is not limited to criminality. Hirschi and Gottfredson (1983) insist that behavior analogous to crime also declines with advancing age. Motor vehicle accidents, for example, drop with age regardless of the social characteristics of the drivers. Data they present on motor vehicle accident rates in New York State among those eligible to drive, by age, closely parallel those

12

for crime. They also refer to several studies showing similar relations between age and rule-breaking in prison, one of them (Flanagan, 1981) reporting that "the most adequately established correlate of misconduct among prison inmates is age". Hirschi and Gottfredson reproduce a figure presenting prison infraction rates by age. When "practically everything" is held relatively constant, the age effect is much like the age effect in the free world.

The age of maximum criminality varies somewhat with the type of crime, with crimes against the person peaking later than property crimes[1]. However, if one is to single out a certain period of life at which criminality reaches its peak, at which individuals are particularly prone to delinquency and crime, then it is the period of adolescence and especially late adolescence. When delinquency rates of the different age groups are compared it becomes clear that the group of 15 to 24 commits much more crime than is expected on the basis of its size within the general population. The decline starts roughly at age 25 and the criminality curve shows a sharp drop after age 30. For reasons that will be discussed later on, a substantial portion of those persons who do have long histories of antisocial behavior show significant remission or improvement with advancing age. As Cormier et al., (1971) point out:

> We know that in the period of late adolescence and early maturity (from age 18 to 25), there is a sharp increase in criminal behavior, that soon after age 25 (the age at which it is generally acknowledged that men achieve biological maturity) this rapid rise begins to show a slow downward trend which is increasingly marked in the 30s and very pronounced after the age of 40 (1971:2).

The popular saying "life begins at 40" surely does not apply to criminal life. Except for the few chronic petty offenders who persist in their criminal careers past their 40th or 50th birthday, conventional antisocial behavior generally comes to an end before or during the fourth or fifth decade of life.

EXPLANATIONS OF THE DECLINE IN CRIMINALITY WITH ADVANCING AGE

Several hypotheses have been advanced to explain the well documented and unquestionable decline in criminality with old age. What follows is a brief summary of some of these hypotheses. Needless to say, some hypotheses sound more plausible than others and further research is needed to confirm or reject them and also to rank them by order of importance.

a)   The Burn-Out Hypothesis

With advancing age, immature, reckless youth reach a stage of adult maturity. They become more settled, less adventurous, less rebellious and less eager to defy authority or to fight the system. Conformity does not necessarily result from a change in beliefs or attitudes but may simply be due to lassitude. Antisocial attitudes may persist while behavior does change. Many of those who have spent long periods of time in prison reach a point at which they feel they have wasted their lives (or at least the best years of their lives) and decide to change their lifestyle before it is too late, to amend their ways and to avoid at

13

any cost further incarceration. In support of this hypothesis one can cite some psychological evidence showing that rebellious and antisocial tendencies decline with age. Testing with the MMPI scales, reported by Weiss (1973), revealed some interesting patterns. Though not clearly statistically significant, the analysis of mean profiles for the various age groups suggested that rebellious and antisocial tendencies tend to be less common or lower in each succeeding age group. Analysis of the "narrative contents" portion of the investigation, based on coded information from the medical records, indicated, on the other hand, statistically significant parameters among the men who were tested. Statements indicating a past history of generally hostile or aggressive behavior toward others and behavior that brought the patient into contact with law enforcement agencies decreased with age. Such statements were present in 62% of the youngest group, but were very rare or absent among the two oldest groups.

Further support for this hypothesis comes from an empirical exploration of "maturational reform" (Jolin and Gibbons,1987). The study shows that career criminals, who have withdrawn from lawbreaking, apparently go through a mid-life transition much the same way as do noncriminal men. According to the authors, at mid-life most of the career criminals in the study went through a reappraisal of their past, which was not infrequently a painful process associated with a lack of psychological well-being. As a result, some aspects of the past were relinquished and replaced with new ways of being. In the case of the ex-offenders, these new ways of being meant changed attitudes, values and behaviors, with the most notable external change being that from criminal to non-criminal behavior.

b)   The Decline in Physical Strength and Agility

Advancing age is invariably accompanied by diminishing strength, a reduction in physical agility, endurance, enterprise and initiative. This diminution is believed to be an important reason for the decline in criminal activity in old age. Aschaffenburg (1913) points out that the weakening body becomes unfit for all those crimes in which physical strength and skill are necessary. Pollak (1941) observes that with advancing years one becomes too weak to lead a criminal life. The same explanation is advanced by Moberg (1953) who points out that older persons are not as active as young people and their physical weakness and slower movements make them less capable of successfully undertaking certain types of crime. Hirschi and Gottfredson (1983) note that some crimes appear only when the strength necessary to inflict injury or coerce others has been attained. One may add that the same crimes are likely to disappear when this strength has been lost or weakened as a result of age or other physical decline. It has been frequently noticed that offenders who persist in their criminal careers usually shift to less physical and less violent types in old age. Robbery and burglary are abandoned in favor of fraud, swindling, counterfeiting or dealing in stolen goods. Anonymous letters and telephone calls replace physical violence as a means of extortion. Active and violent sex offences involving physical force, such as forcible rape, give way to less active, less forceful types like exhibitionism, voyeurism or sexual molestation of non-resisting children.

14

c)   The Decrease in the Volume of Social Interaction

Violent offences against the person are closely related to the volume of social interaction. They increase when human contacts are frequent and intense, and decrease whenever and wherever these contacts are few or sparse. Because many elderly people live alone or in relative isolation, and the volume of their social interactions is much smaller than that of younger individuals, their rates of violent crime against the person are bound to be much lower than the corresponding rates of more youthful age groups.

Furthermore, the elderly's reaction to provocation and challenge tends in general to be slower and less violent than that of young people. For those reasons, the elderly are more likely to be recipients than perpetrators of violence.

Older people are not subject to group pressure as much as or in the same way as younger people are. Peer pressures which are responsible for a significant portion of juvenile delinquency lose much of their strength with advancing age. Even in prison, adherence to the inmate subculture is much more pronounced among younger prisoners than it is among older ones. Respect for institutional rules and regulations, on the other hand, is stronger among older inmates. It should also be noted that the "gang" especially the "delinquent gang", is strictly a phenomenon of early youth, not of old age.

d)   The Change in the Direction of Aggressive Tendencies

Aggressive personalities tend to mellow with age and whatever aggressive tendencies may persist tend to be directed more and more inwards than outwards, towards oneself rather than others, thus contributing to a high rate of suicide. While criminal homicide by older persons is relatively infrequent, the suicide rate among the elderly is generally higher than that of most other age groups(see Chapter Three).

e)   Weaker Motivation and Stronger Inhibitions

Elderly persons are less motivated to commit crime than younger ones. With advancing age, at least until retirement, people earn more money, have less free time and less opportunity, and are less susceptible to temptations and peer pressure than are younger persons. They have less desire to show off and their sexual drive and potency are not as strong as in younger years. Increasing responsibilities and livelihood become more critical considerations in their lives. While young people are generally risk-takers and adventure seekers, looking for thrill, excitement and danger, most old people are risk-avoiders. Not only are they less adventurous and less thrill-oriented, but they also have more to lose if caught, punished and stigmatized, and are, therefore, less willing to take risks. It is well known that growing maturity, stability and responsibilities bring about increased caution and prudence.

f) The Successful Rehabilitation Hypothesis

Successful rehabilitation and treatment are bound to lead to a decrease in crime with advancing age. As offenders come into contact with correctional agencies and personnel (and learn how to cope with their problems), and as they realize that "crime doesn't pay", some are going to become "wiser" and will give up crime as a mode of earning a living or as a lifestyle. In other words, if treatment and rehabilitation of offenders are effective, if they do have some impact on the behavior of those subjected to them, the net result will be that some criminals are going to cease their criminal activities contributing to the decline of criminality with age. And since crime in general (at least conventional crime) is a youth activity, more delinquents will stop than will start their criminal careers in later years. In support of this hypothesis one can cite empirical evidence showing that rates of recidivism never reach 100% and that in adulthood they tend to be lower in each succeeding age group.

There is also the unsubstantiated claim that criminals live a hazardous life and do not grow old (Moberg, 1953). Referring to Tannenbaum (1938), Pollak (1941) states that one of the rather obvious reasons for the general decrease of crime in old age is the fact that criminals lead a very hazardous life under physically submarginal conditions and, therefore, do not grow old.

g) The Lower Detection Rate Hypothesis

This hypothesis is not meant to explain all the differences between the rates of crime of old and young people but to provide a partial explanation of the variance. It is argued that part of the variance could be accounted for by the lower rate of detection of old criminals. Aged offenders, it is claimed, become more skillful and more adept at evading detection and arrest. Moreover, they tend to engage in criminal activities which are harder to detect such as fraud and white collar crime (Jackson, 1981). It is also claimed that old age offenders are more likely to benefit from the sympathy of police, judges and juries than younger ones. This makes it less likely that a senescent criminal will be arrested and convicted. Even when they are, their sentences are likely to be suspended, the defendant is placed on probation, or the sentence is much lighter because of the age of the offender (Moberg, 1953).

A study carried out by Rowe and Tittle (1977) attempted to empirically test four hypotheses explaining the decline in criminality with age: a) higher social integration; b) greater reinforcement of moral standards; c) increased fear of criminal sanctions; and d) lesser motivation to commit crime. They explain the four hypotheses in the following manner:

1. As people mature they are increasingly likely to settle into predictable niches with organized social life; that is, they become more highly integrated. The more involved people become, the more they are likely to take their identities from associations with the community as a whole and from the roles they perform. Furthermore, greater social integration would be expected to lead people to become more attuned to the expectations of others for conformity and to become more dependent upon the social rewards of conformity. Age, then, would seem to imply greater social integration, which in turn should produce conformity.

16

2. Aging may be related to diminished criminality because of greater reinforcement of moral standards that results from the performance of responsible roles. Aging, at least up to the senior years, usually involves greater involvement in the commumity and performances of adult roles rooted in important social institutions. Constant reinforcement of moral standards through role performance may increasingly enmesh one in a moral web which inhibits proclivities toward deviance.

3. The age/crime relationship possibly may be explained by increased fear of sanction as people grow older. With maturity, individuals presumably acquire greater stakes in the social order so that the potential costs of sanctions increase. They accumulate material goods, they develop statuses that are dependent upon favorable reactions from others, and they come to occupy roles which would be jeopardized by non-conformity. Consequently, the older people are, the more they may be deterred by fear of the consequences of non-conformity.

4. A fourth possibility involves the motivation to commit crimes. As people grow older, particularly as they move into late middle- age and the senior years, their physical energy and capability of engaging in many kinds of crime may deteriorate. Thus the desire to steal or take chances through illegal gambling may flag with physical energy. Moreover, with age people may learn to control anger that could lead to physical assault. Therefore, the intrinsic utility of much criminal behavior may recede with age. Rowe and Tittle point out that this explanation is not particularly applicable over the entire age range nor to all crimes (cheating on income tax, for instance). They did, however, include it in their hypotheses-testing due to the fact that theoretical attention to the age problem had been so meagre.

Rowe and Tittle note that the four variables,- social integration, moral commitment, deterrence and motivation - may interact to explain the diminution of criminality with age. They write:

> It is plausible to imagine that aging implies a combination of increased social integration, moral commitment, and fear of sanctions, as well as a decrease in criminal utility. Moreover, these variables may not affect crime in a straightforward additive manner. Rather, there could be a variety of combinations of two or more of these variables which interpret the age/crime relationships. For example, high moral commitment may increase with age, but lead to conformity only when it is coupled with an increasing fear of sanctions. And high social integration may lead to less crime with age only when the utility of the particular act also decreases (1977:232-233).

The results of the statistical analysis were not surprising. They indicated a clear negative relationship between age and criminal propensity which is in part attributed to generational differences and partly to life cycle changes. According to the authors, efforts to account for the association show this relationship to be exceptionally stable and resistant to explanations. The analysis suggested, however, complex interactions among several variables as the appropriate explanation.

17

HOW MUCH CRIME DO THE ELDERLY COMMIT?

Assessments of the volume of crime committed by older citizens and an analysis of the trends and patterns in this type of criminality are subject to serious limitations. Self-report studies, as far as one can tell from the available literature, have never included older people in the populations they surveyed. The assessment of old age criminality, therefore, has to be based on official police or court statistics and to suffer from the shortcomings of these statistics. The problem of using official criminal statistics as measures of the volume and prevalence of crime are too well documented to need any further elaboration. The problems are likely to be more serious in the case of geriatric criminality. The type of offences generally committed in senescence are low visibility offences with a high dark figure: sex offences, shoplifting, fraud, and so on. The reporting rate of offences involving white-haired criminals may also be lower than the corresponding rate for younger age groups contributing further to a higher dark figure. The detection and arrest rate may, on the other hand, be higher for elderly offenders than it is for younger ones because many of the former commit their behavior in an awkward manner and fail to efface the traces of their crimes. It might therefore be easier for the police to clear up offences committed by senior citizens.

There are other problems associated with the use of arrest data as a measure or indicator of the volume of elderly criminality. The vast majority of elderly arrests are not for felonies but for misdemeanors. And the same old person may be arrested dozens of times in the same calendar year. Thus a small number of old petty offenders may inflate the total number of arrests. The same is true for the number of charges. For example, in his study of the relative frequency and pattern of offences of the elderly in Dade County (Miami), Florida, in 1980 and 1982, Wilbanks (1985) found that the large numbers of charges for sleeping on the sidewalk and disorderly intoxication were due to a relatively small number of offenders who were repeatedly arrested for these offences.

Because assessments of old-age criminality can only be based on those reported offences which have been cleared up by an arrest, charge or both, the greater portion of criminality is excluded. All offences which, for one reason or another, have not been reported to the police together with all those reported but not cleared up will not be part of the criminality being assessed. For obvious reasons, offences reported to the police in which the offender remains unknown are of no use to the study of geriatric criminality. Furthermore, there is no reason to believe that elderly offenders arrested and/or convicted constitute a representative sample of the total universe of geriatric delinquents. On the contrary, the sample is probably biased in many respects. These biases mean that generalizations cannot be made from the sample, that the traits and attributes of arrested old offenders are not necessarily those of all elderly criminals. The problems of using official police and court data to examine and analyze temporal trends in old age criminality may not be as serious if one is to assume that the biases in reporting and processing as well as the limitations of detection and prosecution do not change very much from one decade to the next. Because this assumption has never been confirmed empirically, whatever changes or fluctuations may appear in the statistics should be regarded as both tentative and suggestive rather than conclusive and definitive.

There are other problems associated with a quantitative analysis of old age criminality. Population changes require that the volume of crime be measured and presented in the form of rates rather than absolute figures. Rates computed for 10,000 of 100,000 inhabitants are far better indicators of the state of, and changes in, crime than are numbers. Because of the uneven size of the various age groups within the total population, and because crime is not distributed evenly among these groups, it is necessary to further refine the rates by calculating them separately, for different age groups. The differential sex ratio in elderly populations requires further that the rates be calculated separately for each gender.

Neither of the two most commonly used indicators of elderly criminality (namely number of arrests and number of prisoners) is an adequate measure of the volume and extent of crime committed by old people. Arrests are not good indicators not only because they do not account for the dark figure but also because a large number of arrests are alcohol-related. The elderly and the very young are the two most underreported age categories in arrest data. In the USA (and the situation should not be different in Canada) one in every three arrests is for drunkenness.

For varying reasons the number and rate of elderly persons in prisons is a deficient indicator of old age criminality. As mentioned above, the more lenient treatment of the elderly by the police and courts means that many old offenders, especially those guilty of petty offences, will be spared incarceration and will get away with a non-institutional disposition. Moreover, a large number of the elderly in prison did not commit their crimes in old age but grew old in prison. This is true of those sentenced to life imprisonment or to long periods of incarceration.

Estimates of Geriatric Criminality

In his introduction to Malinchak's book Crime and Gerontology (1980), Vernon Fox reports that according to the FBI Uniform Crime statistics for 1976 there were 75,521 arrests of persons aged 65 and over, which is 1.2% of all arrests in the USA. For Index crimes, there were 13,897 arrests of persons aged 65 and over, which is 0.6% of the arrests for these crimes. At the same time, a national survey of twenty-six sample states reported in April, 1977, in the Correctional Compendium, published in Lincoln, Nebraska, indicated that prisoners ages 65 and over average 0.5% of the total adult prisoner population, ranging from 0.2% in Colorado, Delaware, and Wisconsin to 1.3% in West Virginia. This percentage of the total prisoner population represents an estimated 1,400 prisoners aged 65 and over in the United States.

Quoting UCR data without specifying the year, Newman and Newman (1982) note that arrests of elderly criminals for ordinary crimes reach no more than 4% of all arrests reported annually. This, of course, can be higher or lower depending upon the cut-off age for "elderly". If 65 is the age, approximately 2% of arrests are accounted for by 11% of the population. If 55 is the age, then a 4% of arrests are accounted for by about 16% or 17% of the population.

Newman and Newman note that if absolute numbers rather than percentage of arrests are examined, it means that somewhere between 400,000 and

500,000 elderly citizens, over the age of 55, are arrested every year in the USA. They also point out that at the time (1982) there were about 80,000 elderly offenders in state and federal prisons. This does not include local jails and lock-ups which, if surveyed, would increase that number.

Shichor (1985) cites UCR figures indicating that in 1979 there were over 385,000 arrests of people 55 years and older; over 48,0 of these were for one or more of the seven major offences. In 1981 there were over 400,000 arrests in the same age group, out of which over 57,000 were for index offences.

Has Old-Age Criminality Increased in Recent Years?

A report published in May 1982 in the APA Monitor quotes David Shichor, a sociologist at California State University, as saying that the percentage of persons aged 55 or older who are committing crimes in the USA, while small, is increasing. He declared that since 1964 the number of arrests for major crimes committed by the elderly has risen 265% while the number of arrests within the entire population has increased by only 177%.

Another article on geriatric criminality published in *TIME MAGAZINE* (Sept. 20, 1982) reports that during the 1970s, when the number of Americans 55 or older increased by 22%, major felony arrests for that group went up 148%. From 1964 to 1979, arrests for murder by the elderly rose 200%; arrests for rape and larceny each increased by more than 300%. Arrest figures for rape remain, however, quite small.

The same article quotes Professor Donald Newman, of the School of Criminal Justice of the State University of New York, as saying that "of all geriatric crimes, none is now more prevalent than shoplifting.. it is reaching epidemic proportions.. ask any criminal court judge whom he sees across the bench at the end of the month before social security cheques arrive".

Writing in *THE JUSTICE REPORTER* (Vol. no2, No 5, Sept.-Oct. 1982) Newman and Newman point out that over the preceding 15 years the number of elderly arrests has increased faster than the number of arrests of other age categories. Depending upon the index used and the spread between dates, it appears as if the arrest of elderly violators has increased at approximately one-and-a-half times the increase in general population arrests. As Newman and Newman point out, this does not necessarily mean that crimes committed by the elderly are increasing:

> Most observers think this is a phenomenon of a shift in the age demography of our society rather than an increase in the percent of elderly involved in crime. The fact is that the United States is greying. Our population is shifting toward higher proportions of aged in the upper registers while young people have proportionately declined..And as the population shifts toward the upper ranges there will be a large population base from which elderly offenders can be drawn. Put another way, no one knows at present whether the rate of elderly crimes is increasing, but it is clear that actual numbers involved with crime are higher because of this shift in the aging of our population (1982:3-4).

In a paper entitled "White Haired Offenders - An Emergent Social Problem" presented to The Gerontological Society of America (November, 1982), Gary Feinberg analyzed UCR arrest data over a fifteen year period (1966-1980) with particular emphasis on arrest rates for age groups 55-59, 60-64, and 65 years of age and over. The following is a summary of his findings:

First, total elderly arrests by volume and rate are low. In 1980, for example, only about 3% of all arrests were of persons 55 years of age and over. In absolute numbers there were 378,393 such arrests in a field of 9,703,181 total arrests. The arrest rate for the elderly was about 800 per 100,000 as compared to an arrest rate for all ages of about 4,282 per 100,000.

Second, the total crime count by volume and rate is declining for each of the three elderly age classifications. In 1966 there were 2,014 arrests per 100,000 persons aged 55-59. By 1970 it dropped slightly to 2,009 and by 1980 it dropped further to 1,556. The total decline over the fifteen years surveyed was 23%. For ages 60-64 and 65 and over, rates declined even more dramatically: down 32%.

Third, as one advances from one elderly age category to the next, the total Crime Index arrests decline, first by about one-third and then by about one-half respectively. For example, the rate of arrests per 100,000 for Index Crimes of those 55-59 in 1980 was 190, for those 60-64 it was 129 and for those 65 and over it declined further to 64.

Finally, the elderly are significantly less likely than the general population to be arrested for homicide, rape, robbery, aggravated assault, drunkenness, or driving while intoxicated.

Despite these trends, Feinberg concludes that white-haired offenders constitute an emerging social problem. In support of this claim he advances the following evidence:

- A large number of elderly persons are arrested annually in the U.S. The number of those 55 years and over arrested in 1980 was over 378,000.

- Arrests of elderly persons for Index Crimes are increasing. Between 1966-1980 the national rate of arrests for the elderly increased by a higher percentage than the rate for all ages combined. So while it is true that fewer elderly persons are arrested for Index Crimes as compared to other age groups, their rate of increase is higher, and just as steady. This is a critical distinction since Index Crimes tend to reflect a more serious criminal problem. Feinberg adds that during the same period, rates of elderly arrests (65 and over) for each individual Index Crime, except homicide, have increased, although the increase for most of these crimes are less pronounced than for other age groups.

- Elderly arrests for certain minor offences such as vandalism and possession of weapons have also increased between 1966 and 1980.

21

- For crimes of personal violence, crimes against property, and Index Crimes *en toto*, arrest rate increases are higher for the older than the younger elderly.

The above mentioned citations may give the impression that the United States is in the midst of a geriatric crime wave. And it is precisely such statements and the publicity they generated and received in the media that led some criminologists to empirically test the claim that elderly crime has increased and is increasing at a fast pace and that the growth in elderly criminality is far greater than the growth in criminality of other age groups.

Alarmed by reports of a geriatric crime wave, Sunderland (1982) examined national crime statistics in the United States and compared the percentages of older persons arrested in 1975 and 1980. One of the patterns he observed is the relatively few arrests of older citizens (65+). Because of this, insignificant changes in the numbers are represented by big changes in percentages. Sunderland concluded that:

> if there is an "epidemic" of elderly criminality, this investigation to date has not uncovered it...For the present, the " crime wave" has not materialized and the "soaring" crime rates have been vapor. (p.44).

More recent investigations of the trends in elderly crime have used longer periods of time (as long as twenty years) and have relied upon changes in rates rather than percentages. The picture they offer of the elderly crime situation and of the changes that have taken place over the past two decades is a more subtle picture than the one Sunderland provides. The studies show that the general trends observed when aggregate offence data or arrest totals are used might mask important variations among different offences or offence categories. The studies (Covey and Menard, 1987; Inciardi, 1987; Steffensmeier, 1987) demonstrate that while elderly arrest rates in the U.S.A. have been rising sharply in the past two decades for some offences (ex. larceny-theft, driving under the influence), they have sharply declined for other offences such as public drunkenness, disorderly conduct, gambling and vagrancy. The studies further show that while elderly arrests for victimless crime have sharply declined between 1964 and 1984, there has been a sharp rise in elderly arrest rates for the Index crimes, or what the FBI labels serious crimes. However, a further analysis of the increase in elderly arrests for Index crimes over the same period reveals that larceny-theft accounts for virtually all of the increases in Index crimes by the elderly (Steffensmeier, 1987). Although larceny-theft is one of the Index offences and is classified by the FBI as a serious crime, most of elderly arrests for larceny- theft are for shoplifting or related minor thefts[2].

22

The Covey-Menard Study

Covey and Menard (1987) addressed themselves to the question of whether trends in the criminal behavior of the elderly population paralelled those in the non-elderly population or are unique to the elderly group. To explore this and related questions, the authors compared Uniform Crime Report Statistics for those aged 65 and over to totals for those under 65. Data were considered from a continuous 20 year period (1964-1983). The data enabled the authors to make two generalizations about elderly arrests: first, the elderly people were much less likely to be arrested than those in the non-elderly population for every crime, whether arrest rates (normed by the relevant population) or total arrests were the criterion. Secondly, the indexed crimes for which the elderly were most likely to be arrested differ somewhat from those for which the non-elderly were likely to be arrested. For both the elderly and the non-elderly population larceny was the index crime for which most were arrested. For the non-elderly population, burglary resulted in the next highest number of arrests, followed by assault, but for the elderly, assault was next, followed by burglary. For the non-elderly population, auto theft, robbery, rape and murder followed in order, but for the elderly, the order was murder, robbery, auto theft, and rape.

Covey and Menard found that absolute numbers of arrests have been increasing over time for both the non-elderly population and the population 65 and over. For most of the Index crimes, the pattern of increase has been fairly consistent. The exceptions are auto theft, which has had alternating periods of increasing and then decreasing arrests, and homicide, which has had a similar but less pronounced pattern of alteration.

Comparing the elderly to the non-elderly population, overall increases in arrests have been less for the elderly than the non- elderly population for all crimes except auto-theft (and total index offenses). Arrest rates for property crimes (burglary, larceny and motor vehicle theft) among the elderly population have increased faster than those for the non-elderly population, but arrest rates for crimes of violence (homicide, rape, robbery and aggravated assault) have increased more for the non-elderly population than for the elderly.

The Inciardi Study

To find out whether crime among the elderly (defined in terms of their rate of arrest) has increased, Inciardi (1987) undertook an analysis of national arrest statistics for the period 1964 through 1982. He combined the arrest totals for all Part I and Part II offences for the U.S. as a whole and compared them with those of the elderly population (persons 60 and older). He found that in the aggregate, crime within the senior citizen population has decreased and decreased quite substantially. While the general arrest rate during the period under review increased by 77.5 per cent (from 2,448.6 per 100,000 population to 4,346.0 per 100,000 population) the arrest rate of the elderly declined by some 33.1 per cent (from 769.0 per 100,000 elderly population to 528.2). Moreover, while the number of elderly persons arrested in 1964 represented 4.2 per cent of all arrests, by 1982 this proportion had decreased to only 2.0 per cent.

The analysis of individual crime categories represents a radically different picture. Thus, the arrest rate for part I offences as a whole increased by 200 per cent, from 29.0 to 87.9 per 100,000 elderly population. The rate for violent crime (criminal homicide, forcible rape, robbery, and aggravated assault) increased by 76 per cent, from 9.1 to 16.0; and the rate for property crime (burglary, larceny-theft, and vehicle theft) increased by 261 per cent, from 19.9 to 71.9. More specifically, with the exception of criminal homicide, where the rate of arrest remained fairly stable over the 19-year period, the rates in all other Part I offence categories increased. Inciardi points out that the bulk of the increase in the Part I offence arrest rate was attributable to the change in the larceny-theft category, an area that includes such property offences as purse-snatching, shoplifting, pickpocketing, theft of bicycles and motor vehicle accessories, and thefts from coin machines, buildings, and vehicles.

Inciardi draws the following conclusions from his analysis:

First, the marked decline in the general arrest rate of the elderly from 1964 to 1982 is attributable to declining rates of arrest for such offences as gambling, drunkenness, and vagrancy. The declines are not unique to senior citizens but are reflective of a national trend.

Second, while the national arrest rate for property crimes increased by 117 per cent from 1964 through 1982, the rate for elderly persons increased by 261 percent - more than double the national rate.

Third, from 1964 through 1982, the national arrest rate for violent crime increased by 167 percent - from 336.0 to 730.7 per 100,000 population. This growth was not exceeded, or even matched, by the 60-and-above age cohort. However, the arrest rate for violent crime among the elderly did increase by 76 per cent - from 9.1 to 16.0 per 100,000 elderly population, with more than four-fifths of these arrests resulting from aggravated assaults.

Fourth, from 1964 through 1982, DUI (driving under the influence) arrests increased dramatically, from a rate of 38.9 to 117.8 over the 19-year period. Inciardi suggests that this increase might be due to changes in the retirement age which have placed the elderly in social situations and behind the wheels of automobiles for longer periods of time. He adds that advances in medicine, particularly those associated with alcohol-related diseases, have meant that problem drinkers are living, and hence remaining on the highways, longer.

The Steffensmeier Study

Steffensmeier (1987) set out to establish the basic pattern of elderly crime and to determine if this pattern has changed over the past 20 years, 1964 - 1984, a period claimed to have been one of both rising levels of and more serious criminality on the part of elderly persons. Steffensmeier's study addresses three questions: 1) whether the rate of increase in elderly crime is greater than the increase in the elderly population of the United States during 1964 - 1984, 2) whether the rate of increase for elderly persons is greater than the increase for other age groups, and 3) whether within the elderly arrest population there has been a change in the profile of the elderly offender toward involvement in more serious crime.

24

Steffensmeier calculated age-specific arrest rates and used them to measure the level of elderly (65+) crime. To add stability to the arrest figures, they were summed for the 1964-1965 and 1983-1984 years and divided by the sum of the two UCR population coverage figures for those years. Among the findings of the study the following are worth noting:

- There have been sharp rises in elderly arrest rates since 1964 for three offences: larceny-theft, driving under influence and other but traffic. But the rates have fallen sharply for four offences: public drunkenness (PD), disorderly conduct, gambling and vagrancy.

- Both today and 20 years earlier, elderly arrests are overwhelmingly for alcohol-related crimes - PD, DUI, vagrancy, disorderly conduct, and OBT - with one minor intrusion in this profile - there has been a sharp upward trend in arrests for larceny-theft (often shoplifting).

- The total elderly arrest rate is considerably smaller now (that is in 1984) than in the early 1960s. The rate was 1251 per 100,000 in 1964 and 650 per 100,000 in 1984. Steffensmeier attributes this large drop to the whopping decline in the public drunkenness rate that has been only partly offset by moderate rises in DUI, OBT, and larceny-theft rates.

- There has been a sharp rise in elderly arrest rates for the Index crimes from 52 per 100,000 in 1964 to 131 per 100,000 in 1984. Steffensmeier hastens to add that larceny-theft accounts for virtually all of the increases from 1964 to 1984 in Index crimes by the elderly.

- The proportionate elderly involvement in crime has increased for 9 but decreased for 18 offences. The overall pattern is one of very little change, however, in that the absolute change in the PAI (proportionate age involvement) across most offences is small or miniscule. The conclusion is that the relative criminal involvement of the aged is about the same now (that is in 1984) as two decades ago, in spite of dramatic fluctuations in arrest rates for some offences.

- The profile of the elderly offender in the 1980s is much less dominated by arrests for public drunkenness but is equally shaped by arrests for DUI and, to a lesser extent, by arrests for larceny-theft. At present (1984), DUI and PD each make up about 22% of all elderly persons arrested, or about 45% of the total. Thus many arrests of the elderly are still for public drunkenness but far less than the whopping 60% in the early 1960s.

Steffensmeier concludes that his analysis reveals the relative infrequency of elderly criminality for all types of crime both now and in the past. It also documents the comparatively nonserious nature of elderly criminality.

Explaining the Apparent Increases in Elderly Criminality

The rise in elderly Index crime, particularly the larceny-theft category, seems to be well documented even though there is no reason to believe that geriatric criminality is reaching alarming proportions or that it has attained a state that warrants the designation of a "social problem". How can this rise that appears in the official arrest statistics be explained? Naturally without further research one cannot dismiss outright the hypothesis that the elderly, for one reason or another, may be committing some criminal offences with a higher frequency than they did in the past. In the absence of empirical research findings confirming or contradicting this hypothesis, other explanations for the apparent rise in elderly crime should be sought. The following are some suggested explanations:

First and foremost, there is the changing age structure of the population in North america and the shift in age demography resulting in a disproportionate growth of the upper age groups within the general population. As Shichor and Kobrin (1978) point out, both the absolute and relative increase of the elderly in the total population is likely to result in an increase of their number and in their relative share among suspected and actual lawbreakers. This will lead to higher numbers who will be apprehended and processed by the criminal justice system.

Secondly, it might well be that elderly offenders are being more frequently arrested than before as a result of growing intolerance toward their criminality. As the public at large and law enforcement officials become less and less tolerant of geriatric delinquency, more offences that would not have been reported will be reported and more white-haired offenders who would have been dealt with informally will be arrested and processed through the criminal justice system. According to Shichor and Kobrin (1978), there appears to be a link between the civic status of groups and the degree of criminal responsibility attributed to its members for lawbreaking acts. Any gain in political power and rise in civic status by previously powerless and low status groups is therefore likely to be accompanied by an increased attribution of criminal responsibility. With the elderly becoming an effective power block in the political arena, they are bound to incur a loss of whatever informal tolerance for infraction they now enjoy or have enjoyed in the past.

Thirdly, there is a growing availability of programs designed to deal with problems of aging including criminality. As more and more programs become available, many of the elderly who in the past would have been dismissed with a warning or an oral admonition will be processed formally so that they may become eligible for the services now provided. For example, once a new program for elderly shoplifters is set up, many of those who are now eligible for this new service and who, in the past, would simply have been asked to pay for the stolen goods, or shaken up and asked not to do it again, will now be formally processed so that they may be sent to the program.

WHAT OFFENCES DO THE ELDERLY COMMIT?

Information on the offences the elderly commit has to be based again on arrest data despite their obvious limitations.

In the USA Shichor and Kobrin (1978) analyzed UCR arrest data from 1964 to 1974 and point out that the distribution of arrests of the elderly is marked by a distinctive and somewhat surprising pattern. They show a more prominent pattern of crimes of violence than either the total arrested population or the youth group. Within the violent offences, moreover, the single category that stands out is that of aggravated assault with arrests consistent at about 80% of the total arrests for crimes of violence among the 55-plus age group.

That violent offences by the elderly are concentrated in the aggravated assault category is not too surprising. UCR Index crimes comprise four violent offences: murder, forcible rape, robbery and aggravated assault. Since the elderly's involvement in forcible rape and robbery is, for reasons mentioned above, negligible, and since murder is, for all age categories, the least common of these four offences, it is understandable that the elderly will show a concentration of arrests for aggravated assaults.

Arrests of the elderly for the serious property offences were found to be largely concentrated in the general category of larceny-theft. This offence accounted for over 90% of all arrests in this age group for the Index property offences.

Among the non-Index offences, generally misdemeanour offences, Shichor and Kobrin noted five for their prominence in the arrest statistics pertaining to the elderly. These are: drunkenness (which alone accounts for almost half of the arrests for misdemeanour offences: 46.3% in 1974), disorderly conduct, driving under the influence, vagrancy and gambling. Arrest patterns show a marked decline in arrests for drunkenness over the period analyzed, from 61.7% in 1966 to 46.3% in 1974. This is probably due to the establishment of detoxification centres in many American cities during that period. The data, on the other hand, reveal a significant increase in the proportion of arrests for driving under the influence of alcohol which rose from 5.8% in 1964 to 19.4% in 1974. This almost fourfold increase is explained by Shichor and Kobrin by increased longevity of the population and increased use of automobiles generally. An additional factor might be an increase in alcohol consumption by the elderly.

According to Feinberg (1982a), of all crimes reported, driving while intoxicated (DWI) and disorderly conduct are the most common basis for elderly arrests which is also true of criminal arrests for all age groups combined. In line with what Shichor and Kobrin (1978) reported four years earlier, Feinberg equally found that larceny is the most common Index crime resulting in elderly arrests and it also dominates as the leading form of Index arrests for adults in general.

The increase in elderly criminality did not show identical patterns to the increase for other groups. Thus, while for other age groups crimes of violence increased at a faster pace than property crime, the opposite seemed to be true

27

for the elderly whose property crime rate increased more rapidly than did crimes of personal violence.

The Male/Female Ratio

Although the percentage of females is higher than that of males in the upper age groups, arrests of elderly males generally outstrip arrests of elderly females by both volume and rate. Using UCR arrest data for 1980, Feinberg (1982a) reports that the ratio of elderly males to elderly females arrested for all listed crimes was 9.5 to 1 by rate and 5.7 to 1 by volume. This ratio is considerably higher than the national ratio by rate (standing at 5.2 to 1) but is quite similar by volume (5.5 to 1). Feinberg notes that the sex ratio of elderly male to elderly female arrests for Index crimes is very low, 2.8 to 1 using rates. The comparable national figure is almost twice as high, 4.5 to 1. Feinberg interprets this finding as indicating that with advancing age, male and female involvement in Index offences, as measured by arrest rates, becomes more equal. He writes:

> This pattern is especially characteristic for crimes of personal violence (sex ratio 1.8 to 1 by rate as compared to a national of 9.4 to 1 for such crimes). Such figures lead to the generalization that with increasing age there comes a growing similarity in the likelihood of male to female involvement in crime (1982:20-21).

The national pattern reported by Feinberg does not seem to be true of all American cities. In their study of arrests in San Francisco over a period of four months during 1967-1968, Epstein et al. (1971). discovered a substantial male/female ratio in the elderly offender group. They report that in San Francisco there were almost six times as many males as females arrested. In the population aged 60 or over fifteen times as many males were arrested. Of the 41 women arrested, 13 were arrested for charges other than drunkenness. These included eight arrests for petty theft, two for traffic offences, one for minor fraud, one for possession of heroin, one for murder, and the cause of one arrest was unknown. As was true of the male arrests, the causes for women's arrests were, with few exceptions, relatively minor.

Shichor (1985) analyzed 1981 UCR data in an attempt to find out to what degree the patterns of male and female arrests are similar or different as between the general population and the elderly; and if there are differences, to what extent they do vary according to the various offences.

Comparisons of male female arrest rates in the younger (below 55 years old) group indicated that 5.1 times more males than females had been arrested; in the elderly group (55 years old and older) the comparable figure was 8.8.

Shichor found the distribution to be different where the more serious (index) crime arrests are concerned. These arrests account for 22.3 per cent of the total number of arrests. Arrest rates for Index crimes in the younger group were 4.3 times higher for males than for females, while in the elderly group they were only 2.6 times higher! Thus the data indicate a higher proportion of female arrests for serious crimes than for all crimes, especially among the elderly, where the share of female major arrests is considerably higher than in the younger group.

Arrest rates for violent crimes in the younger group were 449.5 for males and 50.7 for females. In the elderly group these rates were 50.2 and 4.2 respectively.

In property index offences the sex differences between the arrest rates indicate that in the younger group, 3.7 times more males are arrested than females; the comparable figure among the elderly is 2.0.

In his previously quoted analysis of elderly crime trends in the U.S., Steffensmeier (1987) devoted a great deal of attention to male/female differences. He observed that while the total crime rate of elderly males dropped about one-half, from 2603/100,000 in 1964 to 1267/100,000 in 1984, the total elderly female rate rose slightly from 149/100,000 in 1964 to 171/100,000 in 1984. This differing movement of total rates is due statistically to very large male/female differences in base rates for several offences (e.g., public drunkenness) that declined dramatically over the 20-year period.

Steffensmeier points out that the proportionate criminal involvement of both elderly males and elderly females has been generally stable, and if anything, in comparison to other age-sex groups in American society, elderly crime levels of both sexes are less now than 20 years ago.

Steffensmeier notes that the offence pattern of both elderly male and female offenders is less differentiated and varied than for other age groups. Elderly males are overwhelmingly arrested for alcohol-related crimes and elderly females for larceny-theft (mainly shoplifting). In fact, about 50% of all arrests of elderly females in 1984 were for larceny-theft compared to 12% for elderly males. According to Steffensmeier, the crime profile of the elderly male is less narrowly that of the chronic or public drunk but still that of the alcohol-related offender, whereas the profile of the elderly female offender has shifted overwhelmingly toward that of a shoplifter or petty thief. Steffensmeier believes the fact that alcohol-related crimes stand out for elderly males and larceny-theft for elderly females is not because of a greater incidence of elderly male or female involvement in these crimes, but because elderly males and females are so unlikely to be arrested for the wider range of offences dominated by younger, male age groups (1985:301).

In Canada, the involvement of elderly females in crime remains very low. It is possible however that this situation will change in the coming years for two reasons:

1. a growing elderly female population;

2. within the last ten years or so female indictable criminality has risen sharply among the younger age groups (below 40). As this cohort advances, it may affect the statistics of female offenders over 60 years (see Jackson, 1981).

IS THE ELDERLY CRIMINAL AN ACADEMIC INVENTION?

In an interesting article entitled "The Rise of the Elderly Offender: Will a New Criminal be Invented?" Cullen et al. (1985) address themselves to the assumption that the aged are committing not only more crimes but also more serious offences, the sort of illegalities that previously were exclusively the domain of the young. The authors tried to find out whether we are witnessing real changes in the criminality of the aged or a socially rooted creation of another "new criminal". Following the methodological framework employed by Steffensmeier (1978) in his assessment of changes in the pattern of female lawlessness, they endeavoured to examine the empirical adequacy of the current imagery depicting the elderly as joining the ranks of serious offenders at an unprecedented rate. The purpose of their analysis was to establish the basic pattern of elderly crime and to determine if this pattern has fluctuated over the past 15 years.

Cullen et al. admit that the analysis is inevitably constrained and biased by the limitations inherent in the data they employed, i.e., FBI arrest data for the period of 1967 to 1982. They note that on the basis of the data it is tempting conclude that crime rates among older Americans have skyrocketed. After arrests for Index crimes indicate that crimes like rape, robbery and assault increased over 100% since 1967. However, they dispute such stance on lowing grounds:

reason for the large increases in percentages is that the raw figures ved are relatively small; as such, small absolute increases will produce jumps in percentages.

- Ti basic crime pattern has remained relatively consistent during the period studied. Thus, at every year studied, larceny-theft constituted the most frequent offence among the elderly, ranging from a low of 64.88% in 1967 to 79.06% in 1982. They admit that some of the increase in 1982 can be attributed to possible changes in the willingness of the police to arrest older shoplifters. They argue, however, that, if anything, the trend has been for increases in elderly illegality to occur in the traditional larceny-theft category as opposed to offence categories (e.g., burglary, robbery) that previously were the domain of the young and hence would be indicative of a fundamental transformation of the criminality of seniors.

- The elderly's rate since 1967 did not rise substantially faster than the rest of the population.

- When fluctuations in the nature of America's age structure are taken into account, the arrest rates show limited participation of the elderly in crime and a distinct tendency for senior citizens to engage in larceny-theft when they do violate the law.

Cullen et al. concluded that the evidence consistently reveals that the elderly continue to constitute less than one percent of the total offender population (as measured by FBI statistics), and that their basic pattern of criminal involvement has remained fairly constant during the period they investigated. The authors make a number of final observations regarding the emergence of the elderly offender as a study and research issue. First, they note that the data they presented should sensitize criminologists to the reality "that patterns of crime are deeply enmeshed in the social structure and will not experience dramatic change in the absence of a fundamental transformation of social arrangements". Secondly, in the absence of any firm evidence confirming the existence of a new elderly criminal, why is it that commentators have been inclined to invent this offender? They offer the following reasons:

- On the broadest level, academic concerns are intimately shaped by the prevailing social climate. The general concern over issues such as elderly rights and the aging of the population have fueled an unprecedented interest in gerontological matters. Criminologists have not remained unaffected by this wider preoccupation with the elderly but instead have begun to actively inspect how crime touches the lives of senior citizens.

- The reason why criminologists came to ask certain questions about crime and the elderly, but not others, is seen to lie in the ideological baggage that criminologists brought with them when they turned their attention to the elderly. The first area of interest investigated was how senior citizens are burdened with fear of crime and impoverish their lives to avoid victimization. This flowed easily from an ideology that saw the elderly as uniformly vulnerable and ineffectual. The replacement of this negative image of the elderly by a positive one asserting that the elderly are capable of performing productive roles brought about a change in research focus. It allowed scholars to entertain the possibility that the elderly are capable of committing crimes, and serious ones at that!

Cullen et al. close their discussion with an attempt to answer the question: when commentators have directed their attention to aged criminals, why have they tended to invent a new offender? Here they quote Hagen and Cole, the latter of whom has observed that the structure of interests within academia places a premium on uncovering interesting premises:

In Cole's words, "a function of theory is to provide puzzles for research". This line of reasoning helps make the proclivity to invent new criminals, whether female or elderly, more understandable. Put directly, what will bring a commentator located in either academic or popular circles more attention: arguing that crime patterns have remained stable or arguing that we now must worry about a new offender who is already making our streets less safe and is prepared to penetrate the sancity of our homes? (1985:160-161).

Despite Cullen et al.'s speculative reasoning, one may look upon the growing interest in elderly criminality and victimization as a natural, logical development resulting from the unprecedented aging of the North American population. An identical development occurred in other countries where the phenomenon of population aging appeared earlier. Because millions of young German men were killed during the Second World War, population aging became a demographic reality in Germany as early as the late 1940s and the 1950s. Several articles on the criminality of old age appeared in criminological and psychiatric journals during the 1950s. This was followed by the publication of at least two books on elderly criminality: one in 1960 by Clemens Amelunxen and another in 1961 by H. Burger-Prinz and H. Lewrenz.

NOTES

1. According to Hirschi and Gottfredson (1983), the consistent difference in the age distribution of person and property offences that appears in official crime data is not supported by self- report data. They point out that formal crime statistics consistently show that person crimes peak later than property crimes, and the rate declines more slowly with age. Self-report data, on the other hand, showed that both types of offence peak at the same time (see e.g., Eliott et al., 1978) and decline at the same rate with age (Tittle, 1980). Hirschi and Gottfredson add that the peak years for person and property offenders in self-report data are the mid-teens, which are also the peak years for property offences in official data. In contrast,person offences in official data peak in the late teens or early twenties.

2. This finding confirms what Shichor and Kobrin(1978) reported four years earlier on the basis of their analysis of UCR arests data for the period 1964-1974. They found that while the share of the elderly (55+) in arrests for all crimes shows a trend of gradual decline (from 7.6% in 1964 to 4.8% in 1974), their share in arrests for all index crimes has risen steadily.

CHAPTER TWO: RECOMMENDED READINGS

Covey, H.C. and Menard S.
1987 Trends in Arrests among the Elderly, The Gerontologist, 27 (5) :666-672.

Cullen, F.T.et al.
1985 The Rise of the Elderly Offender, Will a New Criminal be Invented? Crime and Social Justice, 23:151-165

Hirschi, T. and M. Gottfredson
1983 Age and the Explanation of Crime. American J. of Sociology, 89(3): 552-584.

Inciardi, J.A.
1987 Crime and the Elderly: A Construction of Official Rates. In C.D. Chambers et al. (Eds) The Elderly: Victims and Deviants, Athens, Ohio: Ohio University Press. pp. 177-190.

Rowe, A.R. and C.R. Tittle
1977 Life Cycle Changes and Criminal Propensity. The Sociological Quarterly, 18:223-236

Shichor, D.
1985 Male-female Differences in Elderly Arrests: An Exploratory Analysis. Justice Quarterly, 2 (3): 399-414.

Steffensmeier, D.J.
1987 The Invention of the "New" Senior Citizen Criminal. Research on Aging, 9 (2): 281-311.

CHAPTER THREE

OFFENCES THE ELDERLY COMMIT
AND
THEIR EXPLANATIONS

EXPLAINING ELDERLY CRIME

The Problem in General

Criminal etiology is probably the most problematic and least successful field of study in the discipline of criminology. One reason, of course, is the complex nature of crime. No crime can be traced to a single cause. Causes of crime are multiple, varied and interwoven. Some causes may be endogenic (characteristic of the individual or his or her organism) others are exogenic (characteristic of the natural environment or the social milieu). Another reason is that crime is not a homogeneous category of behavior and criminals are not a homogeneous group. Acts defined as crimes by law consist of a wide variety of heterogeneous and diverse activities which may have nothing in common except that they are all prohibited by some law under the threat of some criminal sanction. This by itself explains why it is difficult, maybe impossible, to come up with a general theory of crime explaining every type of crime and accounting for every type of criminal. It would be both naive and over-optimistic to expect that one day in the near future there will be a comprehensive criminological theory that adequately explains behaviors ranging from criminal homicide to the passing of bad cheques, from price fixing to purse snatching, from armed robbery to child molesting; a theory that succeeds in explaining violent crimes, property crimes, sexual crimes, victimless crimes, white collar crime, organized crime and so on. Furthermore, the root causes of crime might be quite different for different categories of offenders. If this is true, then explanations of juvenile delinquency may not be adequate for explaining elderly criminality; explanations of male criminality may not be appropriate for explaining female delinquency. Different explanations may even be needed to explain the different types of crime committed by each group. Crimes involving violence may need

34

to be explained differently from non-violent offences, and sex offences may need different explanations from those of property offences, and so on.

The Problem of Explaining Elderly Crime

In addition to the general problems mentioned above, elderly crime is difficult to explain because criminal behavior is an atypical activity among those who have reached a certain age. This is probably why most current explanations of elderly criminality are in fact "reverse explanations". That is, instead of explaning why some elderly people commit crime, they try to explain why the elderly, as a group, commit less crime than the young or why criminality declines with age. These so-called reverse explanations are not without merit. If we understand why people stop committing crime we might comprehend better why they start committing crime. In other words, understanding desistance from crime may help explain the onset of crime. Unfortunately, while research on the latter topic is voluminous, research on the former is quite meagre (see for example, Schafer, 1974). Our knowledge of the reasons for desistance from crime remains therefore largely speculative and many of the important questions related to this phenomenon remain without answer. For example,

- Do those who start earlier desist earlier or is it that the earlier one starts, the later one stops? In answer to this, we can only say at this stage of our knowledge that the age of desistance shows considerable variations.

- What accounts for the fact that some offenders quit earlier than others? We actually do not know and in fact we might learn something of interest about criminal behavior if we could find out how those who drop out at different points along this curve of progressive decline in incidence differ from one another (see Roth, 1968).

- Are the offences committed earlier the ones that cease earlier or later? We have some tentative evidence that property offences are usually the first ones committed and are the ones that cease earlier, while offences against the person are committed later and seem to persist longer.

Some of the popular explanations of elderly crime may be qualified as "circular explanations". This is particularly true of the psychiatric explanations. Quite often, the criminal behavior of the elderly individual is used to diagnose her or him as suffering from an organic or inorganic mental disorder, and then the disorder is used to explain the criminal behavior in question!

In order to better understand and explain elderly criminality some preliminary distinctions need to be made and some realities should be kept in mind. The following are a few:

- A distinction between the different types of elderly offenders. A good, specific typology of elderly offenders is needed and a tentative one is elaborated later on (see chapter six). This typology comprises three major types and several subtypes.

- A distinction between the various types of offences the elderly commit. As mentioned above, no single theory can adequately explain largely different

35

types of criminal behavior. For this reason the various types are discussed separately and an attempt is made to explain the most important ones.

- With regard to acts of violence, it should be pointed out that violence by the elderly is predominantly (almost exclusively) expressive or angry violence. It is non-instrumental, that is, it is not employed to accomplish other ends such as rape, robbery, kidnapping, extortion and so on.

- To understand elderly crime in general, and elderly violent and sex crime in particular, equal attention should be paid to the psychological as well as the environmental determinants, to the individual and the situational factors, The latter are characteristic of the milieu rather than the organism: for example, the behavior of the victim, the attitude and behavior of others, the nature and stresses of the environment and so on.

- Further research is needed to answer many of the burning questions regarding elderly crime. For example, are environmental and situational factors more or less important in the criminality of the elderly than they are in crimes committed by younger age groups? Is the role of alcohol as a criminogenic factor more or less pronounced in elderly crime than it is for other age groups? Are the elderly more or less susceptible to some triggering factors (for example, provocation) than other age groups? Are they more likely to react violently to situational stress than others? Does advancing age bring with it increased intolerance, higher degree of irritability, morbid jealousy, and so on? Do the elderly suffer more than the young from the subjective feeling of crowding? Some authors (for example, Wolk et al., 1963) report that a large part of assaults committed by the elderly take place in retirement communities where the aged are in close proximity to one another, and such assaults are often the result of boredom and lack of excitement. They are the outcome of natural strains and irritations of people cooped up together. For the elderly living alone, what is the impact of loneliness on their behavior? Loneliness, as a factor in old age criminality, has been stressed by Hays and Wisotsky (1969) among others.

- Another fact to be borne in mind when trying to understand and explain elderly criminality is the problem of adjustment. The physical, psychological and social changes associated with old age mean that this period of life is a period of adjustment. Coping with these changes will inevitably vary, sometimes greatly, between one individual and another according not only to individual differences but also to the influence of the environment, and the strength or weakness of support systems, in particular the person's own network.

Crime, especially when it occurs for the first time very late in life, may be viewed as a symptom of more or less acute problems of coping and adjustment to the new conditions, the strange experiences and the fundamental changes in old age. In this respect, similarities between elderly criminality and juvenile delinquency might not be totally absent. Moberg (1953) reminds us that many forms of delinquent behavior in youth could be traced to problems of adjustment to physiological, psychological and social changes taking place during adolescence and late adolescence. The next period with as many changes in life is surely that of aging. The aging person often has to adjust to the death of a

36

spouse or partner, to the loss of employment and reduced income, to the loss of status; they have to cope with loneliness, with isolation, boredom, poverty, physical decline, physical infirmity, loss of mobility or freedom and so on. It is not surprising that parallels and analogies have been drawn between senescence and adolescence. Wolk et al. (1963) note that many personality dynamics of aged persons and adolescents are similar:

- Both age groups are in a state of constant flux: during adolescence the change is one of maturation; in old age it is one of decline.

- Both groups are concerned with the future, but only in terms of immediacy.

- Frustration tolerances for both groups are low.

- Both groups are concerned with bodily changes: the adolescent in terms of growth; the elderly in terms of deterioration.

- The focus of living is upon daily and immediate survival. This results in instances of selfishness and an attitude that there is nothing to lose.

- Self-concepts are similar: each has feelings of insecurity and inadequacy and strives to develop and maintain masculinity, femininity or sexuality.

In a paper on the elderly shoplifter, Feinberg (1984) pushes the analogy between the two groups even further. He points to the following similarities:

- Exemption from work responsibilities.

- Relatively unstructured time schedules.

- Relative freedom from future life planning.

- Low prestige or status position.

- Limited financial independence.

- Relative freedom from family responsibilities.

- De-emphasis on production, and emphasis on consumption.

- Emphasis on play and leisure as a way of life.

Feinberg (1984) is prudent enough to also recognize some basic differences between the two groups. He notes that:

- Juveniles can anticipate future engagement in economic, familial and political roles; the elderly can anticipate mainly disengagement from such roles.

- Juveniles expect and are expected to enter mainstream society. The elderly expect and are expected to leave mainstream society, and not return.

- In time, the status, financial and power positions of juveniles become stronger, whereas in time they become weaker for the elderly.

- Juveniles look up to those currently in power for acceptance and their reference groups rest within the ongoing social order. The elderly are outside mainstream society, like the youth, but above it.

- Juveniles tend to have close and intimate role models to follow; the elderly tend to lack such idealized role models.

It is clear that Feinberg's analogy places the emphasis on and highlights the most negative aspects of old age and later life. This is understandable since all of this is presented in the context of explaining some abnormal activity, some atypical behavior: crime. It is natural to expect that only those who have not coped successfully with the changes and problems of old age, only those who have not adjusted and were unable to adapt to their new life conditions, will resort to criminal behavior in some form or another. In other words, the behavior of the elderly who have committed no crime does not need an explanation.

WHAT ROLE DO MENTAL DISORDERS PLAY IN GERIATRIC CRIMINALITY?

Consistent with the belief that different explanations might be necessary for explaining different types of deviant and criminal behavior occurring at different stages in life, some feel that while sociological and socio-cultural theories are more useful in explaining early delinquency and youth crime, psychiatric explanations might be more enlightening when it comes to late criminality. For many years psychiatrists have noticed that brain damage, cerebral disease, traumatic brain injuries, as well as chronic epilepsy, might be associated with disturbances of behavior that sometimes bring the affected individual into conflict with the law. Since some mental disorders, in particular senile dementia, do sometimes accompany or result from old age, it is quite possible that they may play a causative role in certain types of antisocial conduct of elderly citizens in the sense that the deranged patterns of conduct might be attributed, at least in part, to the cerebral disease.

Many psychiatrists are convinced, however, that most offences of old age are expressions of beginning senile dementia although the development of a mental condition may not yet be obvious (see Pollak, p.230). Clinical studies (Whiskin, 1968; Zeegers, 1979) report a very high incidence of organic brain disease among elderly sex offenders. Zeegers reports to have found 18 suffering from arteriosclerotic dementia among 47 aged sex offenders (60 and over); Whiskin found nine of fifteen elderly sex offenders (60 and over) referred to psychiatric clinics by the courts, to be suffering from organic brain disease. In Toronto, on the other hand, Hucker and Ben-Aron (1985) found only 14% of the 43 elderly sex offenders to be suffering from organic brain syndrome. Obviously, the way the diagnosis is made greatly affects the percentages. Whiskin (1968) states in his study that the diagnosis was made on the basis of a history of confused, bizarre behavior and a mental status examination which shows disorientation in one or more spheres of time, place, or person, including disorders of judgement and so on. He adds:

> If it is minimal we may label it "senility", but if more severe, we bring out that most handy weapon of all- the diagnosis "chronic brain syndrome"-either arteriosclerotic or associated with senile brain disease. Although there is nothing wrong with the principle which recommends that we try the simple explanation of a given event before the more complex, in this case I believe that we overwork the principle. In my opinion the diagnosis "organic brain syndrome" oversimplifies the actual state of affairs (1968:248-249).

Hucker and Ben-Aron (1985) also try to explain the significant difference between their findings regarding the organic brain syndrome and those of Whiskin and Zeegers. They note that Whiskin seemed to admit that the diagnostic criteria he employed were vague and he suggested that "social isolation and attempts to regressive solutions" may contribute to a "pseudo-organic syndrome". Similarly, Zeegers stated that among his cases, the main features of dementia were not loss of memory or intellectual deficiency, but a "restriction of their being-in-the-world". Hucker and Ben-Aron comment that:

> This use of existential terminology is somewhat puzzling to North American psychiatrists and it seems likely that many of Zeeger's cases of dementia might fail to satisfy modern criteria for organic dementia (1985:220).

Variations in the criteria used and ultimately in diagnosis can lead to substantial differences in the frequencies reported. They do not, however, alter a psychiatric fact, namely, that organic deterioration of the brain, organic brain disease, progressive cerebral damage, when they really exist, can lead to an impairment of judgement, loss of control, a weakening of inhibitions and to other symptoms that may play a causal role in the genesis of certain offences. What remains to be done is not simply to unequivocally establish the frequency of such disorders in elderly offenders (and to compare this with their frequency in the elderly non-criminal population) but also to establish the process and the mechanisms through which they exercise whatever criminogenic influence they might have.

EXAMINING SPECIFIC OFFENCE PATTERNS

Sex Offences

Among all offences committed by elderly men, sex offences have received the greatest attention. European criminologists, in particular, have always treated sex offences as the leading type of criminality among the elderly (Burger-Prinz, 1961; Korner, 1977; Zeegers, 1966; Roth, 1968). On the basis of earlier American statistics, Pollak (1941) also concluded that sex offences occupy a leading position among the various crimes committed by old people. On the basis of UCR arrest data (five year period 1960-1964) Keller and Vedder (1969) concluded that forcible rape is an offence of younger persons. Those in the 50-54 bracket were subject to fewer arrests than boys in the 13-14 age range. Those in the 55-59, 60-64 groups, and those over 65 were arrested less often for forcible rape than very young boys 11 and 12 years of age. Other sexual offences, however, presented a different picture. These include "statutory rape, offences against chastity, common decency morals, and the like, as well as attempts at such offences". Keller and Vedder found that while this category occupied sixteenth position for men in the 25-29 span, its importance grew greater for the four older groups. These sexual offences consistently occupied twelfth position in all four upper age categories.

Because the greatest majority of sex offences committed by old people do not involve overt violence, and because physical force is not used to subdue or to bring the victim into subjection, the dark figure is extremely high. Fear is also an important factor in the underreporting of sex offences. This is particularly true of incestuous sex offences committed by older persons within the family on young children to whom they are related. In addition to having an unusually high dark figure, the collection of official data on these offences is problematic because of the wide variety of legal classifications under which they may be listed in police and court records, and because many may be hidden under the general listing of "contributing to the delinquency of a minor". It is quite likely, however, that the incidence of non-violent sex offences among the elderly is lower than among other age categories in the population as is the case with all other offences.

There are also no accurate data on the division of cases according to whether they are homosexual or heterosexual in nature and the estimates do vary. According to Newman and Newman (1982) child molestation cases appear to be equally divided between male and female victims. Others, such as Pollak (1941) report that the majority of victims are mainly little girls and less frequently young boys. This is confirmed by Hucker and Ben-Aron (1985). Since both young and elderly sex offenders are predominantly male, it is only natural that the majority of victims are and will continue to be females.

There seems to be general agreement that various forms of child molestation are the major sex offences committed by the elderly. Except for the few truly pedophilic offenders, the predilection for children seems to be in most cases a function of expediency, availability and opportunity than of a real preference for young children as sexual objects. The child is not the preferred sexual target but a substitute sexual target because he/she is less able to resist, easier to bribe, more accesible to threat and less likely to tell. Some psychiatrists, however, see the choice of a child as target, as symptomatic of pathological mental conditions associated with old age or a sign of regression to childhood levels. Feminist explanations of sex offences, on the other hand, stress the role of power relationships in sexual criminality. Sexuality, they argue, is the means by which a male offender can hurt, humiliate and degrade his victim. The choice of a child victim by an elderly sex offender is thus interpreted as a reflection of the declining strength, power and authority of the aggressor who is no longer able to hurt, humiliate or degrade youthful or

40

middle-age females. In her analysis of sexual assault, Sandra Butler (1982) underlines the importance of the imbalance in power. She writes:

In short, almost all approaches to incestuous assault ignore the fundamental problem of an imbalance and abuse of power: by men over women, and by adults over children. While there are multiple factors in incestuous assault which require research, analysis, and explanation, it is this neglected area which most urgently needs to be addressed. For incestuous assault is overwhelmingly the assault of female children by adult males; it takes place on a large scale; and it is against the law. It is important that a feminist analysis take precedence over other interpretations, since it is an analysis which encompasses all existing theories and examines them in the realistic context of gender relations (1982:103).

In contrast to feminist explanations of the various forms of sexual assault which emphasize the violent and aggressive nature of the acts, even when no physical force is used, legal and psychiatric approaches to elderly sex offences point to certain differences between these offences and the ones committed by younger offenders. They point out that contrary to young rapists who more often than not use force, sometimes in extreme forms, against their victims, in general, elderly sex offenders do not use overt violence. In some cases the child is too young to realize the nature of the acts being performed on him/her or that he/she is asked to perform. If the child is old enough to be aware of the sexual nature and the forbidden character of the activities, his/her consent is usually obtained by different means: money, presents, promises, etc. If these do not achieve the result, threats may be used:

The old man usually promises the child candy, a few pennies, or some other little favor or joins children at their play, especially in public gardens, pets them, grasps little girls under their skirts or boys at their genitals, sometimes makes exhibitionist gestures, has his own genitals touched by the children, and attempts substitute actions for the coitus (Pollak, 1941:223).

Pollak's conventional view of the interaction between the elderly offender and the child victim is shared by others. They point out that children's trustful and obedient nature, their respect for elderly persons (who symbolize for them their parents' or grandparents' figures), their craving for affection and their desire to please, make them ideal and easy targets for the sexual advances of those elderly men who are sure to face rejection if they approach more mature prospective sex partners. On the other hand, few precocious and curious young girls (or boys) may try to satisfy their sexual curiosity and/or awakening desires by making advances to old and unsuspecting individuals and may in certain instances be the initiators rather than the seduced. The fact is, most elderly offenders, accused of sexual molestation of young and apparently consenting victims, claim to have been seduced by the little girls or boys themselves. In many cases this is probably a defence, similar to the claim that the offence was committed under the influence of alcohol when the offender was not fully aware of what was happening and not in full control of his actions. It is probable, however, that in some cases, at least, the offender's story is a true account of what really took place. In fact, some authors even report cases of child

41

prostitutes of both genders who prey on elderly males, taking advantage of their weakness and their desperate need to satisfy their fading sexual drives (Pollak, 1941:223).

Although the child's role in initiating, encouraging or consenting to the sexual contact is vehemently denounced by feminist writers on sexual assault, it was highlighted in empirical studies conducted in the 1960s and the 1970s (Maisch, 1970; Virkkunen, 1975; Virkkunen, 1980).

In their extensive study of sex offenders, Gebhard et al. (1965), devote only a few lines to the important question: "to what degree is the offence triggered by the advances, either overt or implied of another person?" On the basis of their material they point out that:

> The "victim" is often a willing sexual partner and even sometimes a seductive one, but if this person is under a certain age our social ethics definitely necessitate legal protection of this "object-victim" in such situation (1965:794).

The authors note that in sexual offences against children, except for aggression offences, there was encouragement, or at least passive behavior, in well over three-quarters of the cases. They also quote a California study by James T. March in which the author stated that, in offences against children "six out of ten cases the so-called victim was an active or passive participant in the offence activity".

In Germany, where the role of the victim in sex offences is systematically examined, Dr. Thea Schonfelder, a psychiatrist, devoted a whole book to the role played by female victims. The second chapter of the book deals with the active participation of the victim. In another paper entitled "The Victim's Initiative" published in 1965, the same author offers figures and percentages. The study was based on 175 cases of convicted sex offenders involving 309 child victims (245 girls and 64 boys). Schonfelder observed active participation on the part of 31% of the girls and 28% of the boys. She further found that the active behavior of the child increased with the age of the offender. In cases where the sexual offender was over 60 years old, the percentage of actively participating victims was 47%. In cases where the offenders were under 40 years old, the corresponding percentage was only 20%.

Further information on the role of the victim in sex offences specifically committed by elderly men comes from the doctoral research carried out by Harold Korner (1975 and 1977). Korner examined 483 cases of men over 55 years old who were charged with sex offences against children in the district court of Frankfurt (West Germany) in the years 1960 to 1969. Although official records, as Korner points out, tend to emphasize the victim's resistance and to downplay the victim's encouragement and participation, he found that in no less than 35% of the cases was there active participation from the victim. Korner notes that since voluntary sexual contacts are rarely reported to the authorities and since a higher percentage of cases where the victim is a willing or initiating partner is likely to remain undetected, the real percentage of actively participating victims should be far higher han 35%. In contrast to Dr. Schonfelder's findings, Korner found that active participation of child male victims was slightly higher than that of their female counterparts. To illustrate the points he makes,

Korner cites detailed case histories from his material to show how some of the elderly sex offenders were persistently and actively seduced by precocious, promiscuous children. It goes without saying that such incidents are difficult to prevent if treatment or rehabilitation efforts are geared to the offender alone. Korner quotes another author, Paulsen, who wondered "how is it possible to prevent such sexual offences when the statistics show that alsmost 50% of the so-called victims are, in fact, the seducers?"

More recent studies of sex offences paint a drastically different picture of the role of the victim. Although Finkelhor's study (1979) of sexually victim-ized children was not limited to offences committed by elderly offenders and covered offenders of all ages, his findings are still relevant to the present discussion. Finkelhor's research was not based on police or court cases but consisted of a survey taken at six New England colleges and universities. The sample used for the data analysis consisted of 796 students, 530 females and 266 males. The sample had the expected college-age distribution with 75% being twenty-one years of age or under. Addressing himself to the issue of initiation and force Finkelhor writes:

> Our data show the children to be the recipients of sexual actions, not the initiators, and also the victims of force and coercion. Only in a tiny minority of cases did the respondents say that they had initiated the sex-ual activity. Ninety-eight percent of the girls and 91% of the boys said it was the older partner who started the sexual behavior. Force was pre-sent more often than not in these experiences. Fifty-five per cent of the girls and almost an equal percentage of boys reported that the partners used some kind of force to gain their participation. The force ranged from actual physical constraint, such as holding the children down, to the threat that they would be punished if they did not cooperate. However, even where respondents did not report overt force, it is hard not to see elements of coercion in the differences in age or authority of the parties involved... It is true that children often did not take actions that might have, from an adult point of view, protected them or prevented a recur-rence of the experience. But in many cases, children were confused about the situation, did not perceive their options, or were deliberately misled by their partners. (1979:63-64).

Naturally, it is to be expected that, studies based on victims accounts of what happened would yield lower percentages of initiation and consent and higher percentages of resistance and use of force than studies based on offenders' versions, on police or court records.

Finkelhor (1979) further reports that, especially for girls, the larger the age difference, the greater the trauma suffered by the victim and the older the partner, the more traumatic the experience. Thus when the childs's partner was another child, even an older child, the sexual experience was not as traumatic as when the partner was an adult. Finkelhor hypothesized that since a larger age difference creates more trauma, a younger child would be more vulnerable. Unexpectedly, he discovered that experiences at earlier ages do not produce more trauma; if anything they produce less. For girls, the most negative experiences occurred between ages sixteen and eighteen. He also found

43

father-daughter incest to be the most traumatic kind of sexual experience that can occur.

In some cases of sex offences committed by the elderly the child victim may be quite young. Newman and Newman (1982) observe that age spreads between perpetrator and victim are sometimes tremendous. They also quote a common saying of treatment personnel in sex offender programs: "the older the man, the younger the child".

One characteristic of elderly offenders arrested for sex offences is their seemingly law-violation-free record. Henninger (1939) reports that there is seldom any evidence of previous delinquencies or misconduct among seniles who commit sex crimes and that such behavior is almost always entirely unexpected by the family and friends of the offender.

In his study of 47 sexual delinquent men over 60 years old, Zeegers (1966) found that only fourteen had been previously sentenced for sexual offences. Of these fourteen recidivists only eleven had been sentenced before the age of 60 years. The author reports that on the basis of Dutch criminal statistics, upwards of 50% of elderly sex offenders have never been sentenced before. If one considers only previous sex offences, the percentage is even higher.

Since many sex offences, particularly incest and child molestation, have a high dark figure (see above), estimates of first offenders, when entirely based on official records and previous convictions, may not be accurate. Newman and Newman (1982) point out that many elderly offenders (and it is unknown how many), apparently were sexually deviant all their lives, perhaps becoming more flagrant in their retirement years. On the other hand, it also appears that many sex deviates, perhaps half, had a clean criminal record and no clinical evidence of sexual deviation until they reached old age.

Roth (1968) also reports that quite often the perverse sexual conduct first appears in old age. He believes, however, that careful inquiry frequently reveals that some of these subjects had experienced considerable difficulties in their sexual adjustment prior to their first conviction in old age.

The predominance of first offenders among those who commit crime in old age led Pollak (1941) to conclude that "In general, it can be said that the older the criminal the greater is the chance that he is a first offender".

In Canada, Cormier et al. (1971) examined the records of offenders aged 40 and over who were admitted to a penitentiary in the Province of Quebec during the calendar years 1967 and 1968 and whose record started after age 20, a total of 129 cases. Among the 129 cases, 33 were found guilty of a sexual offence. Out of these 33, nine had a mixed record (sexual offence or offences with other types of crimial behavior such as crimes against property, public order or person). Eight had a long record of petty offences (vagrancy, loitering, traffic offences, drunkenness, etc.) along with the first sexual offence. One had a serious criminal record and one was sentenced for the first time. There were fourteen cases of incest. Looking at the age on first conviction for sexual offence the following picture emerged: one was found guilty of a sexual offence at age 20 to 24; eight were found guilty of their first sexual offence when they were between 25 and 39. Twenty-four cases were found guilty of their first sexual offence after reaching age 40. These included eleven cases of incest; seven of heterosexual pedophilia or hebephilia; two cases of proxenitism; and one polymorphous sexual deviant[1]. Commenting on their findings the authors write:

Out of these 33 cases (of sexual offenders) six could be considered as sexual deviants whose history started long prior to the legal discovery. For the others, our impression is that sexual offences coincide with a crisis in their life. This is especially well exemplified by the fact that we find fourteen cases of incest, i.e., 42.4% of this group. (It is) to be noticed that most of the other cases also involve sexual practices either with young boys or girls. These cases also correspond to a critical period in the life span as shown by the fact that deviant sexuality appears suddenly at a late age (1971:19).

Another Canadian study of elderly sex offenders was conducted in Toronto by Hucker and Ben-Aron (1985). Between July 1, 1966 and December 31, 1979, seventy individuals aged 60 years or older were seen by the staff of the Forensic Service of the Clarke Institute of Psychiatry in Toronto. The group consisted of 43 sex offenders, 16 violent offenders, and 11 miscellaneous cases. In a paper dealing specifically with the 43 sex offenders, Hucker and Ben-Aron note the absence of rape and attempted rape in this elderly group. The majority were involved usually in rather passive touching and exhibiting. They never used threats or actual force. Their victims, generally children, were known to the offenders in 70% of the cases. Almost half of this group of elderly sex offenders had previous records and nearly a quarter of them were for sex offences. The most frequent psychiatric diagnoses were alcoholism, personality disorders other than the antisocial type, neurosis, and organic brain syndrome. Only 14% were drinking at the time of the offence. Summarizing their findings, Hucker and Ben-Aron point out that:

Certainly, most of the elderly sex offenders in this sample referred for psychiatric examination in relation to their charges had molested children. These victims were usually known to the offender and sometimes were a relative or close friend. The typical non-aggressive nature of the sexual contact is also clear...our figures do not suggest that elderly sex offenders suffer from organic brain syndromes to any greater extent than the elderly population in general (1985:220).

Except for some elderly prostitutes and "Madams" who might be arrested for proxenitism, living off prostitution, running a bawdy house or contribution to the delinquency of a minor, and except for the elderly woman who is occasionally charged as an accessory in a rape, incest, or indecent asssault case, elderly women's involvement in sexual criminality is conspicuous by its absence.

Why would an elderly person, with no previous criminal history, who has r before been arrested for sexual offences, commit a deviant sex act with a d? In trying to answer this complex question a distinction should be made tween the psychiatric and the socio-cultural explanations of sex crimes by the elderly. The former out-number the latter because the behavior in question has been studied mainly by psychiatrists, to whom the offenders were referred, in hospitals, clinics, penal institutions and so on. The following is a brief summary of the psychiatric explanations of sex offences committed in old age:

- Some psychiatrists believe that sex offences in old age are symptoms of in-sanity. Many see them as expressions of beginning senile dementia al-though the development of a mental condition may not yet be obvious (Pollak, 1941).

- Roth (1968) believes that elderly's indecent conduct with the children could often be attributed to cerebral degeneration which releases primitive instinctual urges from the control of higher centres in the brain. In support of this, Roth cites evidence showing that some of these subjects suffer from indubitable cerebrovascular disease and others from the early stages of a senile degenerative process. Roth believes that it is possible to establish the contribution of cerebral degenerative change to perverse sexuality in old age through careful follow-up studies. These should determine the fre-quency with which dementia supervenes, the pathological changes present in the brain, and also the life expectation of such subjects.

- Although the attribution of a senile's sex offences to cerebral degeneration and mental deterioration due to old age is popular among psychiatrists, it should be pointed out that no correlation has yet been found between the degree of deterioration and the likelihood of sex offences (see Henninger, 1939).

- Another psychiatric explanation of sex offences in old age refers to a psychologically persistent libido while the internal mechanisms of self-control are weakened. Henninger (1939) points out that increased libidinous drive, in a period of life when this urge is usually futile so far as procreation is concerned, is a final expression of the aging organism in the unconscious hope of leaving dependents upon this earth.

- Pollak (1941) believes that the psychological changes in old age have a great deal to do with criminality of the aged. Changes in the blood vessels and brain cells as well as senile effects upon the sex glands play, according to Pollak, a role in the causation of many crimes of aged offenders. For sex offences, the probability of irritation of the sex glands in advanced years is particularly noteworthy.

- Alcohol seems to play a major role in sex offences committed by elderly males and its criminogenic effect seems to be greater for the elderly than it is for younger age groups. The importance of alcohol to the offence of incest in particular has been documented in many studies. (see Maisch, 1970)

46

Socio-cultural explanations of sex offences by the elderly stress the un-availability of normal sexual outlets and the strength of sex repression on the level of senescence. Although social attitudes toward the elderly have changed in the past decade, society still equates sex with being young and beautiful. Certainly the situation is not as bad as it was in the 1940s when Pollak (1941) deplored societal attitudes which considers "as the extreme of indecency that an old person should still have sex needs, and nothing seems to shatter our re-spect for aged persons more than to find in them a sex drive without the justifi-cation of procreation". This complete social repression, reasons Pollak, may be responsible for a part of sex offences in old age. The deep mental conflict generated by the severe repression of sex in old age may also be responsible for other non-sex offences committed by the elderly.

Whiskin (1968) points out that in our culture there is, without doubt, less tolerance of overt, or even covert, expressions of sexual interest toward the opposite sex in the elderly than in younger people. It is as if sexuality becomes more verboten as one ages beyond a certain point. The expression "dirty old man" probably finds its origin in these cultural attitudes. Whiskin writes:

The main point to be made here is that society's attitudes towards sexuality in the elderly tend to suppress the healthy expression of sexual feelings. Because of this factor, combined with their need to over-compensate for feelings of impotence, unattractiveness, and rejection by younger persons, it is not surprising that they sometimes turn to an age group who have not yet learned biased, prejudicial attitudes toward the elderly - younger children. Some of these pedophiles undoubtedly had propensities in this direction from earlier years. It is interesting to note that they rarely seek out genital sex relations with the child involved. More often it involves a kind of passive relationship of exhibiting, touch-ing, and being touched. Perhaps in part what they want is contact of some kind to relieve their isolation. The act gratifies their sexual impulse and also relieves their loneliness (1968:250)

The role of isolation and loneliness in the etiology of the elderly's sexual criminality is echoed by Zeegers (1983) who states that a most important factor in these crimes is the isolation in which many aged people find themselves. Terms such as uprootedness, loneliness, detachment and disengagement are certainly applicable to many of them. They need some company; they also need some sense of being of significance for someone. By means of contact with children in their neighborhood some of their needs are satisfied. Zeegers emphasizes that the contacts often start rather harmlessly; more or less far-reaching sexual activities may develop gradually.

The importance of socio-cultural factors in the etiology of sex delinquency among the elderly has also been pointed out even by psychiatrists such as Roth (1968). Roth, citing Hirchmann, notes that elderly males are deterred from establishing personal relationships as a preliminary to courtship with adult sub-jects either by fear of rejection and humiliations or by failure in sexual activity. On the other hand, they find it relatively easy to establish contact with a child in whom a grandfather figure evokes an attitude of trust and affection. This can be readily exploited to lead to exhibitionism, sexual play, or other activity generally falling short of coitus. Roth adds that:

The psychology of these acts, then, has affinities with the perverse conduct of certain inadequate and feeble-minded subjects who likewise find it easy to communicate with small children and in this way establish a sexual relationship that presents little threat or challenge (1968:38).

Criminal Homicide

Because criminal homicide (murder and non-negligent manslaughter) has a relatively low dark figure, statistics on homicide are likely to be more accurate than those of most other offences. And because elderly homicides are usually committed in a specific relationship they are likely to have a higher clearance rate than other types, say stranger-to-stranger homicide or sexual murder.

Elderly individuals commit fewer homicides than their numbers in the population would indicate. Thus according to Newman and Newman (1982):

Arrests, prosecutions, and convictions of elderly people for murder and non-negligent homicide are significantly lower both in proportion to their number in the population and in the proportion of these crimes committed by younger offenders (1982:4).

The authors note that about one-third of elderly suspect arrests in the U.S. are for violence-homicide, aggravated assault, and sex crimes. They are quick to point out that this does not mean that a third of all elderly offences are violent because the proportion is clearly lower. In part, this proportion is an artifact of police arrest practices and of prosecutorial charging policies. That is, elderly violators are much more likely to be arrested and prosecuted for serious crimes against persons while, at the same time, they are under-arrested and diverted to non-criminal justice alternatives for such property offences as shoplifting and check fraud. Since these are much more common than violent crimes, the denominator in the percentage formula is deceptively small thereby giving greater weight to more serious crimes.

In his study of criminal homicide in Philadelphia, Wolfgang (1958) discovered that under age 50 the statistical probability of being an offender in criminal homicide is slightly higher than that of being a victim, while over age 50 the chance of being a victim is two times greater than that of being an offender. He found that the mean annual rate of offenders 50 years of age and over was only 2.3, while the rate for victims in the same age catogory was 4.7.

The high criminal homicide rate which has always been recorded for black Americans does not totally disappear in old age. In a sociological analysis of homicide, published in Federal Probation, Wolfgang (1961) writes:

Although males of both races more frequently commit criminal homicide during their twenties than during any other period of life, negro males in their early sixties as frequently kill as do white males in their early twenties (1961:50).

Newman and Newman (1982) identify major differences in murder patterns of the elderly in contrast to homicides by younger persons. First, felony murder commited by elderly persons in the course of commision of other felonies (i.e, homicide during a bank robbery) is much lower than it is for other age groups. By and large elderly persons do not commit armed robbery, which is the setting for most felony murders. Second, and this is true not only for murder but for all elderly crimes, the older perpetrator is likely to be female than in the lower age categories. Newman and Newman identify yet another difference in murder patterns of the elderly as compared with younger age groups. Elderly persons in the U.S. are more likely to use a gun than other weapons, strangulation, or beating to murder victims. The authors wonder whether this is a function of the frailty of old age, the inability to kill a victim, or a function of the high population of women who may be less physically able to kill without a weapon.

Many years earlier, Von Hentig (1947) had tackled the same issue:

> The criminality of the older man resembles in many ways that of the woman. He is the instigator, or he commits crimes in which craftiness or the use of physical or chemical forces play a role. At the same time, feeling that the normal methods of defeating a competitor are not any longer at his disposal, the older man falls back on primitive means of violence. Even the weak can use force if he chooses a weaker object, a woman or a child, or if he turns to strength-saving devices, weapons, poison, and deceit (1947:152).

The preponderant use of firearms in homicides committed by the elderly is confirmed by other sources. Wilbanks and Murphy (1984) analyzed U.S. national homicide data for 1980 and found that elderly offenders are more likely to use firearms than offenders in other age groups (78.1 percent versus 63.3 percent). Explaining the difference the authors suggest that:

> It is unlikely that an older and presumably weaker person would approach a younger person with a knife, stick or a blunt instrument that could be seized and used by the intended victim. Guns are "equalizers", and thus the elderly are more likely to use this weapon to compensate for lack of physical strength (1984:88).

In a study of homicide in Detroit, Goetting (1985) found that nearly 80 percent of the homicides perpetrated by the elderly were executed with firearms compared with 65.8 percent for the total population. Other methods used by the elderly were: beatings 8.2 percent and burnings 4.1 percent.

Another characteristic of elderly homicide is the intimate relationship that very often exists between the perpetrator and the victim. The latter is usually the wife or another close relative: a daughter, a daughter-in-law, a brother, a nephew, a son and so on. Stranger-to-stranger homicide by the elderly is relatively rare. As with assault and aggravated assault, old age homicides rarely involve a random, unknown victim.

A Canadian study of behavior and aging by Cormier et al. (1971) reports that during the calendar years 1967 and 1968, 71 inmates of the total inmate population in a federal penitentiary in Laval, Quebec, had been admitted for homicides committed in that province. Of these, nine (12.7%) were 40 years and over when the homicide was committed. Seven of these inmates were married of whom five were separated. Four had no previous record; two had a

49

record of misdemeanours, and three had an appreciable criminal record. Three of the nine had a history of mental illness, and in five cases there was a history of heavy drinking. The most important finding, according to the authors, is that for eight of the nine cases, the victim was a specific victim, by which they mean that there was a personal relationship between the offender and the victim, and the conflictual nature of this relationship was a determining factor in the homicide. Four of the victims were wives (legal or commonlaw); one was a brother; three were friends. None of these homicides resulted from the commission of another crime. In the ninth case, the victim was a stranger whose death occurred as an outcome of the commission of another crime.

In his study of the crimes of the aged in Japan, Shimizu (1973) found that while the incidence of sexual offences was low, homicide occupied a conspicuous position. This, he notes, is in contrast to its relative ignorance in other countries. He points out that the majority of the aged homicide criminals were first offenders and their crimes were the result of violent emotional release following an extended duration of intrafamilial conflict. Almost all the victims, mostly spouses or children, were members of the offender's family living within the same household.

Why?

Criminal homicides committed by elderly persons are even more difficult to explain than those committed by younger individuals. Very little information is available on the contexts in which these homicides are perpetrated and on the traits and attributes of both killers and victims.

Richman (1982) agrees with Shichor and Kobrin (1976) that little is known about the circumstances of elderly homicides and aggravated assaults, about the psychological dynamics of such acts, the settings, or the social and interpersonal relationships between the criminal and his victim. The two known facts are that such crimes are unrelated to robbery or any other direct personal gain, and that the victim is almost always someone known to the elderly murderer (p.191).

We do know, however, that certain personality traits commonly associated with acts of violence against the person may persist or even become pronounced in old age. Aggressivity does not completely vanish with advancing age. Moreover, certain individuals become more quarrelsome, more irritable, more suspicious and more mistrustful in their later years. The elderly are likely to suffer from intense frustration and high levels of emotional tensions. And as Richman (1982) points out, with increasing decline there is a decreased tolerance for frustration and a decreased capacity to delay the discharge of impulses. Pathological fears and delusions are also common among the elderly while pathological jealousy may be aggravated by heavy alcohol consumption. The role alcohol plays in elderly homicide is probably as important as its role in homicide committed by younger people. Provocation by the victim is also likely to be a factor in view of the fact that some old people are quite easily provoked. To these might be added the problems associated with the male "menopause," in particular the conscious realization or the subconscious fear of physiological impotence and loss of masculinity. Involuntary institutionalization to which many elderly are subjected against their wish or their will, and the imposed close living, may result in a sense of crowding not previously experienced which, in turn, might bring about problems of adjustment to life in the institution and may produce or trigger aggressive behaviors against other residents or the staff.

A definitive study on elderly homicide remains to be written. In the meantime we can only resort, for explaining this curious phenomenon, to general and vague explanations of elderly violence scattered through the psychiatric, criminological and gerontological literature.

Bergman and Amir (1973) claim that "chronic brain syndrome" may be associated with a loss of inhibitions resulting in illegal sexual behavior, such as exhibitionism, and in rigidity, suspiciousness, and quarrelsomeness with consequent aggressiveness. Feelings of despair and undue dependence on family and social and welfare agencies may lead to violent and aggressive acts against family members and, often, welfare officials. Loss of status as breadwinner and breakdown of authority, at times with paranoid reactions, may lead to physical assaults on family members.

Wolk et al. (1963) point out that an aged person may be moved to acts of physical violence, as a result of close living. The same person, when younger may have been able to channel his aggressiveness and thus not become physically violent.

Shichor and Kobrin(1978) stress increasing opportunities for conflict in old age. They offer what they believe is a plausible hypothesis for the prominence of violent crimes among the elderly. Such a hypothesis would hold that, as the range of social interactions contracts with advancing age, interpersonal primary relationships become intense, with a resulting increase in opportunities for conflict. They claim that this proposition receives indirect support from another element in the pattern of violence among the elderly, namely their serious violent offences are unrelated to predatory gain. This is interesting because the shrinking volume of social interactions may also be advanced as an explanatory hypothesis for the declining rate of offences against the person in old age (see Chapter two).

The role of mental disorders in the etiology of violence by the elderly, and particularly in criminal homicide committed by old people, remains to be established. In England, Roth (1968) observed that offences of violence are almost absent among the aged although they are the second commonest form of offence in all age groups together. He points out that the rare violent acts by aged men often rise in a setting of mental disorder with suicidal tendencies; before committing or attempting suicide the elderly person may attempt to kill his spouse or other relations, often in a most brutal manner[2].

Roth, (1968) firmly believes that violence by the elderly is intimately linked to their suicidal tendencies, tendencies which, in turn, might be linked to cerebral degeneration:

> In rare instances, the violence which is directed into the suicidal attempt overflows into aggressive behavior towards those in the immediate vicinity of the elderly person. It may also find expression in the destruction of belongings or in an attempt to set fire to the house. In very rare instances, aged persons make murderous attacks in the absence of any suicidal tendencies. The aggression is usually directed towards indi-

viduals in the immediate family environment and may be provoked by some trivial rebuff or frustration. Blunting and coarsening of affect are usually prominent, but well established dementia is rare and, although it seems likely that such individuals suffer from a cerebral degenerative process, definite evidence for this is lacking (1968:41-42).

Roth (1968) adds that there is also a small number of hostile and aggressive actions by paranoid subjects - those suffering from pathological jealousy aggravated or released by senility and the advanced stages of chronic alcoholism(see below).

Roth finds the extreme rarity of criminal conduct in old age surprising in view of the fact that a number of the factors generally considered to contribute to the causation of crime in earlier life are no less prominent in old age. They include the relative poverty, lack of social integration and high incidence of mental disorder among the aged. Moreover, cerebral degenerative change or destruction of cerebral neurones due to cerebrovascular disease are both common in a circumscribed form, even among "normal" elderly subjects, and the frequency and extent of such changes increase steeply after the age of 70 years. Such changes, notes Roth, could have been expected to give rise to a coarsening of the emotions and a general heightening of impulsive and aggressive tendencies in conduct. But the opposite is true, and Roth regrets that this curious phenomenon has received very little attention even though its study would likely enhance our understanding of criminal behavior.

Jealousy-Motivated Homicide One type of elderly homicide worthy of particular mention is jealousy-motivated homicide.

In his study of morbid jealousy and murder, Mowat (1966) notes that insane murderers are usually older than sane murderers. He notes further that murderers who are motivated by delusions of infidelity are a good deal older than sane murderers. Although the reasons for this are not clear, Mowat points to the close association between morbid jealousy and paranoid states and to research findings suggesting that the older age groups might be more liable to this form of reaction. The paranoid illness may be an insidiously developing process not reaching its full flowering before the age of 40. There may be many aggressive attacks before the murderous one, and it may well be that the later age of the murderer is related to his insidious illness and the time taken for the morbid process to weaken his restraint and increase his impulsive aggressiveness to the pitch required to perform the murder (p.60).

Mowat (1966) also cites an earlier inquiry by Berg and Fox (1947) into the causative factors in American homicides. The authors found that:

The younger members of the homicide group tend to slay men and to slay them for motives related to economic gain or to avenging a real or fancied insult. The relatively older men , on the other hand, tended to slay women and to slay them for motives usually related to unrequited love, infidelity or arguments which commonly concerned money. It is believed that these relatively older men tended to place a greater value upon security of affection and upon peaceful living. Being older they had accepted and adjusted to a greater degree to whatever economic level they were in. But a younger man might presumably adjust more readily than an older man to the infidelity of a wife or sweetheart by seeking another woman and thus take his wife's defection less personally(1966:56-57).

It is understandable that murders motivated by jealousy will be committed at an older age than most other types of murder. As Mowat (1966) points out, the situation of morbid jealousy is usually the married state and the domestic scene. The jealous man has to have time in his life to be married, presumably when he was reasonably normal, and time for his morbid ideas to develop. Furthermore, according to Mayer-Gross, Slater, and Roth (1945), the paranoid type of reaction is "the most frequent form in the middle aged and elderly". They also refer to "a suggestion that a later age of onset itself predisposes to a paranoid development and jealousy seems only a too natural reaction for the unhappy married husband".

Suicide and Attempted Suicide

Suicide, as well as suicidal attempt, is one form of morbid behavior that appears to rise instead of declining in old age. Early criminological literature contains numerous statements about the high prevalence of this behavior in the later years of life. After noting that the suicide age distribution is much older than the homicide age distribution, Reckless (1950) points out that suicide rates increase steadily "up to 80-84 years of age and then decline (but not sharply)". Jones and Kaplan (1956) agree in substance, but place the peak of self-destruction in the 50s and 60s, "after which the rate remains more or less constant" (see Keller and Vedder, 1969:49). Keller and Vedder (1969) quote East's analysis of English crime (1951) from which he concluded that "In the group of aggressive offenders attempts at suicide occupy the first position in persons over 60".

Stengel (1964) reports that suicide rates have been found to be positively correlated with many factors which include, male sex, increasing age, widowhood, single and divorced state, alcohol consumption, mental disorder, and physical illness. He notes that contrary to popular belief, which associates suicide with frustrated love and "poor moral fibre", the majority of the people who kill themselves are elderly and many of them are physically sick. Their average age is in the late fifties. According to Stengel the peak age for suicide usually lies between fifty-five and sixty-four.

Henry and Short (1965), who examined the relationship between suicide and status, report that the available data confirm the hypothesis that status is generally associated positively with suicide except in the case of age where the decline in status in the later years is accompanied by an increase rather than the predicted decrease in suicide:

Let us return now to our hypothesis of a positive relation between suicide and position in a status hierarchy. A contradiction to the general pattern was the higher suicide rate of the age groupings beyond 65. We had assumed that the older age categories suffer a decline in status and had ranked them lower in a hierarchy of status than the younger age groupings. With this assumption, we would expect the suicide rate to be lower in the age groups past 65 rather than higher as is actually the case (1965:75)

The claim that aggressive tendencies tend in old age to be directed toward oneself rather than toward others, that old people direct their violence inwards rather than outwards, seems to find empirical support in the high rate of suicide among the elderly when compared to their rate of violent crime. Despite their numerous shortcomings, official statistics of crime and suicide tend to confirm Porterfield's hypothesis (1949) that in an aging population homicide rates tend to come down while suicide rates tend to go up.

Moberg (1953) reports that suicide has a higher rate among elderly men than among any other segment of the population. And Roth(1968) points out that successful male suicide reaches a peak in late middle life or old age in every country for which statistical data are available. He also notes that suicide in the elderly is a phenomenon of more general significance than the small number of suicidal subjects would lead one to suppose. According to Roth:

A high proportion of suicidal attempts are of a determined, dangerous or violent nature and more would succeed were it not for ineptitude, ignorance or good fortune. [Cases of] consummated or attempted suicide are merely the visible part of an iceberg. The clinical profile of the severely depressed aged person with physical illness who has few contacts, is living alone, or has recently been bereaved, is commonly seen in community and clinic alike...It is possible that attempts are not made more frequently merely because the forces which impel the individual towards suicidal acts do not converge in time to surmount concern for the feelings of relations, religious scruples and inertia (1968:40).

Why?

Attempts to explain the high rate of suicide among the elderly usually point to the state of hopelessness and despair in which many elderly people inevitably find themselves, or to the boredom and frustration that set in in old age. Gillin (1946) pathetically describes how many elderly feel as strangers in a world that has changed, isolated and cut off from their social network. He writes:

Plumb the depth of their feelings, if they will permit you to do so, and see there the unsatisfied yearning for affection and for gratitude. You will not have great difficulty in understanding why it is that so many old people wish to die. As they so often express it, they have lost their usefulness in the world, and there is no more reason why they should live. They are in the world but not of it. Their ideas, their patterns of conduct belong to an age which has vanished. They find themselves at variance with the accepted behavior of the younger generation. They are strangers to the ideas which have developed since they were young. They live in the past, isolated in the midst of a social world of which they are not part, cut off from the social ties which made life worth while in their earlier years...No wonder these old people give up and pass down hopelessly toward the shades of death (1946:391).

Depression caused by physical ailments and mental disease, triggered or aggravated by retirement, change in life conditions, the loss of a beloved one and so forth, has also been signaled as one of the important factors contributing to a high suicide rate among the aged. Roth (1968) believes that in addition to its association with depression there is a connection between suicide and cerebral degenerative disease. In support if his claim he quotes studies by Batchelor and Napier (1953) in which 10% of those who attempted suicide were diagnosed as having organic dementia. He also refers to Sainsbury (1962) who found that 15% to 20% of suicides had signs of intellectual deterioration and marked cerebrovascular changes in post-mortem. Roth also points to the marked fluctuations in the emotional state of the elderly who suffer from organic dementia. He writes:

> In the elderly organic dement, and particularly in cases of arteriosclerotic psychosis, the emotional state, as also the level of consciousness, tends to undergo marked fluctuations. An elderly subject who has made a violent suicidal attempt by slashing the throat or by trying to hang himself, may, within days or hours, present in a relatively subdued and reasonable frame of mind. Many such violent outbursts occur in a state of clouded consciousness and memory for the events may be partly or wholly obliterated. This marked fluctuation in the mental state may give rise to difficult medico-legal problems (1968:41).

The precarious economic conditions in which many elderly live are also believed by some to be critical factors in suicide. Jackson (1981) cites a high correlation between high suicide rates and lower economic status among the elderly. This pattern is the reverse of that for the overall population where suicide rates are highest in the uppermost levels of socio-economic status (Brown, 1965:145). She also quotes Kaplan (1945) who reported that economic hazard is an important cause of suicide, a fact borne out by the fluctuation of suicide rates with economic conditions.

The disengagement theory, popular among gerontologists, has also been suggested as a possible explanation for the high suicide rate among the elderly. The disengagement theory (Cumming et al., 1960) states that as people grow old some tend to disengage from society and become more internally oriented. Thus with advancing age comes a gradual acceptance of, and a desire for disengagement from, the active societal role. Jackson (1981) suggests that the disengagement hypothesis is consistent with both the low crime and high suicide rate among the elderly. As the older person disengages from society and becomes more internally oriented, there is more attention given to spiritual needs and what may occur as the result of wrongful behavior. This is likely to act as a deterrent against crime. While there is no empirical evidence confirming that this does happen, there is some evidence that the highest suicide rates in the elderly occur in areas where family and neighborhood ties are few (Bromley, 1978:296). This finding makes it reasonable to hypothesize that there is a link between disengagement and suicide.

Roth (1968), on the other hand, is critical of the attempt to explain the marked decline in the rate of criminal offences with age (a decline which runs parallel with a steep decrease in the rate of appearance of fresh cases of drug addiction and a diminution in the prevalence of chronic alcoholism) and the relatively high incidence of consummated suicide and of mental disorder (much of the latter independent of cerebral degeneration) through theories of aging. He writes:

> The changes described cannot be satisfactorily explained by theories vaguely derived from the psychology of senescence. The decrease in the rate of crime and of narcotic addiction begins relatively early in adult life. More precisely formulated and testable hypotheses are needed to investigate areas that may shed light on certain problems of criminal behavior (1968:49-50).

Assault and Aggravated Assault

As with other age groups, assault is the most common violent offence committed by elderly offenders.However, only aggravated assault is included in the seven Index Crimes of the UCR compiled by the FBI.

Both the numbers and rates of elderly arrests for this offence have been rising over the years. Shichor (1984) reports that arests of persons 55 years and older for aggravated assault in the U.S.A. rose from 3,359 in 1964 to 8,927 in 1979, that is an increase of 165.8%. Inciardi (1987) defined the elderly as those 60 years and older. Arrest rates of this age group for aggravated assault went up from 7.1% per 100,000 elderly population in 1964 to 13.4 per 100,000 in 1982, an increase of almost 100% over the 19 year period.

Newman and Newman (1982) point out that assaults which get official attention occur mostly in retirement communities where the aged are in close proximity to one another. They quote a number of observers who think these assaults are the inevitable outcome of natural strains and irritations of people cooped up together. Except for very serious assaults, in the main, these are treated by police like other domestic disturbances, generally with a reprimand and an order to cool down.

This is confirmed by Epstein et al. (1971) who in their study of elderly arrests (60+) in San Fransisco found that assaultive behavior was unusual and tended to occur within the family or rooming house setting. Also of interest was the fact that over the whole period covered (4 months during 1967-1968) there was only one arrest for murder in the age group over 60 and that was the case of a man killed by his wife following an argument.

Wolk et al. (1963) offer an explanation for violent behavior by a specific type of elderly offender, a type they call "the geriatric delinquent". They note that as the geriatric delinquents grow older they find themselves not as well-protected and difficulties arise. Anger, insecurity and feelings of inadequacy, when combined with inability to channel frustration, result in hostile discharges. Frequently status is diminished, so he or she strives for attention and tries to express individuality, sometimes inappropriately. They conclude that the geriatric delinquent, as they define it, is a person who, when placed in a social milieu with which he or she cannot cope, tends to act out his or her conflicts. A basic inability to control impulsivity leads to the acting-out process which is manifested in delinquent behavior.

56

Roth (1968) claims that limited brain damage in elderly individuals will frequently release tendencies to disinhibited and aggressive behavior. This aggressive behavior (as well as the more frequent suicidal tendencies) tend to occur in the early stages of progressive cerebral disease and is particularly characteristic of those conditions in which the degenerative process is of a localized or patchy character. They are more rarely seen in senile dementia than in psychosis with cerebrovascular disease. As the degenerative process advances, the fluctuations in level of awareness die down, aggressive and suicidal tendencies subside, emotional disturbance becomes less prominent and the bland, unresponsive and eventually fatuous or apathetic affect supervenes. Systematized paranoid ideas, depressive symptoms and elaborate delusional ideas of jealousy tend to follow the same course.

Richman (1982) reports that the cases he has seen in the clinic of the elderly assaultive patients whose aggressive behavior stopped short of completed murder seemed similar in many respects to those published reports of elderly people who committed murder. Organic mental syndromes, for example, were common. Richman hypothesizes that there are similarities in the individual dynamics and situational factors of both homicidal attempts and completed homicide. His examination of all the cases, published and clinical, led him to identify six major components of violence in the elderly:

1. A certain premorbid personality is present, in particular one in which violence is ego- and culturally - syntonic and associated with social approval. Several of the assaultive husbands had a "tough kid" history, with much fighting, school failure, and an association of being a "real" man with being violent. Several had a history of alcoholism.

2. The individual is mentally and physically impaired, which has resulted in a drastic difference in self-concept, self-esteem, and the way he or she is regarded by significant others. The difference is due to a decline in the personal resources or coping abilities of the individual, usually on the basis of an organic mental syndrome or a general physiological decline, which weakens the ego, impairs impulse control, and sometimes judgement.

3. There is some provocation from the family and social network. In the majority of the assaultive patients in the clinic, their marriage had been unstable or unhappy, with marital problems that dated back many years. In a manner analogous to messages sent to suicidal persons to harm themselves (Rosenbaum and Richman, 1970), homicidal or assaultive persons may receive messages from the family or significant others to harm others.The family and social network may have a stake in being provocative. The importance of neighbors needs to be stressed, particularly among the elderly for whom the neighbors may have become the major part of their social network. Many old and fixed family patterns and conflicts with those who have died may be transferred with little basic change to these neighbors.

4. The act serves a social as well as psychological function. It may, for example, occur as part of a process of extrusion of the older individual from the social network.

5. There is a crisis, which helps precipitate the homicidal behavior.

6.   Society is brought in. As a result, what begins as an individual and family process becomes part of a social problem.

In summary, the act of homicide in the elderly can best be understood in the light of the personality of the murderer, the nature of the relationship to the victim, and the circumstances surrounding the act. When pursued with full lethal intent, homicide is the extreme example of the effects of frustration and aggression unleashing the destructiveness inherent in human nature (Richman, 1982).

Robbery

Robbery without a weapon is an offence that generally requires physical strength and speed, neither of which is characteristic of old age. The dark streets and alleys and the dimly lit places where robberies tend to be committed are not places where an elderly prospective robber would feel safe. Moreover, he or she runs the danger of falling victim to younger, more agile predators. Consequently, elderly persons who need and/or want to obtain money or other valuables by illegal means are bound to choose acts that do not require them to challenge the victim. They will avoid confrontational situations where, more often than not, they will be the weaker party. Robbery is typical of this kind of situation. It is not surprising, therefore, that elderly involvement in robbery is minimal and that the few incidents they perpetrate are mostly committed by desperate old men who use firearms to compensate for their physical weakness. Shichor and Kobrin(1978) point out that robbery is one of the least frequent of the offences for which elderly people are arrested. In 1974, in the U.S.A., it accounted for 6.3% of arrests for violent offences among the 55 years and over age group. It was lower than murder, and somewhat higher than forcible rape.

On the basis of UCR data for a five year period ending in 1964, Keller and Vedder (1969) concluded that robbery is an activity of the younger offender ranking 19th in the arrests of those between 25 and 29 years. It failed to appear in the top 20 of any of the four older groups.

Although elderly arrests for robbery seem to be increasing in the U.S.A., both the numbers and the rate remain quite insignificant. According to Inciardi (1987), the arrest rate of the elderly (60+) for robbery in 1982 was less than one (0.9) per 100,000 elderly population .

Newman and Newman (1982) suggest that the occasional armed robbery committed on a bank or a store by an elderly person tends for the most part to be perpetrated by a criminal who has grown old rather than an old person who has become criminal in old age. They refer to a real life situation, much like that depicted in the movie "Going in Style" with George Burns, Art Carney and Lee Strasberg, which has been taking place in the Southwest. A group of bank robbers, dubbed the "Over-the-Hill-Gang" robbed several banks in Oklahoma, Texas, and other southwestern States. The leader of the gang is believed to be a man in his sixties who wears a hearing aid. Needless to say, this predatory kind of crime, exemplified by the "Over-the-Hill-Gang" is extremely rare.

TIME MAGAZINE (September 20, 1982) relates the incident of a pair of grey-haired men who looked like any of the retirees at a public supermarket in

Hollywood, Florida. When they reached the cashier, one abruptly pulled out a gun and demanded money. Loot in hand, the two fled from the store, jumped into a get-away car, and were whisked away by another aging driver. According to *TIME*, the trio had played out that scene five times in 1982, and had knocked off Wells Fargo armored cars as well as supermarkets and the bank. At the time the story was published they were still at large.

Property Offences

As for other age groups, non-violent property offences by the elderly far outnumber the sexual offences or offences against the person that they commit. And contrary to numerous affirmations by those who studied old age criminality, fraud, embezzlement and forgery are not prominent among the types of property offences committed by the elderly.

Studies of prison and penitentiary populations sometimes reveal a higher incidence of admission for aggressions against the person and sexual offences than for property offences. For example, Cormier et al. (1971) found, upon analyzing admission to a federal penitentiary in the Province of Quebec, that property offences accounted for 66% in those who started between 20 and 24, 53% in those who started between 25 and 39, and 31% in those who committed their first offence after age 40. On the other hand, crimes against the person, including sexual offences and homicide, accounted for 27% in the 20 to 24 group, 44% in the group between 25 and 39, and 52% in the over 40 group. Needless to say these differences might simply be artifactual, reflecting a more frequent imposition of non-institutional measures and a wider use of alternatives to imprisonment for elderly offenders guilty of less serious property offences.

The high incidence of fraud and embezzlement often reported by students of elderly crime does not seem to be confirmed by UCR arrest data. Pollak (1941), for one, writes that "Our data show again the leading position of sex offences; then come violations of the narcotic and drug laws, embezzlement, fraud and receiving of stolen goods among the violations of property rights while burglary, breaking and entry, robbery, and especially auto theft are to be found on the other end of the list". This is echoed by Moberg (1953) who claims that among older criminals certain types of crime, such as drunkenness, sex offences, embezzlement, fraud, etc.,tend to predominate while crimes which involve physical violence or a quick decision are relatively infrequent. A similar view is expressed by Cavan (1955) who, contrasting the offences of various age groups, insists that crimes of manual skill and mental agility, such as forgery, counterfeiting, embezzlement, and fraud- ways to obtaining money through skillful imitation of handwriting or printing, manipulation of accounts, and outwitting of a victim,are the ones most characteristic of the mature adult and to some extent of the middle and old-age group (1955:47).

Studies of arrest data, however, paint a different picture. Keller and Vedder (1969) found, on the basis of UCR arrest data over a five-year period ending in 1964, little difference among various age groupings with respect to their ranking on larceny. Surprisingly, however, old offenders did not appear any more likely to be arrested for fraud than those in their late 20s! The authors also found that embezzlement does not appear in the "top 20" crimes for any of the five age groups in the Uniform Crime Reports.

In their study of the frequency and causes of arrests in San Francisco of individuals 60 years old and over during a period of four months in 1967-1968, Epstein et al. (1971) found that certain offences which normally constitute about one-third of all adult arrests were absent in the older group. Among these were forgery, fictitious checks, desertion, malicious mischief, arson, extortion, prostitution, as well as a large variety of miscellaneous minor offences.

The discrepancy between the findings of the studies reviewed above is probably due to the differences in the data used. Studies based on arrest figures tend to show that arrests for fraud, embezzlement, forgery, counterfeiting and so on are quite small in proportion to the more dominant types of property offences (such as larceny). Studies of elderly offenders using prison inmates, on the other hand, are more likely to report a high percentage of offenders admitted for these offences. This, again, may simply be due to differences in court practices, namely a higher use of prison sentences for these offences than for ordinary larceny.

Larceny

Larceny is the index crime for which the elderly are most frequently arrested. Shichor and Kobrin (1978) report that arrests of the elderly for the serious property offences are largely concentrated in the general category of larceny-theft. This offence, they write, accounts for virtually all arrests in this age group for the index property offences. Further, the fact that the proportion of arrests for larceny-theft showed a slight tendency to increase over the period they examined, along with a decline in the proportion of arrests for burglary, suggests the possible tendency by the police to reduce potential burglary charges in cases of elderly to the less serious one of theft.

Feinberg (1982) reports that in the U.S.A., between 1975 and 1980, there has been a slight decrease in juvenile arrests for larceny coupled with a strong increase in adult arrests for that offence . He claims that those aged 60-64 and those 65 and older are contributing disproportionately to the aging of larceny arrests. During that period, the volume of larceny arrests for the first group increased from 6,627 to 9,574 and for the second group from 8,566 to 12,857. These figures represent volume increases of 44% and 50% respectively. At the same time, the increase in larceny arrests recorded for those 18 years and over was 35%. For the elderly as a whole, larceny arrests in the U.S.A. went up by 309% (by volume) and 265% (by rate) over the period 1966-1980.

Feinberg (1982) also reports that male arrests for larceny exceed female arrests by about two to one. However, larceny constitutes the Index crime for which the most females are arrested.

More recently, Inciardi (1987), using a different age grouping, found that elderly (60+) arrest rates for larceny-theft went up from 18 per 100,000 in 1964 to 67.6% in 1982.

Shoplifting

Whether in England, Canada or the U.S.A., shoplifting seems to be the most common type of larceny committed by elderly offenders. Roth (1968), a British psychiatrist, reports that the incidence of criminal behavior among the elderly is accounted for by petty theft and shoplifting in both men and women. For men it equals all other forms of petty theft after the age of 60 years. Referring to findings by Gibbins and Prince (1962), Roth states that shoplifting often forms in men the terminal phase in the careers of recidivists previously convicted for a wide range of offences.

In the U.S.A. Newman and Newman (1982) affirm that shoplifting is not only the most common offence of elderly criminals, but, in motivation and skill (or lack of it), is prototypical of behavior patterns in other offences as well. They write:

> shoplifting is an amateur's offence, with the exception of professional "boosters" who make a career of stealing furs, jewels, and other valuable items. Elderly shoplifting is a relatively unskilled opportunistic crime..Shopping is a major activity of retired elderly and opportunities for stealing arise every day..The largest proportion of elderly shoplifters, perhaps as high as 90%, are those who have been law-abiding until detected in this offence (1982:6).

According to the Newmans, elderly shoplifters have some unusual characteristics which are quite different from teenage shoplifters and others who are more professional:

- On the average not only do elderly shoplifters have clean records but they also come from middle and upper middle classes.

- The most commonly shoplifted items are cosmetics and sport clothing. Necessary drugs or vitamin supplements are not high on the list, nor are bread and butter the most common foods stolen. Instead, the elderly steal more esoteric foods, such as imported cheeses, cocktail oysters and the like.

- The major motive in elderly shoplifting is not real economic hardship, but that it provides the perpetrators with discretionary money when they are living close to the subsistence line from retirement income or social security. Sheer economic necessity might, however, become a major motive in elderly shoplifting, especially if the economy continues to deteriorate in the same fashion as it has in recent years.

- Another motive in elderly shoplifting seems to be attention-getting. A number of elderly living in retirement homes distant from their children have discovered that they may get attention by being arrested. The Newmans quote an elderly female shoplifter as saying "My children never visit me no matter how many times I ask, but when I got arrested they came right away".

- Another hypothesis , proposed by Gary Feinberg and cited by the Newmans, is that retired persons and juveniles share many characteristic lifestyles and tend to engage in similar criminal conduct.

- The Newmans finally offer a marxist hypothesis stipulating that some elderly feel that they have been "ripped off" by commercial concerns all their lives and shoplifting is a final chance to get even.

Feinberg (1982a, 1982b), who studied an unrepresentative sample of elderly shoplifters who were referred to an elderly shoplifters clinic in Florida, denies what he calls the myth that elderly shoplifters steal because they are indigent or for subsistence purposes, or because they are lonely or are seeking revenge against a store or an indifferent family. Feinberg is quoted in *TIME* (September 20, 1982) as saying:

Overaged criminals feel they are no longer bound to a system that has no place for them...they are adrift, and society has provided them with nei- ther map nor itinerary nor friendly shore (1982:63).

On another occasion, Feinberg was quoted in the *APA MONITOR* (Vol.13, no.5, May 1982) as saying:

The elderly are drifting. Status roles haven't been well defined and crystalized. They have very few role models and guidelines. All they know is that these are the golden years, a time of leisure. They are left to their own bootstraps...they are clipped free from the normal social controls because social rewards are no longer forthcoming for those behaviors..They have lost respect, power and are no longer important to society. Their amorphous status suddenly puts them in a position to commit deviant behavior, and they say "What have I got to lose?" (1982:32)

Sydney Glugover who counsels elderly shoplifters in Florida's Broward County does not agree . He believes social scientists like to invent poetic theo- ries about alienated subcultures. *TIME* (September 20, 1982) quotes him as saying "Economics is at the root of the crime. If you want a theory for what they are doing, you can call it 'dollar stretch' ".

Organized Crime, Professional Crime and White Collar Crime

Newman and Newman (1982) assert that elderly perpetrators play an important and sometimes a dominant role in three major crime types which are different from ordinary crime: organized crime, professional crime and white collar crime. They note that gangsters and racketeers are generally recruited to a life of crime as young persons but control of organized crime is clearly in the hands of older "family" heads, "godfathers" who by any definition are elderly; the godfather is very likely to be a grandfather.

The Newmans further suggest that Professional crime, which comprises 'behavior as confidence games, shoplifting, picking pockets, and big-time robberies and illicit auto rings, is also dominated by the fessional, they argue, crime is a lifetime career and a group activity, informally structured compared to organized crime, yet organized in its own fashion. It is also much more sophisticated, much more skillful, and much more difficult to detect than ordinary crime. The Newmans write:

> Just as with organized crime, becoming a professional criminal is not an individual decision. To become a true professional the person must be recruited by those already recognized as professionals and trained by them to operate in confidence games and other forms of fraud or theft. They are normally recruited as young men (and occasionally women) but do not reach the zenith of their skills and the professional respect of other thieves (as well as the police), until middle age and beyond. This is not unlike success in any legitimate profession. Some of the most notorious (and most "successful") professional criminals live to a ripe old age practising their skills well into their seventies and beyond (1982:2).

The third major type discussed by Newman and Newman is white collar crime which involves violations of law and trust by persons in the course of their occupations, generally business, politics, or the professions. White collar crimes range from embezzlement to corporate price fixing and from accepting or offering a bribe to systematic tax evasion. By definition white collar crime is not perpetrated by the young. It takes age and maturity to get to a position to commit white collar offences. One must be in an office of trust to embezzle or to engage in systematic fraud and, of course, to accept a bribe, one ordinarily has to be sufficiently mature to occupy an elective or an appointive office (ibid.,p. 3). The Newmans conclude that organized, professional, and white collar crimes are offences of the elderly, not the activities of youngsters. They write:

> Contrary to common notions, then, the elderly do participate in major criminal activities: the elderly, in other words, do not confine themselves merely to shoplifting cans of soup until their social security check arrives. Indeed, the only major type of crime in which the aged are not well represented is ordinary crime, and even this is changing (1982:3).

Alcohol-Related Offences

Alcohol-related offences figure prominently in the overall picture of elderly criminality. In fact, alcohol plays both a direct and indirect role in the offences committed by old age persons. The direct role is demonstrated by the high percentage of arrests for public drunkenness, disorderly conduct and driving under the influence of alcohol. The indirect criminogenic role of alcohol comes from its being a triggering factor and a disinhibitor in crimes of violence against the person (particularly homicide)[3] sexual offences and certain property offences such as shoplifting.

Keller and Vedder (1969) point out that as far as arrests are concerned, people over 50 years of age are apprehended for a great many of the same offences as people 25 years younger and that the offences are ranked in much the same order. This is particularly the case where alcohol is involved. They found that whether the male offender is in age ranges 25-29, 50-54, 55-59, 60-64, or over 65, he is most likely to be arrested for drunkenness. Next, for all age categories, comes disorderly conduct. Driving under the influence of alcohol ranks in the upper half for all five age groupings. The authors add that while more younger than older people were arrested for the various offences, with respect to drunkenness, more individuals in the 50-54 group were arrested than in the group with the highest arrest rate, the 25-29 years old.

A decade later the situation had not changed much. Shichor and Kobrin (1978) reported that among the non-Index, generally misdemeanor offences, five are notable for their prominence in the arrest statistics with reference to the elderly. They include gambling, driving under the influence, drunkenness, disorderly conduct and vagrancy. Of these, the highest proportion of arrests were for drunkenness at each of the three time points examined.

In their study of arrests in San Francisco, Epstein et al. (1971) found that four out of five elderly arrests were for drunkenness whereas this was the cause of only one out of two of all adult arrests. They add that for many of the 18% of the subject population whose arrests were for other than drunkenness, alcoholic intoxication played an important role in the arrest. For example, a woman had her husband arrested for disturbing the peace because she feared for her safety because of his rage while intoxicated; a bartender caused a similar arrest of an elderly patron who insisted upon being served although already intoxicated.

For further study Epstein et al. (1971) drew a sample from the Arrest Ledger. The sample included 200 persons arrested for drunkenness who were 60 years or older (average age was 64). Of this group, 86% were between 60 and 69 years of age. Arrests of persons 70 years of age or over were infrequent and represented only 12% of this group; arrests of persons over age 80 represented 2% of the group; and no one over age 90 was arrested. There were only 10 women (5%) in the sample, and their arrests appeared to be idiosyncratic. The authors found, for example, that whereas the majority of men were arrested lying on the sidewalk or in a doorway or walking with difficulty, arrests of women more frequently were associated with a complaint to the police about their behavior. For example, a woman 75 years old, after drinking relatively little in a neighborhood bar, became insulting and abusive to the bartender, who called the police for aid and "protection".

Epstein et al. (1971) conclude that arrests of the elderly for drunkenness are not often associated with antisocial or assaultive behavior, although they are not infrequently associated with drunk driving. Further they conclude that:

It is... evident that elderly males arrested for drunkenness (and they represent 80% of the arrests of persons aged 60 years or older in San Francisco) are not seen as criminals by the officers who arrest them or by the staff at the jail who supervise them while they are prisoners or by themselves. Despite this, all three groups participate in the arresting process, which is seen by them as a non-punitive procedure and as the only available source for assistance at this time. All three groups tend to view the procedure as tantamount to brief, though at times uncomfortable, hospitalization. The arresting officer and the jailer view these prisoners as ill and in need of supervised care in a sheltered setting: in fact, they spontaneously expressed the view that hospitalization, rather than incarceration in a jail, is preferable. The prisoner himself, moreover, in the majority of cases does not bear resentment toward the arresting officer and with few exceptions expresses the view that he is well treated in jail. A number of anecdotes were told describing the variety of ways in which arrest and imprisonment often are actively sought by this group (1971:40).

In addition to the high toll alcohol generally takes on the aged in terms of death, disease and mental disorders, there is evidence that elderly alcoholics are less tolerated in the home than elderly non-alcoholics (Jackson, 1981). Jackson points out that once established, drinking could lead to further disengagement, deviance, and/or deterioration in the elderly. This, rather than old age *per se*, could lead to criminal deviance. She writes:

When alcoholism accompanies criminal deviance in the elderly, the convergence often results in a shunting back and forth of such individuals from the legal system to the medical or psychiatric systems in order to resolve a "warehousing problem". An old alcoholic may be picked up and charged for vagrancy on one occasion, and on the next taken to a mental facility for bizarre behavior related to drinking (1981:49).

Drug Offences

Roth (1968) wonders why it is that there is a sharp decline in alcoholic and narcotic addiction early in adult life. Citing Percor (1938), Roth notes that the fall in the inception rate of fresh cases of narcotic addiction is already evident in the fourth decade and disappears almost completely in the later decades.

In contrast to this decline in narcotics addiction there seems to be an increase in the use of prescription mood-modifying drugs. Newman and Newman (1982) point out that, for the most part, drug violations by the elderly are simply abuse of common prescription narcotics, that is, the use of these products for other than medical reasons:

No one is certain how frequently this occurs, but those dealing with medical problems of the aged report the incidence of habituation and addiction to be quite high. Since elderly persons are more frequently prescribed drugs than their younger counterparts, there is no way of knowing how widespread this overuse is. In general, these offences involve barbiturates and amphetamines. Use of heroin and other opiates is rare among the aged except for addicts who have grown old. In common use of the term, "junkies" are almost invariably young or middle-aged persons (1982:5).

Newman and Newman (1982) also mention numerous media reports of elderly narcotics violations, mostly involving possession of drugs but, in some cases, sales as well. They refer to a number of arrests of female drug traffickers (labelled the "women's mafia") in California which involved importing and selling hard drugs.

A similar incident occurred in Australia some years ago. On March 23, 1983 the world news agency Reuter reported the release from an Australian prison of two elderly American women aged 66 and 65 both of whom are from La Pine, Oregon. The two women, dubbed the "Drug Grannies" by the Australian news media, were jailed in 1978 for fourteen years for smuggling

65

drugs into Australia. Custom officials had discovered 1.9 tons of hashish with a 1978 street value of $11 million hidden in the women's van after it arrived in Sydney from Bangkok, Thailand.

Whereas the use of, and trafficking in, illicit drugs (cannabis, heroin, cocaine, LSD, etc.) are highly concentrated among the young, the elderly use and abuse prescription and over-the-counter drugs. Abuse of such drugs does increase elderly visits to physicians but does not constitute a criminal offence and does not bring the elderly individual into contact with drug enforcement officers or the criminal justice system. This explains why this is an underresearched area in both criminology and gerontology.

Petersen (1987) recently reviewed the available literature on drug use and misuse in old age and concluded that research on age cohorts other than young adults is comparatively sparse. The few existing studies suggest that the community-dwelling elderly have high rates of use for prescription and over the counter drugs, as well as higher usage rates than any other age categories for several classes of pescription psychoactive drugs, including minor tranquilizers, sedatives and hypnotics. The data Petersen reviewed on prescription psychotropic drug use in institutional setting (nursing homes and hospitals) re-vealed much the same patterns. Major tranquilizers and hypnotics were the classes of psychoactive drugs most frequently prescribed. Petersen deplores the state of current research and suggests that a great deal more information is needed on the nature and extent of drug use by the elderly. He lists the fol-lowing as areas in which research is urgently and badly needed:

- extensive epidemiological studies of drug-use patterns among the general population of community elderly;

- studies of special populations of elderly that are usually underreported in current surveys: studies of women, low-income, institutionalized, minority, and rural aged;

- studies that would examine drug-use patterns over time to assess duration and change;

- information on the social and psychological factors that might predict and explain elderly drug use; studies using control groups aimed at explaining in what key ways drug users differ from non-users;

- studies of the use patterns for all types of prescription drugs (not just psychotropic drugs) and studies concentrating on specific drugs and drug classes;

- studies rigorously testing the various explanatory models that have been advanced to account for elderly drug use and misuse;

- more information about the magnitude of, and the reasons for, the misuse of drugs by the elderly.

CONCLUSION

A decade ago, Shichor and Kobrin (1978) remarked that criminality and criminal behavior among the elderly is a minimally researched field, that there is very limited knowledge of their patterns of criminal involvement and of the associated social and psychological factors. Today, several years later, alas, this remark is still true. Despite repeated statements deploring the dearth of studies on elderly offenders, they continue to be largely neglected by criminological researchers. The abundance of literature, theories and research on juvenile delinquency is in sharp contrast to the paucity of data and the penury of explanations of old age criminality. While a large number of criminologists have studied juvenile delinquency, hardly any have paid more than scant attention to the criminality of the aged (Pollak, 1941:213). As Pollak jokingly remarked, "old criminals offer an ugly picture and it seems as if even scientists do not like to look at it for any considerable amount of time". And while recent criminological literature is paying more and more attention to the victimization of the elderly, their criminality does not seem to elicit much interest or to generate much enthusiasm.

One can only speculate on the reasons for this neglect in the field of criminology where hundreds of books and papers are published every year. One reason seems to be the sharp decline in criminality with age discussed above. Another reason seems to be the respect we have for old people in general. This respect inhibits us from casting them in our minds in the role of predators, aggressors or thieves. We tend to perceive them more as victims than as offenders. Occasionally, it is true, we hear expressions such as "dirty old man" said in connection with some deviant or abnormal act in the sphere of sexuality. But by and large, the image most people have of the elderly fits more the popular stereotype of the victim than that of the criminal.

NOTES

1. Pedophilia is a condition where the exclusive sexual preference is for prepubertal children; in hebephilia the preference is for pubertal children; a proxenete is a person who brings together a prostitute and a client (for example, an operator of a call girl network) and proxenitism is just another word for "pimping".

2. These findings are not confirmed by a more recent study conducted at the Clarke Institute of Psychiatry and quoted by Jackson (1981). Thirty-two individuals aged 60 years or more at the time of the offence were examined: sixteen violent offenders and sixteen non- violent offenders with a control of sixteen violent offenders aged 30 years or less. The elderly violent offenders were no more prone to suicidal behavior after the crime than the younger violent offenders. The elderly offender was more biased toward psychopathology however than the other two groups, which the authors found somewhat striking because the older control group was taken from sexual offenders (Hucker and Ben Aron, 1981 quoted by Jackson).

3. The North Carolina Department of Corrections found that elderly inmates were much more likely to have been intoxicated at the time of their arrest than younger prisoners. And another study of aged convicts in Michigan found that all murders committed by the elderly involved heavy drinking (Krajick, 1979:34).

CHAPTER THREE: RECOMMENDED READINGS

Alston, L.T.
1986 Crime and Older Americans. Springfield, Ill.: Charles C. Thomas. Chapter Five: Counting Older Offenders. pp. 123-156.

Hucker, S.J. and M.H. Ben-Aron
1984 Violent Elderly Offenders: A Comparative Study. In W. Wilbanks and P.K.H. Kim (Eds.). Elderly Criminals. Lanham, MD: University Press of America. pp. 69-81.

1985 Elderly Sex Offenders. In R. Langevin (Ed.). Erotic Preference, Gender Identity, and Aggression in Men: New Research Studies. Hillside, N.J.: Laurence Erlbaum Associates, pp.211-223.

Jackson, M.
1981 Criminal Deviance Among the Elderly. Canadian Criminology Forum. 4:45-54.

Kercher, K.
1987 The Causes and Correlates of Crime Committed by the Elderly. Research on Aging, 9(2):256-280.

Newman, E.S. and D.J. Newman
1982 Senior Citizen Crime. The Justice Reporter. 2(5):1-7.

Richman, J.
1982 Homicidal and Assaultive Behavior in the Elderly. In Danto et al. (Eds.). The Human Side of Homicide New York: Columbia University Press. pp. 190-198.

Roth, M.
1968 Cerebral Disease and Mental Disorder of Old Age as causes of antisocial Behavior. In de Reuck et al. (Eds.). The Mentally Abnormal Offender-A Ciba Foundation Symposium. London: J.& A. Churchill Ltd. pp. 35-58.

Shichor, D. and S. Kobrin
1978 Criminal Behavior Among the Elderly. The Gerontologist, 18(2):213-218.

CHAPTER FOUR

THE ELDERLY OFFENDER
AND
THE CRIMINAL JUSTICE SYSTEM

THE ELDERLY OFFENDER IN THE HANDS OF THE POLICE

The continuing growth in the size of the elderly population means that increasing numbers of elderly people will come into contact with the criminal justice system in one capacity or another. As mentioned in chapter two, the numbers of those who come into conflict with the law and who are handled by the justice authorities seem to be growing. It is important, therefore, to examine how elderly offenders are dealt with by the criminal justice system.

The criminal justice system is supposed to treat people equally regardless of their sex, race, social class and so forth. However, those who work in the criminal justice system are humans, not robots ,and it is impossible for them to be totally objective and impartial in their dealings with everyone they come into contact with. They hold certain attitudes and thus are bound to entertain some favorable as well as some negative biases vis-a-vis various groups. In an article on elderly offenders published in *TIME* magazine (Sept. 20, 1982), Donald Pappa, a municipal court judge in Ashbury Park, N.J. is quoted as saying: "When these people come before me, I feel as if I am standing in judgement over my own parents". Police officers arresting and interrogating elderly individuals suspected of committing violent or non-violent offences might have similar feelings. This begs the question of whether elderly offenders, at present, are treated differently from other offenders by the police. "Different" or "special" treatment does not necessarily mean "preferential" treatment. The police, or at least some members of the police force, might for various reasons deal with the elderly offender more harshly than with younger ones. They might be outraged at a multi-recidivist who continues to commit crime in his sunset years despite the fact that he has been in and out of the system most of his life. They might be incensed at the elderly respectable individual with no criminal record who takes advantage of an unsuspecting child by sexually abusing or molesting him/her. Although police outrage in such cases is quite normal, it is bound to influence their attitudes toward, and treatment, of suspects. After all, the police are part of their community and as such they do share the attitudes, the biases and prejudices of that community. Frustration and moral outrage will give way to a more caring and understanding attitude only when the police are better informed about the nature and causes of elderly criminality.

Alston (1986) cites limited evidence suggesting that police tend to respond to misbehavior in older people primarily in terms of their harmlessness and their need for protection. She adds, however, that this benign picture of police response to the older, minor offender should not be accepted as a universal behavior pattern. At times police may ridicule elderly offenders (for example vagrants, panhandlers, and drunks) and subject them to both verbal and physical abuse as ways to encourage them to leave the street or the area. Alston believes that police treatment of the geriatric delinquent may depend more on the circumstances of the misbehavior than on age.

Police Discretion and the Processing of Elderly Offenders

Police officers enjoy more discretion than most other public officials. Writing in 1970, Bittner pointed out that:

> No other aspects of police practice have received more scholarly attention in the recent past than the procedures and decisions connected with invoking the law. The principal result of these inquiries was the discovery that policemen have, in effect, a greater degree of discretionary freedom in proceeding against public offenders than any other public official...The condition creates something of a legal paradox because, according to the discovered facts, the policeman who is in terms of the official hierarchy of power, competence, and dignity, on the lowest rung of the administration of justice, actually determines that "outer perimeter of law enforcement", and thus actually determines what the business of his betters will be. (Quoted from Fyfe, 1984:105)

Although the police make discretionary decisions in the exercise of their daily duties, the use of this discretion is particularly problematic in the case of elderly offenders. Fyfe (1984) highlights some of the dilemmas police face in processing elderly offenders. One dilemma is that arrests of the elderly, especially for minor offences, are likely to involve both sympathy for arrestees and perception that the police have acted unreasonably. Fyfe notes that if the police are to handle elderly offenders humanely and in a way that minimizes police exposure to civil liability then they need to be allowed more discretion than they currently have. He points out that police often encounter elderly offenders whose criminal acts and general manner suggest that they are mentally disordered - or senile - and who therefore are most appropriately diverted out of the justice system to the care of family or a social service institution as expeditiously as possible. They are often unable to do so, however, because of statutory restrictions. The constraints placed on police discretion by pressure from the victim or outraged citizens' groups often lead to the arrest of the elderly offender. Such elderly offender will be subjected to the trauma of detention prior to court appearances, a detention that accomplishes nothing. Fyfe adds that:

70

While the public is concerned about shoplifting, family violence, and drunken driving, most people retain great sympathy for the elderly. In the abstract, there is great public support for police attempts to deal forcefully with these offenders, but in specific cases there frequently exists the perception of harshness when police arrest individual elderly offenders (1984:107).

In conclusion, Fyfe suggests that police discretion in the handling and processing of elderly offender cases be broadened rather than restricted. It is difficult to agree with Fyfe's suggestion since the police currently enjoy enormous discretion to invoke or not to invoke the criminal process. The discretionary powers of the police, and of other criminal justice officials (particularly the prosecutor), are such that there are at present several attempts in Canada and the United States to structure, control and narrow such discretion. Every study of discretion leads one to conclude that less rather than more discretion is the answer to many of the problems associated with the lack of uniformity in enforcing the law. In Bittner's (1967) study of peace keeping on skid row (and many of skid row dwellers are elderly) he found that the police often do not arrest persons who have committed minor offences in circumstances in which arrest is technically possible. He further observed that on skid row, patrolmen often made decisions based on reasons that the law probably does not recognize as valid:

> whenever there exist means for controlling the troublesome aspects of some person's presence in some way alternative to an arrest, such means are preferentially employed, provided, of course, that the case at hand involves only a minor offence(1967:710).

None of these findings, and they are by no means exclusive to skid row, points to a need for broadening police discretion. Speaking of elderly shoplifters, Fearnside (1976) insists that there are at least seven possible courses of action open to the police all of which rely on personal attitudes, decisions and individual policies of police forces. These range from automatic court proceedings to "cautioning" to, finally, no action whatsoever being taken. Fearnside feels that the final outcome does not rely on the seriousness of the offence but can rely on the decision of an aggrieved or senior police officer or even on a fact so remotely connected with the area of the country where the offence is committed. He finds it absurd that someone who commits an offence in one part of the country is taken to court, while someone else in identical circumstances, apart from the location of the offence, will be cautioned.

Fearnside (1976) believes that an elderly person with no previous criminal convictions, or none during the ten years immediately before, who commits a relatively minor offence, takes the same chance of prosecution as all other offenders, except the young. On the basis of his experience with many elderly offenders he finds debatable whether they should be so classified or whether they should be considered as a separate problem on similar lines to the young. Although he admits that the thought of having to appear in court can have a most harmful effect on an elderly person, he believes that sparing the elderly offender a court appearance is not always in the elderly's own best interest. He writes:

I am of the opinion that throughout this country (England) there are many cases of elderly criminal offenders not made known to the police because of the misguided beliefs of people who feel that they will be adding to the offender's problems by reporting the incident and risking his or her prosecution, whereas in fact, they are probably doing untold harm in denying the offender certain help to prevent repetition of the offence. This problem should not exist and some standardisation of policy might go a long way to reducing this fear. (1976:1297).

Fearnside concludes that along with the tendency to standardize procedure for the young, it might be expedient to consider those who have led mostly blameless lives and then suddenly find themselves a criminal offender, suffering not only the stigma of knowing they have committed an offence but also having to face the ordeal of a court proceeding or a long wait before knowing what action is to be taken against them.

PROSECUTORIAL DISCRETION AND THE PROCESSING OF OLD OFFENDERS

Studies analyzing the processing of elderly offenders through the criminal justice system and comparing dispositions in their cases to those involving younger arrestees are extremely rare and the findings are not conclusive. Clearly this is an area that offers rich possibilities for future research.

Lindquist et al. (1987) highlight some of the problems involved in doing research on dispositions of arrest. They note that the criminal justice system, notorious for lacking organization, divides processing and record keeping among its constituent elements and among the political units into which the United States is divided. Thus, while data regarding arrests and prisoners are available, prosecutional and judicial decisions are not. No single agency collects information on the way prosecutors or trial courts dispose of cases. The authors point out that to conduct research regarding these portions of the criminal justice system, one must examine the files contained in the office of each prosecutor and each court. The situation is made even more difficult because data needed for analysis are normally available only as judicial files, maintained on the bases of individual case folders, stored away in the offices of judges (in those cases in which the offender has been sentenced to probation) or in dead storage. In either event each file must be examined individually in order to reconstruct the events that make up each case. Such reconstructions are extremely time consuming (p.162).

One of the few studies that tries to examine age selectivity in the criminal justice process is a study by Cutshall and Adams (1983). The authors wanted to find out whether decision-makers, or gate-keepers, in the criminal justice process take into account an offender's age in determining an appropriate redressive response; whether older offenders are afforded preferential leniency at key decision-making points of that process. To do so, the authors chose shoplifting because "this offence is subject to greater discretionary processing than a more uniformly repugnant crime, such as murder". The hypothesis that elderly shoplifters were treated more leniently than adult ones in the middle age group was based on previous research which examined the referral/release decision. Cutshall and Adams point out that previous studies with only one major exception (Cohen and Stark, 1974) show that a shoplifter's age is associated with the decision outcome, and it is the young and old who are most likely to be released. Justifying their decision to examine prosecutor's rather than police decision, the authors note that a call summoning the police is most often a call for criminal processing, and not a call for discretionary police intervention. Thus the suspect's age appears to have little or no effect upon formal arrest decisions, and referred shoplifters proceed to the prosecutor with few dropouts. The authors further explain why they selected 50 years of age, rather than 60 or 65 as their cutting point for defining elderly shoplifters.

The analysis of the data indicated that of the older shoplifters charged by the prosecutor, only 28.6% were actually prosecuted compared to 44.9% of adult shoplifters in the middle age group. The data further indicated that older shoplifters were also being prosecuted less often than younger adult shoplifters. Differences in favor of elderly shoplifters persisted when variables such as "prior arrest record", "selected offence characteristics", "strength of the prosecutor's case" were controlled for. In other words, the data demonstrated a fairly consistent pattern of differential prosecution between older shoplifters and those in the middle age group, thus supporting the notion that the prosecutor affords preferential leniency to older shoplifters, and confirming the proposition that age is a mitigating factor in the enforcement of legal norms. The authors point out that this finding was not entirely unexpected given the type of offence they have investigated. Shoplifting, they argue, is a marginally deviant offence of comparatively low seriousness. Such offenses are routinely processed with greater discretion than more serious felony offences.

According to Cutshall and Adams, the Criminal justice system is not responding very well to increasing complaints about petty thievery among older citizens. They observe that the prosecutor's practice of simply dismissing charges against older shoplifters without any feedback about the consequences of charge dismissals, does not solve the problem. They note that some jurisdictions have taken cognizance of the inconsistencies with which petty offences, such as shoplifting, are handled and have implemented information management and offender tracking systems in order to promote greater uniformity and rationality in prosecutorial decision-making. They add that:

> some jurisdictions have already recognized the increasing incidence of complaints about older shoplifters and developed special diversionary community service programs as an alternative to exiting redressive responses (i.e. charge dismissal or prosecution). While these steps may prove adequate for the moment, it has been argued that as our population becomes increasingly older during the next two decades, we may find it necessary to develop a special system for older citizens along lines similar to the current juvenile justice system(1983:7).

Using the judicial files of the Bexar County District Courts for the period between September 1975 and August 1977, Lindquist et al. (1987) examined all cases for which prosecution was being considered by the district attorney. During the two-year period, 3,923 part I offences were processed, of which 85 were committed by persons 55 and over (2.2 per cent of the total).

Since a great deal of discretion is exercised at the police stage, cases of petty non-violent offences involving elderly offenders are more likely to be dealt with informally than cases involving violence. As a result, studies analyzing cases which have reached the prosecutor's office are bound to find a higher percentage of violent crime by the elderly than by younger age groups. Not surprisingly then, Lindquist et al. (1987) discovered that elderly offenders processed by the Bexar County criminal justice system were more violent than were younger offenders. Only one in four of the younger but nearly one-half the elderly arrestees were charged with a violent crime. The difference was statistically significant.

The authors found that at most of the steps in the prosecutorial and judicial processes, elderly offenders were treated differently. Three aspects of the process controlled by the district attorney were examined: outright rejection of the case (refusal to carry forward a case presented for prosecution); being no-billed by the grand jury; and having the case dismissed by a formal motion to the court of jurisdiction for a particular case. This was followed by an examination of three events that take place within the jurisdiction of the courts: the trial outcomes, length of sentence of those convicted, and type of sentence (probation or prison).

In two of the processes within the prosecutors' jurisdiction, elderly arrestees received favourable treatment (were not prosecuted) when their outcomes were compared with those of persons under 55. The elderly had a one-third greater chance of having their case rejected by the prosecutors - that is, of having the prosecutors refuse to present the case to the grand jury. Also, the elderly, compared to those under 55, had twice the chance of having their cases no-billed by the grand jury. The third process within the jurisdiction of the prosecutors - dismissals - showed very little difference between those under and over 55. The nonelderly arrestees had an 8 per cent greater chance of having their cases dismissed than did the elderly. Since Lindquist et al. did not control for the types of offences and did not examine violent and non-violent offences separately, it is not possible to tell what the differences would have been like had these comparisons taken into account the variations in the nature of offences committed by the two populations.

The analysis of court decisions also reflected a more lenient treatment of the elderly. Although there were very few cases for comparison, the elderly were found to be more likely to walk out of the court free than were younger defendants. Both groups were much more likely to be found guilty than not guilty once they went to trial. However, younger defendants (98 per cent) were almost certain to be found guilty while the elderly had a 1 in 6 chance of going free. Here again the authors did not try to match the offences nor to take the nature of the offence into consideration. Summarizing their findings they note that:

In this examination of two of the constituent parts of the criminal justice system, prosecution and adjudication, we found that the elderly fared much better at the hands of prosecutors than at the hands of judges... Over 70 per cent of the cases involving elderly defendants never see the courtroom, compared to less than 55 per cent of the cases in which the defendant is under age 55. This is a statistically significant difference.

If we add "not guilty" verdict to previously discussed actions that resulted in the freeing of the defendants, the elderly obtain "lenient" treatment...nearly 75 per cent of the time their cases get past the police and into the prosecutors' and judges' hands, while younger defendants receive "lenient" treatment only 51 per cent of the time (1987:166).

Comparing the length of sentence assessed against the elderly and the non-elderly, Lindquist et al. found some notable differences though these were not statistically significant. They discovered, for instance, that elderly felons received fewer sentences in the 1-10 year category than did the non-elderly. Thirty-two defendants received sentences in excess of 20 years and none of these were elderly. In general, elderly defendants received shorter sentences than younger ones. The last aspect the authors examined was the type of sentence served and here the differences were less noticeable and were not statistically significant.

The leniency with which the elderly were treated at the hands of prosecutors and the courts, as revealed by the study, gains in significance when one remembers that the offences committed by the elderly (in this study) were more violent (and therefore more serious) to begin with. Many of the differences that proved to be statistically non-significant might have turned out to be such, had the authors matched the two groups by type of offence. It should be pointed out, however, that the small number of offences committed by the elderly in the study (85) means that the numbers in each offence category and subcategory are too small for a statistical analysis of variance.

Lindquist et al. (1987) quote another study, similar to theirs, conducted by Bachand (1983). In an unpublished paper, presented at the Annual meeting of the American Sociological Association (Detroit), Bachand examined the dismissals of Part 1 offences by the police and prosecutors of Detroit, Michigan. His research covered all persons arrested by the police in 1981, those whose cases were forwarded to the prosecutor by the police, and those whose cases were terminated by the police within their own department. Bachand did not do a separate analysis for police and prosecutor dismissals. He concluded that the elderly are treated more leniently than are younger arrestees, because they have their cases dismissed at a statistically higher rate.

DIVERSION OF THE ELDERLY OFFENDER

The psychological trauma the elderly first offender is likely to experience when appearing in a court of law charged with a criminal offence, and the social stigma from which he or she is likely to suffer if convicted, point to the desirability of dealing with some elderly offenders outside of the criminal courts. Pre-trial diversion is one of several alternatives that may be successfully used with certain types of elderly offenders. After noting that most criminal incidents do not end up in the courts, the Law Reform Commission of Canada (1975) points out that in some cases, dealing with trouble in a low key is far more productive of peace and satisfaction for individuals, families and neighbourhoods than an escalation of the conflict into a full-blown criminal trial. Absorption of crime by the community, police screening of cases out of the

75

criminal justice system, settling of incidents at the pre-trial level, or using sanctions other than imprisonment are examples of what is commonly referred to as diversion (working paper no. 7,p.3).

Underlying diversion, writes the Commission, is an attitude of restraint in the use of the criminal law:

> This is only natural for restraint in the use of criminal law is demanded in the name of justice. It is unjust and unreasonable to inflict upon a wrong-doer more harm than necessary. Accordingly, as an incident is investigated by police and passed along the criminal process an onus should rest upon officials to show why the case should proceed further. At different stages in the criminal justice system opportunities arise for police to screen a case from the system, the prosecution to suspend charges pending settlement at the pre-trial level or the Court to exercise discretion to withhold a conviction or to impose a sanction other than imprisonment (1975:3).

The petty nature of most of the offences committed by the elderly, the generally good prognosis of those who are first timers, the seriousness of the consequences a criminal trial or a criminal conviction can have for the elderly offender, make them good candidates for pre-trial diversion. In fact, in discussing situations that might well be screened out rather than dealt with by formal charges, the Law Reform Commission mentions "incidents involving juveniles or the elderly". Another category identified by the Commission is that of "incidents involving mental illness or physical disability". Both are conditions from which the elderly suffer much more frequently than younger offenders. Many of the criteria, suggested by the Commission, for deciding that a charge should not be laid, do apply as well to elderly offences as may be seen from the following:

- The offence is not so serious that the public interest demands a trial.

- Alternative means of dealing with the incident would likely be effective in preventing further incidents by the offender in the light of his/her record and other evidence.

- The impact of arrest or prosecution on the accused or his/her family is likely to be excessive in relation to the harm done.

The Commission suggested in 1975 that pre-trial settlements not be restricted to specific offences such as theft under $200, shoplifting, and so on, since the labels we hang on offences frequently cover a wide range of circumstances. According to the Commission, it is even difficult to rule out offences of violence against the person, for the most common offence in this category is assault and in almost eighty per cent of assaults the victim and offender know each other either in a family context, or in a neighbour or acquaintance relationship. To safeguard against disparities and eventual abuse, the Commission recommends that diversion policies be developed and clearly stated, that express guidelines for decision be formulated and that diversion programs be run under the supervision of the prosecution by competent administrators supported by community service programs. The Commission recommends further that procedures be open and accountable, and that counsel be available to ensure that accused persons fully understand what they are consenting to.

To our knowledge, no pretrial diversion program has been specifically developed in Canada for the exclusive diversion of elderly offenders. Some exist in the United States. An example of these programs, mentioned by Alston (1986), is the Advocate for Seniors Program in Dade County, Florida. This program is part of a larger one developed for the alternative treatment of first offenders regardless of age. Alston notes that if the offender is elderly, he/she is more likely than not a shoplifter. Restitution or other method of accountability is determined for each case, counseling is available, and offenders are referred to other agencies and services if they need them. Another program, described in detail by Feinberg (1984), is the Broward Senior Intervention and Education Program of Broward County, Florida, which focuses exclusively on first-offender shoplifters who are over sixty years of age.

Alston (1986) points out that these are only two of a growing number of diversion programs for older offenders. While some operate exclusively for the elderly, many are for first offenders of any age. She suggests that any attempt to provide alternatives to arrest and protective custody in jail requires some attention to the needs of law enforcement as well as offenders. Any alternative must be more attractive than the traditional solution both in terms of convenience to the police and in terms of its ability to live up to its promise. According to Alston:

> The short-term programs of most detoxification centers and the long-standing problems that most patients have with alcohol mean that programs cannot promise "to do something" about public drunkenness, but can only provide a humane alternative to jail for most offenders. Community mental health centers which have in-patient facilities also provide police with another option in their dealing with minor offenders. An older person who is fighting or creating public nuisance may be disoriented rather than inebriated. He or she may be in even more need of protective custody than the drunken offender. In theory, these two kinds of facilities could provide incarceration alternatives for the majority of old offenders. In practice, however, they are not as widely available as they should be. Some communities do not have them. In those which do, the extent to which older minor offenders can be accomodated depends on the size of the facility and the volume of demand for services. Yet another potential barrier to the use of these alternatives by police is described by Regier: A rejection of all but "treatable clientele" (1986:205).

THE ELDERLY OFFENDER IN COURT

Old Age as a Criminal Defense

Criminal codes that are based on the concepts of moral responsibility and moral guilt usually recognize young age as a reason for exempting from or reducing the criminal responsibility of the person who commits the crime. Children under the age of discernment (usually fixed at seven years) are regarded as incapable of formulating intent. Their actions are believed to be lacking the moral element necessary for intentional crime, that is "mens rea". Young offenders under a certain age are generally considered to be unable to fully appreciate the nature and consequences of their actions, or to make a clear-cut distincion between right and wrong, hence they are treated more leniently than others. They benefit from "reduced", "diminished", or "partial responsibility" like those who suffer from some mental disorder without being completely insane. In other words, in cases of children and juveniles who commit crime, the criminal law recognizes age as a factor affecting their degree of responsibility. What the law actually does is to create a legal presumption in favor of the offender based solely on a chronological age, an age that is determined in an arbitrary manner and therefore varies from one jurisdiction to the other.

Should a similar legal presumption be created for elderly offenders, for those who are beyond a certain age? Should old age by itself be recognized as a criminal defense even in the absence of mental impairment? Should the criminal law treat old offenders as individuals not fully responsible for their actions even when their mental faculties are intact?

Cohen (1984) affirms that chronological age is a poor guide to the state of a person's mental alertness. He believes that it is neither necessary nor desirable to create a presumption of incapacity or impairment. He equally believes that there is a powerful case against the creation of legal presumptions based only on age,despite the fact that the older the person is, the greater the possibility that he/she has some impairment relevant to law. Although Cohen's concern about, and criticism of, a legal presumption based only on age is understandable, the alternative seems much less appealing. The alternative would be to let psychiatrists decide who is and who is not impaired, who is suffering from some mental disability and who is not. The problems of disparity, accuracy, reliability would simply be enormous. Injustices will inevitably ensue. In many cases there might be no detectable signs of mental disorder or brain degeneration. The criminal behavior might be the first visible symptom of the underlying problem. If the reduction in responsibility is based not on age but on impairment, the elderly offender might be treated as fully responsible whereas in fact he/she is not.

Cohen (1984) addresses as well the question of whether there are certain characteristics associated with aging that are relevant to the legal issue of criminal responsibility - whether the criminal law should provide some special doctrine or procedural treatment for the elderly offender, and if so, what? According to Cohen, there are five different possibilities:

1. Aggravated culpability. The first alternative might be to view the older offender as more culpable than younger offenders, the rationale being that with age and experience there should be a concomitant increase in responsibility and consequently in sanctions. The popular saying "old enough to know better" epitomizes this view. Cohen correctly points out that this position speaks less to criminal responsibility than it does to penal policy at the sentencing and correction stage.

2. Diminished responsibility. Another alternative would be to consider old age not as a reason for total exemption from criminal responsibility but as grounds for either diminished or partial responsibility. The elderly defendant would, for example, be permitted to show that by virtue of age and consequent changes in physical and psychological makeup he/she lacked "the equipment to deal reasonably with life's stresses".

3. Incapacity: no responsibility. A third alternative is to provide that above a certain age there should be a total exemption from criminal responsibility and, along with this, a rebuttable assumption of irresponsibility between certain advanced ages.

4. Age neutrality. This fourth possible option requires that the criminal responsibility of the elderly offender be dealt with on the same basis as any other adult accused of crime. Thus age per se would not be a defense to a criminal charge. While ruling out age *per se* as an exculpatory or even a mitigating factor, this option need not foreclose the allowance of evidence of the functional impairments commonly associated with old age.

5. EOs and OPINS - benevolence and prediction. According to this final position, the elderly offender should not be subjected to the same procedures and institutional arrangements as other offenders. Their needs are different, and the objectives of the law necessarily are different. Thus, as a matter of benevolence and wise policy, a special court for the elderly, a Geriatric Court,should be created. Such a court would assure due process prior to any adjudication as an Elderly Offender (EO) and would have available a number of dispositional options designed especially for older people. It also may be desirable to invent a noncriminal category for the elderly person who appears to need help not otherwise or as easily available or who may be diagnosed as a pre-Elderly Offender. This new category might be termed Older Persons in Need of Supervision (OPINS). Behavior which might be subject to an OPINS petition includes the non criminal category of "wandering about", placing oneself in situations dangerous to life and limb, failing to maintain minimal dietary and personal hygiene practices and thereby causing a danger to oneself, and attempting to engage in shoplifting. Cohen sees the objectives of an OPINS category as protective and preventive, to deal with the struggling older person in a way that is physically and socially protective while striving also to cut short either further harm to the person or to the rights of others. Thus the creation of this special tribunal and the OPINS category could,in his view, entirely displace guardianship proceedings, euphemistically called protective services, which often deprive the elderly of their personal autonomy, and often of their dignity, integrity and self-esteem as well.

The system described by Cohen is fraught with dangers. One obvious danger is the widening of the net of social control. Another danger is subjecting elderly people who have committed no criminal offence to measures (sometimes drastic measures) of control under the guise of protection and preventon. As happened with juveniles, the use of such humane-sounding terms might ultimately lead to the sacrifice of legal and procedural safeguards. Another distinct danger is that of creating categories of behaviors justifying legal intervention that for other age groups do not constitute conduct warranting state control. All this militates against the creation of stigmatizing labels such as "elderly offender" and especially "elderly person in need of supervision".

Cohen is not unaware of these dangers. He writes:

> Efforts to create a special offender category or special benevolent court for the elderly offender would appear to be particularly dangerous to the public held concept of older persons and to self-image, and dangerous because of the risks of creating another treatment-rehabilitation establishment (1984:134).

Is a Special Geriatric Court Needed?

In his foreword to Newman, Newman and Gewirtz's book (1984), Albert Abrams makes a strong plea for a senior citizen court. He argues that elderly people who fall into the chaotic judicial system today are often victimized by it. Noting that it is easy for the aged to become traumatized by the system when they are herded together with pimps, punks, and prostitutes in local holding "tanks" and shoved before overworked judges dealing with life-and-death situations stemming from complex interpersonal relationships, Abrams suggests that:

> Today we have family courts, juvenile courts, and a large variety of speciality courts to handle specific problems ranging from admiralty cases to immigration. A special court to handle cases of senior citizens charged with crimes would bring greater justice to bear. We need a court informed on geriatrics and gerontology that can assure the proper counseling service, the proper referral service, the proper family and community support when dealing with the frail elderly caught in the judicial administration system (1984:xvi).

Arguments for a geriatric court are usually based on the specific and special needs of elderly offenders and often draw an analogy with the system that now exists, and has existed for many decades, for juvenile offenders. Society has seen fit to create a special "criminal code" for young offenders (The Juvenile Delinquent Act, The Young Offenders Act) and a parallel justice system with its own courts, judges, prosecutors, probation service and even separate institutions. It is true that the number of elderly offenders is minute compared to that of juvenile offenders. However, numbers were not the reason for the establishment of the juvenile justice system. The underlying rationale was the need to treat young offenders differently from other offenders and to have them dealt with by specially trained and specialized professionals. This rationale applies as well to elderly offenders. Yet before proceeding with the creation of a geriatric court or a geriatric justice system we need to look critically at the experience with the juvenile justice system, and the experience is not a happy one. Juvenile justice has been under heavy criticism for many years. The criticism, much of which is fully justified, ought to caution us against the creation of other separate and specialized systems of justice for other categories such as women or elderly offenders.

After a lengthy recitation of the inadequacies of the administration of juvenile justice, and after documenting the failure of the juvenile court and juvenile institutions to approximate the designs outlined in their rhetoric or to protect their charges from injury, historian David Rothman (1980) suggests that this situation raises two recurring and troubling questions: why did such dismal conditions come to exist, and why did they continue to exist? Thinking along the same lines, Cohen (1984) suggests that in the infancy of our legal concern for the elderly offender, we can extrapolate from Rothman's questions about a system-in-being and ask "why" in advance of spawning a new bureaucracy, new institutions and procedures, and new experts. He reminds us that institutions and experts, once in place, have a remarkable penchant for remaining in place and using the fact of existence as the strongest argument for their own survival. Cohen proceeds to analyze some of the possible reasons for the failure of the juvenile justice system only to conclude that an elderly offender system is not likely to fare much better. He cites for example the performance of legislatures that never provided budgets to match the high-blown rhetoric of the child-savers movement. He refers to a lack of knowledge concerning the causes and control of delinquent behavior as another important factor in the failure of the juvenile justice system. This factor suggests that larger budgets would simply have contributed to a more expensive failure. He writes:

> Where theory pointed to causes of delinquency as a part of the socioeconomic fabric, it was clear that ultimate solutions lay outside the jurisdiction of the juvenile system, a system that at best could apply only palliatives. The juvenile justice system was built on the flawed vision of superimposing a medical model over a model based on fault or individual blame, and it could never reconcile the incompatibility between coerced custody and treatment or that between the role of keeper and that of helper (1984:128).

Cohen suggests that prior to proceeding with the establishment of a new geriatric justice system we should ask questions based on the lessons learned from the failure of the juvenile system: Do we know more about the "elderly delinquent" than about the juvenile offender? Do we have a clear vision of how to treat or rehabilitate? Are legislatures going to open the purse strings for the elderly where they would not for the young? Can we reconcile keeper and kept roles for the older person where we could not for the younger? Would we not, in fact, face the prospect of yet another liberal reform gone awry, constructed on a flawed and destructive incompetence model, of increasing the stigma associated with age through the invention of such new terms as OPINS (older persons in need of supervision), and ultimately, of enlargening the number of people under the control of the state? Having formulated all these relevant questions which, if answered in a sincere manner, would all militate against the establishment of a separate geriatric justice system, Cohen suggests that a less cynical approach would frame questions on the premise that we can learn from the disasters of the juvenile system and use the Geriatric Court as a second chance. For example, the benefits of the procedural informality model could be preserved within a due process model without insisting on procedural parity with the criminal court:

> Punishment and blame would have to give way to rehabilitation, which would form the core of the Geriatric Court System. Rehabilitation for

the elderly must have highly specific, attainable and measurable objectives. The Geriatric Court System would not tolerate the rhetorical and programmatic hoaxes of the juvenile justice system... As troublesome as these questions may be for a punitive system, they can be avoided in a rehabilitation system. Since rehabilitation necessarily relates to achieving some desired change in the individual, and since one cannot know in advance when such change will occur, the dispositional structure must remain open-ended. Release from custody or confinement would be based on the achievement of some rehabilitative objective and not on any relationship between the seriousness of the offense and the amount of deserved punishment (1984:128-129).

Individualization and the Geriatric Offender

Rehabilitation and treatment have lost favor in recent years. In some places they are gradually becoming a thing from the past. Be this as it may, when dealing with elderly offenders, a good number of whom might be suffering from cerebral degeneration, senile dementia, inorganic psychoses, chronic alcoholism and so forth, an enlightened justice system would be remiss if it were to discard a priori treatment and rehabilitation as legitimate goals of the penal measure imposed upon the offender. Making the punishment fit the crime, a principle based on the belief in the metaphysical notion of free will, seems to be particularly inappropriate when dealing with elderly offenders. The majority of offences committed by elderly first time offenders can be traced for the most part to psychiatric, environmental and socio-economic factors over which they have little or no control. In many cases the offenders may be regarded more as victims than victimizers. In such instances, retribution is undoubtedly an ill-advised and unjustified response.

If rehabilitation and treatment are accepted as goals (or as the primary goals) of sentencing elderly offenders, individualization becomes an integral component in the choice of sanction. Individualization means that the penal measure imposed should fit the particular offender and should meet the specific rehabilitation needs of that offender. In sentencing, the criminal court judge has a choice from a range of punitive and non-punitive sanctions, custodial and non-custodial dispositions. The Young Offenders Act (Section 20) provides the judge with a wide variety of dispositions to choose from when sentencing a young offender. Although the adult court judge might not have as many available options, he/she still enjoys a great deal of discretion. To help the judge in the effort to individualize the sentence in cases of elderly offenders, it might not be a bad idea for the criminal code to require a mandatory predisposition report together with a medical or psychological examination. Section 14 (1) of the Young Offenders Act stipulates that "where a youth court deems it advisable before making a disposition under section 20 in respect of a young person who is found guilty of an offence it may, and where a youth court is required under this Act to consider a pre-disposition report before making an order or a disposition in respect of a young person it shall, require the provincial director to cause to be prepared a pre-disposition report in respect of the young person and to submit the report to the court". Section 24 (11) of the same Act requires that "Before making an order of committal to custody under paragraph 20 (1) (K), the youth court shall consider a pre-disposition report". Introducing similar

82

provisions in the Canadian Criminal Code where elderly offenders are concerned would no doubt be of great help to the sentencing judge in individualizing the measure imposed upon the geriatric delinquent.

Another provision of the Young Offenders Act which needs to be considered for elderly offenders is the one urging the youth court to seek in certain circumstances a medical or psychological report. Section 13 (d and e) stipulates that a youth court may, at any stage of proceedings against a young person, with the consent of the young person and the prosecutor, or on its own motion or on the application of either the young person or the prosecutor "where the court had reasonable grounds to believe that the young person may be suffering from a physical or mental illness or disorder, a psychological disorder, an emotional disturbance, a learning disability or mental retardation and where the court believes a medical, psychological or psychiatric report in respect of the young person might be helpful in making any decision pursuant to this Act, by order require that the young person be examined by a qualified person and that the person who conducts the examination report the results thereof in writing to the court".

In the case of geriatric delinquents the terms "learning disability or mental retardation" could be replaced with the term "mental deterioration". And since elderly offenders are more likely to suffer from the afflictions contained in the above section than young offenders, it does not seem unreasonable to suggest that the examination in their case be made mandatory rather than leaving it to the discretion of the court or upon the application of the offender or the prosecutor.

Another provision of the Young Offenders Act which is particularly relevant to elderly offenders is the one related to the protection of privacy. Section 38 of the Act prohibits the disclosure of identity and the publication of names of young persons and children who have committed criminal offences as well as those of children and young persons aggrieved by the offence or who appeared as witnesses in connection with the offence. Elderly offenders would greatly benefit from a similar prohibition. As mentioned earlier, many elderly offenders are first time delinquents who have led a law-abiding life. They are respected members of their communities. Publicity surrounding their offence, their arrest, their court appearance, their sentence, is likely to lead not only to a loss of standing and reputation, but also to severe emotional distress and deep psychological trauma. Cases of elderly offenders who could not endure the loss and distress and who decided to face death rather than shame are not uncommon. Protecting the privacy of elderly offenders, prohibiting the disclosure of their identities and the publication of their names would spare them the pain and suffering resulting from such disclosure and would probably prevent some of the ensuing tragedies.

The Right to Counsel

The right to legal counsel is a basic right in democratic societies. An elderly offender who might be disoriented or confused, who might be suffering from some mental illness or disorder, is in much greater need of legal counsel than an adult, normal offender in full possession of his/her mental and intellectual faculties. Since many elderly offenders live alone, in isolation, they are not likely to have family members, relatives or friends who can come to their rescue once they are arrested or charged with a criminal offence. Furthermore, the immediate need for legal counsel might not be evident to the elderly offender in such a situation. Some might not fully realize the implications of what they have done and what they are facing. Others might not have the necessary presence of mind or the financial means to seek and retain legal counsel. Since most elderly people live on meagre, fixed income, and since those with the lowest income are the ones most likely to be arrested and charged with a criminal offence, their need for some type of state funded legal aid is particularly pressing. Due to budgetary cuts, legal aid has been restricted not only to those who are extremely needy, but also to serious offences. As a result, the bulk of elderly offenders, whose offences are usually minor, find themselves excluded from the realm of legal aid services. This is particularly unfortunate since the consequences of a criminal conviction are usually more drastic for the elderly offender than they are for a younger one. Requiring mandatory legal representation in the case of elderly offenders regardless of the nature of the offence and relaxing the conditions of eligibility for public legal aid in their case would help solve this problem.

CHAPTER FOUR: RECOMMENDED READINGS

Alston, L.T.
1986 Crime and Older Americans. Springfield, Ill.: Charles C. Thomas. Chapter Seven: Response to the Older Offender. pp. 201-224.

Cohen, A.
1984 Old Age as a Criminal Defence. In Newman,E.S., Newman, D.J. and Gewirtz, M.L. (Eds.) Elderly Criminals. Cambridge, Mass.: Oelgeschlager, Gunn, and Hain Publishers. pp. 113-141.

Cutshall, C.R. and K. Adams
1983 Responding to Older Offenders: Age Selectivity in the Processing of Shoplifters. Criminal Justice Review, 8(2):1-8.

Fyfe, J.J.
1984 Police Dilemmas in Processing Elderly Offenders. In Newman, E.S. et al. (Eds.) Elderly Criminals. Cambridge, Mass.: Oelgeschlager, Gunn & Hain Publishers. pp. 97-111.

Lindquist, J.H., White, O.Z. and Chambers, C.D.
1987 Elderly Felons: Dispositions of Arrests. In C.D. Chambers et al. (Eds.)
    The Elderly: Victims and Deviants. Athens: Ohio University Press. pp.
    161-176.

CHAPTER FIVE

THE ELDERLY OFFENDER IN PRISON

INCARCERATION AND OLDER CRIMINALS

Elderly Offenders in Canadian Penal Institutions

It is difficult to trace the movement of elderly offenders in and out of the provincial prison and federal penitentiary systems in Canada. It is also difficult to tell how many old inmates there are at any given time in Canadian prisons and penitentiaries. The numbers will vary according to which age is taken as the starting point beyond which a prisoner is considered old: 50, 55, 60 or 65 years. Statistics on admissions to prisons and penitentiaries are published annually by Statistics Canada in its catalogue no. 85-211 Adult Correctional Services in Canada. The distribution by age of those admitted is given in absolute numbers for the penitentiaries and in percentages for provincial prisons. The rationale for this different presentation is not clear. Furthermore, the breakdown of the "50 and over" category is not provided. According to the latest statistics available, 126 offenders age 50 and over were admitted to the federal penitentiaries in Canada under a warrant of committal in 1984-1985. The corresponding figure for the year 1985-1986 is 153, a 20% increase. Because the total number is relatively small, no conclusion should be drawn from this increase. Out of the 153 admissions in 1985-1986, 13 came from the Atlantic provinces, 48 from the province of Quebec, 35 from Ontario, 25 from the Prairies and 32 from British Columbia. These crude figures are not very useful unless related to the population size and the rates of serious crimes in each region.

According to the same document, in 1985-1986, 6% of all offenders admitted to a Provincial facility, following a court sentence, were 50 years and over. The same age group accounted for only 4% of admissions on remand. Since the total number of sentencing admissions to provincial facilities in 1985-1986 was almost one hundred and twenty-thousand (119,631), it is fair to assume that there were more than 7,000 admissions of offenders 50 years and

86

over that year. The number of admissions does not automatically correspond to number of offenders. As the majority of sentences to provincial institutions are for less than one year and many are even for less than one month, the same offender might be readmitted several times during the same year.

In the Historic Statistics of Canada, second edition (1982), admissions of males to federal penitentiaries are given for a fifteen year period: 1961 to 1975. Figures for 1961 to 1968 were for the fiscal year ending 31 March, while those for the years 1969 to 1975 were for calendar years. Numbers of admissions of those 50 years and over fluctuated from a high of 180 in 1970 to a low of 109 in 1974. There were no visible trends. Admissions of those 60 and over oscillated between a high of 43 in 1970 and a low of 18 in 1974. The percentage of those who were 60 and over on admission to those who were 50-59 varied from a high of one-third in 1969 (40/120) to a low of one-sixth two years later, i.e., in 1971, (18/115).

The number of admissions is the best available indicator for the study of the use of, and trends in, incarceration of elderly offenders. This is because the population of elderly inmates in Canadian penitentiaries contains, in addition to those who were admitted when old, a large number of those who aged in prison. Some middle-aged offenders, convicted of serious crimes and sentenced to life imprisonment or lengthy prison terms, are not released on parole and grow old in the penitentiary. The number of inmates in this group will continue to rise since in 1976 the Canadian Criminal Code imposed a minimum of 25 years before eligibility for release on parole on those sentenced to life imprisonment upon conviction of first degree murder.

The United States

Ann Goetting (1984) reports that on December 31, 1981, an estimated total of 8,853 persons aged fifty-five and older were incarcerated in state and federal prisons in the United States. This figure, she suggests, has increased and will continue to do so as the prison population continues its upswing, with an increasingly higher proportion of arrests of senior citizens for serious offences.

On the basis of two studies, Krajick (1979), quoted by Rubenstein (1984), reports that 1% of the prison population in the U.S. are 60 and over and 0.5% (1500 persons) are 65 and over. Reed and Glamser (1979) estimate that prisoners over age 50 account for 5% of persons under correctional supervision for a total of approximately 10,000 persons. Golden (1984) affirms that at any given time 3% of American jail inmates are over the age of 55.

Chaneles (1987) claims that in the U.S.A. there were nearly 600,000 inmates 18 and over in federal, state, county and municipal prisons on January 1, 1987. He estimates that about 10 percent of these were over 50 and facing the prospect of release only when they are well past 60. He estimates further that by the year 2000, if present trends continue, the number of long term prisoners over 50 will be around 125,000, with 40,000 to 50,000 over 65. As to women, Chaneles figures out that there are probably no more than a thousand women over 65 in U.S. prisons.

Numbers of admissions to State prisons in 1982, quoted by Chaneles, show that 1,109 between 55 and 64 and 196 sixty-five years and over were admitted that year. The total number of admissions was 100,814. In other words, elderly (55+) admissions accounted for 1.3 percent of the total. Murder and manslaughter accounted for 6.9 per cent of total admissions but their share of elderly admissions was far greater: 20.8 per cent in the 55-64 group and more than a third (35.2 per cent) in the 65 years and over group! For the population as a whole, burglary was the leading offence resulting in admission to State prisons (27.2 per cent). For the 55-64 years group, burglary resulted in 7.3 per cent admissions and for those 65 years and over in 4.1 per cent admissions.

Types of Elderly Inmates

Based on incarceration history, Teller and Howell (1981) distinguish between two types of older prisoners: the first incarcerated and the multiply incarcerated. They found the second type to be similar to the younger inmate in terms of crime classification. Similar proportions of these two inmate categories (64 and 69 per cent, respectively) were serving sentences for property crimes. First incarcerated offenders, on the other hand, were more likely to be sentenced for crimes against persons.

Metzler (1981) delineates three types of elderly inmates. His typology is similar to that of Teller and Howell (1981) except that he divides the first type in their classification, that is the first incarcerated, into two subtypes: those incarcerated for the first time in older years and those incarcerated while young who grew old in prison.

Goetting (1984) developed a four class typology :

Type 1: Old offenders. This category consists of those inmates who were 55 years of age or older at their first incarceration. They constituted 41.38% of her sample. The sample consisted of the 248 individuals age fifty-five and older who comprised a subsample of the 11,397 prisoners selected by the U.S. Bureau of the Census for the Bureau of Justice Statistics for their Survey of Inmates of State Correctional Facilities, 1979.

Type 2: Oldtimers. This category consists of those inmates who had grown old in prison. They had been incarcerated for their current offence before the age of 55, and had served at least 20 years on that sentence. They constituted 2.32% of the sample.

Type 3: Career criminals. This category consists of recidivists whose first incarceration had been before the age of 55, and excludes oldtimers. They constituted 45.6% of the sample.

Type 4: Young short-term first offenders who were incarcerated before the age of 55, and excludes oldtimers. They constituted 10.68% of the sample.

It is difficult to tell, without further study, what the size of each of these four types is in the general prison population in the United States or Canada. In one study conducted in the State of Illinois, Baum and Berman (1980) report that, contrary to expectations, most older prisoners were not in prison for crimes committed when young, but had received their sentences after age 50. Over two-thirds of the prisoners sentenced after age 50 were first offenders. The study further reports that the crimes of the older prisoners tended to be more severe than those of the general population. For example, 35% of the older prisoners were serving a sentence for murder compared to 15% of the general prison population.

Alston (1986) estimates that up to half of the older prison population in the United States is serving time for first offences. She adds that elderly first-time offenders are more likely to have been sentenced for violent crimes while older multiple offenders are more likely to have been sentenced for property crimes.

Due to differences in characteristics, in reaction to incarceration, in the problems they encounter in prison and in the problems they pose for prison administrators, it does not seem justified to discuss elderly inmates as if they were a homogeneous population. It is necessary to divide them according to typologies like the ones outlined above. Prior incarceration experience, length and frequency of such incarceration are important variables along which elderly inmates may be classified. And while the different types may share some common problems related to their imprisonment, there are certain problems that are specific to each type. The older first offender, for example, is likely to suffer from some form of cultural shock and may find it difficult to adjust to the deculturalization process that is part of prison socialization. Rubenstein (1984) believes, however, that they are extremely successful at resisting dependence on the prison and being socialized into the prison system. Multi-recidivists and those who grew old in prison, on the other hand, are likely to exhibit symptoms of prisonization and to be assimilated into the prison culture.

Some authors, however, claim that age is an insignificant variable in explaining shifts in degree of prisonization. In his longitudinal research of patterns of change in prisonization, Alpert (1979) claims that all age groups become prisonized. The oldest group (40 and above) in the prison population he studied reported the lowest levels of prisonization at time 1, yet became slightly more prisonized than other groups.

NEGATIVE AND POSITIVE EFFECTS OF IMPRISONMENT ON ELDERLY INMATES

Inmates

Prisons are generally considered total institutions (in the sense employed by Goffman, 1961) that share many characteristics with other institutions such as the asylum, the psychiatric hospital, the nursing home and so on. It is commonly believed that all these institutions have deleterious effects caused by the "dehumanizing" and "depersonalizing" characteristics of institutional environments (see Lieberman,1969). Summarizing these effects, Townsend (1962) writes:

In the institution people live communally with a minimum of privacy and yet their relationships with each other are slender. Many subsist in a kind of defensive shell of isolation. Their mobility is restricted, and they have little access to a general society. The social experiences are limited, and the staff lead a rather separate existence from them. They are subtly oriented toward a system in which they submit to orderly routine, non-creative occupation, and cannot exercise as much self-determination. They are deprived of intimate family relationships and can rarely find substitutes which seem to be more than a pale imitation of those enjoyed by most people in a general community. The result for the individual seems fairly often to be a gradual process of depersonalization. He has too little opportunity to develop the talents he possesses and they atrophy through disuse. He may become resigned and depressed and may display no interest in the future or in things not immediately personal. He sometimes becomes apathetic, talks little, and lacks initiative. His personal habits and toilet deteriorate. Occasionally he seems to withdraw into a private world of fantasy. (Quoted in Lieberman, 1969:330).

Studies of the elderly residing in homes for the aged, domiciliaries, and nursing homes, as cited by Lieberman (1969), suggest that they share common characteristics: poor adjustment, depression and unhappiness, intellectual ineffectiveness because of increased rigidity and low energy (but not necessarily intellectual incompetence), negative self-image, feelings of personal insignificance and impotency, and a view of self as old. Residents tend to be docile, submissive, show a low range of interests and activities, and to live in the past rather than the future. They are withdrawn and unresponsive in relationships to others. There is some suggestion that they have increased anxiety, which at times focuses on feelings of death. Other investigators have reported marked increases in mortality rates for aged persons entering mental institutions or homes for the aged. Lieberman cautions that these effects should not be automatically attributed to living in institutions since they may be due to population differences between those living in the community and those residing in institutions. After scrutinizing these findings, Lieberman suggests that the common stereotype about the destructive influences on the aged of living in institutional settings is overdrawn. He feels that many of the supposed psychological effects are characteristics of the person prior to his coming to an institution (and are related in part to the reasons for institutionalization) while others appear to be associated with aspects of entering the institution (making a radical change in the environment) which occurred before the individual actually entered the institution.

Notwithstanding Lieberman's views, most researchers believe that incarceration can have serious negative effects on the elderly person, particularly the first time elderly offender, who suddenly finds himself/herself in the strictly regulated and confined environment of the prison. Reporting on elderly male prisoners in Israel, Bergman and Amir (1973) point to a rapid deterioration in their physical and mental conditions. The aging prisoners were found to be at the mercy of younger, more aggressive, and difficult prisoners who tended to frighten, ridicule, or even harm them. The aged prisoners became depressed, anxious and consequently dependent on the warden and prison staff for protection.

90

While many studies report differences between old and young inmates, it is usually difficult to tell whether the negative characteristics did exist prior to institutionalization or whether they were a result of the prison experience. One such study is reported by Panton (1977). The author analyzed MMPI test differences between a sample of 120 aged inmates (age sixty and above) and a representative population sample of 2,551 male inmates. The test responses showed that the aged inmates demonstrated greater anxiety, despondency, apprehension and concern with physical functioning. They appeared somewhat naive and self-centered, were likely to be demanding of attention and support, and appeared inclined toward the avoidance of responsibility. They expressed feelings of inadequacy and insecurity and were likely to be easily influenced and intimidated by younger, more aggressive inmates. They appeared to have difficulty in personal adaptability and resourcefulness. And they demonstrated difficulty in concentration and fear and apprehension over possible loss of mental functioning.

Although the effects of imprisonment on both young and elderly inmates are overwhelmingly negative, the prison might have some positive effects on few older offenders. For those who were suffering from extreme loneliness on the outside, the prison offers new contacts and increased opportunities for social interaction, especially with younger age groups. For those who were living in unhealthy, substandard conditions or who were leading a self-destructive life-style (for example chronic alcoholics), the prison provides a healthier, more regulated and less destructive environment. Speaking of prisonization, Aday and Webster (1979) explain that it gives the prisoner a new subculture, new role, new identity and new social group - which are vital for social and psychological well-being. They add that the longer the normal roles of the life-cycle are disrupted, the more likely the older prisoner will establish new roles in the inmate social system.

Some researchers cite evidence suggesting that for some elderly inmates the prison might delay rather than hasten the aging process. Jackson (1969) cites one inmate as saying:

There's something else funny that happens to some people; they come down here and their age seems to fix at what it was when they came in. And something else: I don't think they age as much in appearance as they do in the free world. Down here I see guys all the time that are 60 or 75 who look like 40 to 45. Physically they stay younger. (quoted after Reed and Glamser, 1979:354).

Reed and Glamser quote another study of aging in prison which tends to support such a description. The study by Gillespie and Galliher (1972) found the belief that prison retards the aging process prevalent among middle-aged prisoners (30 to 59). The authors write:

The inmates supported their claim in two ways: first from the standpoint of their physical well-being they argued that life in prison offers some advantages over life in the streets. Prison, they said, removed them from temptations of liquour, drugs, prostitution and other attractions of an active night life. On a more positive side, prison offered regular meals, sleep, and the opportunity to keep physically fit by participating in varied sports programs. Second, many inmates argued that prison maintained their mental health by freeing them from the worries and responsibilities which were confronted in the streets. (Quoted from Reed and Glamser, 1979:354-355).

Gillespie and Galliher (1972) report that this belief is a part of prison lore to which younger inmates are exposed. On the other hand, among prisoners in their 60s and 70s, they found a belief that prison has aged them. This is explained in terms of bitterness, resentment and hopelessness.

In their own study, (Reed and Glamser ,1979), 15 out of the 19 subjects (with an age range from 42 to 77 years with a median of 60) reported they felt younger, and only one reported feeling older. The authors believe this perception to be accurate given the social class background of most prisoners. Older prisoners are not exposed to heavy industry, hard labor or heavy drinking. They eat well, rest often, and have ready access to medical care. This is unlikely to be the case among lower and working class men on the outside. The authors conclude that much of what is viewed as part of normal aging does not take place in the prison setting. They write:

> Many of the losses associated with normal aging take place in young adulthood among prisoners. Retirement and widowhood are not meaningful. Chronological age does not possess such salience for prisoners. Even some of the cosmetic effects of environmental stress appear to be mitigated (1979:359).

Commenting on the divergent and sometimes conflicting findings reported by various researchers, Goetting (1983) points out that the fact that some observers view prison life for the elderly as reasonably satisfying, while others perceive it as a miserable existence, suggests the possibility of a broad spectrum of settings for older prisoners in the United States. While such variation exists the literature provides little insight into the specifics of this difference in quality of life.

PROBLEMS OF ELDERLY OFFENDERS IN A PRISON SETTING

Environmental Change

For the elderly first-time offender, who is living alone or with family or friends, the move to a prison setting is a radical environmental change, bound to have profound effects on the individual. Lieberman (1969) provides us with a summary of studies which examined the effects of radical environmental changes on the psychological well-being and physical survival of the aged. Many of these studies have involved changes from community living to life in an institution; others have studied relocation from one institutional setting to another. The studies suggest that the conditions associated with moving into an institution create many of the effects usually attributed to living in an institutional setting. The majority showed that changing the environment of elderly persons sharply increased the death rate. While some studies failed to show increased mortality, they revealed other negative effects. In the Lawton and Yaffe study (1967), the relocated group was judged to have declined more frequently on measures of health compared to the control group. In the Miller and Lieberman study

(1965), half the Ss declined either psychologically (occurrences of confusion, memory defects, bizarre behavior) or physically (hospitalization, restrictions of activity, health failures). A third study (Lieberman et al., 1968) showed that inquiry based on the psychology of loss may offer a more effective framework for identifying factors leading to noxious effects of institutionalization than analyses of institutional characteristics.

Lieberman (1969) also refers to studies that examined characteristics of environmental change in terms of "overload". Tentative findings suggest that the larger the difference between old and new situations, the greater the possibility that the aged individual will need to develop adaptive responses often beyond his/her capacity. Lieberman suggests that:

> In this light, the effect of an institution can be viewed less as a product of its quality or characteristics than of the degree to which it forces the person to make new adaptive responses or employ adaptive responses from the previous environment... This review of the effects of selection and degree of environmental change suggests that these two factors may explain many of the deleterious effects on the aged which are associated with living in an institution (1969:334).

Institutional Dependency

Institutional dependency is more of a problem in the case of the multi-recidivist and the person who grew old in prison than it is in the case of the first time elderly offender. There are countless cases of inmates for whom, after many years of incarceration, the prison became a home. They refuse to be released when they are paroled and if let go against their wishes will commit new offences to be sent back to prison.

CORRECTIONS MAGAZINE (1979) tells the story of an 84-year-old New York State inmate who, the magazine claims, has served the longest prison term in U.S. history - 67 years. Paul Geidel, sentenced to life in prison for second-degree murder on Sept. 5, 1911, remained in prison at his own request. He was offered parole in 1974 and turned it down. He considered prison as his home and felt it was too late for him to try to survive in the outside world. Geidel, who was 17 at the time he was sent to prison, is quoted as saying:

> It's very nice where I am, people treat me fine. Why should I leave? There is nothing for me outside. I would be completely lost in strange surroundings.

CORRECTIONS MAGAZINE reports that Geidel refused parole again in 1976 and when called up for his hearing in 1978, he declined to show up. According to the magazine, Geidel will take the place in the *GUINNESS BOOK OF WORLD RECORDS* held until 1978 by Van Dyke Grisby, who was released from an Indiana prison in 1974 after serving 66 years. He was 88 at the time.

Another pathetic story comes from Texas and was reported in the *VANCOUVER SUN* on August 6, 1980. Santos Casarez Rios, aged 74 and alone, robbed a bank and then sat back to wait for the police so he could die in a federal prison, where his death could at least be noticed. According to Sgt. Manuel

Benavides, the man told him he had been wandering all over Texas, trying to commit a crime so he could be arrested. He wanted to die in a federal prison, so he robbed a bank. The bank vice-president quoted Rios as telling him "I'm old, I'm sick, I'm going blind, I'm lonely, I want to go back to the penitentiary and die".

On April 23, 1983, the Canadian Press reported (in the *VANCOUVER SUN*) that Canada's oldest and most enduring "con" was convicted again for theft - 59 years after his first conviction for stealing a car in Columbus, Ohio, in 1924. Victor (Ace) Hamel, 86, has such a long criminal record that the Crown Attorney needed a police van to bring the record to court. Hamel's last lengthy sentence was 14 years, served in several Canadian penitentiaries for uttering forged documents. He was released in 1978 at the age of 81 when he probably was the oldest inmate in Canada. Although he admits to doing 18 years in prison, Hamel's record indicates he has amassed 63 years in sentences in Canada and the United States.

Morton and Anderson (1982) insist that with recent lengthy mandatory sentencing statutes and the trend toward longer sentences, increasing numbers of people will grow old in prison in the United States. In Canada, the life sentence with a mandatory 25 years minimum before eligibility for parole, introduced in 1976 when the death penalty was abolished, is bound to create in the years to come a large group of aged inmates who will grow old in federal penitentiaries, become "prisonized", and if released are likely to commit new crimes so that they may be returned to the institution.

Ham (1976) wonders if the elderly who have been incarcerated for an extremely long period of time (25 years and more) do develop a dependency from a man-made disease which may be called "institutional neurosis" that manifests itself in their not wanting to leave or be released from prison. Gaddis (1972), in his article "Home at last: The prison habit" concludes that one characteristic of the maximum-security prison is the reality of prison as a seduction.

The theory of prisonization, enunciated by Clemmer (1940), examined the length of time served and the socialization processes within the prison environment and, particularly, the relationship between what inmates experience within the prison vis-a-vis their attachment to the outside world. Because the theory does not deal specifically with various phases of the institutional career important to the study of older prisoners, Aday and Webster (1979) set out to construct and test a tentative theoretical framework of institutionalization while focusing on the older prisoner. The theoretical model in their study is based on the assumption of institutional dependency, including the premise that it may be the only alternative for certain aging prisoners. The authors measured institutional dependency among two groups of older male prisoners whose ages ranged from 55 to 82 in both samples, with the mean age of the selected respondents being 61 years. The first group (40) was housed in an age-segregated facility (Lexington Regional Treatment Center in Oklahoma) and the other (55) in a more traditional integrated prison structure (Cummins Prison, a maximum security prison in Arkansas). Subjects were highly homogeneous concerning variables such as social class, education, occupation, and health status. Only 29% of the sample reported being married; 38% were black, 60% were Caucasian, with the remaining 2% being of an Indian heritage. Aday and

Webster found no significant difference in dependency associated with the social structure of the prison. They did discover, however, that marital status, age at first incarceration, and criminal classification were important variables in predicting institutional dependency among older prisoners. High degrees of dependency were found among the unmarried, those first incarcerated at an early age, and chronic offenders when compared with late offenders. Inmates in these categories may have fewer alternative sources of emotional support such as family and friends, which may force them to seek such support from the prison environment. Aday and Webster admit that their study suffers from certain weaknesses and feel that their tentative model needs further testing, preferably focusing on single dimensions within the model. They believe that their study did not adequately assess "reference group orientation". Friendship patterns were based on the perceptions of older prisoners and not actual interaction patterns. They suggest further that in order to determine the validity of the model based on age itself, future studies should use younger cohorts thus examining the development of institutional dependency from a life cycle perspective.

Alston (1986) points out that while institutional dependency is not limited to older prisoners, it can easily become more pronounced for them. Long or frequent prison terms take their toll on relationships with people in the free world at any age. For older prisoners, adds Alston, the deaths of friends and relatives are added to other strains which sever ties with those outside. Declining health and diminishing job skills can also encourage dependence on the protective environment of the prison.

The Physical and Social Settings

Golden (1984) points out that the physical layout of a jail (and one may add of a prison or a penitentiary) can present problems for the older (male) inmate. The lack of privacy sometimes frustrates the individual to the extent that medical or mental health help is necessary. She notes that everything is secured in a fixed position for additional security. This is particularly problematic for older inmates who, because of reduced physical flexibility, may have difficulties with standard seating and raised sleeping heights. In addition, fixed lighting can present a reading problem for the sight-impaired. Golden adds that:

> The layout of the jail can create additional problems for older inmates if worship services, recreation, family visits, or other programs are located at some distance from the cell area... Because of the age of most prisoners, jails are geared toward younger offenders. This presents a major problem for older inmates. Younger inmates are often noisy and assaultive. Programs are geared toward younger inmates, and even the physical layout of the jail is meant for people in good physical condition. Older inmates are subject to various abuses by their younger counterparts, from harassment to assault and robbery (1984:146).

Impairment and/or fear of younger inmates, suggests Golden, forces most older inmates to remain inside their cells, which further reduces their physical activity and may cause emotional problems. Most often they serve their entire sentences in idleness.

Because prisons are microcosms of society, there is a general impression that elderly (male) inmates are at the mercy of younger and more aggressive prisoners, that they can be easily threatened, intimidated, exploited and victimized. There are no empirical data to back up the belief that older prisoners are more easily and more frequently victimized than younger inmates. In fact, in view of the general patterns of victimization, the opposite might be true. But, since the elderly population in general seem to entertain a higher fear of victimization than do younger age groups, it might well be that there is a similarly higher level of fear among older inmates. This fear is likely to keep them apart from younger prisoners, thus restricting the volume of social interaction they have inside the prison and placing them in relative isolation.

In addition, the social isolation of some elderly inmates may be almost complete. Older prisoners in general are primarily loners. As Wiegand and Burger (1980) point out, they do not join into groups and often live quietly, not bothering anybody and nobody bothering with them. This is confirmed by Reed and Glamser (1979), though their study was based on a relatively small sample (19 male subjects). The authors note that older people who live in an age dense situation are particularly likely to have a number of friends. The situation among the older prisoners they studied was, on the other hand, quite different. Although inmates knew each other by name, friendship as it exists in the community was uncommon. Older prisoners were not likely to trust anybody, rarely formed friendships or had confidants.This seems to be in contrast   with what takes place in women's prisons where older female prisoners often serve "maternal" functions for younger inmates.

While having few if any social relations in the institution, incarceration is likely to cut off many elderly offenders from whatever family and friends they might have on the outside. In Goetting's (1984) sample of 284 elderly inmates, 39.57% reported never receiving visits from family members. An even higher percentage (45.84%) reported no family communication by telephone, while over a quarter (26.29%) reported none by mail. Less than 20% of the older prisoners received at least monthly visits from friends and others whereas (62.33%) reported never receiving visits from friends and others. While frequency distributions associated with visiting patterns with families and with friends/others did not differ significantly between older and younger inmates, those associated with telephone and mail patterns of interaction were significantly different.   Older inmates participated in less telephone and mail communications with family and with friends/others than did the younger prisoners.

Lack of Programs for Elderly Inmates

Prisons were not designed with the elderly offender in mind. They were planned for the bulk of the criminal population most of whom are males in their early, mid or late twenties. Elderly offenders are usually thirty or forty years older than the average inmate. Prison programs were equally designed to meet the needs of an incarcerated youthful population. Educational, vocational and recreational programs were all meant to provide these mostly young adults with opportunities to learn how to read and write or to upgrade their education, learn a trade and acquire some vocational skills that can facilitate the task of finding

96

a job upon release, or to provide some sport and cultural activities to relieve the monotony and alleviate the boredom that is one of the facts of life in a penal institution. Since there are very few programs, if any, designed specifically for elderly inmates, this group inevitably finds it difficult to take advantage of the existing ones which, more often than not, do not suit their needs. Even in prisons where there are opportunities for work, elderly inmates are likely to be at a disadvantage and this might hamper their chances for early release or parole. As Alston (1986) points out:

the system for earning greater freedom and other privileges often involves work as well as good behaviour. For the healthy, fit older prisoners this system may present few problems since most states assign work on the basis of health and strength. For frail or infirm older prisoners, the absence of suitable work can deny them a means for improving their positions in the prison hierarchy.. It has also been charged that recreational, therapy and educational programs are designed for the younger prisoner and have little or no appeal for the older one. Job training, for example, would be of less interest to a man reaching retirement age...Recreational opportunities such as basketball are obviously not appropriate for frail or ailing older inmates, but limiting them to sedentary activities such as checkers is not in their best interest either(1986:219).

These views are echoed by Goetting (1983). Referring to formal educational programs, she notes that most older prisoners have left the education system decades ago, and have no desire to resume their studies. Even those who do show an interest in educational programs are often discouraged by prison officials who believe that the limited openings should be offered to younger men and women who would more likely benefit occupationally from them. Goetting writes:

Often the staff are unwilling to place older prisoners in educational programs. The same situation holds true for vocational training programs; they are of little interest or value to the elderly because chances are slim that an older ex-convict will find work available to him in the community (1983:298).

In addition ,there seems to be a widespread belief that older prisoners are not interested in prison education and are unwilling to participate in institutional activities which are open to the general inmate population (Shinbaum, 1977; Bintz, 1974). Such perception (or misperception) is confirmed by a prison administrator (cited by Krajick, 1979), who said:

The older inmates are not as easy to motivate as the younger guys. They need a lot of coaxing to do anything at all. It would be good for them if we could do that, shake them out of their boredom...there isn't much we have here that's of interest to them.

In another study, based on a sample of 248 (male) inmates aged 55 and older, housed in American correctional facilities, Goetting (1984) found that the most common recreational activities among these older prisoners were reading books, magazines, and papers and watching television daily. Additionally, the following proportions of the sample participated in the following activities at least once a week: 60.92% used the prison store or commissary, 28.96% played cards or participated in games, 29.63% attended movies, and 15.25% participated in sports. Regarding work, Goetting reported that over half (56.75%) of the older prisoners had work assignments, and over half (53.98%) of those were paid for their work. Those with such job assignments worked a mean of 36.22 hours per week. The type of work varied with slightly over a quarter doing general janitorial duties, and slightly less than a quarter working in prison services (library, stockroom, store, office, help, etc.). Smaller percentages performed duties such as "grounds or road maintenance", "food preparation or related duties", "maintenance or repair", "goods production", "farming/forestry", "hospital infirmary, or other medical services", and "laundry".

Goetting (1984) found certain differences among elderly male inmates and their younger counterparts. Older prisoners, for example, reported a higher mean number of hours outdoors in the average week (23.00 hours compared with 18.21 hours). Furthermore, the distributions of weekday prison activities across eight categories of activities differed significantly for the two age categories.

The lack of special programs for elderly inmates was highlighted in a telephone/mail survey conducted by Goetting (1983) during the first half of 1982. She solicited information on the existence or lack thereof of special policies, programs and facilities for elderly inmates in United States prisons. She reports a one hundred per cent response from prison officials approached. Of the fifty states, forty-seven, as well as the Federal Prison System, reported no formal special consideration to elderly inmates. Only three states and the District of Columbia reported the operation of special policies, programs, and/or facilities designed to accomodate elderly prison inmates through standards based on chronological age. On the basis of the information provided, Goetting concluded that a chronological age system independent of health status is not recognized by prison policy. She sees this as reflecting a lack of recognition and responsiveness to the special needs of institutionalized senior citizens.

Health Problems of the Elderly Inmate

Elderly inmates are likely to be suffering from physical ailments and mental impairment at a rate higher than that of younger inmates. Many might not be able to receive adequate treatment in the prison setting. McCarthy (1983) points out that although alcoholism has been recognized as a leading medical and social problem among the elderly, it often goes untreated in prison, except for enforced abstinence. She adds that excessive use of drugs and alcohol may have precipitated the behavior that violated the law since alcohol exacerbates mental illness and suicidal as well as homicidal behavior in addition to inducing bizarre behavior.

As age advances, individuals develop all kinds of physical ailments. Such ailments may be found among elderly inmates whether they have aged in prison or whether they were committed in old age. Baier (1961) notes that in addition to the physical change, inmates who are arteriosclerotic and senile undergo characteristic mental and personality changes. Their tolerance for stress and strain of all types is diminished. Their ability to maintain equilibrium is slow and imperfect, as is the healing of wounds.

While some conditions, for example malnutrition or excessive alcohol consumption, might improve as a result of confinement in a penal institution, most other conditions are unlikely to improve and might become distinctly worse due to incarceration. The elderly inmate might suffer a marked decline in his physical and mental status. New health problems might develop as a consequence of institutionalization. Ham (1980) points out that when institutionally isolated older persons are confronted with unusually high levels of environmental regimentation, rigid discipline, pressure and stress, the end result is the development and manifestation of institutional neurosis. Ham further notes that forced inactivity in prison leads to sensory deprivation which is extremely hazardous to physical and mental well-being, replicating the effects of chronic debilitation. Quoting Oster (1976), Ham adds that:

Sensory deprivation speeds up the degenerative changes normally associated with aging and enhances the loss of functional cells in the central nervous system. Since it connotes reduction or absence of stimulation of the senses, it involves physical activity, social relationships, intellectual status and the overall value system. Older individuals with various illnesses are particularly vulnerable to sensory deprivation, which becomes increasingly pronounced as physical or mental deterioration progresses. For instance, with immobility, a decrease in muscle strength and a weakening of the bones will occur (1980:29).

In one of the few studies of health problems among older inmates, McCarthy (1983) found that physical fitness programs geared to them were noticeably lacking, as was preventive physical therapy for those suffering from debilitating illnesses. Some older inmates could not consume sufficient amounts of food to sustain them between meals or during the night, yet supplemental kitchen snacks seemed to be nonexistent. Among those who were 65 and over, lack of a hearing aid or other medical prosthetic devices was a general concern, as was the diet and type of medical services available.

In another study, Ham (1980) reviewed the medical records of the 93 inmates in Ohio who were housed at the Limited Duty Unit (Columbus Correctional Facility) to report on the conditions of confinement as they affect aged, aged-infirm, and young-infirm male prison inmates. The review revealed a wide range of medical and psychological disorders and impairments characterized by or typical of human aging. Physical and mental functioning for all inmates at the Unit were diminished and levels of morbidity did not appear to vary with age.

Alston(1986) suggests that the health facilities of prisons are geared to deal with the acute illnesses and injuries of younger persons and are not generally equipped to handle the chronic, long-term health problems of old age. She quotes one prison counselor who had this to say about older inmates : "They're a corrections problem, they're a parole problem, they're a welfare problem, they're a mental health problem, and no one takes care of them". (1986:219).

Integration Versus Segregation

Should senior citizens live in age-segregated or age-integrated communities, housing projects, housing units? This controversial issue has been the subject of lengthy debates among gerontologists and sociologists with strong arguments on each side. Recently, the debate has been extended to the situation of older inmates who are serving time in prison. Those who argue for segregation believe it is necessary to protect elderly, and often weak, male prisoners against victimization, exploitation, and harassment by younger, aggressive inmates. Older prisoners, they point out, are vulnerable and their safety should be a primary concern of the prison administration. Their safety could best be secured by separating them from other inmates. By housing them in separate facilities and units,they can also benefit from extended care and specialized services and programs designed specifically to meet their particular needs. Segregation, it is further suggested, provides the older inmate with optimal opportunity for forming peer networks and the administration with the chance to cater to the unfulfilled needs of the elderly prison population. Having older prisoners engage in age-specific group activities within the institution is also seen as beneficial to their mental health. Among the desirable effects that might ensue are the ones summarized by Rubenstein (1984). He cites research suggesting that participation in age-specific groups in institutions: 1) increases self-respect; 2) diminishes feelings of loneliness and depression: 3) re-activates desire for social exchange; 4) reawakens intellectual interest; 5) creates a sense of identification among members and a shared feeling of shared historical legacy; and 6) increases capability to resume community life.

Because of the relatively small number of elderly prisoners, and because of the economic restraints imposed on the correctional system, it seems unrealistic to expect that specially designed correctional facilities will be constructed for them in the near future or that specialized services will be provided to them in the general prisons by highly trained staff. The question of segregation versus integration should not, however, be regarded as merely a theoretical one. Though not on a large scale, the principle of segregation has already been implemented in a few correctional facilities in the United States. Goetting (1984) cites a couple of places where elderly inmates are segregated from the general prison population. Virginia, for example, operates the Aged Offender Program at its state penitentiary. This program accommodates sixty-two men over age 50, which represents approximately 13% of the total Virginia inmate population in that age category. The District of Columbia Department of Corrections houses inmates aged 55 and older (except those with medical problems requiring hospitalization) apart from the general inmate population in two special dormitories, which are described as quieter, cleaner, and better controlled than other residential facilities.

Another example of segregation is the Limited Duty Unit at the Columbus Correctional Facility in Ohio. The unit, with a maximum capacity of 120 to 130 men, is isolated from the larger part of the prison and the general inmate population. According to Ham (1980), the expressed function of this unit is to provide institutional housing for aged inmates to "alleviate discrimination of aged inmates in the Columbus Correctional Facility by virtue of the fact that present programming is not commensurate with their physiological, psychological and sociological needs". Ham adds, however, that the same services are provided

100

young inmates who are physically unable to function in the routine correctional setting. In addition to the aged and aged infirm, there are also younger, medically indigent inmates housed at the Unit. Ham found that the Unit was administered in reality in the same fashion as the various cell blocks and other units of confinement at the Columbus Correctional Facility. He writes:

> Furthermore, despite the fact that a small nurses' station and physical therapy room are located in this three-story building, it is devoid of anything remotely related to a "geriatric unit" or therapeutic environment. Inmates housed here, regardless of age and physical infirmities, are afforded no special privileges, treatment, or programs. In fact, because of isolation, immobility, and physical infirmities, the inmates are worse off than those housed in the main section of the prison (1980:24).

While acknowledging the need to give special consideration to elderly inmates and to provide them with extended health care and even more specialized services, critics of segregation point to some of the detrimental effects that could result from isolating aged prisoners in geriatric units or facilities. Although segregation is often justified and advocated as being in their own best interest, it could easily be turned into age discrimination. Elderly inmates might easily be deprived of some of the services and opportunities that are available to the general population. They might suffer from being treated with undue paternalism and from the stigma attached to being old, weak, helpless and in need of particular care. Possibilities for social interaction within the prison will necessarily shrink, their relationships and communications with the outside world might suffer, and isolation might enhance their institutional dependency. Removing them from mainstream life and activities in the institution can only heighten their sense of inadequacy.

In addition to challenging the need for, and the appropriateness of, segregating older prisoners from younger ones, proponents of age integration stress the benefits of such policy to both the institution and the elderly inmates themselves. They suggest that dispersing older prisoners throughout the institution can have a stabilizing effect on the general inmate population and can positively contribute to the general climate in the prison. They point to the findings of research showing that older prisoners, in general, present fewer discipline problems, commit less rule infractions, are more cooperative and get along better with other inmates. To counter this argument, advocates of segregation point out that old-timers, professional and career criminals, can have a negative effect on younger, inexperienced ones and can teach them many of the secrets of the crime trade. They add that the interests of elderly inmates should prevail over administrative considerations. Concern for their safety and the need to protect them against victimization, exploitation and harassment outweigh any stabilizing effect their integration might have. Responding to the argument of vulnerability and potential victimization integrationists point to information indicating that older prisoners are not frequently victimized and that most victimization is limited to harassment in the form of verbal abuse and the petty thefts of personal items (see for example Krajick, 1979). Others cite information showing that, within the prison status hierarchy, elderly inmates are accorded prestige and deference. Wiltz (1978) describes the inmate status hierarchy as one based partially on seniority, with recently admitted prisoners occupying the lowest place, and "old cons" with long experience in prison ways initiating norms and occupying leadership roles. Wiltz believes that older inmates are respected by their younger counterparts because of their accumulated wisdom regarding the workings of life which allows them to manipulate the system to their advantage.

While the debate on the advantages and drawbacks of both segregation and integration is raging among gerontologists, sociologists, criminologists and penologists, very little attention is paid to what the elderly inmates themselves want. A policy that has the best interests of the older prison population at heart should be based on the findings of studies of the elderly's life and position in various institutions and on surveys asking the older prisoners about their personal preferences and the reasons for such preferences.

Last but not least, it should be pointed out that complete segregation or total integration are not the only options; between these two extremes there exists a range of alternative and intermediate options. One idea suggested by Wiltz (1978), is to incarcerate aged inmates with other adult inmates, with special accomodation for the aged that would include specific housing areas, special diets, and job assignments. Another alternative offered by Wiltz might be even better: releasing the aged inmates from prison, but reinstitutionalizing them into homes for the aged in the general society. He feels this alternative would be particularly appropriate for inmates with no family, or for those with families that are unwilling to assume responsibility for them.

Parole and the Elderly Offender

Habitual and chronic offenders who have spent most of their adult life in prison, together with offenders who aged in prison while spending a life or a very long sentence, are not likely to look favorably upon the prospect of parole. As discussed earlier, many of them suffer from "prisonization' or institutional dependency. The prison is their home. Many are likely to reject the possibility of release on parole when offered. Aday and Webster (1979) report that several subjects in their study declared that they intended to "flatten" their time instead of taking early parole. Their rationale was based on the inconvenience of having to report to the parole counselor. The authors feel it could also be interpreted as a fear of being unable to cope with life on the outside.

The attitude of the first time elderly inmate, the offender whose first experience with the prison occurred at a very late age, is likely to be very different. The change in environment, the deprivation of liberty, the pains of imprisonment, and the problems of adjusting to life inside the walls mean that the elderly inmate will be counting the days remaining before release. He or she is likely to apply for parole immediately upon eligibility and to be terribly disappointed and upset if parole is denied. Such an offender is likely to be unfamiliar with the parole process and may therefore be unprepared when the time comes for appearance before the parole board. Compared with other younger inmates serving time for the same or similar offences, the elderly inmate is also more likely to be handicapped. Since criteria such as housing and employment weigh heavily in the consideration for parole, the elderly inmate is disadvantaged in more ways than one. In their discussion of the elderly offender and parole, Wiegand and Burger (1979) point out that the elderly inmate is often a sorry spectacle as he or she presents himself or herself for parole consideration. The fact that he or she typically hasn't been active in existing correctional programs is only one of the strikes agaist the elderly inmate, but it is by no means the only one. They add that:

> All parole boards have specific criteria that must be fulfilled if the inmate's parole plan is to be accepted. Of primary importance is housing. An inmate must have a place to live before he (or she) can be paroled. This condition is usually met by friends or family providing housing, at least until the parolee is back on the street and can make other arrangements. This issue becomes a much larger problem for the older offender... The employment/financial aspect of parole is also a difficult issue for the elderly offender. Parole typically calls for employment as a prerequisite for release. But what of the older inmate who is unemployable because of age or health difficulties? In some cases parole boards will waive the employment requirement for the older man/woman. But this still leaves financial difficulties. A parolee must show that he (or she) is able to support himself (or herself) financially. For many elderly parolees this support is some type of pension or welfare promising, at best, a minimal level of existence (1979:51-52).

One American program designed to help elderly inmates prepare for parole is based in Pittsburg, Pennsylvania. According to Wiegand and Burger (1979) the program is unique in working with the elderly offender and ex-offender. They describe the project as providing services continuously from the time an older person comes into prison until the time he/she can function independently. The program provides each client with a wide variety of direct services including group and family counseling, release planning, and assistance with housing, financial, medical and employment problems. The project also acts as an advocate for release in many cases. It serves as a client liaison with community agencies which can be of assistance in meeting the needs of the elderly prisoner. The rationale for the project is a simple one: the belief that one of the largest factors involved in parole violation and recidivism is the system's lack of adequate preparation for release. According to Wiegand and Burger (1979):

> Lack of appropriate programming for the older offender, combined with the prison staff's lack of insight into the dynamics of aging, make the elderly parolee's chances for reintegration into the community very poor. Particularly in cases of long periods of incarceration, the elderly parolee is returning to an unfamiliar environment, surrounded by strangers. His (or her) personal support system and points of reference are gone (1979:52).

The authors recommend that the prison take some responsibility for how it prepares inmates for return to free society. They argue that unless a systematic effort is made by prison officials to overcome and reverse the effects of long term incarceration, parole becomes a time bomb, rather than a calculated risk.

CHAPTER FIVE: RECOMMENDED READINGS

Goetting, Ann
1983 The Elderly in Prison: Issues and Perspectives. Journal of Research in Crime and Delinquency, 20:291-309

Goetting, Ann
1984 The Elderly in Prison: A Profile. Criminal Justice Review, 9(2):14-24.

Krajick,K.
1979 Growing Old in Prison. Corrections Magazine, March, 33-39.

Reed, M.B. and F.D.Glamser
1979 Aging in a Total Institution: The Case of Older Prisoners. Gerontologist, 19 (August):354-360.

Rubenstein,D.
1984 The Elderly in Prison: A Review of the Literature In Newman, E.S. et al.(Eds.) Elderly Criminals. Cambridge, Mass.: Oelgeschlager, Gunn & Hain Publishers. pp. 153-168.

Wiegand, D. and J.C. Burger
1979 The Elderly Offender and Parole. Prison Journal, 59(2):48-57.

CHAPTER SIX

RESPONDING TO ELDERLY CRIMINALITY: SENTENCING, PUNISHMENT, PREVENTION

A TENTATIVE TYPOLOGY OF GERIATRIC OFFENDERS

As mentioned earlier, elderly offenders are, like the criminal population in general, a very heterogeneous group. Their only common denominator is their old age. They differ as to the age of onset of their delinquency, the nature, frequency and intensity of their criminal activities, the length and persistence of their delinquent careers, the time periods between their delinquent episodes, and so on. They also differ in their personal characteristics, their socioeconomic and sociocultural backgrounds, their motivation as well as the causative and triggering factors underlying their criminality. It seems essential, therefore, for better understanding and better dealing with their criminal behavior, to categorize them in more or less homogeneous groups using one or more criteria. Differentiating between various types is also indispensable for individualizing the justice system's response and for choosing the most appropriate penal measure in each individual case.

Although there are several typologies of delinquents and criminals (Ferdinand, 1966; Clinard and Quinney, 1973; Roebuck, 1967; Gibbons, 1975; Megargee et al., 1979) specific typologies of elderly offenders are extremely rare. Wolk (1963) talks about one single type he calls the geriatric delinquent. The term is used to describe a person over 60 years of age who commits antisocial acts within his or her own specific social milieu, but whose previous social history is devoid of such behavior. So defined, the geriatric delinquent is an old person who has managed to make an adequate adjustment through most of his or her adult life; only in the late years has the asocial or antisocial behavior emerged.

105

Cormier et al.(1971) identify three types of elderly offenders. They distinguish between the late offender whom they define as someone "whose delinquent behavior is confined to a single episode" and the episodic offender defined as "a recidivist whose life is characterized, apart from two or more short delinquent episodes, by law-abiding behavior". The third type, a late delinquent,is defined as a multi-recidivist whose social adjustment is governed by delinquent values. This terminology is rather confusing. Not only are the terms "late offender" and "late delinquent" similar, but also they do not correspond to the definitional content given to them by the authors.

Cormier et al.(1971) state that we could expect the proportion of "late delinquents" to decrease as the age of legal onset increases. They point out that the earlier delinquency starts, the more likely it is that it will continue beyond age 40 (the age at which delinquent behavior usually comes to an end). On the other hand, the later delinquent activities begin the more likely it is that they will cease in late adulthood and that they will not persist in old age. In their sample, 73% of those who became delinquent between the ages of 20 and 24 were found to have become late delinquents (according to their definition) after age 40. The proportion of late delinquents fell to 47% among those with a legal onset between ages of 25 and 39. As for the group of offenders with a legal onset at age 40 or over, late delinquents numbered only 6%.

A typology of geriatric offenders is necessary for understanding their criminal behavior and for developing policies, strategies and techniques to deal with that behavior. Some of the existing criminal typologies may be applied to elderly offenders. Such is the one that classifies criminals on the basis of the types of offenses they commit, whether the offenses are violent or nonviolent, committed against the person or against property, whether they are sexual or non-sexual in nature, and so forth. Within each type several subtypes may also be identified. Thus among those committing non-violent property offenses one may distinguish subtypes like the professional thief, the embezzler, the swindler, the safe-cracker, the shoplifter and so on. Even a subtype like the shoplifter may be further divided into two subtypes: the booster and the snitch. Among the general type of sexual offenders one can distinguish specific subtypes such as the rapist, the pedophile, the non-pedophilic child molester, the incestuous father, the exhibitionist, the peeping-tom, the obscene phone-caller, and so on.

Applying existing typologies to elderly offenders does not satisfy the need for a specific typology of this group which differs from the general population of criminals by its old age. Such a specific typology can use a combination of criteria related to the time of onset, the length of the criminal career, the time periods between the criminal acts and so on. Among the general category, referred to for convenience purposes as "elderly offenders" or "geriatric delinquents", one may distinguish between those who started committing crimes at an early age and continued to do so over their entire adult life, those who might also have started early or in middle age but whose criminality is intermittent, occurring at long or very long intervals, and finally those who committed their first crime ever (officially or unofficially) late in life, at an age at which most individuals are leading an existence free from law violations. If elderly offenders are to be classified according to these criteria, three major types emerge:

106

1. **The inveterate aging offender**

Elderly offenders of this type (and they may also be called aging persistent offenders or elderly chronic offenders) are those who start their criminal career as juvenile delinquents or as young adults and continue their activities into senescence. As noted earlier, the majority of recidivists abandon their career in criminality before reaching old age. A few, however, persist in their criminal activities way past the age at which most criminals retire. They are the veterans of crime. The main characteristic of this type is a chronic, persistent pattern of repetitive criminality; the perseverance in a life of crime started in adolescence, late adolescence or youth.

Empirical studies (see Cormier et al.,1971) of recidivism suggest that "the earlier one is fixated in repetitive delinquency, the greater are the chances that this pattern will persist". Yet, even the most persistent offenders cease their criminal activities by age 40, and the question therefore is: why does this small particular group continue far beyond that age when the majority have usually abated?

The criminality of these veteran offenders may be continuous or episodic but it is spread over a very long period of time (in many cases over a lifetime) and is characterized by the relatively brief intervals between the commission of various crimes, interrupted only by short or long periods of incarceration. Some may spend more time in prison than in freedom. And while some may stick to one type of offence (for example drunkenness, fraud, sex offenses, petty theft) many of these chronic offenders switch from one type of criminality to another. The natural criminal history of those who switch usually exhibits a certain progression in their early criminal career and a certain regression in their later life. This is generally reflected in the offenses they commit over the years. Shoplifting or the passing of bad cheques may represent the terminal phase in the career of recidivists previously convicted of a wide range of offenses (see Roth,1968).

The inveterate aging offender is not to be confused with the aging incarcerated offender. The latter type is usually a middle-aged person who receives a life or a very long sentence for a serious crime such as murder or manslaughter, is not released on parole, and is thus doomed to spend his senior years in the penitentiary.

Several subtypes of the inveterate aging offender may be identified:

a. **The professional criminal**

What differentiates the professional criminal from the habitual criminal is the sophisticated forms of crime in which the former engages and the petty forms to which the latter seems committed. It is possible to identify a wide variety of professional criminals, for example the professional counterfeiter, the professional safecracker, the professional swindler, the professional blackmailer, the professional con man, the professional jewel thief, the professional art forger, to name but a few. The natural criminal history of some of these professional criminals has been immortalized in the annals of criminology through books such as Sutherland's *THE PROFESSIONAL THIEF*; Shaw's *THE NATURAL HISTORY OF A DELINQUENT CAREER; BOX MAN: A PROFESSIONAL THIEF'S JOURNAL*, as told to and edited by Bill Chambliss. Among the ones less known to criminologists is *"YELLOW KID" WEIL - CON MAN: A MASTER SWINDLER'S OWN STORY* as told to W.T. Brannon. The book's blurb informs the reader that in his long and checkered career as a confidence man, "Yellow Kid" Weil mulcted the public of over $8,000,000 and established a reputation for connivery that has never been equalled.

Inciardi (1974) maintains that the professional who has supplied such colorful characters to criminology is probably a figure of the past. Improvements in the technology of identification and record-keeping, and the creation of cooperative arrangements among law-enforcement agencies, have made it less possible to pursue a single criminal activity for a lifetime. (see Alston, 1986, p.149). Inciardi maintains that:

> more and more, the latter day professional seems to forfeit any pursuit of focused specialization in lieu of the less-skilled and more haphazard "hustling" way of life (1974:342).

b.   The chronic drunkenness offender

The old, chronic drunkenness offender is a subtype frequently found in the skid row of every major city in North America. One typical case suffices to illustrate the dilemma this particular type poses for the criminal justice system. The May 1966 issue of the *NEW HAMPSHIRE ALCOHOLISM BULLETIN* mentions an alcoholic, age 59, in Durham County, North Carolina, who has been arrested "possibly for his 300th or 400th" time for intoxication. Court records showed that the man had been jailed for drunkenness more than 200 times. The Bulletin article reports that he has spent nearly two-thirds of his life in prison for the same infraction of the law - being drunk in public.

Morris (1973) cites another case, this one in Washington, D.C., of six habitual drunks who were arrested for public drunkenness a total of 1,409 times and had collectively served 125 years in the city's penal institutions. Their arrests, prosecutions and incarcerations had cost Washington more than $600,000.

c.   The habitual criminal / the chronic petty offender

In their book on habitual offenders, Hammond and Chayen (1961) discuss the persistent petty thief or false pretence offender who is often quite old and who has failed to make a satisfactory adjustment to life generally. Most commonly male, he has few ties, holds a job for a short period only, tends to have no roots and lives from day to day in cheap hotels, lodging houses or on the streets, and he tends to be a drain on the social services whether in prison or not. Moreover, he has been in and out of prison most of his life and appears to be better adjusted to prison life than to any other.

d. **The organized crime godfather**

Becoming an organized crime Godfather is usually the crowning achievement of a long career extending over a lifetime in organized crime. Many of those identified by the police in the United States as "Mafia Dons" are elderly individuals and some of them are even septuagenarian(see Newman and Newman,1982).

e. **The inveterate psychopath**

Psychopathy is a loose nosological concept used by psychiatrists who rely mainly on emotional and behavioral problems the individual manifests to reach the diagnosis of "psychopath" . Thus, according to Weinberg (1952), a true psychopath presents a distinctive set of characteristics. He (or she) lacks, for example, the ability to postpone the satisfaction of each urge as it comes upon him, and he has little capacity for remorse or guilt. Although he can relate adequately on an impersonal, casual level, he is rarely able to sustain intimate relationships, because his emotional responses to others are very limited. He is egocentric, irresponsible in the extreme, and emotionally shallow.

Another psychiatrist,Guttmacher (1958) notes that the psychopathic criminal is an individual who is not psychotic (insane) but who indulges in irrational, antisocial behavior, probably resulting from hidden unconscious neurotic conflicts which constitute the driving force underlying the criminal conduct. Among psychopaths, argues Guttmacher, are to be found some of the most malignant and recidivistic offenders. They exhibit the following characteristics:

*   evidences of life-long social maladjustment reaching back into early childhood;

*   overwhelming hostility skilfully hidden behind a mask of amiability;

*   they look upon other people as mere objects to be manipulated for their own hedonistic purposes;

*   they possess no loyalties and are suspicious of others;

*   they exhibit an incapacity for establishing satisfying and meaningful relationships with other individuals;

*   they do not learn by experience and despite admonitions and punishments they continue their same pattern of objectionable behavior.

McCord and McCord (1964) define the psychopath as "an asocial, aggressive , highly impulsive person, who feels little or no guilt and is unable to form lasting bonds of affection with other human beings."

Among the old persistent offenders in prisons and penitentiaries, a good number fit the diagnostic label of a

109

"psychopath" described above. A long persistent career of offending is actually an important criterion in the diagnosis of a psychopathic personality. In fact, some psychiatrists, for example Karpman (1946), have used "incurability" as a major criterion of psychopathy (see McCord and McCord, 1964:43).

f.   **The chronic, non-violent sex offender**

The truly pedophilic sex offender, who is exclusively attracted to prepubertal children - girls, boys or both - can persist in his sexual activities with non-discerning or seemingly "consenting" children long after his libido has weakened or subsided. Most of these offenders exhibit no other antisocial attitudes and are law-abiding, conforming citizens except for the sexual sphere. Because of this and because of the type of victims they select ,they can go on with their deviant sexual activities for many years (or even for a lifetime) without being detected. And since their sexual preference or fixation does not change over time, their offenses persist, whether detected or not, until late in life. One such case came recently to light in Australia. It is the case of a small, lonely, obsessive and not very likeable man living in a middle-class suburb in Brisbane. For over twenty years he was able to have a physical relationship with at least 2,500 boys before his case, just by chance, came to the attention of the police. In his book, *THE MAN THEY CALLED A MONSTER*, Paul Wilson (1981) provides a socio-psychological analysis of the case which ended with the offender committing suicide rather than going to trial.

2.   **The relapsing old offender**

Some old offenders, long thought to have been rehabilitated, suddenly relapse into crime after a very long period of successful adjustment and after having stayed away from crime for two, three or four decades. Those who continue to commit crime through adult age and middle life without being detected do not actually belong to this type, but to the first one, the "inveterate aging offender". Those who belong to this second type of elderly offenders are individuals with a long or short history of delinquency or criminality in their younger years (a history that may well extend into their late twenties), followed by a long or a very long period of latency or remission. During this period of remission, these individuals were living in society and were not engaged in criminal activities of any kind. The relapse into crime occurs after they have reached the age of fifty or sixty and is usually triggered by some life crisis or by some problems or changes brought about by old age.

A distinction may be made between two subtypes: the monomorphic and the polymorphic.

a.   **The monomorphic**

The monomorphic is an elderly offender who, after a long period of remission, re-offends in the same way, committing the same offence (or category of offence) as when he/she was a young person.

b. **The polymorphic**

The polymorphic is an elderly offender whose later criminal activities are of a different type than the ones committed during his youth. For example, a person might have committed violent offenses when he was young, subsequently ceased to be violent and after reaching old age commits one or several offenses such as shoplifting, swindling or fraud. Another may have committed property offenses in his youth, ceased to engage in criminal activities and then commits a sexual offence, an assault or a homicide in his senior years.

3. **The elderly first offender / The late starter / The late-comer to crime**

This is the most atypical, most intriguing and probably the most problematic of all offenders. It is a person whose first criminal offence ever is committed in old age. Those who belong to this type are individuals with no prior history (official or unofficial) of delinquency or criminality who commit their first offence after reaching the age of 55, 60 or 65. The criminality of this particular type poses a formidable challenge to criminologists and to the criminal justice system.

For criminologists, the question is: why, after so many decades, after an entire life of conformity and law-abiding behavior, do they break the laws they have previously respected? Why is it that social controls which seem to have been operative and effective hitherto have failed so late in life? Could their criminality be the outcome of factors or conditions related to aging? Could it be the result of physiological, psychological, sociological, economical or environmental changes associated with old age?

For the criminal justice system, the major problem stems from the fact that the system is designed to deal with young delinquents or youthful offenders. It does not seem to have a place or a plan for those who come into conflict with the law very late in life. Neither the underlying philosophy nor the traditional measures and institutions seem appropriate for this particular type. In reality, what may be functional for young or adult offenders may be dysfunctional when applied to elderly or geriatric delinquents.

The suspected origin of the criminality of these late-comers to crime may be useful in distinguishing between different subtypes. The following are some of these subtypes:

a. elderly first offenders who exhibit psychiatric and behavioral changes caused by, connected with, or symptomatic of, an organic brain disease, such as cerebral damage, cerebral degenerative change, arteriosclerotic psychosis, or other organic brain deterioration leading to loss of memory, impairment of judgement, loss of inhibitions, break-down of the inner mechanisms of self-control or to the sudden (and not too sudden) release of primitive instinctual urges, morbid jealousy, morbid irritability, suspicion and mistrust.

b. elderly first offenders suffering from senile dementia either in an early or advanced stage as well as those suffering from some functional

111

psychosis such as paranoid schizophrenia, depression (acute or chronic) or neurosis.

c. elderly first offenders whose criminality can be traced directly or indirectly to alcohol abuse or to chronic alcoholism, whether this is in combination with any of the aforementioned states or not. This subtype also includes elderly first offenders whose criminality can be traced directly or indirectly to the influence of some drug or medication (obtained with or without prescription).

d. elderly first offenders suffering from specific personality changes associated with, or resulting from, old age. Offenses committed by this subtype are usually, though not exclusively, violent acts consisting of aggressive reactions triggered by increasing rigidity, suspiciousness, quarrelsomeness, extreme excitability and irritability. One may also observe aggressive reactions related to the male and female menopause, to the conscious or sub-conscious realization of physiological impotence.

e. elderly first offenders whose criminality can be related directly to the influence of the environment. Some elderly individuals with offending-free history start committing crime, mostly minor offenses, after a fundamental environmental change such as the placement in a nursery home or a residence for senior citizens. In some cases, assaults and other attacks against the person may be a result of aggressive reactions to institutionalization and close living, to a personal (and subjective) sense of crowding not previously experienced. Problems of adjustment to life in an institution, to forced company, to daily interactions with virtual strangers, may also manifest themselves in other forms of criminal or deviant behavior.

The three major types of elderly offenders identified above raise different etiological and social control questions:

1. Regarding the first type, the aging persistent offender, the multirecidivist, the lifetime criminal grown old, the basic question is "Why does an individual persist in criminal activity far beyond the age at which most criminals cease their criminal involvement?" Most existing criminological theories attempt to explain the onset of delinquency. Rare are the theories (for example the labelling approach) that try to explain the persistence of criminality. Theories offering explanations for recidivism do not answer the question of why a minority of multi-recidivists continue in old age.

From a social viewpoint, elderly chronic offenders are the most difficult to treat. The inveterate aging offender, whether a professional criminal, a habitual offender, or an inveterate psychopath, is the living proof of the failure of the criminal law, the criminal justice system and the system of punishment in dealing with certain problems of criminality. Many of the persistent offenders who have been incarcerated for interrupted or uninterrupted long periods of time suffer from the syndrome of "prisonization" well described by Clemmer (1941). As a result, they feel more at home in prison than they do on the outside. For them, the prison is a niche, a peaceful spot in contrast with the uncontrolled jungle outside

112

the walls. To continue to send them to prison is both futile and a waste of public funds. A totally different approach needs to be taken to deal with their persistent (and often petty) criminality.

2. Regarding the second type, the relapsing old offender, whether of the monomorphic or the polymorphic variety, the fundamental problem is to find out why, after so many years free from criminal activity, there is a relapse, i.e., renewed criminal behavior. What stresses, frustrations, crises, or other conditions in old age brought about an end to a long period of successful adjustment? The criminological prognosis for this type of elderly offender is certainly brighter than that for the first type. Understanding and dealing with the problems suspected of having led to the relapse, and providing the offender with the necessary personal and social support, is likely to prevent future recidivism and to ensure an existence free of law violations.

3. the third type of elderly offender, the late starter, is the most enigmatic. Why is it that someone who has been a law-abiding and often an exemplary citizen all of his/her life, suddenly commits an act (or a series of acts) of delinquency? How should society respond to such late and often unpredictable criminality? What is to be done with such a late first offender depends on a wide variety of factors, not the least of which is the offender himself/herself, the make-up of the individual, his or her social network and other support systems, the nature of the offence(s) committed and the circumstances surrounding the offence, aspects of the offender's physical and mental health and so forth. If individualized sentencing and treatment are necessary in the case of other young or old offenders, they are absolutely imperative in the case of the late-comer to crime. Here again the criminological prognosis is usually good, provided the problems underlying this late criminality have been identified and adequately dealt with. Psychiatric treatment is necessary for those exhibiting the symptoms of an organic brain disease or a functional psychosis. In cases where the offence can be traced directly or indirectly to chronic alcoholism, any individualized treatment program will have to deal with the alcohol condition. Senile personality changes are well known to psychiatrists and clinical psychologists and although it may be difficult to reverse them or to arrest their progress, illegal forms of behavior stemming directly from these changes can be easily controlled or modified. Finally, elderly offenders whose late criminality can be attributed directly to the influence of the environment need to be treated with care and understanding. The initial shock of a change in the environment usually wears out with the passage of time. Minor changes in the elderly person's new environment might be all that is needed to facilitate the person's adjustment and to put an end to the disruptive or aggressive behavior.

Table 1

A Typology of Elderly Offenders		
The aging persistent offender **The elderly chronic Offender**	**The relapsing old Offender**	**The elderly First offender** **The late starter** **The latecomer to crime**
The elderly profes- sional criminal	The monomorphic	Those who exibit psychiatric and behavioral changes caused by/or con- nected with an organic disease
The elderly habitual criminal		
Organized crime god fathers	The polymorphic	Those who suffer from some functional psychosis
The inveterate psychopath		Those whose criminality can be traced directly or in- directly to chronic alcoholism
The chronic drunkenness offender		
The chronic sex offender		Those who suffer from senile person- ality changes
		Those whose criminality can be re- lated directly to the influence of the environment

SENTENCING THE ELDERLY OFFENDER

We know very little about the sanctions the elderly get when convicted of various offenses. Statistics Canada have not released court/judicial statistics since the early 1970s. It is therefore difficult to surmise what percentage of elderly offenders are sent to penitentiaries and prisons, or what percentage are given fines, placed on probation, or receive some other disposition. Do imprisonment rates for elderly criminals vary from those for other offender groups? Do the elderly receive fines and probation more often than younger offenders sentenced for the same offenses? Are the amounts of fines imposed on the elderly generally lower than those imposed on adults found guilty of similar crimes? In other words, are elderly offenders treated more leniently or more harshly by the courts? Research is needed to find answers to all these questions.

Old age is considered by many to be a mitigating factor (see Chapter Four). The American Convention on Human Rights contains a prohibition against the imposition of the death penalty upon persons below eighteen years of age or on persons over 70 years of age. According to Alston (1986), there is impressionistic evidence that serious old offenders have routinely received more lenient dispositions of their cases than younger people guilty of the same crimes. Alston adds that:

> Given the discretion that has been built into our criminal justice system, there is probably considerable variation in the disposition of the cases of older offenders depending upon both type of offence, and the individual judge. The population composition of the community may also play a part in sentencing. It is possible to handle older offenders more leniently in small communities where their numbers are relatively small. Small numbers and low offence rates mean that they rarely come before the court as offenders. Their cases are more likely to appear to be unique and therefore call for unique solutions (1986:211).

According to Alston, the growth of retirement communities has meant that there are areas of the United States where older citizens make up increasingly large proportions of the population. In these communities, their crimes are more numerous and cannot be easily dismissed as exceptions. Under such circumstances, the problem of how to treat the elderly offender has to be dealt with in a more systematic way. And since the majority of their index crimes are commercial property offenses such as shoplifting, there may also be more insistence on the part of merchants that the justice system not go easy on them.

Occasional mention of sentences received by the elderly appears in the sporadic literature on elderly crime. A study of elderly sex offenders conducted by the Forensic Service of the Clark Institute of Psychiatry in Toronto (Hucker and Ben-Aron, 1985) compared 43 elderly sex offenders (60 years or older) with a similar size group aged 30 years or younger. Both groups were referred to the Institute by the courts for psychiatric evaluation. The problem is that no attempt was made by the authors to match the groups on legal charges. Be this as it may, the study found a marked difference in the percentage of those sentenced to prison in the two groups. Only 2% of the elderly group were sent to prison compared with 25% of the younger group. In addition, the number of cases for elderly offenders that were adjourned sine die (i.e., indefinitely), or for which charges were dropped, was somewhat greater than those for younger offenders. The percentage of court verdicts and sentences are reproduced in the following tables.

Table 2

Elderly Sex Offenders: Court Verdict Hucker and Ben-Aron (1985)		
Verdict	**Elderly sex offenders**	**Young sex offenders**
Guilty as charged	77%	91%
Adjourned sine die	5%	2%
Not guilty	7%	2%
Charges dropped	9%	0%
Unknown	2%	5%

Table 3

Elderly Sex Offenders: Court Sentence Hucker and Ben-Aron (1985)		
Sentence	**Elderly sex offenders**	**Young sex offenders**
Fine, caution	7%	7%
Suspended sentence with probation	61%	58%
Prison sentence	2%	25%
Not applicable	23%	5%
Unknown	7%	5%

In another study by the same authors (Hucker and Ben-Aron, 1984) in which they focus on violent offenders, 16 elderly violent offenders (60 years and over) were compared with a group of violent offenders 30 years or younger, matched on the same offence. According to the authors, similar numbers of elderly and young offenders were found guilty of the offence with which they were charged. Considerably more (44%) of the elderly group than the young (19%) were found guilty of lesser offenses, but fewer of the elderly were found "not guilty by reason of insanity" (19%) compared with the young group (31%). No significant differences were found in the two groups with respect to the various sentences imposed.

Due to the small numbers in both studies, the specific nature of the samples, and because of the methodological limitations involved, no general conclusions can be drawn as to the treatment of elderly violent and sex offenders by Ontario courts.

A Florida study (Curran, 1984) used data from the Palm Beach Sheriff's Office to compare the dispositions of elderly shoplifters arrested in 1981 (N=176) with the dispositions of a 10% sample of other adult shoplifters arrested the same year (N=37). The study found that the only factor to have a statistically significant effect on severity of disposition is prior arrest. Those shoplifters with prior arrest records received more severe dispositions than those who had no record of previous arrest, regardless of age. Consequently, elderly offenders were treated more leniently than non-elderly offenders not because they were old, but because they were more likely to have no prior record. The author notes that her results are consistent with the notion that legal factors (e.g., prior arrest) are more important predictors of severity of disposition than non-legal factors (e.g., age). She affirms that in her sample of shoplifters there was no apparent differential treatment based purely on the age of the offender. Another interesting finding of the same study was that once apprehended, elderly shoplifters were not likely to be involved in a subsequent arrest for shoplifting regardless of the sanction applied. On the basis of this, Curran suggests that elderly shoplifters are good candidates for diversion programs like the one called "pre-trial intervention", a first-offender program that is not age specific, the aim of which is to divert first offenders from the criminal justice system and to spare them the stigma of a formal conviction.

Another Florida study (Feinberg and Khosla, 1985) examined judges' attitudes to elderly misdemeanant offenders. All 121 judges sitting on Florida's County Court in 1980 who heard non-traffic criminal cases were sent a five part questionnaire. Ninety-seven answered it - an impressive 80% response rate. When asked whether elderly misdemeanants should be accorded special consideration by the criminal justice system, most respondents disagreed. Only 38% approved the proposition. Older and more experienced judges did not demonstrate greater likelihood of approving special consideration. Surprisingly, despite this apparent disapproval of special consideration, most judges confessed to sanctioning elderly misdemeanants with probation, fines and/or court costs, or community service. Pretrial intervention and counseling were the sanctions most commonly perceived by the judges as ideal sanctions for misdemeanant elderly shoplifters, while incarceration, fines and/or court costs were rarely, if at all, recommended.

Data from other countries also suggest that very few elderly offenders are sentenced to prison. A study in Germany by Albrecht and Dunkel (1981) reports that only a very small part of aged offenders (60 years and older) is sentenced to prison or probation, whereas over 90% are fined. In the year 1979 the proportion of aged prisoners in the Federal Republic of Germany was slightly more than 1% of the total prison population. Since the low percentage of elderly offenders sentenced to prison may be due not to their old age but to the volume, nature and type of offenses they commit, it is difficult to conclude on the basis of this study whether or not elderly offenders are treated leniently by German courts.

PUNISHMENT AND THE ELDERLY OFFENDER

Crime by the elderly raises important criminological and penological questions, questions that challenge the basic philosophy of our criminal law and the fundamental goals of our criminal justice system. Elderly offenders, whether first-timers or multi-recidivists, pose a formidable challenge to the existing justice system and force us to take a hard look at the underlying philosophies as well as current practices. The aging persistent offender, i.e., the elderly chronic offender, as mentioned above, is the living proof of the failure of the justice system and the system of sanctions. These are offenders who have been frequently and repeatedly punished, who have been in and out of the system, and in and out of prison, for most of their lives. They have not been rehabilitated nor are they being deterred by the prospect of further punishment. Evidently, punishment, whether in the form of a monetary penalty or imprisonment, is not the answer to their problem. Repeated punishment has not been effective in stopping their criminal behavior. If anything, punishment might have been responsible for, or at least a contributing factor to, the persistence of their criminality. To continue to punish these multi-recidivists despite the evident failure and negative effects of punishment, is not only futile, it is outright counter-productive. Obviously, other means of dealing with these chronic and habitual offenders are needed, depending naturally on the type of offence they are in the habit of committing. Some kind of intensive supervision might be all that is needed to make it more difficult for them to engage in further criminal activity.

The problems of the older person who commits his/her first offence in old age are of a completely different order. The traditional forms of punishment, namely incarceration and fines, seem particularly inappropriate for this type of elderly offender. The problems of incarceration for the elderly offender have been discussed in the previous chapter. It might simply be added here that a prison sentence for a person who is seventy or eighty years old is a much harsher punishment than one of equal length for a younger offender. And since the discussion here is about elderly first offenders, it should be noted that the emotional shock and psychological trauma of incarceration are generally much greater for a very old person than they are for a young one. Equal fines can also mean greater hardship for elderly offenders with modest means and fixed income than they are for more youthful offenders. Alternative forms of punishment are thus needed to deal with the relatively small number of individuals who commit their first offence in old age. However, before responding to elderly criminality by means of punishment, regardless of what form this punishment may take, we have to ask some serious questions not only about the negative impact of punishment on elderly offenders but also about the goals and ends we hope to achieve by punishing them.

Societies punish criminals for a variety of reasons, to accomplish various aims, and these aims do change over time. Throughout history offenders have been punished to achieve one or more of the following: revenge, retaliation, expiation, retribution, reprobation, denunciation, humiliation, degradation, ostracism, stigmatization, deterrence, intimidation, isolation, segregation, neutralization, incapacitation, correction, treatment, reformation, rehabilitation, re-education, resocialization and so forth.

In modern times, the main objectives of punishment are believed to be retribution, deterrence, incapacitation, rehabilitation and denunciation. In his book on the Principles of Sentencing, David Thomas (1970) examines the principles that govern current sentencing practice in England and Wales. He notes that during the past fifty years sentencing policy has undergone an important change. He says that as late as 1932 the Department Committee on Persistent Offenders could describe sentencing behavior almost entirely in terms of a tariff system - based primarily on the concepts of retribution and general deterrence. But by 1961 the report of the Streatfield Committee was aware of a shift:

> the courts had increasingly come to consider the offender as an individual, whose needs, rather than whose guilt, would form the basis of the sentence passed (not always, of course, to his immediate advantage in terms of the extent of deprivation of liberty) (Thomas, 1970:3 and Box-Grainger, 1986:34).

The question remains whether for offenders in general, and for elderly offenders in particular, the choice of sentence should be governed principally by the "needs" or the "guilt" of the offender. Opting for need as the primary (or sole) criterion requires individualized sentencing, where the characteristics of the offender, rather than the nature and circumstances of his offence, are the major factors determining the choice and the type of sanction. Using guilt as the main or only criterion leads, on the other hand, to punish those guilty of the same offence in much the same way.

The traditional aims of sentencing appear problematic when examined in the context of elderly crime.

Retribution

Retribution requires that the offender be made to pay for his crime. It requires that the punishment fit the crime and that offenders convicted of the same offence be subjected to the same amount of pain and suffering, to the same degree of unpleasantness, to identical deprivations, and that they be made to suffer similar consequences regardless of their individual characteristics and background. Retribution as a sentencing goal raises insoluble problems of equating a certain amount of fine or a certain length of deprivation of liberty with the degree of moral guilt or with the extent of harm done to the victim or to society. How can we determine what term of prison should expiate an attack on property and how can we equate physical and sexual assaults with a certain fine or a certain number of days, months or years in prison? Furthermore, the pains of imprisonment, well-described by Sykes (1958), are not the same for all those who experience it. Even when they are kept in the same or similar institutions for the same length of time, the pain and consequences of losing one's liberty vary greatly from one individual to the other. The age of the offender is likely to be a crucial variable in this respect. In other words, a month or a year in prison can have very different punitive values to offenders of different age groups and according to their previous experience (or lack of it) with incarceration. As long as it remains impossible to measure the pains of

119

imprisonment and to weigh the sufferings and deprivations resulting from it for each individual offender, the use of incarceration as a retributive sanction will always be an arbitrary, capricious, unfair and inequitable exercise. The use of imprisonment for elderly first offenders is particularly problematic because the negative and traumatic effects of incarceration in their case are quite often dramatic and irreversible.

Since, very frequently, incapacitation is not a consideration in sentencing these offenders (most of whom do not pose a further threat to society), other means of dealing with them seem much more appropriate than prison. So if we decide that retribution IS the goal, and that they have to pay for their crimes, it is preferable to make them pay by means other than deprivation of liberty.

Deterrence

Criminal sanctions are supposed to have a deterrent effect on the punished offender, preventing him/her from repeating the offence or committing others (special deterrence), and preventing others from following his/her example (general deterrence). The issue of deterrence remains a very controversial one, and research on the deterrent effect of criminal sanctions, despite some progress in the last two decades, is still in its infancy. In its working paper on *THE PRINCIPLES OF SENTENCING AND DISPOSITIONS, THE LAW REFORM COMMISSION OF CANADA* (1974) noted that an accumulating body of research and writing throws growing doubts upon the deterrent effects of sentencing itself as opposed to the total deterrent effect of apprehension, arrest, trial and public conviction. According to the Commission:

> Ignorance and uncertainty respecting deterrence... raise deep moral and practical problems for the legislator or judge who bases dispositions on the false assumption that a bigger stick is the answer to crime. While criminal laws, arrest and trial procedures, sentencing and the experience of jail probably do have a collective deterrent effect for some classes of persons in respect of some types of crimes, the deterrent effect of sentences *per se* is problematical. Longer terms, generally, do not appear more effective than shorter terms in reducing recidivism and prison appears no more effective than release under supervision in preventing recidivism (1974:4).

If incarceration is no more effective than non-custodial dispositions, then using it for the elderly, whose offenses are usually petty, whose prognosis is generally better than more youthful offenders , and who are likely to suffer more from imprisonment than their younger counterparts, is neither warranted nor justified. Whether examined from a criminological or humanitarian viewpoint, incarceration is likely to be judged an inappropriate sanction for most elderly offenders, be they multi-recidivists or first-timers. Furthermore, the issue of general deterrence raises the thorny ethical question of whether society has the moral right to use one of its members, young or old, as an example to others in order to dissuade them from doing what he or she has done.

Last but not least, imprisonment seems to be an inopportune and unsuitable sanction for elderly offenders who are senile, terminally ill, or whose criminality is directly linked to mental or psychiatric problems associated with advancing age, Punishment, regardless of its form, is unlikely to have any special deterrent effect on this particular group of elderly offenders.

Incapacitation

Incapacitation as a penal philosophy is being increasingly advocated by the public at large and by politicians as an effective means of neutralizing violent and dangerous offenders. The costs and benefits of a policy of incapacitation are frequently discussed in the criminological literature. What is important here is to reiterate what has been mentioned earlier, namely that the vast majority of offenses by the elderly are neither serious nor violent. While incapacitation for periods of varying length may be necessary in rare, isolated cases, it is irrelevant, as a correctional goal, for the bulk of those who continue to commit crime or who commit their first crime past the age of sixty or sixty-five.

Newman et al. (1984) suggest that incarceration not be used in the case of elderly offenders unless incapacitation is absolutely necessary to neutralize a continuing threat of committing further violent crimes. They point out that:

Incarceration would never be used to punish, to deter others, or to rehabilitate. The sole criterion would be incapacitation to prevent imminent further crimes. Such sentences would be rare. In fixing the length of imprisonment the court should take into account the offender's advanced age and should not impose a term so long as to be a life sentence, unless the particular crime carries a mandatory life sentence (1984:234).

While drastic forms of control and incapacitation are unnecessary in the vast majority of cases involving elderly offenders, it may become evident in some cases that the person is in need of supervision, assistance, support or treatment. In such cases, the court might find it necessary or desirable, as a condition of probation or discharge, to require the elderly to seek treatment or to undertake a specific program to upgrade certain skills. The latter condition could be imposed for instance when the offence is related to the elderly's motor vehicle driving skills. The need for treatment is usually pronounced in cases where the elderly is charged with a sexual offence, where alcohol is a contributing factor to the crime, or where the offender is clearly suffering from some mental disorder or is exhibiting some psychiatric symptoms.

121

Denunciation

In its working paper on imprisonment and release (1975), the Law Reform Commission of Canada recognizes "denunciation" as one of the principal aims of sentencing. Sentencing, affirms the Commission, is a very clear expression of the disapproval of certain acts by society. By demonstrating that certain acts are unacceptable, society reaffirms the importance of certain social norms and, thus, repeatedly reassures law-abiding citizens that their behavior is approved. According to the Commission:

> Some offenses not representing a continuing threat to the life and security of others, may, nonetheless, constitute such an affront to fundamental values that society could not tolerate their punishment or denunciation by any sanction other than imprisonment ...However, we believe that, as a general rule, we should attempt to achieve the social effect sought by denunciation through the publicity of trial, conviction and pronouncement of sentence without resort to imprisonment (1975:12).

Elderly offenders seem to be particularly good candidates for the enforcement of this principle enunciated by the Law Reform Commission, namely denunciation without imprisonment. In most cases, the nature, the gravity and circumstances of the offence are such that proper denunciation is achieved simply by the arrest, prosecution and trial of the elderly person. The sentence itself could therefore be geared toward the accomplishment of goals other than denunciation. Still, in many cases, a non-punitive disposition such as absolute discharge,conditional discharge, or short term probation, may be all that is needed to put an end to what is often a real life drama, a painful episode in the life of the senior citizen brought before justice. Even caution, which is widely used in the cases of juveniles, may be quite appropriate in cases of elderly offenders where it is clear that the offence is an isolated incident, a deviation from the normal behavioral patterns of the person charged.

Rehabilitation

As a correctional goal, rehabilitation has lost favor in recent years. The correct or incorrect belief that rehabilitation does not work, and the return to a neo-classic philosophy of punishment based on retribution, have relegated rehabilitation to a low priority on the lists of politicians and correctional policymakers. And yet, rehabilitation, in the sense of improving the offender's ability to cope with life, may not be, as the Law Reform Commission of Canada (1974) pointed out, an unimportant factor in sentencing. The Commission deplored the fact that too frequently rehabilitation is measured only in terms of reduced recidivism, a measure that has repeatedly demonstrated the limited capacity of treatment or rehabilitation to control crime:

> Yet, to improve an offender's life skills or to reduce his personal suffering are simple, humane gestures that should have a proper place in sentencing policy. Such rehabilitative efforts, indeed, may even have indirect benefits in reducing recidivism in particular cases (1974:4).

Rehabilitation, as correctional objective, is often dismissed in the case of elderly offenders on the grounds that it is neither feasible nor desirable. Re-education or vocational training are usually seen as appropriate aims of a penal philosophy geared towards offenders who are in their teens, twenties or even thirties. They are deemed unnecessary and impractical for those who have already celebrated their fiftieth or sixtieth birthday. This view overlooks the fact that many elderly offenders need help, assistance and support as much as, or even more than, younger ones. Furthermore, rehabilitation programs for offenders over fifty or sixty need not be identical or similar to those developed for youthful offenders. The nature and content of programs designed specifically for grey-haired offenders may be, and in fact need be, quite different from the traditional ones that have been used in corrections for many decades. If what has been said earlier about sparing elderly offenders the traumatic and stigmatizing consequences of imprisonment is accepted, then they will have to be dealt with in a community, non-custodial setting. Their rehabilitation and treatment programs will have to be community-based in contrast to the ones for young and adult offenders which more often than not are institution-based programs.

An example of a community-based, non-custodial program designed specifically for elderly shoplifters, is "The Broward Senior Intervention and Education Program" described by Feinberg et al. (see chapter 12 in Newman, Newman and Gewirtz, 1984). This pilot program which combines individual counseling, socio-cultural participation, and externships at manpower-poor community agencies is by no means perfect or ideal. Its significance lies mainly in its recognition of the fact that the problems of many elderly offenders are substantially different from those of other younger ones and thus they need programs that are designed specifically for them and tailored to their own particular needs.

The need to adopt new methods in dealing with elderly offenders, to take new approaches, and to design and develop new programs might bring a windfall and have beneficial effects on the criminal justice system at large. According to Newman, Newman and Gerwirtz (1984), the existence and the continued growth of an elderly criminal population gives us an opportunity to experiment with new policies in handling offenders that may indeed be more generalizable than it seems at first. A non-restrictive approach in processing criminals is a departure from traditional crime control, and it is precisely the opportunity to try this approach that elderly offenders provide for us. They note further that the:

> one contribution elderly offenders may make to the criminal justice system may be to demonstrate that least restrictive methods work just as well as, and perhaps better than, traditional forms of strict prosecution and maximum restriction will be effective with elderly criminals and can serve as a model for younger adults..this criminal sub-population gives us an opportunity to experiment, to try new approaches with minimum risk and little threat to our social order(1984;235).

Reconciliation with the injured party, in offences against a specific victim, seems to be a particularly suitable approach to most property offences committed by elderly persons as well as offences against the person involving mild forms of violence. Dispute settlement centres and victim-offender reconcil-

123

iation programs (VORP) now exist in many places in Canada and the United States. Reconciliation in most cases is based upon, or accompanied by, some sort of restitution or compensation to the victim. In cases where the goods or money stolen or obtained by fraudulent means have not been disposed of, restitution is not a problem. It can be a problem in the case of an elderly offender with limited resources and income who has already spent or disposed of what he or she has obtained by illegal means. A wide use of reconciliation coupled with restitution for elderly offenders might ultimately help transform our criminal justice system from one based on retaliation and disablement to a system whose ultimate goal is to achieve the restoration of a harmonious and peaceful relationship between the offender and the victim.

Reconciliation, however desirable it may be, should not be viewed as a panacea for all elderly crimes. In cases of white collar crimes committed by wealthy elderly individuals, compensation to the victims may not be enough to prevent the reoccurrence of the offence. Hefty fines might be necessary to achieve the other goals of sentencing such as deterrence, denunciation and retribution.

PREVENTING ELDERLY CRIME

Prevention, needless to say, should be the immediate and the ultimate goal of any criminal or social policy dealing with crime. This is more so in the case of elderly criminality than it is in the case of juvenile delinquency. Juvenile delinquency, in one form or another, is a "normal", "developmental" and "transitory" phase in the life of most male teenagers. If certain delinquent activities are typical of a certain stage of development, there might be little that can be done, at least in the short run, to prevent them. And if many of these activities are by their very nature transitory, they will tend to cease, with or without prevention programs, once those who commit them have reached a certain age. Crime in old age is, on the other hand, an atypical and abnormal phenomenon. Juvenile delinquency, in most incidents, is not a product or even a reflection of any specific pathology. In the case of elderly offenders who commit their very first offence, be it an act of violence, a sexual or a property offence in old age, the criminal behavior is more often than not symptomatic of the existence of some personal problems, problems of aging, of adjustment or of mental health. The commission of the crime is generally an indication that the underlying problems were not identified, or in case they had been identified, nothing effective was done to stop them from leading to criminal behavior. As the saying goes "an ounce of prevention is better than a pound of cure". Since there are reasons to believe that crimes by elderly first offenders are intimately linked to the physiological, psychological, social and economic changes of old age, an effective preventive policy will have to deal with the problems resulting from these changes prior to the occurrence of crime. In other words, effective prevention of elderly crime requires a proactive policy rather than a reactive one. The following is a very brief outline of a general preventive policy aimed at elderly crime:

Improved Mental Health

Since mental health problems seem to play a significant role in crimes committed by first time elderly offenders, an effective prevention strategy should have as one of its principal dimensions the improvement of mental health for the elderly population. This requires early detection and better intervention. Much has been done in recent years to improve the physical health of the Canadian population. That is why Canada's level of life expectancy for both sexes at age 65 is one of the highest among developed countries. Unfortunately, advances in mental.health have not kept pace with other medical advances. And while the rate of hospitalization of those 65 and over has increased during the early 1970s, there was at the same time a positive trend to deinstitutionalize mental patients. If both trends continue we can expect an ever growing number of senior citizens with either undetected or untreated mental health problems. These problems might lead, in some instances, to behavior in conflict with the law. Better health care requires that equal attention be paid to mental health as to physical health, that mental hygiene be given the same priority as,or even a higher priority than physical hygiene. Physical check-ups are now regular and systematic for those who have attained a certain age. Voluntary check-ups to detect cerebral changes and organic deterioration of the brain should also be encouraged while safeguarding the individual against whatever unwanted or unnecessary measures may be recommended by the psychiatrist. The social stigma attached to mental disturbances and psychiatric hospitals is likely to discourage many senior citizens who are experiencing early symptoms of an organic brain disease from seeking help or treatment. Special clinics and hospitals for the elderly where they can undergo comprehensive health examinations on a regular basis may be one answer to this problem.

Since alcohol seems to play an important role in elderly criminality, discouraging heavy regular drinking coupled with treatment programs and facilities for alcohol abuse, drinking problems and chronic alcoholism are sensible ways of reducing both health and behavioral problems resulting from, or associated with, alcohol. In his study of alcohol-related crime among older people, Meyers (1984) offers some suggestions about what may be done to address the special needs and circumstances of older drinkers and drivers. For example, special labels may be put on bottled alcohol warning that older adults may be more sensitive to its effects. Graphs and charts that correlate alcohol consumption and blood alcohol content - which are often posted in bars and restaurants - may have to be modified to demonstrate the effects of aging, or of chronic illness associated with aging, or of prescription drug use.

Strengthening the Elderly's Social Network

Older people are more likely to live alone and this social isolation may act as a victimogenic and/or as a criminogenic factor. The role of loneliness and boredom in certain offences committed by the elderly has been discussed earlier. A policy aimed at reducing crime by, and victimization against, the elderly should have as one of its goals the strengthening of the social networks of older people. If the normal family network has been weakened by reason of death, geographical mobility or sickness, alternative networks of friends, age peers and neighbors could be developed as substitutes and gradually strengthened to perform the same preventive, protective and supportive social functions.

There is an important role for self-help groups and self-help activities in preventing future crimes by those elderly who have already come into conflict with the law and have been diverted from or processed through the criminal justice system. Such groups and programs can provide the advice, assistance and support the elderly offender may need to prevent a relapse into crime. Rather than being placed under the supervision of a regular probation or parole officer, the elderly offender may simply be referred to a program run by other elderly volunteers. In view of their own life experiences, elderly helpers are probably more likely than young professional workers to understand the stresses, the frustrations and the problems that led the elderly to commit the crime.

Improving Social Services and Social Support Systems for the Elderly

Many offences committed by elderly citizens can be traced directly or indirectly to the difficulties they have had in coping with the various changes resulting from or accompanying old age. It is only natural, therefore, that an effective policy aimed at reducing or preventing elderly crime should aim at providing the social services needed to help the elderly cope with such problems. If poor economics are, as many believe, an important factor in property as well as other crimes committed by senior citizens, then improving their economic lot needs to be part of any preventive strategy. And although most elderly cope quite well either on their own or with the help of their social networks with the negative changes of aging, better services that are available and handy are needed to cater to the small minority who might need some help overcoming the series of losses that accompany old age (see Chapter One).

Gewirtz (1984) notes that in an era of tightening budgets, it would be difficult to create new systems as old ones are abolished for lack of funding. The challenge, he suggests, is to effectively link and integrate services within existing frameworks and to use those services to provide the best care possible for those in need. Moreover, the formal systems may not need to become even minimally involved. More thoughtful use of the informal system can thus free the formal supports to help people who cannot be served in another way. According to Gewirtz, the informal supports can act to enrich the formal supports. The informal support system is also superior because it motivates family, friends, and peers to care for the elderly offender.

Changing the Structure of Opportunity

Many have suggested that a great deal of leisure time, boredom, and lack of meaningful activities have a criminogenic effect and are totally or partially responsible for crimes committed by retired people (see Chapter Three). Providing the elderly with meaningful work opportunities, paid or benevolent, is likely to have a salutary effect on their physical/mental health and on their behavior.

Elderly sex crimes may be blamed, at least in part, on the absence of normal, socially acceptable outlets for sexual expression and contact. Changing social attitudes toward elderly sexuality is a *sine qua non* requirement for any preventive policy. A positive attitude change requires that society recognize that sexual urges, drives and needs do persist for both sexes into advanced age. Seeking to satisfy those needs is to be regarded as both normal and healthy. Once this is recognized and accepted, social programs aimed at bringing together elderly persons of both sexes are likely to provide them with the opportunity to engage in social activities and to establish social (and eventually sexual) rapport with members of their age-peer group. Non-sexual expressions of affection, with or without physical contact and towards children and adults alike, if encouraged, may provide a substitute for sexual activities rendered difficult or strenuous by advancing age and weakening libido.

While in some areas increasing opportunities might be a means of preventing elderly crime, in others, prevention may be achieved by reducing available opportunities. As mentioned earlier, elderly killers are more likely to employ firearms than younger killers, a problem that is more acute in the United States than it is in Canada. In fact, many American researchers (Block and Zimring, 1973; Rushforth et al. 1977; Stark, 1975; Zimring, 1968; Goetting, 1985a) have suggested that availability of firearms, particularly handguns, seriously inflates homicide in the U.S. and it appears that this is especially true among the elderly. An effective, carefully enforced gun control policy is likely to prevent many of the killings where the aggressor is elderly. Gun control, by itself, is not the answer unless coupled with an educational campaign informing the elderly of the dangers and liabilities of keeping firearms in their residence. Like young people, many elderly wrongly believe that firearms - be it rifles or handguns - are good protective devices in the case of an attack. Because of their vulnerability many are likely to feel safer with a firearm at home. Empirical evidence, however, shows that such a weapon is more of a liability than an asset, that it is more likely to be used as an instrument of aggression (either by or against the person who keeps it) than as a means of self-defence. In view of this, an elderly person might be much better off without such a weapon in his or her possession.

What is most important in preventing acts of violence by the elderly is to reduce the enormous frustrations from which many suffer and which occasionally explode into aggressive, expressive violence. The social and economic situations of the elderly in our society generate deep frustrations. While most senior citizens are able to cope with these frustrations without resorting to violence, and while many are able to channel their frustrations into positive, productive activities, a small minority will continue to react with violence. And it is the violence of this tiny minority that can be prevented or reduced by a social policy aimed at improving the quality of life of the general elderly population.

CHAPTER SIX: RECOMMENDED READINGS

Cormier, B. et al.
1971 Behavior and Ageing: Offenders Aged 40 and Over. Laval Medical, 42 (Jan.) :15-21.

Curran, D.
1984 Characteristics of the Elderly Shoplifter and the Effects of Sanctions on Recidivism. In W. Wilbanks and P.K.H. Kim (Eds.). Elderly Criminals. Lanham, MD: University Press of America.

Feinberg, G. and D. Khosla
1985 Sanctioning Elderly Delinquents. Trial, Sept.,46-50.

Gewirtz, M.S.
1984 Social Work Practice with Elderly Offenders. In Newman, E.S. et al. (Eds.) Elderly Criminals. Cambridge, Mass.: Oelgeschlager, Gunn & Hain Publishers. pp. 193-208.

BIBLIOGRAPHY: PART I

Abrams,A.J.
1984 Foreword to Elderly Criminals, Newman, Newman and Gewirtz (Eds.), Cambridge, Mass.: Oelgeschlager, Gunn & Hain. pp. xi-xvii.

Adams, M.E. and C.B. Vedder
1961 Age and Crime: Medical and Sociological Characteristics of Prisoners Over 50. Geriatrics, 16:177-181.

Aday, R.H.
1976 Institutional Dependency: A Theory of Aging in Prison. Ph.D. dissertation, Oklahoma State University.

Aday, R.H.
1977 Toward the Development of a Therapeutic Program for Older Prisoners. Offender Rehabilitation, 1:343-348.

Aday, R.H., and E.L. Webster
1979 Aging in Prisons: The Development of a Preliminary Model. Offender Rehabilitation, 3:271-282.

Albrecht, H.J. and F. Dunkel
1981 Die vergessene Minderheit--alte Menschen als Straftater. Zeitschrift fur Gerontologie, 14:259-273.

Allersma, J.
1971 Ouderdom en Criminaliteit. (Old Age and Criminality.) Ned. T. Geront. (Netherlands J. Of Gerontology). 2(4):285-293.

Alston, L.T.
1986 Crime and Older Americans. Springfield, Ill. Charles C. Thomas.

Alpert, G.
1979 Patterns of Change in Prisonization: A Longitudinal Analysis. Criminal Justice and Behavior, 6(2):159-173.

Amelunxen, Cl.
1960 Alterskriminalitat. Hamburg: Kriminalistik Verlag.

Anonymous
1982 Experts Debate Elderly Crime--the Offender as Victim. In APA Monitor, May 13(5):17 and 32.

Aschaffenburg, G.
1913 Crime and Its Repression. Boston: Little, Brown and Co.

Baier, G.F.
1961 The Aged Inmate. American J. of Correction, 23:4-6, 30, 34.

Barrett, J.G.
1972 Aging and Delinquency. In Gerontological Psychology, Springfield, Ill.: Charles C. Thomas.

Baum, S., and H. Berman
1984 Older Prisoners: Who are They? The Gerontologist, 24:160.

Bengston, V.L. and D.A. Haber
1975 Sociological Approaches to Aging. In D.S. Woodruff and J.E. Birren (Eds.). Aging. New York: Van Nostrand Reinhold.

Bensinger, G.
1981 As People Get Older, the Crime Gets Bolder. Law Enforcement News, 7:10(5/25/1981), p. 6.

Berg, J.A. and V. Fox
1947 Factors in Homicides Committed by 200 Males. J.of Social Psychology, 26:109-119.

Bergman, S. and M. Amir
1973 Crime and Delinquency Among the Aged in Israel. Geriatrics, 28(Jan.):149-157.

Bernocchi, F.
1974 La Senilita dal punto di vista criminologico. (Old Age from a Criminological Point of View.) Quaderni di Criminologia Clinica, 16(3):321-342.

Bintz, M.T.
1974 Recreation for the Older Population in Correctional Institutions. Therapeutic Recreation Journal, 8:87-89.

Bittner, E.
1967 The Police on Skid-Row: A Study of Peace Keeping. American Sociological Review, 32(5):699-715.

Block, R. and F. Zimring
1973 Homicide in Chicago, 1965-1970. J. of Research in Crime and Delinquency. 10(1):1-12.

Blumstein, A. and J. Cohen
1979 Estimation of Individual Crime Rates From Arrest Records. J. of Criminal Law and Criminology, 70:4.

Bonitz, G.
1971 Die Delinquenz der alten Frau unter sozial psychiatrischem Aspekt. Medizinisch-Juristische Grenzfragen. Heft 11, pp. 109-117.

Box-Grainger, J.
1986 Sentencing Rapists. In R. Matthews and J. Young (Eds.). Confronting Crime. London: Sage Publications, pp. 31-52.

Brannon, W.T.
1957 "Yellow Kid" Weil -- Con Man: a Master Swindler's Own Story of a Life of Crime. New York: Pyramid Books.

Bromley, D.B.
1978 The Psychology of Human Aging. Middlesex, England: Penguin Books.

Brown, R.
1965 Social Psychology. New York: The Free Press.

Burger-Prinz, H. and H. Lewrenz
1961 Die Alterskriminalitat. Stuttgart: Ferdinand Enke Verlag.

Burnett, C. and S.T. Ortega
1984 Elderly Offenders: A Descriptive Analysis. In Wilbanks and Kim (Eds.) Elderly Criminals. Lanham, MD. University Press of America. pp. 17-40.

Butler, R.N.
1975 Why Survive? Being Old in America. New York: Harper and Row.

Butler, R.N. and I.L. Lewis
1982 Aging and Mental Health (3rd edition). Toronto: The C.V. Mosby Co.

Butler, S.
1982 The Politics of Sexual Assault-Facing the Challenge. In Sue Davidson (Ed.). Justice For Young Women: Close-up On Critical Issues. Tucson, Arizona: New Directions for Young Women. pp. 99-109.

Canada. Government of Canada
1982 Canadian Governmental Report on Aging. Ottawa: Minister of Supply and Service.

Canada. Statistics Canada
1979 Canada's Elderly -- One of a Series from the 1976 Census of Canada. Catalogue 98-800E. Ottawa: Minister of Supply and Service.

Canada. Statistics Canada
1984 The Elderly in Canada. Ottawa: Minister of Supply and Service.

Carlie, M.K.
1970 The Older Arrestee: Crime in the Later Years of Life. Ph.D. dissertation, Washington University.

Carriero, F. and D. Torelli
1970 Considerazioni crimino-genetiche sui reati sessuali dei vecchi. (Criminogenetic considerations on sexual crimes by old people.) Acta Neurologica (Naples), 25(4):497-504.

Cavan, R.
1955 Criminology. New York: Thomas Y. Crowell. p. 47.

Chambliss, W.J.
1972 Box Man: A Professional Thief's Journey. New York: Harper and Row.

Chaneles, S.
1987 Growing Old Behind Bars. Psychology Today (October), pp. 47-51.

Clemmer, D.
1940 The Prison Community, New York: Holt, Rinehart and Winston.

Clinard, M. and R. Quinney
1967 Criminal Behavior Systems: A Typology. New York: Holt, Rinehart and Winston.

Cohen, F.
1984 Old Age as a Criminal Defense. In Newman, Newman and Gewirtz (eds.). Elderly Criminals. Cambridge, Mass.: Oelgeschlager, Gunn and Hain. pp. 113-141.

Cohen,L. and R. Stark
1974 Discriminatory Labeling and the Five Finger Discount: An Empirical Analysis of Differential Shoplifting Dispositions. J. of Research in Crime and Delinquency, 11:25-39.

Cormier, B. et al.
1958 The Natural History of Criminality and Some Tentative Hypotheses on its Abatement. Canadian J. of Corrections, 1(4):35-49.

Cormier, B. et al.
1961 The Latecomer to Crime. Canadian J. of Corrections, 3(1):2-17.

Cormier, B. et al.
1961 The Problem of Recidivism and Treatment of the Latecomer to Crime. Canadian J. of Corrections, 3:51-64.

Cormier, B.M. et al.
1971 Behaviour and Ageing: Offenders Aged 40 and Over. Laval Medical, 42(Jan.):15-21.

Covey, H.C. and Menard, S.
1987 Trends in Arrests among the Elderly. The Gerontologist, 27(5):666-672.

Cullen, F.T., J.F. Wozniak and J. Frank
1985 The Rise of the Elderly Offender-Will a "New" Criminal be Invented? Crime and Social Justice, 23:151-165.

Cumming, E. et al.
1960 Disengagement: A Tentative Theory of Aging. Sociometry, 23(1).

Curran, D.
1984 Characteristics of the Elderly Shoplifter and the Effects of Sanctions on Recidivism. In Wilbanks and Kim (Eds.). Elderly Criminals. Lanham, MD. University Press of America. pp. 123-141.

Cutshall, C.R. and K. Adams
1983 Responding to Older Offenders: Age Selectivity in the Processing of Shoplifters. Criminal Justice Review, 8(2):1-8.

East, N.W.
1944 Crime, Senescence and Senility. J. of Mental Science, 90:836-849.

East, N.W.
1945 Crime, Senescence and Senility. The J. of the American Medical Association, 127:460.

Economic Council of Canada
1979 One in Three: Pensions for Canadians to 2030. Ottawa: Supply and Services Canada.

Elliott, D. et al.
1978 1977 Self-Reported Delinquency Estimates by Sex, Race, Class, and Age. Mimeographed. Boulder, Colorado: Behavioral Research Institute.

Epstein, L.J., C. Mills and A. Simon
1970 Antisocial Behavior of the Elderly. Comprehensive Psychiatry, 11(1):36-42.

Fearnside, J.R.
1976 Treatment of Elderly Criminal Offenders. Police Review, Oct. 15, 1976:1296-1297.

Feinberg, G.
1982a White-Haired Offenders: An Emergent Social Problem. Paper presented to the Gerontological Society of America. Boston, Mass. Mimeograph. 30p. (Revised version published in 1984 in W. Wilbanks and P.K.H. Kim (Eds.). Elderly Criminals. Lanham, MD: University Press of America. pp. 83-108.)

Feinberg, G.
1982b Shoplifting by the Elderly and One Community's Innovative Response. Prepublication chapter for a book titled Elderly Criminals. E. Newman et al. (Eds.) mimeographed.

Feinberg, G.
1984 Profile of the Elderly Shoplifter. In E.S. Newman et al. (Eds.) Elderly Criminals. Cambridge, Mass.: Oelgeschlager, Gunn and Hain. pp. 35-50.

Feinberg, G. and D. Khosla
1985 Sanctioning Elderly Delinquents. TRIAL (September) 46-50.

Ferdinand, T.N.
1966 Typologies of Delinquency: A Typical Analysis. New York: Random House.

133

Finkelhor, D.
1979 Sexually Victimized Children. New York: The Free Press.

Flanagan, T.
1981 Correlates of Institutional Misconduct Among State Prisoners. Mimeographed. Albany, N.Y.: Criminal Justice Research Center.

Fleszar-Szumigajo, W.A.J.
1971 The Problems of Delinquency in Offenders Found by Expert Examination to Suffer from Senile Mental Disorders. In Medizinisch-juristische Grenzfragen. Heft 11, pp. 119-123.

Fletcher, S. and L.o. Stone
1982 The Living Arrangements of Canada's Older Women. Statistics Canada, Catalogue 86-503. Ottawa: Minister of Supply and Service.

Fry, L.
1984 The Implications of Diversion for Older Offenders. In Wilbanks and Kim (Eds.). Elderly Criminals. Lanham, MD. University Press of America. pp. 143-156.

Fyfe, J.J.
1984 Police Dilemmas in Processing Elderly Offenders. In Newman, Newman and Gewirtz (Eds.). Elderly Criminals. Cambridge, Mass.: Oelgeschlager, Gunn and Hain. pp. 97-111.

Gaddis, T.E.
1972 Home at Last: The Prison Habit. Nation, 214:719-721.

Galiani, I.
1978 Criminological and Medico-legal Aspects of Sex Crimes Committed by Elderly. Giornale di Gerontologia, 26:O190-0199.

Gebhard, P.H. et al.
1965 Sex Offenders: An Analysis of Types. New York: Harper & Row.

Gewirtz, M.S.
1983 Social Work Practice with Elderly Offenders. In Newman, E.S. et al. (Eds.) Elderly Criminals.. Cambridge, Mass.: Oelgeschlager, Gunn & Hain Publishers. pp. 193-208.

Gibbons, D.
1975 Offender Typologies -- Two Decades Later. British J. of Criminology 15(April):140-156.

Gibbons, D.
1982 Society, Crime and Criminal Careers. 4th edition. Englewood Cliffs: Prentice-Hall, Inc.

Gillespie M.W. and J.F. Galliher
1972 Age, Anomie, and the Inmates Definition of Aging in Prison: An Exploratory Study. In Donald P. Kent et al. (Eds.) Research Planning and Action for the Elderly. New York: Behavioral Publications.

Gillin, J.L.
1946 Social Pathology. New York: Appleton-Century.

Glueck, S. and E. Glueck
1950 Later Criminal Careers. New York: The Commonwealth Fund.

Goetting, A.
1983 The Elderly in Prison: Issues and Perspectives. J. of Research in Crime and Delinquency, 20:291-309.

Goetting, A.
1984a The Elderly in Prison: A Profile. Criminal Justice Review, 9(2):14-24.

Goetting, A.
1984b Prison Programs and Facilities for Elderly Inmates. In Newman, Newman and Gewirtz (Eds.). Elderly Criminals. New York: Oelgeschlager, Gunn and Hain Publishers. pp.169-176.

Goetting, A.
1985a Patterns of Homicide Among the Elderly. Paper presented at the annual meeting of the American Society of Criminology, San Diego, California.

Goetting, A.
1985b Racism, Sexism and Ageism in the Prison Community. Federal Probation, 49:10-23.

Goffman, E.
1961 Asylums. Chicago: Aldine, also New York: Doubleday.

Golden, Delores
1984 Elderly Offenders in Jail. In Newman, Newman, Gewirtz (Eds.). Elderly Criminals. Cambridge, Mass.: Oelgeschlager, Gunn and Hain Publishers, Inc.pp.143-152.

Guttmacher, M.
1958 The Psychiatric Approach to Crime and Correction. Law and Contemporary Problems, 23(4):633-649.

Ham, J.N.
1976 The Forgotten Minority ... An Exploration of Long-term Institutionalized Aged and Aging Male Prison Inmates. Washington, D.C.: National Institute of Law, U.S. Department of Justice.

Ham, J.N.
1980 Aged and Infirm Male Prison Inmates. Aging. Washington, D.C.: U.S. Department of Health and Human Services.

Hammond, W.H. and E. Chayen
1963 Persistent Criminals. A Home Office Research Unit Report. London: H.M.S.O.

Harter, M.T. and Chambers, C.D.
1987 Alcohol and the Elderly: Abuser and Abused. In C.D. Chambers et al. (Eds.) The Elderly: Victims and Deviants. Athens, Ohio: Ohio University Press. pp. 191-205.

Hartman, A.A. and P.L. Schroeder
1943 Criminality and the Age Factor. J. of Criminal Psychopathology, 5:351-362.

Havens, B.
1981 Population Projections: Certainties and Uncertainties. in G.M. Gutman (Ed.) Canada's Changing Age Structure: Implications for the Future. Burnaby: SFU Publications, pp. 1-31.

Hays, D.S. and M. Wisotsky
1969 The Aged Offender: A Review of the Literature and Two Current Studies from the New York State Division of Parole. J. of the American Geriatrics Society, 17(11):1064-1073.

Henninger, J.M.
1939 The Senile Sex Offender. Mental Hygiene, 23:436-444.

Henry, A.F. and J.F. Short, Jr.
1965 Suicide and Homicide. New York: The Free Press.

Hentig, H. von
1947 Crime: Causes and Conditions. New York: McGraw-Hill.

Hirschmann, J.
1962 Zur kriminologie der Sexualdelikte des alternden Mannes. Gerontologica Clinica Additamentum, 4:115-119.

Hirschi, T. and M. Gottfredson
1983 Age and the Explanation of Crime. American J. of Sociology, 89(3):552-584.

Hucker, S.J. and M.H. Ben-Aron
1984 Violent Elderly Offenders: A Comparative Study. In W. Wilbanks and P.K.H. Kim (Eds.). Elderly Criminals. Lanham, MD: University Press of America. pp. 69-81.

Hucker, S.J. and M.H. Ben-Aron
1985 Elderly Sex Offenders. In Ron Langevin (Ed.). Erotic Preference, Gender Identity, and Aggression in Men: New Research Studies. Hillsdale, N.J.: Laurence Erlbaum Associates. pp. 211-223.

Inciardi, J.A.
1974 Vocational Crime. In D. Glaser (Ed.). Handbook of Criminology. Chicago: Rand McNally. pp. 342-344.

Inciardi, J.A.
1987 Crime and the Elderly: A Construction of Official Rates. In C.D. Chambers et al (Editors). The Elderly: Victims and Deviants. Athens, Ohio: Ohio University Press. pp. 177-190.

Jackson, B.
1969 A Thief's Primer. London: Macmillan Co.

Jackson, M.A.
1981 Criminal Deviance Among the Elderly. Canadian Criminology Forum, 4(1):45-53.

Jensen, G.
1977 Age and Rule-Breaking in Prison: A Test of Sociocultural Interpretations. Criminology, 14:555-568.

Jolin, A. and Gibbons, D.C.
1987 Growing Old and Going Straight: An Exploration of "Maturational Reform". Paper presented at the American Society of Criminology Meeting. (manuscript). 26 pages.

Keller, O.J. and C.B. Vedder
1968 The Crimes that Old People Commit. The Gerontologist, 8(1)43-50.

Kercher, K.
1987 The Causes and Correlates of Crime Committed by the Elderly. Research on Aging, 9(2): 256-280.

Korner, H.H.
1975 Sexualentgleisungen Alternder Menschen im Umgang mit Minderjahrigen. Ph.D. dissertation, Mainz University.

Korner, H.H.
1977 Sexualkriminalitat im Alter. Stuttgart: Ferdinand Enke Verlag.

Krajick, K.
1979 Growing Old in Prison. Corrections Magazine, March, 32-42. ᴜᴧ 33-39
 ✢ See p. 104, Chp. 5

LaWall, J.
1982 Profile of the Older Criminal. American J. of Forensic Psychiatry, 141-146.

Lamy, P.P.
1980 Misuse and Abuse of Drugs by the Elderly. American Pharmacy, NS20(5):14-17.

Law Reform Commission of Canada. Working papers:
1974 No. 3 The Principles of Sentencing and Dispositions;
1975 No. 7 Diversion; and
1975 No. 11 Imprisonment and Release. Ottawa: Information Canada.

Lawton, M. and S. Yaffe
1967 Mortality, Morbidity and Voluntary Change of Residence. Paper presented at the meeting of the American Psychological Association

Lieberman, M.A.
1969 Institutionalization of the Aged: Effects on Behavior. J. of Gerontology, 24:330-340.

Lindquist, J.H. et al.
1987 Elderly Felons: Dispositions of Arrests. In C.D. Chambers et al. (Editors) The Elderly: Victims and Deviants. Athens, Ohio: Ohio University Press. pp. 161-176.

Long, J.
1982 Serious Crime by the Elderly is on the Rise. Wall Street Journal, June 21, 1982:19.

Maisch, H.
1970 L'inceste. Paris: Robert Laffont S.A.

Malinchak, A.A.
1980 Crime and Gerontology. Englewood Cliffs: Prentice Hall.

Malley, A.
1981 The Advocate Program Sees the Elderly Through. The Florida Bar Journal, March, 207-210.

Matthes, I.
1978 Alt Menschen als Tater und Opfer von Straftaten. (Old People as Offenders and victims of crime.), In Deutsche Polizei, 1:20-21.

Mayer-Gross, W.E., E. Slater and M. Roth
1954 Clinical Psychiatry. London: Cassell.

McCarthy, M.
1983 The Health Status of Elderly Inmates. Corrections Today, Feb., 64-74.

McCord, W. and J. McCord
1964 The Psychopath: An Essay on the Criminal Mind. New York: D. Van Nostrand Co. Inc.

McCreary, C.P., and I.N. Mensh
1977 Personality Differences Associated with Age in Law Offenders. Journal of Gerontology, 32:164-167.

Megargee, E.I. et al.
1979 Classifying Criminal Offenders: A New System Based on the MMPI. Beverly Hills, California: Sage Publications.

Metzler, C.
1981 Senior Citizens in Massachusetts State Correctional Facilities from 1972 Through 1979. Massachusetts Department of Correction, unpublished manuscript.

Meyers, A.R.
1984 Drinking, Problem Drinking, and Alcohol Related Crime Among Older People. In Newman, Newman and Gewirtz (Ed.). Elderly Criminals. Cambridge, Mass.: Oelgeschlager, Gunn and Hain. pp. 51-65.

Miller, D. and M.A. Lieberman
1965 The Relationship of Affect State Adaptive Reactions to Stress. J. of Gerontology, 20:492-497.

Moberg, D.
1953 Old Age and Crime. J. of Criminal Law, Criminology and Police Science, 43:764-776.

Moore, E.O., and R. Phillips
1979 Two Prison Environments: Their Effect on the Elderly. Unpublished manuscript.

Morris, N.
1973 The Law is a Busy Body. Originally published by the New York Times. Reprinted by World Correctional Service Center.

Morton, J.B., and J.C. Anderson
1982 Elderly Offenders: The Forgotten Minority. Corrections Today, December, 14-20.

Mowat, R.R.
1966 Morbid Jealousy and Murder. London: Tavistock Publications.

Myles, J.F.
1981 Social Implications of a Changing Age Structure. In G.M. Gutman (Ed.). Canada's Changing Age Structure: Implications for the Future. Burnaby: SFU Publications. pp. 33-58.

Newman, D.J. and E.S. Newman
1982 Senior Citizen Crime. The Justice Reporter, 2(5, Sept.-Oct.):1-7.

Newman, E.S., D.J. Newman and M. Gewirtz
1984 Elderly Criminals. Cambridge, Mass.: Oelgeschlager, Gunn and Hain, Publishers, Inc.

Oster, C.D.O.
1976 Sensory Deprivation in Geriatric Patients. J. of the American Geriatrics Society, 24(16).

Panton, J.H.
1977 Personality Characteristics of Aged Inmates Within a State Prison Population. Offender Rehabilitation, 1(2):203-208.

Petersilia, J.
1979 Which Inmates Participate in Prison Treatment Programs? J. of Offender Counseling Services and Rehabilitation. 1(2)Winter:121-135.

Petrie, W.M. et al.
1982 Violence in Geriatric Patients. Journal of the American Medical Association, 248: 443-444.

Pheiffer, E.
1971 The Use of Leisure-time in Middle Life. The Gerontologist, 11(3):187-195.

Pollak, O.
1941 The Criminality of Old Age. J. of Criminal Psychopathology, 3:213-235.

Pollak, O.
1948 Social Adjustment in Old Age -- A Research Planning Report. New York: Social Science Research Council. Bulletin 59.

Quetelet, A.J.
1839 Treatise on Man. Reproduced in S.F. Sylvester Jr. (1972) The Heritage of Modern Criminology. Cambridge, Mass.: Schenkman Publishing Co. p. 38.

Reckless, W.C.
1950 The Crime Problem. New York: Appleton-Century-Crofts Co.

Reed, M.B.
1978 Aging in a Total Institution: The Case of Older Prisoners. Nashville: Tennessee Corrections Institute. 75 pages.

Reed, M. and F.D. Glamser
1979 Aging in a Total Institution: The Case of Older Prisoners. The Gerontologist, 19(August):354-360.

Richman, J.   (Dante?)
1982 Homicidal and Assaultive Behavior in the Elderly. In B.L. Dants et al. (Eds.). The Human Side of Homicide. New York: Columbia University Press. pp. 190-198.

Ritzel, G.
1972 Untersuchungen zur Altersdelinquenz. Monatsschrift fur Kriminologie, 55(8):345-356.

Roebuck, J.B.
1966 Criminal Typology. Springfield, Ill.: Charles C. Thomas.

Romaniuc, A.
1974 Potentials for Population Growth in Canada--A Long Term Projection. In A Population Policy in Canada. Toronto: Conservation Council of Ontario and Family Planning Federation of Canada.

Rose, H.K.
1978 Alte Menschen als Tater (old people as offenders) Deutsche Polizel, 1:18-19.

Rosner, R. et al.
1985 Geriatric Felons Examined at a Forensic Psychiatry Clinic. Journal of Forensic Sciences. 30:730-740.

Roth, M.
1968 Cerebral Disease and Mental Disorders of Old Age as Causes of Antisocial Behavior. In International Psychiatry Clinics, 5(3):35-58. Also in A.V.S. de Reuck and R. Porter (Eds.). The Mentally Abnormal Offender. London: J. and A. Churchill.

Rothman, D.
1980 Conscience and Convenience: The Asylum and its Alternatives in Progressive America. Boston: Little, Brown. p. 282.

Rowe, Alan R.
1983 Race, Age and Conformity in Prison. Psychological Reports, 52:445-446.

Rowe, A.R. and C.R. Tittle
1977 Life Cycle Changes and Criminal Propensity. The Sociological Quarterly, 18:223-236.

Rubenstein, D.
1984 The Elderly in Prisons: A Review of the Literature. In Newman et al. (Eds.). Elderly Criminals, Cambridge,Mass: Oelgeschlager, Gunn and Hain Publishers. pp. 153-168.

Rushforth, N.B. et al.
1977 Violent Death in a Metropolitan County. New England J. of Medicine, 297:531-538.

Schafer, H.
1974 Alter und Kriminalitat-Zum Problem des Abbruchs Krimineller Karrieren. (Age and Crime -- The Problem of Ending a Criminal Career.) Kriminol. J., 6(3):209-216.

Schonfelder, T.
1965 Die initiative des opfers. In F.G. v. Stockert (Ed.) Das sexuell gefahrdete kind. Stuttgart: Ferdinand Enke Verlag. pp. 109-115.

Schonfelder, T.
1968 Die Rolle des Madchens bei Sexualdelikten. Stuttgart: Ferdinand Enke Verlag.

Schroeder, P.L.
1936 Criminal Behaviour in the Latter Period of Life. American J. of Psychiatry, 92:915-924.

Schwarz, H.
1971 Gibt es eine spezifische Alterskriminalitat? (Is There a Specific Senile Delinquency?) In Medizinisch-Juristische Grenzfragen, Heft 11, pp. 71-77.

Shaw, C.R.
1930 The Jack Roller. Chicago: Chicago University Press.

Shichor, D.
1984a Patterns of Elderly Lawbreaking in Urban, Suburban and Rural Areas: What do Arrest Statistics Tell Us? In Wilbanks and Kim (Eds.). Elderly Criminals. Lanham,MD. University Press of America. pp. 53-68.

Shichor, D.
1984b The Extent and Nature of Lawbreaking by the Elderly: A Review of Arrest Statistics. in E.S. Newman et al. (Eds.) Elderly Criminals. Cambridge, Mass.: Oelgeschlager, Gunn and Hain.pp. 17-32.

Shichor, D.
1985 Male-Female Differences in Elderly Arrests: An Exploratory Analysis. Justice Quarterly, 2(3):399-414.

Shichor, D. and S. Kobrin
1978 Criminal Behavior Among the Elderly. The Gerontologist. 18(2):213-218.

Shimizu, M.
1973 A Study on the Crimes of the Aged in Japan. Acta Criminologica and Medicina-legalis Japonica, 39:202-213.

Shinbaum, M.G.
1977 Development of a Model for Prediction of Inmate Interest in Prison Sponsored Academic and Vocational Education. Unpublished Ph.D. Dissertation, Auburn University.

Shover, N.
1985 Aging Criminals. Beverly Hills: Sage Publications.

Siegal, H.A.
1987 The Older Drunk Driving Offender. In C.D. Chambers et al. (Editors) The Elderly: Victims and Deviants. Athens, Ohio: Ohio University Press. pp. 206-219.

Silfen, P.
1977 Adaptation of the Older Prisoner in Israel. Int. J. of Offender Theraphy and Comparative Criminology, 20 (1) : 18-25.

Sluga, W. et al.
1973 Geronto-Psychiatrie im Strafvollzug. (Gerontopsychiatry in Prison.) Mschr. Kriminol. u. Strafrechtsref., 56(2):49-57.

Snodgrass, J., and the Jack Roller
1982 The Jack Roller at Seventy. Lexington, Mass.: Lexington Books.

Sordo, I. and G. Fishman
1981 The Elderly Offender in the Israeli Criminal Justice System. Society and Welfare, 4(1):27-41.

Stark, R.
1975 Social Problems. New York: Random House.

Statistics Canada
1979 Canada's Elderly. Ottawa: Ministry of Supply and Services. Catalogue No. 98-800E.

Statistics Canada
1982 Historical Statistics of Canada. 2nd ed., Ottawa: Ministry of Supply and Services.

Statistics Canada
1984 The Elderly in Canada. Ottawa: Ministry of Supply and Services. Catalogue No. 99-932.

Statistics Canada
1985 &
1986 Adult Correctional Services in Canada. Ottawa: Ministry of Supply and Services. Catalogue no. 85-211, annual.

Steffensmeier, D.J.
1987 The Invention of the "New" Senior Citizen Criminal: An Analysis of Crime Trends of Elderly Males and Elderly Females, 1964-1984. Research on Aging, 9(2):281-311.

Stengel, E.
1964 Suicide and Attempted Suicide. Hammondsworth: Penguin Books.

Stone, L.O. and S. Fletcher
1980 A Profile of Canada's Older Population. Montreal: The Institute for Research on Public Policy.

Strauss, A.C. and R. Sherwin
1975 Inmate Rioters and Non-rioters--A Comparative Analysis. American Journal of Corrections, July-August:34-35.

Sutherland, E.
1937 The Professional Thief. Chicago: University of Chicago Press.

Sunderland, G.
1982 Geriatric Crime Wave: The Great Debate. Police Chief, 49(10):40, 42, 44.

Sykes, G.
1958 The Society of Captives. Princeton, N.J.: Princeton University Press.

Szewczyk, H. and Drechsler, I.
1971 Untersuchungen von Alterssittlichkeitstatern. Medizinisch-Juristische Grenzfragen. Heft 11, pp. 93-100.

Tannenbaum. F.
1938 Crime and the Community. Lexington, Mass.: Ginn.

Teller, F.E.
1980 Criminal and Psychological Characteristics of the Older Prisoner. Ph.D. dissertation, Brigham Young University.

Teller, F.E. and R.J. Howell
1981 The Older Prisoner. Criminology, 18(4):549-555.

Thomas, D.A.
1970 Principles of Sentencing. London: Heinemann.

Time Magazine
1982 Old Enough to Know Better: A Stunning Rise in Crime by Senior Citizens Creates a Quandary. Sept. 20, 1982, p. 83.

Townsend, P.
1962 The Last Refuge: A Survey of Residential Institutions and Homes for the Aged in England and Wales. London: Routledge and Kegan, Paul.

Ulrich, H.
1971 Die Sexualdelikte des alteren Mannes. Medizinisch-Juristische Grenzfragen. Heft 11, pp. 87-91.

Virkkunen, M.
1975 Victim-Precipitated Pedophilia Offences. British J. of Criminology, 15(2):175-180.

Virkkunen, M.
1980 The Child as Participating Victim. Reprint, pp. 122-134.

Von Wormer, K.
1981 To be Old and in Prison. In Contemporary Issues in Corrections, Society of Police and Criminal Psychology.

Vedder, C.G. and O.J. Keller Jr.
1958 The Elderly Offender, Probation and Parole. Police Chief, 311:14-16.

Weinberg, S.K.
1952 Society and Personality Disorders. Englewood Cliffs: Prentice Hall.

Weiss, J.M.A.
1973 The Natural History of Antisocial Attitudes--What Happens to Psychopaths? J. of Geriatric Psychiatry, 6(2):236-242.

Whiskin, F.E.
1967 The Geriatric Sex Offender. Geriatrics, 22:168-172.

Whiskin, F.E.
1968 Delinquency in the Aged. J. of Geriatric Psychiatry, 1:242-262.

Wiegand, D., and J.C. Burger
1979 The Elderly Offender and Parole. Prison Journal, 59(2):57-58. *(in 48-57?)*
(1980? → See p. 95) *See p. 104, Chp5*

Wilbanks, W.
1984a The Elderly Offender: Placing the Problem in Perspective. In W. Wilbanks and P.K.H. Kim (Eds.) Elderly Criminals. Lanham,MD. University Press of America. pp. 1-15.

Wilbanks, W.
1984b The Elderly Offender: Sex and Race Variations in Frequency and Pattern. In W. Wilbanks and P.K.H. Kim (Eds.) Elderly Criminals. Lanham,MD. University Press of America. pp. 41-52.

Wilbanks, W.
1985 The Elderly Offender: Relative Frequency and Pattern of Offences. Int. J. of Aging and Human Development, 20(4):269-281.

Wilbanks, W. and P.K.H. Kim
1984 Elderly Criminals. Lanham, MD. University Press of America.

Wilbanks, W. and D.D. Murphy
1984 The Elderly Homicide Offender. In Newman, Newman and Gewirtz (Eds.) Elderly Criminals. Cambridge, Mass.: Oelgeschlager, Gunn & Hain Publishers. pp. 79-91

Wilson, P.
1981 The Man They Called a Monster. Sydney, Australia.

Wiltz, C.J.
1973 The Aged Prisoner: A Case Study of Age and Aging in Prison. Kansas State University, unpublished M.A. thesis.

Wiltz, C.J.
1978 The Influence of Age on Length of Incarceration. Ph.D. dissertation, University of Iowa.

Vito, G.F. and Wilson, D.G.
1985 Forgotten People: Elderly Inmates. Federal Probation, XLIX (1):18-23.

Wolfgang, M.E.
1958 Patterns in Criminal Homicide. Philadelphia: University of Pennsylvania Press.

Wolfgang, M.E.
1961 A Sociological Analysis of Criminal Homicide. In Federal Probation, 25(March).

Wolinsky, J.
1982 The Offender as Victim. In APA Monitor. 13(5):17-32.

Wolk, A.
1963 The Geriatric Delinquent. J. of American Geriatrics. 11(7):653-659.

Wooden, W. and J. Parker
1980 Aged Men in a Prison Environment: Life Satisfaction and Coping Strategies. Ph.D. dissertation, California State University. Also an abstract in the Gerontologist. (1980), 20, Nov. p. 231.

Wooden, W.S. and J. Parker
1980 Aged Men in a Prison Environment: Life Satisfaction and Coping Strategies. The Gerontologist, 20 (Part 2, Nov.) :231.

Zeegers, M.
(n.d.) Sexual Delinquency in Men Over 60 Years Old. Mimeograph.

Zimring, F.
1968 Is Gun Control Likely to Reduce Violent Killings? University of Chicago Law Review, 35:721-737.

PART II

VICTIMIZATION OF THE ELDERLY

CHAPTER SEVEN

AGE AS A VICTIMOLOGICAL VARIABLE

INTRODUCTION

The next several chapters shift attention away from the study of elderly persons as offenders and toward the study of elderly victims of crime. Social scientific interest in the analysis of victim processes is relatively recent and may be seen as representing one aspect of a significant broadening of the criminological paradigm which began in the 1960s and which continues to the present day (Gibbons, 1979; Short and Meier, 1981; Pfohl, 1985). The development of victimology during this period has reflected the influence of several other methodological and theoretical innovations such as the increased use of survey research methods, and the movement toward labeling and situational theories of crime (Elias, 1986; Fattah, 1979; Friedrichs, 1983). In general terms, the growth of victimology has underlined a widespread perception that the traditional criminological preoccupation with the offender has provided a focus that is both narrow and limiting. Despite its relatively short history, the victimological literature is indeed vast and, a significant proportion of this literature concerns the special problems faced by the elderly as actual and potential victims of crime. In the next several chapters, the attempt will be made to sort through a variety of competing theoretical and empirical claims in order to uncover the salient dimensions of the relationship between being "elderly" and being "victimized".

The present chapter will overview and organize our approach to the problem. An effort will be made to clarify the nature of the conceptual and methodological foundations upon which the victimological study of the elderly is predicated. We begin with a consideration of some popular cultural views of the problem of elderly victimization.

148

ELDERLY VICTIMIZATION: CULTURAL IMAGES

The Content of Cultural Imagery

Until recently, the elderly were largely invisible to the average consumer of news and entertainment media. Rarely did television comedies, dramas or commercials feature older characters and when they did, their portrayal tended to be highly stereotyped. A reliance upon stock characterizations such as the "kindly grandmother", the "old wino" or the "senile neighbor" meant that such offerings did not, as a matter of course, treat older persons as well- rounded characters whose emotions and life-experiences were as varied as those of other characters in the script. Similarly, until the recent past, we read relatively little about the elderly in newsreports or editorials; although we would (and still do) see the front page picture of the resident of a retirement home blowing out the candles on a birthday cake or read about the "little old lady" and her acts of good work or the "dirty old man" and his sexual indiscretions. While we routinely encountered news about elderly individuals, we were rarely exposed to news about the elderly as a social group. (Buchholz and Bynum, 1982).

Admittedly, this situation has changed somewhat in recent years. The "greying of society" and the political organization of seniors have had the effect of modifying some of the dominant cultural images relating to aging. Still, a strong tendency exists to portray the elderly in both news and entertainment media in ways that stereotype and simplify complex realities. (Bishop and Krause, 1984).

Particularly pertinent in this regard is the media portrayal of the elderly as "people in trouble". Many of the newsreports that we do encounter are concerned with the financial, medical, psychological and social difficulties of later life. The pervasive definition of the elderly as people in trouble reflects a more generalized propensity on the part of media managers to emphasize the reporting of "bad news".

One type of bad news about the elderly to which we are frequently exposed relates to the subject of criminal victimization (Cumberbatch and Beardsworth, 1976; Dominick, 1978; Gordon and Heath, 1981; Graber, 1980; Mawby and Brown, 1984; Sherizan, 1978). With respect to elderly crime problems (as with respect to crime more generally), the mass media may be criticized for creating a "social reality of crime" (Quinney, 1970) which distorts and sensationalizes the empirical dimensions of the problems which they purport to describe. In part, this is because the media provide a forum for "claims- making activities" (Spector and Kitsuse, 1977) by which politicians, crusading journalists and other moral entrepreneurs (Becker, 1963) construct an image of crime that is consistent with and supportive of particular sets of social interests.

As a result, much of what the mass media tell us about the crime problems of the elderly is couched in what Cook and Cook (1976) have termed a "rhetoric of crisis". In this respect, several specific themes may be identified:

1. **The Elderly Have a Particularly High Rate of Victimization**. Much of what we read about in the mass media and much of what passes for conventional wisdom would seem to suggest that older persons have very high rates of criminal victimization. Some politicians and elderly advocates

149

have claimed that the elderly have the highest rate of victimization of any group in society (Cook and Cook, 1976). Not only is it maintained that older persons have excessive rates of many traditional offences such as robbery, assault and theft of personal property but that they are also particularly vulnerable to several other specific crimes such as fraud, domestic abuse and abuse within the context of long-term care institutions.

2. **Rates of Crime Against the Elderly Are Increasing.** Public opinion polls suggest a widespread perception that rates of all types of crime have been increasing in recent years and that particularly pernicious crimes have been increasing at an alarming rate (Brillon, 1987). It is also widely maintained that for some groups in society, such as the elderly, life is becoming even more dangerous (Cutler, 1980). Being vulnerable and feeling vulnerable are viewed by many as incontrovertible aspects of growing old in the 1980s.

3. **Elderly Persons Are More Likely to be Victims of More Serious Rather Than Less Serious Crimes.** Not only is it popularly held that crimes against the elderly are widespread and increasing, but it is also maintained by many that the victimization experience is more serious in its consequences for older as compared to younger members of the population. A random sample of news reports of crimes against the elderly would probably confirm the belief that they are more likely to be robbed, murdered or assaulted than to be the victims of acts of petty theft or vandalism. The selective reporting of "sensationalist" and therefore newsworthy crimes helps to foster the perception that elderly victimization implies serious victimization. A corollary of this argument suggests that due to their greater physical and economic vulnerability, eldery persons will experience greater loss and hardship than younger people even when the type of offence is held constant.

4. **The Elderly Are More Likely than Younger People to Anticipate the Threat of Criminal Victimization and Experience the Psychological and Social Discomfort Which the Anticipation of these Threats Implies.** The elderly, it is claimed, are particularly sensitive to the negative consequences which flow from vicarious exposure to victimization experiences. For many older persons, it is argued, their homes have become "fortresses of fear" in which they cower in the face of ominpresent criminal danger. The anxieties which accompany these perceptions are seen to reduce the quality of life for older persons to the degree that some observers have argued that it is the fear of crime rather than crime itself which is the real problem for the elderly (Clemente and Kleiman, 1976; Logan, 1979).

There fortunately exists much empirical research which speaks to the claims embedded in the rhetoric of crisis regarding the victimization of the elderly; and, the fruits of these analyses will be discussed in subsequent chapters. Suffice it to say for the moment that these cultural images of the elderly victim have wide currency and are reinforced not only by the mass media but also in the more informal conversations that people have about crime. In the latter respect, Skogan and Maxfield's (1981) study of public reactions to crime

150

in three American cities revealed the degree to which the imagery of the rhetoric of crisis was supported by the stories and rumors that circulated throughout local networks. They found that these stories tended to disproportionately focus upon the plight of those elderly neighborhood residents who had been victimized by serious violent crimes despite (or possibly because of) the atypical nature of such incidents.

The Sources of Popular Views of Elderly Victimization

The forces which shape the social reality of crime are many and complex. As stated, "special interests" are frequently active in the promotion of particular views of the problem of crime (Elias, 1986). Research attention has also focused upon the ways in which the newsgathering activities of media professionals systematically determine media images of crime (Chibnall, 1977; Roshier, 1973; Sherizen, 1978).

One important attempt to investigate the ways in which images of elderly victimization emerge from routine newsgathering practices is provided by Fishman (1978) who studied a "crime wave" against the elderly in New York City in 1976. Late during the year in question, the city's three daily newspapers and five local television stations reported a surge of violence against elderly people. The crime wave lasted approximately seven weeks and eventually received national media coverage. According to Fishman, the crime wave resulted in a public outcry as police, politicians and lawmakers were mobilized to respond to this new and pressing threat.

Despite the wave of media publicity, however, Fishman contends that it is most likely that no dramatic increase in crimes against the elderly occurred during the study period. In fact, in the case of some crimes such as homicide, rates of elderly victimization actually decreased.

For Fishman, the theoretical problem was to account for the inconsistency between recorded and perceived crime and thus to explain the development of the crime wave. According to Fishman, the dynamics of crime waves originate in the professional newsgathering and news-structuring processes in which agency personnel are involved. In their attempt to impose order upon disparate stories that come in over the "police wire", editorial gatekeepers seek to define news themes that will organize the day's news by facilitating the presentation of different stories as though they were elements of some bigger story.

Fishman contends that "rising crimes against the elderly" represented one such news theme. Moreover, the tendency of each local media outlet to augment the themes marketed by other media outlets may be seen as further contributing to the climate of concern and worry. Fishman also argues that the police tend to support "crime waves" by making readily available to media agencies crime stories that fit into established themes. On this latter point, Fishman concludes:

I do not want to assert from this brief history of one crime wave that all crime waves are inspired by the police or politicians. It is not that simple. The crime wave against the elderly in New York seems to have resulted from a mixture of happenstance and police assistance. The history of the crime wave, however, does show that officials can and do use their positions to nurture fledgling crime waves first identified by journalists (1978:542).

The correspondence (or lack thereof) between popular views of elderly victimization and the definition of the problem provided by the accumulated literature of victimological theory and research will be a central theme of our discussion. The substance of that analysis must be preceded, however, by an examination of some of the more general conceptual and empirical issues which this literature presents.

AGE AND VICTIMOLOGY

At a general level, the theoretical question in which we are interested can be stated simply: What is the relationship between aging and victim processes? This question subsumes a number of more specific issues:

1. Overall, when compared to the rest of the population do the elderly experience higher or lower rates of criminal victimization?

2. Does being elderly increase or decrease the probability of specific types of victimization?

3. Does being elderly exacerbate or ameliorate the consequences of criminal victimization?

4. Do elderly persons differ from younger persons in terms of the degree to which they are amenable to social and criminal justice policies intended to reduce the burden of criminal victimization?

5. Recognizing that the elderly are not a homogeneous group, for which elderly persons is victimization a particular problem?

These questions suggest the need to develop "theories of the middle range" (Merton, 1957) which provide generalized answers that are consistent with relevant empirical data. These theoretical accounts, in turn, require conceptual and terminological distinctions that are meaningful and useful. Realistically, however, the rapid development of the victimological literature has produced a considerable degree of inconsistency and uncertainty regarding such matters. This discussion, therefore, recognizes the tentative character of the conceptualization process and aims toward an exploration of "sensitizing concepts" which are intended to give the analyst "a general sense of reference with respect to empirical instances" (Blumer, 1969:147-148) rather than to close off discussion with respect to their definitional character.

152

Victimization

At first glance, we might conclude that the concept of victimization is relatively nonproblematic. As we have said, we routinely encounter the term in the context of personal conversations and in the accounts of crime made available in news and entertainment media. In such instances, the term is self-explanatory and does not appear to be one over which we need to agonize. For present purposes, however, it must be recognized that the concept is somewhat more complex than we might suspect.

In simple terms, the concept of victimization implies a kind of social transaction in which an individual or group is the object of some sort of harm authored by another individual or group. The essence of victimization, therefore, is predation and we recognize this explicitly when we use the term, "victim" to describe one person who has been raped, robbed, murdered or assaulted by another person.

While we may experience little trouble in recognizing what is essential to an appropriate conceptualization of victimization, we may confront somewhat greater difficulty in attempting to determine the proper conceptual limits of the term. In other words, what sorts of predations are to be included in a definition of victimization and what sorts of predations are to be excluded?

For many writers, the tendency to equate victimization with criminal victimization is too restricting (Elias, 1986; Mendelsohn, 1976; Reiman, 1976). They argue that we are all subject to a wide variety of victimization experiences that have grave consequences and yet fall outside the scope of criminal law. Our governments lie to us; corporations manufacture dangerous products, employers engage in racist and sexist hiring practices; commercial institutions charge excessive costs for goods and services; and many members of the medical profession prescribe unecessary drugs and perform unnecessary surgery (Ermann and Lundman, 1982; Goff and Reasons, 1986; Snider, 1988). Such cases present us with obvious examples of how some in society exploit and prey upon others in ways that frequently extend beyond the scope of criminal law.

The haziness of the boundary separating criminal from non-criminal forms of victimization is a particularly relevant consideration in the study of the elderly. It has been argued that because the social role of the elderly is a devalued one in our society (Berg and Johnson, 1979; Stearns, 1986; Teski, 1981) older persons are the objects of a wide variety of social harms and that any criminal-non- criminal distinction is largely arbitrary.

Spitzer (1975) claims that the elderly in capitalist societies are regarded as "social junk" because they do not play an important role in the system of capitalist production. Frequently, their incomes are insufficient (Smith, 1976; Teski, 1981), they experience difficulty in finding affordable housing (Hoyer, 1979; Braungart et al., 1979; Morello, 1982), they are excluded from meaningful spheres of social interaction (Rathbone-McCuan and Hashimi, 1982) and they are often responded to, even by members of the "helping professions" in prejudicial and stereotypical ways that ignore their problems and their needs (Geiger, 1978; Lumbomadrou, 1987; Schmall et al., 1977; Solomon. 1⁰⁰⁻ terms of the consequences which such conditions have for th⁻

the elderly, it can be argued that we are forced to see the elderly as victims of society, generally defined. Accordingly, Reiman (1976:77) suggests:

> Victimization of the aged cannot be fully understood unless it is seen in a larger social context in which *aging itself has been rendered a process of victimization*. We have created and sustain (in a variety of ways) a society in which becoming old is not merely becoming different; Becoming old is moving away from optimal human characteristics; becoming old is becoming less human and more dead. So, when the process ends in physical death it appears as the culmination of a dying that started at the close of middle age and is indeed sometimes greeted by those still living with a sigh of relief as if the death has put the survivors out of their misery - the ambiguous misery of waiting for the living dead to become the dead dead.

It is claimed that the failure to employ a broad definition of victimization results in a victimology that is insufficiently critical (Elias, 1986). If we see victims as only those who are the objects of legally proscribed harms, we may give comfort to those interests in society which are powerful enough to shape criminal law in some directions and not others. To be critical, it is argued, we must acknowledge that people are victimized in a variety of ways which the laws of an unequal society permit and in some cases encourage.

While we recognize that there is considerable value to be derived from a broad definition of victimization (particularly with respect to the development of a critical posture toward existing social arrangements) we will, in this and subsequent chapters adopt a somewhat narrower focus by concentrating analytical attention - explicitly at least - upon **criminal victimization**.

However, our examination of those types of predation that involve criminal harm at the exclusion of more diverse victim experiences is undertaken with three caveats in mind. First, we realize that it is not only crime (legally defined) that makes victims of the elderly but other social experiences as well. We do not deny the reality of those experiences but in view of pragmatic limitations and because of broader disciplinary concerns, we do not give them detailed treatment. If we were to define victimization in the broadest possible terms, we would be able to say little that did not require constant qualification.

Second, our utilization of a narrow definition of victimization is not meant to imply that more inclusive definitions are incorrect, only that they are not useful for our purposes.

Finally, although we concentrate upon criminal victimization, this is not to sugggest that we can examine the problem of crime among the elderly in a way that ignores the other kinds of problems that the elderly experience or the other kinds of exploitation to which they are subjected. The crime problems faced by the elderly are not separable from other aspects of their lives. The threats of criminal victimization that many elderly people face are exacerbated by the fact that they lack many of the social and economic resources that most of the rest of us take for granted. To the extent that we are willing to view the deprivation of such resources as a form of social victimization, we are forced to conclude that victim experiences tend to be correlated (Hoyer, 1979; Kahana et al., 1977; Croake et al., 1988; Rifai and Ames, 1977); and that the key to understanding one type of victim experience (such as criminal victimization) may be to understand other types of victim experiences (such as the deprivation of resources or the forced dependence upon others).

Victimization Costs

It may appear obvious to suggest that victimization is regarded as a social problem because of the negative consequences which such experiences generate. Still, there is some practical value to be derived from a conceptual distinction between victimization incidents *per se* and the costs associated with such incidents.

An appreciation of the victimization cost as a conceptually distinguishable aspect of the victimization episode alerts us to the fact that similar victimization episodes may produce quite different costs depending upon the social, economical or physical resources of the victim. A "petty theft" will impose a lesser cost upon a multimillionaire than upon someone living at or below the poverty line. In addition, the costs of victimization - as opposed to the victimization itself - may suggest a distinctive point of policy intervention. Thus, although public programs may be directed toward preventing victimizations from occurring, they may also be directed toward ameliorating the costs of those victimization events which do occur.

As we will discover in subsequent chapters, the concept of victimization cost, like the concept of victimization is complex and multi-faceted. Most generally, there does not exist any simple and convenient metric by which such costs may be calculated or summed. The costs of victimization may be obvious and immediate (as in the case of a broken jaw that results from the strong-arm tactics of a robber) or subtle and long-term (when, for instance, the victimization incident contributes to chronic health problems).

In recent years, many victimologists have argued that it is short-sighted to suggest that the concept of victimization cost is applicable only to those who are directly and immediately affected (Conklin, 1975). Instead, they have insisted that it is useful to recognize that there are also indirect costs of victimization. In the context of such arguments, individuals are said to be indirectly affected by crime when they react to media or interpersonal reports of crime in ways that suggest a lessening of the quality of their lives. Understood in this way, criminal events may be said to send out "shock waves" (Taylor and Hale, 1986) which generate negative outcomes for those who vicariously experience the criminal victimization of others. It is argued that vicarious experiences with crime may be no less real in their impact than direct experiences.

These impacts may be manifested in a pervasive fear of criminal victimization and in the psychological discomfort which it implies. The fear of victimization may make people apprehensive about taking a walk in the local park and thus they remain at home on warm summer evenings; it may cause them to think twice about attending a concert or recital because they believe that the streets are not safe; it may lead them to use some portion of their disposable income to purchase alarm systems or extra locks for doors and windows; or, it might lead them to isolate themselves from neighbors and strangers because they feel that a failure to do so may result in harm to themselves or their property.

155

It is important to recognize that direct and indirect experiences with crime may be related in some rather complex ways. Most obviously, being a victim of crime may accentuate a fear of future victimization. Alternatively, being afraid of crime may reduce the probability of being a victim of crime (if, for instance, a fear of being on the street at night reduces exposure to crimes which occur in such settings). There have been several attempts to disentangle these relationships and we will discuss some of this research in later chapters.

Risk

The concept of risk refers to variations in the level and type of exposure to threats of criminal harm. For purposes of the present discussion, it might be suggested that differences between elderly and non-elderly levels of criminal victimization may be related to socially patterned, age-graded differences in opportunities to be victimized. Several variations on this theme may be identified.

A number of writers, for instance, have argued that residential variables provide a linkage between age and exposure to criminal harm (Braungart et al., 1979; Kosberg, 1985; Morello, 1982; Smith, 1979; Teski, 1981). It is claimed that the economic precariousness of the elderly and their generally low rates of mobility have combined to produce inner-city "geriatric ghettoes" (Clark, 1971). As a result, many elderly people find themselves living in socially heterogeneous and economically disadvantaged neighborhoods where crime levels and thus victimization risks are high (Nettler, 1984).

In a somewhat different way it might be suggested that the elderly have higher levels of exposure to the sensationalist crime messages that are encoded in mass media content and which, it is claimed, aggravate the fear of personal criminal victimization (Gerbner and Gross, 1976).

Perhaps the most influential arguments linking age to exposure to risk are those which have emerged out of an attempt to establish a theoretical relationship between criminal victimization and the concepts of "lifestyle" (Garofalo, 1986; Gottfredson, 1981; Hindelang et al., 1978; Miethe et al., 1987; Sampson, 1987) or "routine activities" (Cohen and Felson, 1979; Cohen et al., 1981). Such accounts focus attention upon the ways in which the relative involvement in particular patterns of vocational or avocational activity increases or decreases the probability that individuals will come into contact with persons or situations that threaten criminal harm.

It is argued that aging brings with it important changes in the ways in which time, interest and talent are distributed across social roles and activities. Retirement, for instance, is normally accompanied by significant changes in lifestyle. The day may be less rigidly controlled by the clock and the definition and use of leisure time may undergo important modifications (Hindelang et al., 1978). All such changes may affect quite dramatically the degree of risk to which people are typically exposed.

An important corollary of lifestyle arguments relates to the role which social relationships play in the aggravation or reduction of victimization risks. There is much research to suggest that being married, for instance, or not living

156

alone reduce the risk of criminal victimization (Hindelang et al., 1978; Liang and Sengstock, 1983; Timrots and Rand, 1987) as well as the level of fear and anxiety relating to criminal victimization (Braungart et al., 1980; DeFronzo, 1979; Toseland, 1982).

Alternatively, it is evident that particular types of relationships may increase the risk of being victimized. For instance, it is well known that much violence occurs among intimates particularly in the context of familial associations (Wolfgang, 1958, Luckenbill, 1977). Black (1983) has argued that many of the behaviors that we refer to as criminal victimizations represent efforts on the part of one party, particularly in the context of enduring relationships, to impose social control upon another party.

The changing nature of social relationships in old age may affect victimization risks in a number of conflicting ways. The fact that elderly people are somewhat more likely to live alone and to be widowed (Brillon, 1987; Hoyer, 1979) may increase insecurities relating to personal safety. It is also argued that for some people, advanced age may bring with it debilitating physical or mental conditions which increase the degree to which they are dependent upon others who might subject them to physical or other forms of abuse (Pillemer, 1985; Scharlach, 1987; Steinmetz and Amsden, 1983). At the same time, however, the age-segregated nature of much social interaction means that elderly people will less frequently develop associations with members of those groups (i.e. young males) that most likely threaten criminal harm (Hindelang et al., 1978).

In general, it is clear that there are major differences in the lifestyles of retired persons, university students and young married couples with children and that these differences relate to matters as diverse as patterns of consumption, degree of involvement in the local community, the frequency of evening activities, the nature of personal associations and the amount of time spent at home. Since victimization risk varies temporally, spatially and situationally, it is reasonable to suggest that particular types of lifestyles may increase or decrease exposure to these risks. Thus, in order to understand why some groups in society have higher or lower rates of victimization, we must appreciate the ways in which their lifestyles make them more or less available to be victimized.

Quite obviously, the concept of risk may be understood as having subjective as well as objective dimensions; and these dimensions may vary quite independently of each other. In other words, people may subjectively perceive the level of risk associated with a particular location, activity or situation as being higher or lower than "objective" empirical data suggest that it is. The point is an important one since it is, in the final analysis, the subjective probability rather than the objective probability of victimization that is the principal determinant of the strategies which people employ for the purpose of managing or avoiding criminal danger (Merry, 1981).

Vunlnerability

The concept of vulnerability is intended to designate an openness or susceptibility to the occurrence or consequences of victimization (Dussich and Eichman, 1976; Kosberg, 1985; Perloff, 1983; Sacco and Glackman, 1987; Skogan and Maxfield, 1981). The concept draws our attention to the social, physical and economic characteristics of elderly persons and the ways in which these characteristics affect the sensitivity to risk and the ability to cope with the aftermath of the victimization experience. Vulnerability to victimization is not a unidimensional concept and thus it is possible to identify a variety of ways in which people may vary in their susceptibility to criminal harm (Brillon, 1987; Dussich and Eichman, 1976; Kosberg, 1985; Skogan and Maxfield, 1981). The major types of vulnerability that may be distinguished are physical, economic and social. Later life, it is argued, may exacerbate all three conditions.

On a physical level, advanced age brings with it a decline in physical strength and agility and an increase in chronic health problems (Brillon, 1987; Hoyer, 1979). These changes may mean that older people are "less likely to resist an attack, flee from adversity or engage in effective self-protection activities" (Kosberg, 1985:377). The perception by potential offenders of the reduced physical efficacy of the elderly may mean that they come to be defined as more attractive targets (Grayson and Stein, 1981). In a related way, various forms of sensory impairment may increase the susceptibility to financial fraud and medical quackery (Mc Ghee, 1983). Other potential effects of the general diminishment of physical capacity may involve the development of a subjective sense of vulnerability which increases feelings of fear and insecurity (Skogan and Maxfield, 1981; Braungart et al., 1979) and impairs recovery and adjustment processes in the post-victimization phase.

Earlier reference was made to the economic precariousness of many seniors and the role that it plays in the promotion of risk-factors associated with criminal victimization. In addition, inadequate economic resources may mean that elderly persons are less able to absorb the financial losses that result from criminal victimization and that as a result, the burden of victimization falls more heavily upon them (Elmore, 1981; Skogan and Maxfield, 1981). It is also argued that the state of financial insecurity in which many seniors live makes them desirable targets of fraudulent "get rich" schemes (Pepper, 1983; Geis, 1977) and, in combination with long-term physical disabilities, forces them into situations in which they are easily exploited by those to whom their care has been entrusted (Solomon, 1983).

The social vulnerability of older persons may be said to be related to the devaluation of aged roles in contemporary society. The relegation of the elderly to the margins of social life increases the social isolation of older persons (Rathbone-McCuan and Hashimi, 1982) and perpetuates ageist attitudes and practices (Smith, 1979; Teski, 1981; Stearns, 1986). Discriminatory behavior and prejudicial attitudes toward the elderly may reinforce perceptions of them as "culturally legitimate victims" (Fattah, 1979; Viano, 1983) since for many in society, the elderly are viewed as "intellectually unfit, narrow- minded, ineffective and ready to die momentarily" (Davidson et al., 1979). The concept of social vulnerability encourages us to understand the aged not as a biologically defined aggregate but as a group occupying a subordinate position in a social hierarchy (Miethe et al., 1987). The ideological system which underwrites this subordination may be an important factor in the facilitation of the victimization of older persons (Kosberg, 1985).

As this discussion makes clear, vulnerability, like risk, may be understood in ways that emphasize the subjectivity or the objectivity of the concept. In the former sense, we may argue that vulnerability is a subjective matter by focusing upon variations in the ways in which people perceive their abilities to cope with the threat or consequences of criminal harm (Perloff, 1983). Vulnerability as an objective characteristic is somewhat more problematic. While it may be argued that physical strength or agility represent characteristics that "in some objective manner" increase or decrease the individual's ability to manage criminal danger, such characteristics are indicators of vulnerability only to the degree that they are subjectively understood as such by potential offenders. Stated differently, there is nothing inherent in the physical, social or economic descriptions of individuals that in some a priori way predisposes them to victimization. What is at issue is the offender's definition of such characteristics as legitimating the victimization of those who possess them (Fattah, 1976).

THE VICTIM AS DECISION-MAKER

The perspective taken in subsequent chapters emphasizes the understanding of elderly victimization as a collection of complex social processes (Berg and Johnson, 1979; Fattah, 1981; Lejeune and Alex, 1973) rather than as discrete and static events.

Such a framework stresses the active role of the victim as a decision-maker (Gottfredson and Gottfredson; 1980; Henshel and Silverman, 1975), and of the victimization and its aftermath as an inter-connected series of decision-making stages. At each stage, the decisions made by the victim both influence and are influenced by the decisions made by others involved in the process; and, decisions made at any one stage reflect decisions made at earlier stages and impact upon those made at later stages.

At an intial stage, individuals make decisions about the risks that they are willing to take and about the ways in which they will manage danger in the situations that they define as threatening. They must decide if they will take actions intended to reduce their vulnerability and how they will interpret information that speaks to their potential for criminal harm.

In those situations in which the victmization involves an interaction between offender and victim a second major stage of decision-making may be recognized. Does the victim attempt to resist or cooperate with the offender? Does he or she use physical force, make a verbal plea or try to outwit the victimizer? Does the victim try to remember important details about the offender for the purposes of making a subsequent police report or try to enlist the assistance of available bystanders?

During the aftermath of the victimization the victim must again make several decisions. Should the victimization be reported to the police, or other authorities? Should an attempt be made to seek reparation through private or public compensation schemes? How can he or she most adequately cope with the losses sustained in the victimization? If an offender is apprehended, what

159

role, if any, should the victim attempt to play in the judicial process? Should the individual embrace or reject the victim role and how should the social stigma and the psychological strain associated with criminal victimization be managed?

The conceptualization of the victim as a decision-maker proceeds from a model of victim behavior which stresses rationality and volition (Henshel and Silverman, 1975). It implies that at each stage of the decision-making process, the victim is able to formulate goals towards which behavior is directed and to consider alternative behavioral options with respect to these goals. It further assumes that the choice among alternatives is based upon the information to which the decision-maker has access (Gottfredson and Gottfredson, 1980). This information may be accurate or inaccurate and the decisions which are based upon it may serve or defeat the decision-maker's interests.

This emphasis upon voluntarism and rationality may seem to be inconsistent with the mainstream of criminological theory which stresses the role of causality and "social forces" in understanding behavior. The inconsistency, however, is more apparent than real. Decisions must be made in institutional and cultural contexts and in the face of structural constraints and impartial and inaccurate information. While we may be free to choose among available behavioral options, this does not mean that our choices are not influenced by our place in the stratification order, our cultural environment, the wishes of significant others or what we understand our role obligations to be. In this respect, we are in agreement with Henshel and Silverman (1975:4) who state:

> As we see it, on the one hand, man's actions are indeed purposive, the direct product of consciousness and choice, and the individual ascribes meaning to a situation by interpreting the information he obtains about it. This is a process unique for each individual, but on the other hand, certain common tendencies in how interpretation is done can be found in persons with similar previous experiences, while persons occupying similar social positions will tend to receive similar information out of the total information matrix. To that extent, it does seem legitimate to speak of "factors" being involved in human behavior, and we must part company with those who feel that acceptance of a voluntaristic component precludes the possibility of social forces.

Thus, the decision-making framework does not preclude the utilization of empirical data that are generated through the traditional methodologies of criminology. The principals and shortcomings of these methodological approaches are considered below.

DATA ON ELDERLY VICTIMIZATION

Researchers interested in the investigation of the problem of crimes against the elderly have, in general, attempted to gather data from one or some combination of three sources. These sources include the victims, the victimizers and the agents of social control whose professional mandates involve the acquisition of information pertinent to elderly victimization.

The Agents of Social Control

The data source with the longest history of usage in criminological research derives from the official records maintained by criminal justice agencies, most notably the police. In Canada and the United States, these data are gathered by local law enforcment agencies, according to standardized rules and procedures and subsequently collated and summarized at the federal level (Brannigan, 1984; Evans and Himelfarb, 1987; Hagan, 1984; Nettler, 1984; O'Brien, 1985; Silverman and Teevan, 1986).

Although these Uniform Crime Report data are collected through standardized procedures and although they are readily accessible to criminal justice researchers, they are known to have a number of significant shortcomings. First, it is recognized that, since these data are based only on those crimes about which the police have knowledge, they underestimate the total volume of crime. Such distortions are likely to be particularly evident in the case of those "less serious" crimes which are unlikely to come to public attention (Nettler, 1984). Second, it may be argued that the data are more accurately seen as describing the political and administrative priorities of local policing agencies and the preferences of the citizenry for police action rather than some external universe of criminal events (Black, 1970). Third, it is maintained that the administrative procedures which guide the generation of these data are fraught with problems which produce a distorted picture of crime levels (O'Brien, 1985; Silverman and Teevan, 1986). Fourth, the data are categorized in terms that are legally rather than conceptually meaningful and thus it is not possible to separate out, for example, domestic assaults from other types of assaults.

· While such criticisms suggest some general factors which limit the utility of official crime data, there is one problem that is particularly relevant in the present context. Specifically, with the exception of homicide, Uniform Crime Reports do not include information on the victims of crime (O'Brien, 1985). This means that it is not possible to determine the way in which rates of victimization are distributed across age groups.

Researchers interested in the investigation of the problem of elder abuse have also made use of data gathered from social control professionals (Block and Sinnott, 1979; Chen et al., 1981; Hickey and Douglass, 1981a; Lau and Kosberg, 1979; O'Malley et al., 1983). Studies of this type normally involve the examination of case records relating to the abuse of elder persons and/or the detailed interviews with physicians, nurses, social workers, police officers, coroners or other health or social service professionals who are directly involved in the investigation of, or intervention in such cases.

Reviews of such studies suggest that they are limited in several important ways:

1. They tend to use small, and in many cases, unrepresentative samples which limit the generalizability of the findings (Pillemer and Suitor, 1988; U.S. Department of Health and Human Services, 1980; Quinn and Tomita, 1986). Not all older persons are equally likely to come under the purview of social service agencies and to the extent that distinctive socially or demographically defined groups are over-represented in the clientele of

161

such agencies, they are likely to be over- represented in estimates of abuse and neglect as well.

2. These studies employ widely variable operational definitions of abuse and neglect which mitigate against the development of systematic information (King, 1983; Hooyman et al., 1982; Pillemer and Suitor, 1988). As we will see in Chapter 11, there is little agreement among criminologists, gerontologists or practitioners regarding the most apporopriate way to conceptualize the phenomena of elder abuse and neglect and these inconcistencies in operational definitions promote inconsistencies in estimates.

3. Studies of this type may over-represent the more serious types elder abuse which, for instance result in death or emergency-room medical treatment, and to underestimate less serious abuse incidents (Sengstock and Hwaleck, 1987).

4. The methods of data collection do not necessarily ensure unduplicated counts of abuse cases (Shell, 1982). Because these studies rely upon second-hand accounts of abuse (Pillemer and Suitor, 1988) it is not always possible to ensure that reports provided by social service professionals refer to distinct cases.

5. The categorization of elder abuse by the professionals involved tends to reflect the "professional ideologies" to which they are committed (Douglass and Hickey, 1983). In other words, the data reflect the influence of the professional filters of the groups in question. Police officers, social workers and physicians may differ not only with respect to the types of abuse with which they come into contact but also in terms of what they are prepared to define as abuse (Quinn and Tomita, 1986; Hudson, 1986). The various problems that characterize the data generated by those involved in social control activities suggest that they may be more useful for some purposes than others. While they reveal the nature of the incidents or persons that come to official attention, they do not necessarily address in adequate fashion the larger population of cases from which that sample is drawn. Thus, it might be argued that the data speak more directly to the control activities relevant to such events rather than to the events themselves.

The Victims

One alternative to official data sources is the victimization survey which attempts to elicit information directly from the victims of crimes themselves. The information generated by such studies has the advantage of not having been mediated and therefore distorted by the professional activities of social control agents. Also, because this research focuses upon the victim directly, it is possible to generate a wealth of information about the social and demographic characteristics of the victim, the social context and consequences of the victimization, and the relationship between the victim and the offender.

Numerous victim surveys have been undertaken in Canada, the United States, as well as in several European countries and we will, in subsequent chapters, review the findings of several such studies. For the present, it is important to note that despite their value, victimization surveys are problematic in several respects (Biderman, 1981; Block and Block, 1984; Evans and Himelfarb, 1987; Gottfredson and Hindelang, 1981; Johnson and Wasielewski, 1982; Nettler, 1984; O'Brien, 1985; Sparks et al., 1977; Schneider, 1981). With respect to the problems of victim surveys, Skogan (1986:82) has recently noted:

> Respondents sometimes do not know of things about which we quiz them. They might also have forgotten about them, a fallibility which in practice we cannot distinguish from their deliberately not telling us about them. Respondents may also either inadvertently or malevolently tell us something that is incorrect. Finally, some people are better respondents than others: they more readily grasp the nature of the task presented to them; they work harder at it; and they tire of the demands of a survey less rapidly. All of these factors conspire to shape the volume and character of reports of victimization, sometimes independently and sometimes in conjunction with the true distribution of criminal incidents.

Such criticisms should not be interpreted as suggesting that victim surveys are without value, only that their use must be judicious. It will become apparent in the chapters that follow that studies of this type provide one of the most important data sources on the subject of elderly victimization.

In addition to providing information about specific criminal victimization incidents in which individuals have been involved, surveys are also a useful technique for ascertaining the ways in which people are indirectly affected by crime. Respondents may be asked about their perceptions of local crime problems, the degree to which they fear the possibility of criminal victimization, the types of limitations which they place upon their behavior because of crime, and the sources of their information about crime. Research of this type may be undertaken in conjunction with a victimization survey or it may form the focus of independent inquiry in the context of a crime perception survey. These investigations of "perceptual victimization" (Johnson and Wasielewski, 1982) like the investigation of more direct forms of victimization involve complex sampling and measurement issues which will be discussed in greater detail in Chapter 10.

Finally, it should be noted that victim accounts have also been utilized to a somewhat lesser extent in the investigation of the abuse and neglect of the elderly by informal careproviders (Pillemer and Finkelhor, 1988; Pillemer, 1985; Steur and Austin, 1980; Block and Sinnott, 1979).

The infrequency of such studies is no doubt in part attributable to the methodological assumption that the population of interest is likely to be inaccessible to the researcher. In other words, it is popularly believed that the seclusion and isolation of the elderly victim may be implicit in the nature of domestic abuse.

Moreover, there may be several reasons why the elderly are reluctant to label the situations in which they find themselves as abusive or to report to researchers those situations which are so defined. They may fear reprisals from the abuser or define the abuse as a private matter (Kosberg, 1988). They may experience embarrassment about their mistreatment or, feel guilty because they believe that they have brought the mistreatment upon themselves (King, 1983; Kosberg, 1983). There may, in addition, be strong inhibitions working against the admission on the part of a parent that he or she has raised an abusive child (Steinmetz, 1981). In the case of families in which there is a history of violence, the elder may not define even extreme abuse as anything other than normal (Anderson, 1981). In particular, Quinn and Tomita (1986) suggest, women who have been abused as children or as wives may in old age define abuse as a routine expectation. Finally, elderly persons may not even be aware of some forms of abuse to which they are subjected. This may be the situation when for instance, an elderly person is financially exploited by a caregiver (Gordon, 1987).

Victimizers

A final empirical approach to the problem of elderly victimization focuses not upon the victims of harm but upon those who are its authors. In the context of such research, offenders are asked to detail the nature and the circumstances of the crimes which they have perpetrated.

Studies of self-reported crime and delinquency like victim surveys, emerged as a response to problems of official data; and like victim surveys, they were intended to generate data that are uncontaminated by the errors implicit in social control agency processing.

Critics argue that, despite their popularity, self-report surveys have not fulfilled their original promise (Nettler, 1984). Serious problems of validity and reliability and a narrow focus upon primarily juvenile populations have undermined the generalizability of the findings of such studies (Hagan, 1984; O'Brien, 1985). A further problem that seriously limits the applicability of the findings of self-report studies to present concerns is discussed by O'Brien (1985:71):

> The focus of SR studies has been on the offender. This is, to some extent, inherent in the method that involves questions about the criminal/delinquent behaviors of the respondents. SR studies have not been used to examine the characteristics of victims of crime. They could, of course, do so by asking respondents to identify characteristics such as the sex, age and race of their victims. Thus, this method provides us almost no information about the victims of crime.

An important exception to this general pattern may be found in the area of elder abuse and neglect. Specifically, some researchers (Scharlach, 1987; Anetzberger, 1987; Steinmetz, 1983) have attempted to generate samples of individuals who are responsible for providing informal care to the elderly. The purpose of such research is to facilitate the indentification of the social and psychological characteristics of those who are involved in abusive relationships as well as to yield estimates of the frequency and intensity of the abusive and neglectful conduct itself. Like all research that attempts to investigate disreputable behavior by eliciting confessions from those who perform the behavior, these studies risk unrepresentative samples and they potentially confuse the victimizers's definition of the situation with the empirical reality in which the researcher is interested.

SUMMARY

This chapter has attempted to lay a foundation for the more focused discussion of elderly victimization that is found in the following chapters. We have examined the concepts of victimization, risk and vulnerability and have made explicit the nature of the theoretical perspective that will guide subsequent analyses. In addition, we have considered the major methodological approaches to the problem of crime against the elderly and commented upon some of the factors that compromise the quality of the data which these strategies generate.

The chapters that follow give substance to the issues raised in this chapter. By drawing heavily on the findings of major victimization surveys, Chapter 8 details what is currently know about crimes against the elderly and offers a theoretical interpretation of these findings.

Chapter 9 analyzes the behavior of the elderly in the aftermath of the victimization experience and considers the ways in which older persons cope with such events. Chapters 10 and 11 analyze two additional problems which have attracted considerable research attention. The former analyzes the issue of the indirect costs of victimization by discussing the fear of crime among the elderly and the manner in which older persons manage the risks of criminal danger. The latter chapter discusses the emergent problem of elder abuse and neglect. Finally, Chapter 12 details the policy dimensions of elderly victimization and discusses what has been and could be done to ameliorate the problem.

CHAPTER SEVEN: RECOMMENDED READINGS

Buchholz, M. and J.E. Bynum
1982 Newspaper Presentation of America's Aged: A Content Analysis of Image and Role. The Gerontologist, 22:83-87.

Cook, F.L.
1981 Crime and the Elderly: The Emergence of a Policy Issue. in D.A. Lewis (Ed.). Reactions to Crime, Beverly Hills: Sage Publications. pp. 177-190.

Fattah, E.A.
1979 Some Recent Theoretical Developments in Victimology. Victimology, 4:198-213.

Gottfredson, M.R. and M.J. Hindelang
1981 Sociological Aspects of Criminal Victimization. Annual Review of Sociology, 7:107-128.

Hindelang, M.J., M.R. Gottfredson and J. Garofalo
1978 Victims of Personal Crime: An Empirical Foundation of a Theory of Personal Victimization. Cambridge, Mass.: Ballinger Publishing Co.

Maddox, G.
1979 Sociology of Later Life. Annual Review of Sociology, 5:113-135.

Reiman, J.R.
1975 Aging as Victimization: Reflections on the American Way of (Ending) Life. in J. Goldsmith and S.S. Goldsmith (Eds.). Crime and the Elderly, Lexington Mass.: D.C. Heath.pp.7-82.

CHAPTER EIGHT

GENERAL PATTERNS OF ELDERLY VICTIMIZATION

INTRODUCTION

In this chapter we will explore patterns and causes of criminal victimization of the elderly. More specifically, we are interested in an exploration of the types and levels of victimization risks, the social settings within which elderly victimizations occur and the theoretical accounts that are intended to explain these patterns. In order to accomplish this objective, we will review the findings of victimization studies conducted in Canada, the United States and elsewhere. Because several of these studies employ general population samples, they allow us to compare elderly and non-elderly groups with respect to the frequency and content of victimization experiences.

In the last chapter, we commented upon the general methodology of victimization surveys and some of the issues that compromise the validity of their findings. In this regard, it may be advantageous to raise some additional matters that are salient with respect to the following discussion.

First, it should be pointed out that all victimization studies ask respondents about a relatively limited range of victimization incidents. Therefore, the general picture of elderly victimization that we draw is one that is influenced, in the first instance, by the narrowness or the breadth of the crimes about which repondents are queried. Moreover, because a survey routinely proceeds from a fairly specific assumption about what kinds of events do and do not qualify as victimizations, there is always the risk that the study will reflect researcher rather than respondent definitions of criminal harm. Most of these studies ignore victimization by governments, corporations and other bureaucracies and focus rather narrowly upon conventional street crime. This occurs despite the fact that there is research to indicate that the public does define certain corporate and government abuses, such as fraudulent advertising and the sale of known dangerous products, as victimizing (Johnson and Wasielewski, 1982).

Second, most of the studies described below have been conducted in urban areas and while they permit generalizations to be made with respect to such populations, they may tell us little about people who reside outside urban areas where patterns of victimization may be quite distinctive.

Third, even within urban areas, there are important sub-populations that are likely to be under-represented or not represented at all. The homeless, the poor and those living on "skid row", for instance, may not be captured by more general sampling procedures. This may be a particular problem in those studies in which respondents are selected through telephone sampling procedures such as "Random Digit Dialing" (Tuchfarber and Klecka, 1976). Omissions of this type are particularly noteworthy in that the excluded groups may experience atypically high victimizations risks.

Finally, it should be noted that the studies reviewed below do not employ a consistent definition of "old age". While they generally distinguish elderly from non-elderly groups in chronological terms, they employ variable operationalizations. Thus, in some studies elderly persons are those who are over 65 years of age, in other studies they are over 60 and in still others they are over 55. This lack of agreement reflects the more general uncertainty among criminologists and gerontologists regarding the way in which elderly status is most appropriately conceptualized.

In spite of these problems, we must be careful not to present too negative a view of victimization surveys. As this chapter will hopefully demonstrate, a judicious review of their findings can be quite instructive.

THE FINDINGS OF VICTIM SURVEYS

The Volume of Victimization

As discussed in the last chapter, the "rhetoric of crisis" in which popular discussions of elderly victimization are frequently phrased, suggests that older persons experience criminal victimization at a rate exceeding that experienced by other age groups.

A preliminary review of victimization data and a knowledge of the social composition of elderly populations should raise suspicions in our minds regarding the validity of such a conclusion. The findings of victim surveys suggest that criminal victimization is socially distributed such that the greatest overall risks are experienced by males, minority group members, urban dwellers, the poor and those who have never been married (Hindelang et al., 1978; Skogan and Maxfield, 1981; Canada, 1983b; Hough, 1986). The group that we call the elderly, when compared to the rest of the population, contains a greater number of people who are female, poor and married or widowed and fewer people who are minority group members and urban residents. Thus, with the exception of the socioeconomic variable, the social composition of the elderly population would lead us to expect lower and not higher rates of criminal victimization.

When we focus more specifically upon the comparative analysis of elderly rates of victimization, it becomes readily apparent that the rhetoric of crisis regarding the volume of criminal victimization is quite inaccurate and that the

168

elderly are victimized much less frequently than the rest of the population. Moreover, the difference between elderly and non- elderly rates of victimization exists quite independently of the social and demographic characteristics of the aged. In other words, being older seems to make a separate and independent contribution to the reduction in victimization risk. This finding has been consistently reported by victimization researchers for almost two decades and in a number of different countries.

Perhaps the best known and most comprehensive data that speak to the issue of elderly victimization are derived from the American National Crime Surveys (Gottfredson and Hindelang, 1981; O'Brien, 1985). The National Crime Survey, which was initiated by the Law Enforcement Assistance Administration in the early 1970s, can be divided into two major types of programs. The first program involved a series of city surveys which were conducted in 26 major American urban areas between 1972 and 1975. The second is a survey of a national sample that has been conducted on a regular basis since 1972. Currently, the national sample includes about 60,000 households and elicits detailed data from approximately 136,000 individuals. The research strategy of the national study involves a panel design in which interviews of respondents are conducted at six-month intervals for a maximum of three years.

Taken collectively, the data from the National Crime Survey programs allow a rather rigorous assessment of claims regarding levels of elderly victimization. In summary, the research supports the following conclusions:

1. When the rates of several personal crimes (rape, aggravated assault, simple assault, robbery, larceny with contact and personal larceny without contact) are aggregated, elderly rates of criminal victimization are lower than those of other age groups (Hochstedler, 1981; Cook and Cook, 1976; Cook et al., 1981; U.S. Department of Justice, 1981; Skogan and Maxfield, 1981; Liang and Sengstock, 1981; 1983)

2. A similar age-reduction in risk obtains in the case of crimes against property such as burglary, household larceny and motor-vehicle theft (U.S. Department of Justice, 1981; Cook and Cook, 1976)

3. The "mix" of personal victimization incidents for the elderly is different than for younger population groups such that older victims tend to be objects of economic predation while younger victims are more likely to be objects of violence (Timrots and Rand, 1987; U.S. Department of Justice, 1981; Cook and Cook, 1976; Cook et al., 1981; Antunes et al., 1977; U.S. Department of Justice, 1981; Liang and Sengstock, 1983; Hochstedler, 1981). The data suggest that the elderly have high rates of theft with contact (such as purse-snatching and pickpocketing) and robbery, but low rates of sexual and non-sexual assault. In other words, "elderly victims are more likely to be preyed upon than to be victimized with intent to do personal injury; younger victims are more likely to be treated violently than to be preyed upon" (Cook et al., 1981:231).

In general, then, the NCS data indicate that aging brings with it a significant and dramatic decline in the risk of criminal victimization and that when the elderly are affected by crime they seem to be somewhat more susceptible to crimes motivated by economic gain. Such findings are not unique in any

169

sense to the methodology or sampling procedures of the National Crime Survey but are consistent with data generated by numerous other victim surveys conducted in particular cities or regions of the United States (Forstan, 1974; Lindquist and Duke, 1982; Smith, 1979; Yin, 1985; Alston, 1986; Burkhardt and Norton, 1977; Rifai, 1977; Eve, 1985; Ollenburger, 1981; Kosberg, 1985).

Nor is the pattern unique to criminal victimization in the United States. A major victimization survey conducted in seven large Canadian urban areas in 1982 revealed that for four categories of personal crime (assault, sexual assault, personal theft and robbery) the rates of victimization of elderly people were about one-sixth those of all adult residents and that those in the 16 to 24 age catgory were twelve times more likely than elderly people to suffer personal victimizations (Canada, 1983b; 1985). Less extensive victim surveys in Canadian urban and rural areas are consistent with the findings of the national study (Brillon, 1987).

The age decline in victimization risks has also been revealed in the victimization data generated by surveys in Great Britain and several other European countries (Hough, 1987; Jones, 1987; Sparks et al, 1977; Colijn, 1981).

Trends in Elderly Victimization

The fact that rates of elderly victimization are lower than the rates associated with younger age groups leaves unanswered questions about the ways in which these rates may change over time. The investigation of this issue requires an examination of longitudinal data which permit an assessment of the fluctuations in victimization levels over some extended period.

Unfortunately, there are relatively few data sets that cover a period of time sufficient to allow a meaningful examination of temporal variations. Although the official Uniform Crime Reports do provide long-term, continuous data, it will be recalled that they do not record victim information. Moreover, because victim surveys are generally costly exercises, they generally have not been undertaken with the intention that the data collection would be replicated on any regular basis.

An early attempt to investigate trends in elderly victimization by Cook and Cook (1976) compared National Crime Survey data collected in 1973 with a 1966 victimization survey which was conducted by the National Opinion Research Center. While the data were not entirely comparable, they did permit a crude estimate of crime trends over the period. In general, the researchers found that, for those crimes for which comparisons could be made, rates of elderly victimization appeared to be increasing in an absolute sense but there was no indication that they were increasing more quickly than for other age groups. An examination of 13 years of the national samples from the NCS provides a somewhat more sophisticated basis for the analysis of temporal trends (Rand, 1987). The analysis which focused upon changes in violent victimization of the elderly for the period 1973 to 1985 indicated that for most violent offences, rates of victimization appeared to be gradually declining during the period in question. The relative stability of the elderly victimization pattern was in marked contrast to the upward and downward shifts in the victimization rates of younger population groups.

The best available evidence would seem to indicate that concerns about a disproportionate increase in levels of crimes against the elderly are not supported empirically.

The Social Distribution of Elderly Victimization

While gross comparisons between elderly and non-elderly groups inform our understanding of the relationship between age and victimization, they mask important distinctions within the elderly population with respect to the distribution of risk. In other words, not all older persons are equally likely to be objects of criminal harm and thus several variables may be identified which are related to differentials in the probability of victimization.

One such variable is gender. With respect to the types of crimes that victimization surveys measure, it appears that males are more frequently victimized than females and that they are more likely to be the victims of serious crime (Alston, 1986; Brillon, 1987; Eve, 1985; Liang and Sengstock, 1983; Lindquist and Duke, 1982; Ollenburger, 1981). Thus, men tend to outnumber women among victims of assault and robbery while more women than men are victims of personal theft (Hochstedler, 1981; Canada, 1985a). This gender differential in rates of victimization is greater among non-elderly than elderly populations (Brillon, 1987; Colijn, 1981; Alston, 1986).

The probability of victimization is also seen to vary by the marital status of the victim. The relationship is such that those who are married and those who are widowed have the lowest rates of victimization while rates are higher for those who are divorced, separated or never married (Eve, 1985; Liang and Sengstock, 1983).

Racial or economic minority group membership has also been found to be related to increased victimization risks. In the American context, non-whites tend to face significantly greater victimization risks and generally, crime is more likely to threaten the poor than the non-poor (Eve, 1985; Forstan, 1974; Liang and Sengstock, 1983; Ragan, 1977).

To some considerable extent, these racial and economic characteristics may be interpreted as indicators of residential location such that minority areas frequently tend to be high crime areas. As Alston (1986) notes, black burglarly rates are higher than rates for Whites among high income groups quite possibly because pervasive racial discrimination restricts housing opportunities even among the highest income members of racial minorities.

More generally, it is not surprising to discover that elderly residents of high crime rate areas are more likely to be victimized than those who reside in lower risk locations. Thus, rates of elderly victimization are higher in more urban areas (Liang and Sengstock, 1983), in high crime neighborhoods (Morello, 1982; Smith, 1979) and in housing environments which decrease the distance between the aged and minority youth (Gubrium, 1974; Kosberg, 1985). A study of elderly victims in Kansas City Missouri found, for instance, that

171

neighborhood residence could increase the risk of criminal victimization by a factor of eight (Cunningham, 1975). Similarly, Jones' (1977) examination of victimization among the elderly on the "skid row" of Portland Oregon revealed that in this particular setting, older persons tended to be victimized seriously and frequently.

Finally, it should be noted that even among the elderly the risk of victimization decreases with age. Thus, the "young old" - those between the ages of, for instance, 65 and 80 - are more likely to be victimized than those over the age of 80 (Eve, 1985; Liang and Sengstock, 1983).

It should be pointed out that these social and demographic characteristics combine in additive fashion to create substantial disparities in victimization rates across sub-categories of the elderly population. Liang and Sengstock (1983), for example, use National Crime Survey data to argue that, on average, an elderly Black male has a risk of criminal victimization that is three times greater than that of an older Black female and fourteen times greater than an older White female.

The Social Context of Victimization

We have seen that when compared to younger population groups, the elderly are less likely to be victimized and when they are victimized they are more likely to be the objects of economic predation. Data available from victimization surveys indicate that there are some distinctive characteristics of the situations in which elderly victimizations occur. Like all such data, however, they may reflect intentional or unintentional tendencies on the part of respondents to inaccurately recall events.

In contrast with the victimization of younger adults, those involving elderly persons are more likely to occur during the day rather than in the evening (Cook et al., 1981; Richardson, 1975; Liang and Sengstock, 1983). The National Crime Survey, for instance, indicated that about three-fourths of elderly victimizations were daylight occurrences as compared to only one-half of the victimizations involving younger adults (Hochstedler, 1981).

With respect to high risk locations, available data suggest that elderly persons, like younger adults, are most likely to be victimized in open public places (such as the street) but when compared to those younger than themselves, they are somewhat more likely to become victims of crime in a public building or in or near their homes (Hochstedler, 1981; Jones, 1977; Jones, 1987; Liang and Sengstock, 1983; Forstan, 1974). The increase in victimization risk associated with the area around the home seems to be particularly evident in the case of violent crimes such as assault and rape (Antunes et al, 1977; Cook et al, 1981).

Victim Offender Interaction

There is a rich body of social psychological literature which sugges[s] need to be suspicious of the "eyewitness evidence" offered by those who exposed to criminal events (Brannigan, 1984). We also have reason to be cautious in approaching victims' descriptions of those who victimized them. Particularly in serious situations, the trauma of the victimization experience may interfere with the victim's ability to accurately perceive or recall offender characteristics. Nevertheless, we can use the information gathered in victim surveys to "estimate" some of the characteristics of offenders as perceived by their victims.

When compared to younger adults, elderly victims are more likely to report that the people who victimize them are strangers rather than relatives or acquaintances (Cook et al., 1981; Timrots and Rand, 1987). In part, this reflects the nature of the offences to which older people are typically subjected. Crimes like personal theft and robbery, unlike assaults, for example, more typically involve offenders and victims who are unknown to each other.

Like victims of all ages, the elderly report that the vast majority of offenders are male (Hochstedler, 1981) but unlike younger adults, elderly victimization appears to have a considerably greater inter-racial component (Cook et al., 1981; Forstan, 1974); black victims of all ages and elderly white victims are most often the prey of black offenders (Smith, 1979).

The popular assumption that elderly persons are particularly susceptible to the predatory activities of youths, especially those involved in delinquent gangs is only partially supported by the empirical evidence (Alston, 1986). While a number of studies such as Jones' (1977) analysis of victimization on Portland's skid row, Morello's (1982) examination of elderly crime problems in the Bronx and Conklin's (1976) research into robbery patterns in Boston provide data in support of the conclusion that teenage gangs contribute substantially to the volume of elderly victimization, other studies suggest a less extreme view (Cunningham, 1976).

The National Crime Survey data, for instance, suggest that the elderly are not more likely to be the object of gang attacks. Only about one-half of elderly victimizations involve more than one offender; and in such cases, the elderly are typically the target of pairs of offenders, whereas younger victims are more often preyed on by offender groups of three or more (Hochstedler, 1981). These data also indicate that while the elderly, moreso than other adults, fall victim to crimes committed by youth, they are less likely to be victimized by members of this group than are other youths (Antunes et al, 1977; Cook et al., 1981; Hochstedler, 1981; Liang and Sengstock, 1983; Skogan, 1977).

Elderly persons are somewhat more likely than younger people to be alone when victimized and they are less likely than their younger counterparts to be involved in multiple-victim incidents (Hochstedler, 1981).

The National Crime Survey data indicate that weapons are used relatively infrequently in elderly victimization situations and that when weapons are used, they tend not to be firearms (Antunes et al., 1977; Cook et al., 1981; Hochstedler, 1981). Not surprisingly, weapon use is related to the nature of the

173

offence such that elderly victims of robbery are more often confronted by armed offenders than are victims of other types of crimes. Even in the case of robbery, however, it appears that elderly victimizations are less likely to involve the use of a weapon than are robberies of younger victims.

It also appears that, in general, older victims are somewhat less often the objects of physical attacks in the context of victimization incidents and that when attacks do occur they more likely involve male than female victims. The lower probability of physical attack again reflects the age-specific risks associated with particular types of offences. As noted, the elderly are more likely to be victims of offences involving economic predation, while younger victims are more likely to suffer assaults. Hochstedler (1981) reports that in the case of single offenders, elderly victims are attacked less frequently than younger victims and that when multiple offenders are involved the difference between younger and older victims with respect to the likelihood of attack is marginal. Skogan (1977) notes, however, that when elderly robbery victims are attacked by their assailants, much of the violence is "capricious" in that it appears to be unrelated to an immediate instrumental need on the part of the offender to control the behavior of the victim.

The NCS data also indicate that elderly victims are unlikely in the majority of cases to take action intended to protect themselves from an offender (Hochstedler, 1981; Skogan, 1977). Liang and Sengstock (1983) note that the tendency to take preventive action is unrelated to the social and demographic characteristics of the victim and that the probability of engaging in such behavior increases with the seriousness of the offence.

Because the NCS data include information on completed as well as attempted offences, it is possible to make a determination as to whether differences exist with respect to the completion of elderly and non-elderly offences. In general, it appears that crimes against the elderly have a higher completion rate than do crimes against younger persons. Moreover, the data suggest that victimizations are more likely to be completed when the offender is a stranger, when there are multiple offenders, and when the offence is committed in the daytime (Hochstedler, 1981).

Many of these contextual variables such as the presence of a weapon, the use of force, the number of offenders and the level of victim resistance have important implications for the physical and economic injuries which victims sustain. We shall return to this issue in the next chapter.

FRAUD AND THE ELDERLY

Thus far we have been concerned with the patterns of elderly victimization as revealed in victim surveys. As noted, however, general studies of this type are more effective in capturing some types of crimes than others. Elder abuse and neglect, for instance, which are discussed in Chapter 11 may be inadequately tapped by the narrowly focused questions which ususally comprise the victimization survey questionnaire.

In a somewhat similar way, it is sometimes argued that although elderly persons are frequent victims of frauds and cons of various kinds (Geis, 1977;

174

Pepper, 1983) the victim survey does not tap this empirical reality (Johnson and Wasielewski, 1982). There are several reasons for this.

First, many frauds perpetrated against the elderly are in a sense, "perfect crimes" such that they are never defined as crimes by their victims. Consider, for example, those cons which involve the use of high pressure sales tactics to sell to elderly homeowners housing repairs that are overpriced and unecessary (or ultimately never even delivered to the consumer). The homeowner may never realize that he or she has been victimized and thus would not report such an event in the context of a victimization survey.

Second, because most frauds and cons involve the exploitation of elderly persons in their roles as consumers or clients of social or financial agencies, they are forms of victimization that may involve considerable embarrassment on the part of the victim. There is a pervasive sense that people should be aware enough to see through a fraud and that a failure to do so may indicate a lack of critical insight or an inability to exercise proper judgment. Such factors may inhibit the reporting of fraud victimization not only to authorities but also to the survey interviewer.

Third, many frauds involve forms of economic manipulation which may be of questionable ethical character but legal nonetheless. The use, for instance, of sales tactics which appeal to the fears and concerns of older persons or which encourage financial expenditures which the consumer cannot afford may operate quite squarely within the law. As we have seen, however, most victimization surveys focus upon a rather limited range of traditional criminal offences.

To be sure, victim interviews are not the only possible source of information about fraud and the elderly. Data can be and have been gathered from public and private agencies that are responsible for the processing of consumer complaints. Yet, data of this type, like all forms of agency data, may misrepresent the nature of the larger population of cases from which this sample is derived. Elderly persons, for example, may be more reluctant to report such experiences to the police or to consumer complaint agencies and thus appear to be experiencing fewer such problems. Or, they may be reluctant to report any but the most serious forms of victimization which would result in the underrepresentation of less serious cases.

Taken together, these factors suggest that even if the elderly are disproportionately victimized by con operators, our major methodological tools may fail to yield the relevant data. As a result, our knowledge of frauds perpetrated against the elderly is much less systematic than is our knowledge of more traditional criminal offences.

Elmore (1981) has catalogued six major categories of consumer frauds to which it is popularly believed the elderly frequently fall victim:

1. Health and Medical Frauds. These include various forms of medical quackery which involve abuses within the context of the doctor-patient relationship or in the merchandising of drugs, health-aids or insurance.

2. General Merchandising Frauds. This category includes the many and varied consumer frauds operated by unscrupulous business operators such as "bait and switch" advertising and the sale of shoddy and unsafe products.

3. Mail-Order Frauds. Although the mails may be used as a channel for the commission of any type of fraud, there are several which rely upon the impersonal nature of the postal system in order to take unfair advantage of consumers. Thus, mail order schemes frequently preclude comparison shopping and prevent the consumer from developing a familiarity with the product prior to purchase.

4. Income Creation, Protection and Investment Frauds. This category references a variety of "get rich quick" schemes such as pyramid selling, work at home scams and the sale of fraudulent franschises and business opportunities.

5. Social Psychological Frauds. Frauds of this type involve the merchandising of products and services that exploit fears and worries of consumers by unrealistically promising solutions to loneliness or other personal problems.

6. Con Games/Bunco. This includes the full range of traditional bunco operations such as the "pigeon drop", "the bank swindle" and other schemes that tend to be the domain of professional con operators.

The factors which might increase the susceptibility of older persons to all such frauds are well known and were briefly discussed in the preceding chapter. It is argued that the social isolation, the economic precariousness, and the increased physical vulnerability of the aged make them the preferred targets of con operators. However, as stated above, serious measurement problems mitigate against precise statements regarding either the prevalence or the social distribution of this type of elderly victimization.

In the latter respect, it has been argued that women may be more susceptible than men to many of these schemes. This is in part because of the greater longevity of women and their associated tendency to be the beneficiaries of spousal life insurance policies. It is also maintained that the traditional socialization of women has resulted in a lower degree of familiarity with the complexities of many aspects of consumer economies (Block, 1983; Geis, 1977).

Other writers have suggested that residence in a retirement community may increase victimization risk since such areas may serve as "magnets" for fraud operators (Hahn, 1976; Kosberg, 1985).

It may also be the case that many of these frauds and cons shift the burden of crime away from the poor elderly and toward those who are somewhat more affluent since greater access to discretionary income may increase the attractiveness of the potential victim. A number of studies relevant to the victimization of the elderly by consumer fraud have been reviewed by Mc Ghee (1983). Among the conclusions drawn by the author are the following:

1. Elderly persons do not report a greater level of dissatisfaction with consumer services than do younger persons. Quite possibly, however, the high level of satisfaction reported by the elderly may be interpreted as evidence

of an unwillingness to report consumer problems rather than the absence of difficulties in the marketplace.

2. Older and younger consumers do not differ markedly with respect to types of consumer complaints; although, older persons seem somewhat more likely to complain about repairs and a failure to perform services. This difference may reflect the decreased proclivity on the part of elderly consmers to purchase durable goods and an increased tendency to repair and service consumer goods purchased at an earlier point in life.

3. Elderly persons are more likely to be alone when victimized and more likely to be victimized at home by mail order transactions.

4. Elderly victims may be more susceptible to victimizers who are polite, who appear knowledgeable and who are in positions of authority.

5. Older consumers, in general, have a more positive attitude toward businesses and a more tolerant attitude toward ethically marginal business practices.

6. Those elderly persons who are not socially isolated are able to cope more effectively with consumer problems and are more likely to take corrective action when victimization occurs.

Mc Ghee's review suggests that the consumer fraud problems faced by the elderly may be more subtle and more complex than popular stereotypes suggest. Moreover, as the analysis makes clear, there is a need for more rigorous research that would permit informed estimates of the incidence and social location of these victim experiences. In the absence of such research, we risk perpetuating an image that is informed only by anecdote and which often implies, in ageist fashion, that older people are by definition the easy prey of fast-talking con artists.

EXPLAINING GENERAL PATTERNS OF ELDERLY VICTIMIZATION

As we have seen, our best empirical information indicates that when compared to younger population groups, the elderly are less frequently the victims of most personal and household crimes. The important exceptions in this regard concern crimes that appear to have as their primary motivation, economic gain on the part of the offender. Thus, the elderly have relatively high rates of crimes that involve personal theft with contact (such as purse snatching and pocketpicking) and perhaps fraud. With respect to the former type of crime, about which our knowledge is most complete, it appears that older people are likely to be victimized during the daytime and disproportionately in the area around their homes. The offender is often a stranger and the interaction is typically brief and fleeting. The victim rarely resists the predation in any active fashion. The salient issue at this point is to account for these patterns of victimization in some theoretical fashion. The previous chapter discussed the concepts of risk and vulnerability and their potential utility in this regard. Our intention, therefore, is to employ these concepts, within a decision-making framework, in order to render these empirical patterns meaningful.

Elderly Victimization and Risk

One way to approach the problem of elderly victimization is to examine the situations and settings within which categories of crimes occur and to account for the relative degree of involvement of elderly persons in such situations and settings. Thus, the greater the degree of involvement the greater the level of risk and the lower the degree of involvement the lower the risk.

The accumulated body of victimization research quite clearly demonstrates that, in general, the risks of criminal victimization are not randomly distributed across time and space. Personal crimes are most likely to occur in the evening hours and in public places (Hindelang et al., 1978; Canada, 1983b; U.S. Department of Justice, 1981). Those studies which include appropriate measures indicate that the more frequently people engage in evening activities outside the home, the more likely they are to become victims of a variety of personal crimes (Garofalo, 1986). These studies also suggest that some types of evening activities pose greater risks than others. There is potentially greater danger associated with visits to pubs, bars and sporting events than with visits to the homes of friends or relatives or attendance at meetings (Canada, 1987). The "high risk" nature of the former activities in part reflects the fact that such locations tend to be frequented by large numbers of young males who consitute the majority of criminal offenders.

In the case of household crime, there is a striking pattern which involves the correlation between the occurrence of such offences and the level of occupancy of households (Cohen and Felson, 1979). Thus, the greater the tendency for homes to be unoccupied, the higher the risk of household victimization. A low rate of occupancy means that "guardianship" of the home and its possessions is decreased (Cohen and Felson, 1979); and not suprisingly, the absence of occupants is an important choice criterion employed by offenders in the selection of locations to be victmized (Reppetto, 1974). A significant proportion of household victimizations occur in the evening and as in the case of personal crimes, the offenders tend to be young and to be male.

Such empirical observations take us far in our attempt to understand the comparatively low rates of elderly victimization in that they establish a linkage between the social relationships and activities of older persons and their victimization risks. In a preliminary way, we may note that the social relationships in which each of us is involved are in one sense a matter of free choice but in another sense they reflect the opportunities for sociability which our environments make available. Thus, the attachments that we develop to others reflect the influence of residence, economic position, culture, kinship, gender, occupation and class.

Of particular relevance in the present context is the extent to which such relationships are circumscribed by the social realities of age segregation. Relationships more frequently involve those who occupy roughly equivalent positions in the life cycle rather than those who occupy radically different positions (Hindelang et al., 1978). This means that older persons are more likely to associate with other older persons and that within this group, inter- _____ mally be further delimited by gender, occupational, cultural and tions.

178

The overall effect of such patterns of association is to increase the social distance between the elderly and those groups in which criminal offending is most heavily concentrated. Thus, retirees are more likely to know, visit or spend leisure time with other retirees than with teenage males and in so doing, to lower the probability of regular and sustained contact with those who are at high risk with respect to offending. Moreover, as Antunes et al. (1977:324) note, "the elderly typically live alone and have fewer opportunities to become involved in rancorous intra-familial disputes". While the prolonged social relationships in which we engage may increase the probability that others will do us harm, they appear in the case of the elderly - in the aggregate at least - to do the opposite.

An examination of the routine social patterns of the elderly suggests that they less fequently engage in evening activities outside the home; and when they do, their preference is for low- rather than high-risk activities (Golant, 1984). Because older persons are less likely to find themselves in public places at night in the presence of those who statistically resemble typical offenders, they experience a lower rate of exposure to the threat of criminal victimization. Similarly, a greater presence in the home means that elderly housholds are in general subject to greater guardianship which discourages the opportunistic offender.

It is worth noting that the attempts to demonstrate that age differences in rates of victimization are attributable to differences in exposure to risk as measured by, for instance, the number of evening activities have produced inconsistent results. Corrado et al. (1980) used data collected in a victimization survey in Vancouver to try to determine if age differentials in victimization persisted even when variability in the amount of evening acitivity outside the home was held constant. The analysis revealed that age differences in victimization rates remained even after differences in these lifestyle variables were taken into accout. Using NCS data, Miethe et al. (1987) found, however, that evening activity patterns did mediate the effects of relevant demographic variables but only with respect to property crime. Such inconsistencies probably reflect the tendency to use rather crude, aggregate indicators of activity which are not sensitive to variations in the nature of the activities, their community context or the social or demographic characteristics of the associates with whom the activities are undertaken (Garofalo, 1986; Sampson, 1987). Nevertheless, the claim that elderly lifestyles (as manifested in social relationships and routine activities) attenuate victimization risk is both logical and consistent with a large body of empirical evidence.

If the linkages between lifestyle and risk are useful in explaining why older persons are not victimized , they also facilitate our understanding of the conditions under which they do become the objects of criminal harm. We have noted that crimes against the elderly tend to occur in large numbers during the day, in or near the household and that they tend to involve offenders who are strangers. In a sense, these empirical patterns also emerge quite logically from the activities and associations in which older persons routinely engage. We have said that, compared to younger people, the locus of much elderly activity is the home and its immediate vicinity and that involvement in nighttime acitivities is low. Moreover, there is a low probability that they will be victimized by friends and acquaintances, many of whom are themselves elderly. Patterns of

179

victimization, therefore, reflect the spatial, temporal and associational constraints which elderly lifestyles place upon risk.

The crimes to which elderly persons are subjected in such situations - purse snatching and other personal thefts and to a lesser extent robberies - appear to be largely opportunistic in nature. The youthful offenders are interested in an easy and not necessarily a big score. In the case of purses snatched or packages or wallets stolen, the offender depends upon stealth and there is little opportunity for the victim to react. When reactions are possible, the victim behaves in ways that reflect a realistic awareness of disparities in strength and agility, and the willingness to use force. Judged from one perspective, it may appear that the elderly are relatively adept at managing victimization risks. Success in this regard, however, is achieved at certain costs. Victimization risks are low, in part because the elderly reduce their levels of social activity and because the society in which they live is age-segregated. These conditions represent aspects of elderly lifestyle that may themselves be regarded as problematic.

It is worth noting that in many ways the elderly are somewhat freer than younger population groups to manage risk through the avoidance of persons or situations that they may perceive as threatening. This is because, in general, the elderly are less constrained by occupational and work-related roles which sometimes increase the risk of victimization (Conklin, 1975). This gives the aged somewhat greater flexibility in the construction of personal schedules. For example, if it is unsafe to ride the subways in the evening, the retiree, unlike the shiftworker, may exercise the option of not doing so. It has been argued that the smaller disparity between male and female victimization rates among the elderly, as compared to younger populations, is in part attributable to the fact that gender differences which characterize labor force participation are largely eradicated in later life (Alston, 1986; Colijn, 1981).

An issue which may be raised at this point, but which will be addressed more fully in Chapter 10 concerns the extent to which this tendency to circumscribe activities is itself a reaction to the potential for criminal danger. As we will see, however, the fear of crime plays a secondary role in determining how, where and with whom the elderly spend their time. More generally, the avoidance of high-risk activities such as rock concerts or visits to taverns, or the preference for friends from one's own age-cohort reflect age-specific tastes and customs, perceptions of appropriate behavior and the structural limitations placed upon social opportunities.

Elderly Victimization and Vulnerability

We have already discussed the factors which it might reasonably be argued increase the vulnerability of older persons to criminal victimization. These factors include diminished economic resources, the decline in physical strength and agility, the reduction in social participation and the stigmatizing character of aged roles. It has been suggested that as offenders perceive elderly persons as generally less efficacious, they may be encouraged to seek them out.

There is empirical evidence to support such a position. In an innovative study, Grayson and Stein (1981) videotaped persons selected at random walking through one of the highest assault areas of New York City. They subsequently showed the videotapes to offenders who had been incarcerated for assault and asked them to rate the vulnerability of potential victims. The analysis revealed that older persons were most likely to be rated as potential victims and that several physical characteristics such as stride length, body movement and type of walk were interpreted as providing cues to victim vulnerability. In a related way, Mc Ghee (1983:239) has argued that, with respect to elderly consumers, a "lesser sensitivity to deceptive practices and lack of knowledge in complex product-services may predispose them to abusive situations" (Mc Ghee, 1983:239).

Arguments about the unique vulnerability of the elderly may appear to be inconsistent with empirical evidence reviewed earlier in this chapter. We have seen that for most crimes, the elderly have rates of victimization lower than - not higher than - the rest of the population. If the elderly are particularly vulnerable to crime and thus actively sought out by offenders, we might expect that they would be victimized at rates that exceed the rest of the population.

Any attempt to reconcile the argument that older persons are more vulnerable to criminal victimization with the empirical observation that their rates are indeed lower must take into account the reduced level of exposure to risk that is characteristic of elderly lifestyles. In somewhat more complex fashion, we might therefore ask if older persons have a high rate of victimization after their rate of exposure to risk is statistically adjusted or taken into account in some other way. In other words, if we "hold constant" the amount of exposure across age groups, are older persons more likely to be victims of crime than the members of other age groups? If this question is answered in the affirmative then arguments about the greater vulnerability of the elderly would appear to be empirically supported. Correcting rates of victimization for differential patterns of exposure to risk is not, however, a simple matter in that it involves some potentially complex methodological issues. Most notably, we require a suitable measure of exposure and as we have already seen, most attempts to operationalize exposure to victimization risk are rather crude.

There are a few studies which speak to this issue. Lindquist and Duke (1982) utilize an "at-risk" hypothesis to explain the age-decline in victimization rates among a sample of San Antonio victims. Although they do not employ a direct measure of exposure they suggest that combinations of age and gender categories are themselves proxy measures of the degrees to which people risk specific offences such as rape, robbery and assault. While they lack a specific test of the hypothesis, they conclude that:

> the apparent low rate of victimization of the elderly is a function of the analytical techniques used rather than a function of age. We believe that when the extent to which the elderly are "at risk" is taken into consideration, the victimization rate for the elderly will equal or exceed the victimization rate for other age categories (1982:124-125).

Stafford and Galle (1984) utilized National Crime Survey data in order to more directly examine this question. For combinations of age, race and gender categories, Stafford and Galle calculated conventional victimization rates, which were standardized in terms of the size of the population group in question, and adjusted victimization rates, which were standardized in terms of exposure levels. Since the NCS data with which the authors were working did not contain measures of exposure, they obtained these data from another survey which had asked a broad sample of respondents about the amount of time that they spent away from home on weekdays and weekends. The comparison of conventional and adjusted rates allowed some assessment to be made of the degree to which the age-decline in victimization levels was influenced by reductions in levels of risk-exposure. The analysis revealed that for all groups except black males, those over age 65 continued to have the lowest rate of personal victimization even when differences in exposure were taken into account. For black males, the elderly had an unadjusted rate second only to those aged 20 to 24 but when the rates were adjusted, those over 65 had the highest rate. While for other groups, the age-decline in victimization risks persisted even when rates were adjusted, it is important to note that the recalculation diminished the differences between age groups. For white males, for instance, those between the ages of 20 and 24 (who had the highest victimization rate) were four times more likely to be victimized than the elderly. When these rates were adjusted for exposure they were only about twice as likely to be victimized. Similar but less extreme reductions obtained in the case of white and black females.

Skogan (1980) also employed National Crime Survey Data as well as additional data sets to estimate "what would happen if the low levels of exposure to risk typically reported by the elderly (and the high rates recalled by youth) were to shift to an age-independent pattern" (Skogan, 1980:7). Like other researchers, Skogan acknowledges that in the absence of longitudinal or panel data, the conclusions that can be drawn are tentative.

Nonetheless, the analysis is revealing. It suggests that in the case of burglary, when rates are adjusted for a variety of exposure measures, the elderly are not particularly vulnerable to this form of victimization. Instead, they are victimized in an "exposure-adjusted" fashion at about the same rate as other mature adults. Skogan also examined the effects of exposure upon rates of "mugging" (defined in this analysis as robberies and purse-snatchings). He suggests that elderly victimization rates, adjusted for exposure, are lower than those of youths and young adults. However, elderly rates are higher than those of persons between the ages of 30 and 59 implying a weak tendency to be "over-victimized" when patterns of exposure to risk are held constant.

Taken together, these studies reveal that much of what has been written and said about the special vulnerability of the elderly may tend towards hyperbole. In particular, the Stafford and Galle and Skogan studies indicate that while elderly victimization rates, adjusted for exposure, are higher than conventional rates, they do not clearly exceed the rates of younger groups as the vulnerability argument would suggest. The possible exception is Skogan's finding regarding the somewhat greater vulnerability of elderly persons to muggings. In view of the measurement and analytical limitations of these studies, however, it is necessary to draw any general conclusions with caution.

This discussion may alert us to the need in future research to examine not only how the social and economic circumstances of the elderly may increase vulnerability but also how they may reduce it. In other words, there are many ways in which older persons may be less rather than more attractive to

182

offenders. Dominant cultural images of femininity, for instance, may mean that elderly females are less desirable as victims of sexual assault. The tendency of older persons to spend discretionary income on services rather than portable, durable consumer goods may make their homes and possessions less attractive to burglars. While older persons may be preferred targets of young opportunistic pursesnatchers, they may because of their reduced incomes, be less desirable targets of older, more experienced robbers. The lack of economic resources may also decrease the probability that they will be the preferred quarry of professional con and swindle operators (Alston, 1986; Yin, 1985).

CONCLUSION

This chapter has discussed the disparity between the rhetoric of crisis regarding the criminal victimization of the elderly and the empirical dimensions of that problem as revealed in the findings of victim surveys. We have seen that when they are compared to other age groups, older persons in general experience lower levels of victimization. The discussion has also documented the crimes which most frequently victimize the old and the ways in which these risks are distributed across sub- groups of the elderly population. The patterns which these studies reveal have been intepreted in terms of the risks and vulnerabilities that characterize later life.

Within the social science community, reactions to the apparent disjunction between popular and criminological knowledge regarding criminal victimization of the elderly has been mixed.

According to some commentators, any insistence that older persons are plagued by serious crime problems when the evidence suggests that they may not be, is clear proof of an ageist tendency to perpetuate a stereotyped view of older persons as a burden with which the rest of us must deal.

Others have claimed that direct victimization may never have been the problem and there is a need to focus more attention upon the ways in which the elderly are indirectly affected by a pervasive fear of crime. Other critics have maintained that a demonstration that the elderly are victimized less often misses the essential point. Their position is that the elderly are less able to cope with the consequences of even minor victimizations, and thus the burden of crime affects them disproportionately. This claim, which requires detailed attention, is examined in the next chapter.

CHAPTER EIGHT: RECOMMENDED READINGS

Antunes, G.E., F.L. Cook, T.D. Cook and W.G. Skogan
1977 Patterns of Personal Crime against the Elderly: Findings from a National Survey. The Geronotologist, 17:321-327.

Canada
1985 Canadian Urban Victimization Survey: Victimization of Elderly Canadians. Ottawa: Ministry of the Solicitor General.

Cook, F.L. and T.D. Cook
1976 Evaluating the Rhetoric of Crisis. Social Service Review, 50:632-646.

Cunningham, C.L.
1975 Pattern and Effect of Crime Against the Aging: The Kansas City Study. in J. Goldsmith and S.S. Goldsmith (Eds.). Crime and the Elderly. Lexington Mass.: D.C. Heath. pp. 31-50.

Eve, S.B.
1985 Criminal Victimization and Fear of Crime among the Non-Institutionalized Elderly in the United States. Victimology, 10:397-409.

Liang, J. and M.C. Sengstock
1981 The Risk of Personal Victimization among the Aged. Journal of Gerontology, 36:463-471.

Skogan, W.G. and M.G. Maxfield
1981 Coping with Crime. Beverly Hills: Sage Publications.

CHAPTER NINE

THE COSTS OF ELDERLY VICTIMIZATION

INTRODUCTION

What occurs in the aftermath of criminal vicitmization? How do individuals assess the problems that victimization has created for them and how do they cope with these problems? Thus far in our examination of criminal victimization of the elderly we have focused upon the determinants and the content of victimization experiences. We have discussed the rates of such crimes and their distributional properties but we have not been concerned with the consequences which flow from them. This is the principal issue considered in the present chapter.

We have observed that much of the popular wisdom regarding crimes against the elderly is not supported by empirical data. Both the levels and the types of elderly victimization are somewhat different than the "rhetoric of crisis" would lead us to expect. Yet, it might be argued that even if the elderly are victimized less often and less seriously than the members of other age groups, the issue of elderly victimization may remain a serious one due to the unique problems which criminal victimization creates for older persons (Cook and Cook, 1976; Skogan, 1977). This implies that the elderly, in general, may suffer more from criminal victimization than others (Eve, 1985). In statistical terms, this amounts to a hypothesis of an "interaction effect" involving victimization and age such that the effects of the former variable are dependent upon categories of the latter (Berg and Johnson, 1979; Fattah, 1984).

There are several reasons why we might expect the costs of victimization to be more severe for older persons. First, we know that, as a group, the elderly have fewer economic resources than do younger segments of the population. As a result, the economic costs of even relatively minor property crimes may be exacerbated (Cook and Cook, 1976). Liang and Sengstock's (1983) analysis of National Crime Survey data, for instance, revealed that among elderly victims only a very small proportion were insured for the losses that they had sustained or were able to recover cash or property stolen.

185

Second, although older persons tend to be in generally good health, they are more likely to suffer from chronic ailments. This could mean that any physical injuries sustained in victimization may require a longer and more difficult recovery period. Thus, being pushed or jostled during a purse snatching or robbery could result in greater suffering for older than for younger people (Cook et al., 1978).

It is also the case that the elderly are somewhat more likely than the non-elderly to live alone or to be socially isolated in other ways. This could imply that much of the trauma associated with serious victimization must be endured in the absence of social support which might mitigate the psychological distress that victimization creates.

Further, because older people feel more vulnerable, they may be less able to effectively seek redress for crimes committed against them. They may feel less competent in any attempt to identify an offender to the police, to use the courts or to seek some other forms of legal or social assistance. To the extent that the mobilization of social control helps people deal with the effects of victimization, the elderly may be at a distinct disadvantage.

Finally, the elderly may have a more traditional understanding of the problem of criminal victimization and may as a result internalize some considerable degree of self-blame for what has happened to them. This may complicate the social and psychological adjustments which individuals attempt to make in the post-victimization phase.

Consistent with themes developed earlier, we attempt in this chapter to determine whether popular claims regarding the severity of the effects of elderly victimization are warranted. We proceed by first describing some of the major criteria according to which "the costs of victimization" may be identified.

ESTIMATING THE COSTS OF VICTIMIZATION

It will become apparent in our discussion that there are very real methodological problems involved in any attempt to come to terms with the theoretical and empirical issues that are of interest to us in this context. Most generally, these problems concern the conceptualization and operationalization of "victimization cost" (Canada, 1984c).

Perhaps the most fundamental problem is one of specification. The difficulty here relates to the ambiguity regarding the measurement processes by which the concept of victimization cost should be circumscribed. In other words, what should and what should not be considered a cost of victimization?

An extended example will clarify the nature and the implications of the specification problem. Suppose that an elderly woman, walking in the area near is victimized by a young offender who approaches her from behind The force of the physical confrontation pushes the cause the woman in question was on her way to pay g $500 in cash in her purse. It would seem quite e missing $500 as a cost of victimization and it would to that sum the cost of the purse and the replacement

186

cost of the documents contained in the wallet. Although, most researchers would agree that these costs are directly attributable to the victimization, there might be less agreement regarding the following expenditures:

1. The experience has impressed upon the victim that there may really be a serious crime problem in her neighborhood. For a long time she has been considering the purchase of a deadbolt lock for her apartment door and the incident has served as a catalyst with respect to that purchase. Should the cost of the lock and its installation be added to the other victimization costs?

2. The victim is so distressed by the attack that she phones her sister who has always been a very supportive person. Because her sister lives in another part of the country, the call involves long-distance charges. Is the cost of the call a victimization cost?

3. Not unexpectedly, the victim becomes curious as to whether or not attacks like the one that she has experienced have happened to other people in the community. While she never did so before, she begins to buy the local newspaper. Is it legitimate to consider the cost of the newspaper a cost of victimization?

4. Because of the incident, the victim no longer hand delivers her rent money. This means that she now must pay postage and banking charges that she did not previously pay. Moreover, because her cheques have on occasion been lost in the mail, she has been assessed a penalty by her landlord. Again, these costs would not have been incurred if the victim had not been victimized in the first place.

5. When she fell to the ground, the victim sustained minor physical injuries which resulted in some medical costs not covered by her health insurance. Are these victimization costs as well?

It should be made clear that there are no right or wrong answers regarding the inclusion or exclusion of these costs. In essence, the issue revolves around our judgments regarding how broadly or how narrowly we wish to assess victimization impact (Burt and Katz, 1985). The problems that we confront in this regard are underscored by the fact that the financial impact of victimization is pehaps the least difficult type of cost to estimate, given the convenience of the counting units involved. Thus, the attempt to specify the boundaries of physical, psychological or behavioral costs of criminal victimization is rendered even more difficult because of the somewhat more abstract nature of the domains of interest. In all cases, however, estimates of victimization costs are made according to assumptions about what is to be and what is not to be included in such an estimate.

It should also be pointed out that there may be significant ideological dimensions to the estimation procedures (Elias, 1986). In the above example, for instance, it is unclear whether some of the items represent direct costs of the victimization or instead, costs levied by public and private agencies upon victims who are attempting to respond to the victimization. For example, if a retailer in the private security industry is able to effectively exploit victims' fears by charging exorbitant prices for deadbolt locks (or other security equipment), we must ask whether the retailer's profit should be considered a victimization cost. Similarly, the attempt on the part of the crime victim to follow the legal prosecution of his or her victimizer may require taking time off work, hiring a babysitter and arranging transportation. If the victim makes repeated appearances in court because bureaucratic inefficiency halts the progress of the trial, we might suggest that the justice system contributes practically to the cost of being victimized.

What should be clear from the above example is that any attempt to develop an inclusive definition of victimization costs is likely to be hampered by the reseacher's inability to know in advance what types of questions to ask about what types of costs. The economic, physical and social effects of victimization may be subtle and far reaching and it is extremely difficult to anticipate fully and accurately the extent and nature of these effects. The pragmatic response taken by many researchers has been to concentrate attention upon the most visible and most immediate costs to the victim. As a result, we risk losing perspective on the ways in which victimization might create hardship. In particular, the research literature has been generally more attentive to the short-run rather than the long- term costs that criminal victimization might create (Fattah, 1979).

It may also be worth noting that the term, "cost" itself constrains our analysis in particular ways in that it focuses our attention upon the negative impact of criminal victimization to the exclusion of potentially functional consequences. While it is true that victimization is, in the main, an event that produces undesirable effects, it should be recognized that the analytical emphasis upon costs closes off in an *a priori* manner the search for positive outcomes. The argument that victimization may produce some benefits in addition to its costs will be considered later in this chapter.

Before proceeding to a discussion of empirical data relevant to the costs of victimization, it may be advantageous to describe briefly the major forms that these costs are generally said to take.

Financial Costs

As the previous discussion made clear, financial loss is one of the most obvious types of victimization costs. If an individual is the victim of a robbery, theft, burglary, vandalism or any one of a variety of other offences, it is reasonable to speak of a direct financial impact.

As stated, there may be indirect financial costs as well. These are recognized, for instance, in those cases in which a physical assault or court appearance results in lost work time.

In view of what was said in the previous chapter, however, it is important to recall that very frequently people may not be aware what crime has cost or is costing them. This may be particulary true with respect to the variety of frauds committed against the elderly which remain undetected even by their victims.

Physical Costs

The major concern with crimes of violence is that they impose physical costs upon their victims. In addition to whatever financial loss may occur there is in cases of rape, assault and homicide, pain and injury as well.

As with financial costs, there may also be less obvious physical costs. The injuries sustained in violent encounters may exacerbate existing health problems (Main and Johnson, 1978). Or, physical injury may make it more difficult for an individual to exercise or meet appropriate nutritional requirements and therefore interfere with health needs (Alston, 1986).

While we can, in a general way, recognize levels of physical cost, such that a broken bone is more "costly" than a laceration, there is not, as in the case of financial loss, an easy and convenient metric for the standardization of physical costs.

Psychological Costs

To the extent that criminal victimization is a traumatic life experience, it may have severe repercussions for the ways in which people feel and for the ways in which they perceive the world (Berg and Johnson, 1979; Fattah, 1979; Janoff-Bulman, 1985; Sykes and Johnson, 1985).

Particularly pertinent in this regard are the ways in which such experiences may contribute to a sense of personal vulnerability, a perceived lack of safety, depression and feelings of helplessness. Such reactions suggest that victimization may be understood as a source of psychological stress which, in the extreme, may undermine personal adjustments to the victimization experience.

The psychological costs of criminal victimization may also be exacerbated by the actions of criminal justice officials, who show insensitivity to the needs and concerns of the victims, and by cumbersome bureaucratic procedures which increase victims' anxieties about themselves and their experiences (Canada, 1984c).

That such psychological costs are not as obvious or as easily measurable as those of a financial or physical nature does not deny their empirical reality.

Behavioral Costs

If victimization makes people fearful, or if such experiences depress and sadden them, we would expect that these mental states would be given a variety of behavioral expressions. Thus, people may not merely feel fearful, they may act fearfully.

There is however, good reason for maintaining a distinction between the social psychological and the behavioral; and thus for analyzing differences in behavior independent of perceptions. Few of us, after all, are completely free to act on the basis of our perceptions and moods and must frequently conform

189

to requirements of the situations in which we find ourselves, the organizations to which we belong and the social roles which we occupy.

We might anticipate several distinctive behavioral reactions among those who have been victimized (DuBow et al, 1979). They might engage in **target hardening**, that is purchasing or installing new locks or lights in order to prevent the reoccurrence of victimization. They might engage in **avoidance behavior**, such as avoiding contact with strangers, staying home in the evening or taking taxis rather than walking to local stores.

In a similar way, feelings of depression and paranoia may manifest themselves in terms of a withdrawl from social networks or an increasing disengagement from normal patterns of activity. Social life may become more difficult as the assumptions of trust upon which it is predicated are increasingly defined by the victim as untenable.

It should be clear that the distinctions that we have made among various types of victimizaton costs are conceptually valuable although the empirical realities which they are intended to describe are not as clearly distinguishable. When a victim pauses to turn on an alarm purchased in response to a burglary, we may have evidence of both a financial and a behavioral cost of that vicitimization. When physical injuries sustained in an assault lead to physical pain and depression, we may recognize costs that are not easily separable. As is always the case, the empirical world is not as uncomplicated as our conceptual categories would imply.

THE EMPIRICAL INVESTIGATION OF VICTIMIZATION COSTS

Most of the data that allow us to make assessments about the costs of elderly victimization come, not surprisingly, from victim surveys. The use of survey methodologies for the purpose of investigating such issues normally involves one of two analytical strategies.

The first strategy employs survey questions specifically designed to elicit from respondents detailed information about their victimizations. Respondents may be asked to indicate the amount of cash or the value of goods stolen or vandalized. Or, they may be asked about the nature and extent of injuries sustained as a result of a victimization episode. Data acquired in this way are subject to all of the usual limitations regarding faulty memory and all of the other factors that intentionally or unintentionally undermine the accuracy of the information. Such an approach, as previously stated, also tends to proceed from a rather narrow and short-sighted understanding of victimization costs in that it focuses analytical attention upon costs directly incurred during or in the period immediately following the victimization (Burt and Katz, 1985). Moreover, because the approach begins with a rather definite notion of what relevant costs are, it prevents a comprehensive view of the phenomenology of victimization as a source of hardship.

A variation on this analytical theme involves the attempt to elicit from respondents, perceptions, attitudes or behaviors that they believe have changed as a result of the victimization experience. Thus, if we are interested in determining the way in which the respondent has changed as a result of the victimization we may conclude that the most direct means of doing so is to ask the victim about these changes.

The simplicity of such an approach may make it a desirable option, but it is also open to criticism. First, since such investigations usually involve reports of behavior rather than direct observations of behavior, they do not truly tell us how behavior has changed; more correctly, they tell us how people perceive their behavior to have changed. Second, even when these perceptions are accurate, the respondent's claim that the victimization episode is the source of the change may be inaccurate. People do not always have insight into their own behavior and it is important not to confuse the reasons which they give to explain their behavior with the causes of their behavior (Nettler, 1984).

An alternative strategy is to compare victims and non-victims with respect to their relative scores on measures thought by the researcher to represent various types of victimization costs. Thus, the analyst might compare victims and non-victims with respect to their feelings of personal safety and discover that overall, those who have been victimized are significantly more concerned about their personal security. The obvious conclusion to be drawn is that victimization experiences decrease feelings of safety.

Such a conslusion, however, may be inaccurate if we are unable to specify the temporal ordering of the variables of interest. Since most victimization surveys yield cross-sectional rather than longitudinal data, they do not allow unequivocal judgments to be made about causal order. This means that to find that victims are more depressed than non-victims does not prove that victimization leads to depression any more than it proves that depression leads to victimization.

It should also be recalled that victimization surveys usually only ask about criminal victimizations experienced within some specified reference period. As a result, respondents whose victimization experiences occur prior to the reference period are considered, for analytical purposes, as non-victims (Hough, 1985). If the effects of victimization are enduring and if, for instance, many such non-victims are depressed as a result of victimizations occurring prior to the reference period, the strength of the relationship between being victimized and being depressed will be inaccurately specified (Dubow et al, 1979).

Financial Costs of Elderly Crime

Material reviewed in the previous chapter indicated that the crimes most frequently committed against the elderly are those that involve some form of material deprivation. Because older victims are "preyed upon" we might expect financial loss to be a particularly salient aspect of elderly victimization. Because the estimation of economic impact involves the use of a convenient measure, the immediate losses which result from victimization may be easily ascertained by simply asking victims to describe these losses.

Cook and Cook (1976) and their colleagues (Cook et al., 1981; Cook et al., 1978) have used National Crime Survey data to investigate differentials in the economic impact of victimization upon elderly and non-elderly victims of personal and household crime. Their analyses focus upon three types of estimation of financial loss:

1. **absolute loss** which refers to the unadjusted loss of cash and property

2. **net loss** which exludes the portion of the loss that is either recovered or for which the victim is reimbursed by, for instance, private insurance plans

3. **catastrophic loss** which is somewhat arbitrarily defined in operational terms as financial losses in excess of one month's income.

With respect to household crimes (burglary and household theft), an examination of the 1973 and 1974 NCS data revealed that when absolute losses are considered, those victims over the age of 65 did not appear to suffer disproportionately (Cook et al., 1978). With respect to both types of household crimes, elderly victims were at or near the bottom of each dollar loss category. An examination of net losses suggests a somewhat different perspective on the issue, however. In general, the data indicate some curvilinearity in the relationship between age and loss. The greatest net losses were experienced by the youngest and the oldest members of the sample; yet, the elderly victims experienced losses somewhat below those of the youngest victims. In the case of catastrophic loss, rates were again highest among the youngest crime victims. As in the case of net loss, the percentage of catastrophic losses decreased with age until later life at which point it began to rise again.

With respect to personal crimes (robbery, theft with and without contact and assault), the data indicate that teenagers experienced the smallest losses in absolute terms but that among adults, losses were lowest among the elderly. An analysis of net and catastrophic losses resulting from personal crime reveals that these measures do not vary significantly across age categories.

Overall, these findings reveal that with respect to the types of financial loss that are measured in the National Crime Survey data, the elderly do not experience financial costs from criminal victimization that are indicative of an extreme susceptibility. When absolute losses are considered, they lose the same or less than other adults; and when losses are adjusted for income, they lose the same or more than other adults.

Data from the Canadian Urban Victimization Survey provide a picture of the costs of elderly victimization that is largely consistent with the findings of the NCS studies (Canada, 1984c; 1985b; 1986). In general, in the seven cities surveyed during the year 1982, victims of all ages lost $211,500,000 in unrecovered cash and property; $41,900,000 in damage to property; and a further $7,000,000 in associated medical expenses and lost wages. Overall, financial losses were sustained in 70% of the total incidents, in 59% of the personal incidents and in 78% of the household incidents.

With respect to aggregated incident categories, the CUVS data indicate that elderly victims, on average, do not suffer gross financial losses in excess of those experienced by other age groups. When these losses are standardized in terms of income, however, the rate of loss of older persons is approximately twice that of others. The relationship between age and economic loss is not significantly affected when loss recovery is taken into account. Thus the mean net dollar loss for the elderly is almost twice that of the 50 to 59 age group which sustained the next highest loss level. It will be recalled that with respect to household crime, the NCS data indicated the existence of a curvilinear relationship between age and net loss adjusted for income. It is not possible to detect a similar trend in the Canadian data since the analysis combines household and personal incidents.

Despite these relatively subtle differences, however, it seems that the same general lesson emerges from both the American and the Canadian data. The direct economic costs that victimization imposes upon elderly persons do not seem to result primarily from the fact that elderly victims are the objects of "big scores". This is after all consistent with our knowledge of the types of offenders who prey upon them and the types of crime to which they are subjected. It will be recalled that offenders are typically unprofessional opportunists and that the crimes typically involve purses snatched and pockets picked. Instead, the relevant research would seem to indicate that the economic problems which victimization creates for the elderly are rooted in the economically precarious positions that they occupy in society. While the losses sustained by elderly victims may be smaller or about the same as those experienced by younger victims, they impinge more dramatically upon the diminished economic resources of older persons.

It must also be recalled that these data do not speak to a variety of offences which result in the economic predation of elderly persons. Most particularly, they leave unaddressed the losses incurred through frauds and other forms of economic exploitation to which reference has already been made.

Nor do these data inform us regarding the potentially numerous other secondary economic costs that criminal victimization might impose upon older persons. We learn nothing of the extent to which economic resources might have been diverted away from other priorities and toward the purchase of hardware or services intended to alleviate the anxieties associated with the victimization experience.

Physical Costs of Elderly Victimization

By all accounts, the vast majority of criminal victimizations involve offences against property rather than against persons. National Crime Survey data indicate that although one in four American households was "touched by crime" in 1986, only one in thirteen was touched by a "crime of high concern" - rape, robbery, assault or burglarly committed by a stranger (U.S. Department of Justice, 1987). Moreover, in a typical year, most of these high concern crimes involve burglaries rather than personal crimes (Karmen, 1984). Even in the case of personal crimes, the overwhelming majority do not result in physical injury. Bulmer's analysis of personal crimes described in the NCS data, for example, revealed that in general, only 23% of theft-related and 29% of nontheft-related crimes resulted in injuries to victims. We have already seen that when the elderly are victimized they tend to be preyed upon rather than treated as objects of violence. We might expect, therefore, that in a comparative sense, physical injury may be a lesser problem for elderly as compared to younger victims. Alternatively, however, it is recognized that the greater physical frailty of the elderly might increase their sensitivity to the use of phys-

193

ical force and thereby exacerbate their propensity to injury. Fortunately, there is a large body of empirical evidence that speaks to these issues.

Analyses of National Crime Survey data indicate that of all age groups, the elderly are the least likely to be attacked in the context of a criminal victimization but that when they are attacked, they are one of the groups most likely to be injured (Blumberg, 1979; Cook et al., 1978; Cook et al., 1981; Hochstedler, 1981; Liang and Sengstock, 1983). Elderly males are more likely than elderly females to be attacked but less likely to be injured if attacked (Hochstedler, 1981). The nature of the injuries suffered by older people are also found to differ from those incurred by more youthful victims. Elderly victims are less likely to experience knife or gunshot wounds or broken bones and more likely to receive bruises, scratches, cuts and blackened eyes. Although victims over the age of 40 are more likely than younger victims to require medical care, the elderly are least likely to require medical attention.

Not surprisingly, elderly victims are most likely to receive their injuries in the context of a robbery (Hochstedler, 1981). However, the injuries sustained in such incidents are not markedly different from those of younger age groups "even when differences in attack patterns are taken into account" (Skogan, 1978:7).

The findings of the National Crime Survey are largely consistent with those of other victim studies such as the Canadian Urban Victimization Survey (Canada, 1984c; 1985b). The Canadian survey results show that elderly victims had a comparatively low rate of physical injury; and, that slightly fewer elderly victims of personal violent crime suffered injury as a result of their victimizations than did younger victims. These studies reveal that while the elderly may be less likely to suffer physical attack (particularly serious physical attack), they may be somewhat more sensitive to the effects of these attacks. It may appear, therefore that the physical costs which criminal victimization imposes upon the elderly may be only marginally greater than those borne by other age groups. Again, however, these data may tell only part of a much more complex story.

First, such data do not describe age variations in the periods of recovery associated with patterns of injury (Skogan, 1977). While the physical, like the economic costs of criminal victimization may erode over time (Hough, 1985), it is not at all clear that these processes occur as rapidly for older as for younger victims (Burt and Katz, 1985; Main and Johnson, 1978).

Second, the effects of physical injury may be long-term and subtle - a consideration not normally taken into account by victimization surveys. Physical injury may complicate existing health conditions and reduce the ability to function independently (Burt and Katz, 1985). A study by Feinberg (1981) of elderly victims referred to a victims' compensation program supports this observation. She found that aside from obvious injuries, some of the victims reported that additional problems such as heart ailments or hypertension had worsened and that they were less able to carry out certain daily activity patterns such as shopping or cooking.

Third, because the range of offences covered in victim surveys is normally restricted, this means that many forms of physical injury resulting from criminal

194

victimization are neglected. For instance, it is frequently claimed that the elderly may be particularly vulnerable to medical fraud and quackery (Elmore, 1981). The consequences of such victimization may be to deflect the elderly away from more traditional forms of medical treatment which hold greater promise for the amelioration of medical problems (Smith, 1979).

Finally, it should be noted that the physical costs of victimization are intricately bound up in complex ways with other problems which victimization creates. The psychological stress which results from the victimization experience may result in physical problems (Coakley and Woodford-Williams, 1979). Similarly, the physical costs of elderly victimization may exert substantial economic impact. Cook et al. (1978) found that although the elderly were not more likely to receive medical care with an associated dollar charge, the charges which older persons did incur represented a substantially higher portion of their monthly incomes.

The Psychological and Emotional Costs of Elderly Victimization

To what extent does the victimization experience impair the mental well-being and the perceived quality of life of victims? Admittedly, the data available to answer this question are somewhat more ambiguous than in the case of physical and psychological costs owing in part to the generally more amorphous nature of the effects in question (Burt and Katz, 1985). The area is, however, one that has attracted considerable research attention.

Sykes and Johnson (1985) utilized data from a general victim survey of Kentucky residents to examine the relationship between victimization and a measure of psychological depression. The analysis revealed that in households touched by crime, both victims and those who resided with victims were likely to score higher on the depression scale. Further, they found that depression scores were higher in households that had experienced a violent crime than in those that had experienced a crime against property. Data from a partial replication of the Canadian Urban Victimization Survey, which was conducted in Edmonton Alberta, indicated that about three-fourths of crime victims suffered emotional or physical reactions following the incident (Canada, 1987). The most common reaction to violent victimization was anger although a substantial minority reported feeling anxious, nervous or confused. Feinberg's study, which focused upon elderly victims, suggests a wide array of psychological consequences including an increased reliance upon tranquilizers and heightened feelings of nervousness and sleeplessness. Victims were also more likely to report disliking loud noises, having bad dreams, forgetfulness and a loss of appetite.

Perhaps the most frequently discussed aspect of the psychological cost of criminal victimization relates to the way in which the experience impacts upon feelings of personal safety. As we will see in the next chapter, older persons whether they have been victimized or not, are somewhat more likely than younger persons to be afraid of crime. For present purposes, however, we are not interested in attempting to explain why the elderly have a higher level of fear (depsite their lower victimization rate) but only in attempting to determine the ways in which victimization affects feelings of personal safety.

195

Early victimization studies tended to cast doubt upon the significance of the relationship between victimization experience and feelings of personal insecurity. In general, the lack of a relationship in this regard has been explained as a methodological artifact that emerges out of inconsistent and inappropriate operationalizations of the independent variable (DuBow et al., 1979; Fattah, 1979). In other words, when researchers looked at very crude categories comprised of "victims" and "non-victims" they obscured important differences between categories of victims. As we have said, the vast majority of victim experiences are "non-serious" and involve thefts and other crimes against property. Many of these crimes are not significant life-events and do not have profound influence upon perceptions of self or society. However, when we examine the smaller number of offences which do involve an actual or potential assault upon personal safety, a relationship between criminal victimization and fearfulness quite clearly emerges (Canada, 1983b; 1987; Elias, 1986; Eve, 1985; Fattah,1979; Smith, 1976; Sykes and Johnson, 1985).

More central to the present discussion is the degree to which the relationship between victimization and fear of crime is given unique expression in elderly populations. The Canadian Urban Victimization Survey yields data which address this issue (Canada, 1985b). That study, like several that we will review in the next chapter, discovered that older people were more likely to be concerned about their personal safety than younger people, that females were more fearful than males and that victims were more fearful than non-victims. The most fearful respondents were elderly women who had recently been victims of violent crimes. However, the data also indicated that the size of the effect of victimization upon fear did not increase with advancing age. In other words, the level of fear exhibited by elderly female victims represented the additive effects of being elderly, being female and being victimized rather than an interaction among these variables. In contrast, the analysis of NCS data by Cook et al. (1981) suggests that victimization may have a stronger effect upon fear for elderly as opposed to younger people. Thus, although victimization influences perceptions of safety at all age levels, it does so more strongly when the victims are older.

The social psychological processes by which victimization affects feelings of safety has been explored by a number of writers. Lejeune and Alex (1973) who conducted in-depth interviews with mugging victims in New York argued that the victimization experience results in a "vulnerability conversion" which dramatically transforms perceptions of self and the environment. Thus, the mugging is interpreted by the victim as symbolizing the degree to which the individual is a potential target and "an environment previously perceived as benign has become a jungle" (1973:273). They argue that although the resulting insecurity about personal safety may be generalized, it is most closely associated with the time, place and circumstances of the victimization incident. Similarly, drawing on a broad body of literature, Perloff (1983) maintains that the consequence of negative life events such as ciminal victimization is to shatter illusions of invulnerability. She suggests that such experiences force people to see the world as a dangerous place and require them to come to terms with their own mortality. In addition, Perloff argues, the new sense of vulnerability may extend to the victim's friends and relatives. Janoff-Bulman (1985) like Perloff and Lejeune and Alex maintains that the long- term effect of victimization may be to undermine basic beliefs about social life and that the attempt to cope with

196

victimization "involves rebuilding shattered assumptions about the world and oneself" (1985:508).

Berg and Johnson (1979) argue that the anxiety about personal safety, which criminial victimization promotes, along with associated feelings of depression, helplessness and mistrust coalesce into a "victim role". According to Berg and Johnson, the victim role, like all social roles, is learned in the context of interaction with significant others who define the content of the role and attempt to ensure conformity to its normative requirements. Thus, the acquisition of the role involves social processes which encourage victims "to act like persons who have been violated or compromised" (1979:60)

Berg and Johnson go on to suggest that all of those who undergo victim experiences may not be equally likely to embrace the victim role. Instead, there is a greater likelihood that those who occupy positions of powerlessness within a stratified society will view the victim role as a logical extension of their place in the social order. Berg and Johnson maintain that the elderly and women are among those most likely to acquire the victim role and to exhibit role-related behavior and attitudes.

It would be inappropriate to conclude a consideration of the psychological costs of victimization without some reference to the ways in which psychological and emotional stress may be exacerbated by the very agencies which (ostensibly at least) are intended to help victims deal with the victimization experience. Criminal justice and social service agencies have frequently been criticized for their insensitivity to the needs of victims and for their collective tendency to treat victims of crime as irrelevant to justice processes.

Since the police are the only agency with whom many victims come into contact, it is not surprising that they have most frequently been the brunt of criticism in this respect. It has been suggested, for instance, that the police are too frequently uninformed about victim services (Sykes, 1976; Alston, 1986; Hamel, 1979). It has also been argued that certain bureaucratic procedures (such as the failure of the police to return to victims stolen merchandise which is required for evidence) are frequently a source of victim frustration (Canada, 1985b). Further, the professional attitude which the police adopt in the investigation of reported victimizations may be interpereted by many elderly persons as non-supportive and insensitive (Arcuri, 1981). Although elderly persons generally have positive attitudes towards the police (Alston, 1986; Canada, 1985b), there is some evidence to suggest that contact with the police reduces these favorable attitudes.

In Chapter 12 we will return to a discussion of the problems that characterize the relationship between elderly victims and criminal justice officials. For the moment, it is important to note that these relationships sometimes add insult to the emotional and psychological injury of criminal victimization.

The Behavioral Costs of Elderly Victimization

There are several different ways in which behavioral reactions to crime may be categorized. Dubow et al. (1979), however, suggest a fivefold typology that is particularly useful:

1. **Avoidance.** This includes behavior by which the victim intends to distance him- or herself from those persons and situations which are perceived as a potential source of criminal harm (Lejeune and Alex, 1973). Thus, as a result of having been victimized, the individual may go out less in the evening, take taxis instead of walking in the neighborhood, and avoid contact with strangers (Fattah, 1979; Feinberg, 1981). In extreme cases, the victim may change residences (Skogan and Maxfield, 1981).

2. **Home Protection.** The measures subsumed under this category represent a wide range of "target hardening" practices (Conklin, 1975) intended to make the household more resistant to victimization (Sengstock and Liang, 1977). These may include, for instance, the installation of new locks or lights which are supposed to deter potential offenders by increasing the level of household surveillance. Fences may be built, burglar alarms installed or neighbors asked to remain vigilant.

3. **Self-Protection.** Victims may purchase or begin to carry a gun or some other type of impromptu weapon such as a hatpin or keys clenched firmly between the fingers (Elias, 1986). Alternatively, they may take instruction in judo or one of the other martial arts (Cohn et al., 1978). Self-protection may involve more subtle and less militaristic responses. People may engage in behaviors expressive of a "street savy" (Riger et al., 1982). In this way, they may attempt to affect their demeanor in public so as to be more aware of themselves and their surroundings and more sensitive to cues to criminal danger.

4. **Communicative Behavior.** Victims may respond to vicitmization by becoming increasingly vocal about their experiences (Lejeune and Alex, 1973). They may attempt to construct the social meaning of the victimization and in so doing elicit from others similar accounts which validate or modify their own understanding of the event.

5. **Collective Participation.** This refers most obviously to involvement in community-based organizations relevant to crime control (Skogan and Maxfield, 1981). Thus, the victim may occasionally attend the meetings of or become an active participant in police-sponsored community-based crime prevention programs such as Operation Identification or Neighborhood Watch. Alternatively, the individual may respond to victimization by seeking affiliation with one of the victim support or victims' rights groups which have rapidly prolifierated during the last several years.

This typology, is meant to describe reactions to rather than costs of victimization. The former term is descriptive while the latter implies some form of evaluation of the behavior in question. Thus while it would be appropriate to designate a behavior a cost if it is thought to reduce the quality of life, it would seem inappropriate to so so if the behavioral change resulted in benefits to the victim that in some sense outweigh the negative impact of the crime. Quite obviously, the distinction proceeds from a particular set of value judgements about which there may be disagreement. Moreover, it is also the case that arguments about "net costs" and "net benefits" cannot be made with any degree of precision. Still, it is important to recognize that, as stated earlier, the effects of victimization may be positive as well as negative.

Feinberg (1981) found, for instance, that the elderly victims that she studied tended to be people who before their victimization experiences were likely to be socially isolated; and that the effect of the victimization was to mobilize friends and relatives and thus, in the short run at least, reduce the level of isolation. The analysis of the reports of mugging victims by Lejeune and Alex (1973) revealed that many of them were able to achieve some degree of celebrity by recounting their experiences and thus proving that he or she has been "where the action is" (Lejeune and Alex, 1973:279). Additionally, Cohn et al. (1978) suggest that reactions to crime which involve the acquisition of new "self-defence" skills can contribute positively and significantly to one's self-confidence.

While it may not be possible to make conclusive statements about the comparative behavioral impact of victimization, a more general position may be advanced. The categories of behavioral change described above suggest responses that are distinguishable in some rather fundamental ways. Most significant in this respect is the degree to which they suggest victims becoming increasingly integrated into or increasingly alienated from social life. To the extent that victims respond to crime through avoidance and protection they begin to erect barriers between themselves and others (Conklin, 1975). To the extent that they seek social interaction or involve themselves in community groups, they may be observed to increase their involvement in social life.

At a general level then, we may ask whether victimization has effects upon behavior which are integrative or disintegrative. While the accumulated evidence on this point is of necessity equivocal, it does appear that the net effects of victimization experiences tend to be in the direction of decreasing rather than increasing involvment in community life (Burt and Katz, 1985; Skogan, 1981). This is, in large part, because victimization has the effect of encouraging feelings of fear, mistrust and other attitudes that are not particularly conducive to the intensification of communal activity.

The suggestion that victimization frequently tends to result in behaviors that are restricting and limiting is not meant to imply that all victims of even serious, personal crime place themselves under "house arrest". While some do respond this way, there has been much written in both the popular and professional literature that paints a picture of the post-victimization phase that is too extreme. As Hindelang et al. (1978:224) observe, many of the effects of crime, "appear more as subtle adjustments in behavior than as major shifts in what may be called 'behavioral policies'".

199

COPING WITH THE COSTS OF VICTIMIZATION

We have seen that the costs of victimization are highly variable; they differ not only in kind but also in intensity and duration (Antunes et al., 1977; Hough, 1985). It is also the case that some victims, because of their social and economic situations may be more able to cope effectively with the costs of victimization than others. This section explores some of the factors that might mitigate the costs of crime for its victims.

Mobilizing Social Control

Perhaps one of the most important decisions that the victim must make in the post-victimization phase is whether to report the incident to police authorities (Fattah, 1979). It can be argued that such action might do much of both an instrumental and retributive nature, to alleviate the pains of the victimization experience. Reporting to police authorities may lead to the apprehension of the offender and thus, in some jurisdictions, make possible the payment of restitution. Reporting the victimization may also be necessary if the intention is to collect insurance payments. Further, contacting the police may provide access to advice at a time of crisis and may facilitate referral to social agencies that assist crime victims. Finally, the reporting of a criminal victimization may vent feelings of anger or frustration and thereby provide a cathartic release (Ernst et al, 1978).

Despite such potential advantages, victimization surveys consistently demonstrate that a large proportion of crime is not reported by victims. Data from the 1986 National Crime Survey, for instance, indicate that only about 37% of all crimes measured by the NCS were reported to the police (U.S. Department of Justice, 1987). Similarly, the Canadian Urban Victimization Survey revealed that for the year 1982 more than half of the incidents described to the survey interviewers were never brought to the attention of authorities (Canada, 1984a). Such findings are consistent with the larger body of victimization literature (Kidd and Chayet, 1984; Ruback et al., 1984).

In view of a general tendency toward non-reporting, it might be expected that older victims may be even less likely than others in the population to notify the police. Arcuri (1981) argues, for instance, that the older victims may be more likely to blame themselves for what has happened and thus less likely to involve themselves in legal processes. Additionally, the elderly victim may be more fearful of retaliation from the offender or more anxious regarding the bureaucratic entanglements that police reporting may imply.

The best available data, however, indicate that older victims are somewhat more likely than others to report criminal victimizations (Brillon, 1987; Yin, 1985). Hochstedler's (1981) analysis of the National Crime Survey data indicated that 51% of the victimizations of the elderly were reported to the police compared to 47% of the crimes committed against those 12 through 64. The Canadian Victimization Survey also found that reporting increased with age, from 40% of incidents reported when the victims were under the age of 25, to 53% when victims were over 65 years of age (Canada, 1985a).

When those who do not report their victimizations are asked to explain their failure to do so, the reasons that they provide are not substantially different from those given by younger victims. In general, non-reporting seems to reflect perceptions that the event is "too minor" and thus not worth the time and energy that reporting the event would involve; or that, because of the nature of the offence, there is little that the police can do and thus little reason to notify them (Hochstedler, 1981; Canada, 1984a). Contrary to popular stereotypes, a fear of reprisal seems to be a relatively minor factor in the decision not to report a criminal victimization.

It also appears to be the case that for elderly and non-elderly victims alike, the probability of reporting the crime to the police increases with the seriousness of the offence (Gottfredson and Gottfredson, 1980; Gottfredson and Hindelang, 1979; Liang and Sengstock, 1983; Skogan, 1976). Hochstedler, reports, for instance, that several characteristics of crime seriousness such as the presence of a weapon, physical attack, physical injury and whether the offence was completed, affected the likelihood of reporting.

Taken together, these data suggest that decisions regarding the reporting of victimizations to the police reflect a rational cost-benefit analysis of the situations in which victims find themselves (Gottfredson and Gottfredson, 1980). In other words victims weigh the advantages and disadvantages of reporting, assess the gains to be made and the losses to be incurred from doing so and make their decisions accordingly. If the crime is a particularly serious or a particularly threatening one they are more likely to notify the police of its occurrence than if the offence is of a minor nature. If the reporting is unlikely to result in the apprehension of the offender or the return of stolen property there is a reduced probability that the police will be told about the incident. With respect to the elderly specifically, it appears that the generally positive regard in which the police are held by older people may contribute positively to reporting decisions (Canada, 1985a).

To argue that the reporting decision is a rational one does not deny that the reporting process may itself be a source of problems and anxiety for the victim. Reference has already been made to the nature of police-victim interaction and some of the reasons why it may increase rather than diffuse the victim's frustration.

Lejeune and Alex (1973) describe another important dimension of this issue. They argue that because the police officer may be among the first with whom the victim has contact following the victimization, he or she will importantly influence the way in which the victim constructs the meaning of the event. The police officer may convey to the victim the ordinariness of his or her plight and indicate that there is little likelihood that the offender will be apprhended or that justice will be served. As a result of these revelations, the victim may come to see his or her situation as common and trivial compared to the enormity of the crime problem. Thus, with respect to the muggers in their sample, they concluded:

When the victim's definition of the situation is initially structured by the policeman, as is often the case, he is learning to see and experience the world from the police point of view. The more urban citizens become exposed to the police perspective, the more this view becomes dominant in the society. Thus the mugger, the police, the victim-and the media which disseminate the victim's plight - each contribute to the collective image of the city as an urban jungle (Lejeune and Alex, 1973:284)

Social Support

The degree to which people are located within supportive interpersonal networks may be an important factor in mitigating the psychological and other costs of criminal victimization (Janoff-Bulman and Frieze, 1983; Sales et al., 1984; Ruback et al., 1984; Perloff, 1983).

Supportive others may assist the victim in shaping the meaning of the event and in choosing among available options in the aftermath of the victimization experience (Ruback et al., 1984; Taylor et al., 1983). Ruback et al. (1984) argue that victims may be particularly sensitive to the influence of others in the context of the distress caused by a victim experience and that those to whom the victim has access may be a resource that importantly determines how adequately the victim copes with the pains of victimization.

There are, of course, much more practical and mundane ways in which supportive others may assist the victim. They may take the initiative in informing the police or other social service agency about the incident. They may drive the victim to the hospital or help assess property damage resulting from the victimization. Should a case proceed to trial, they may make arrangements for babysitting services or transportation and assist in seeking legal advice.

It is well known that the elderly are more likely than the younger persons to live alone (Brillon, 1987) and it is often claimed that they may experience more serious problems of social isolation (Rathbone-McCuan and Hashimi, 1982). This may imply that, in general, there may be less support for elderly, as opposed to non-elderly victims (Heller and Mansbach, 1984; Vaux, 1985). It is important to note, however, that there do exist significant individual differences in this regard.

Perceptions of Victimization

The social meaning of victimization is frequently ambiguous. In constructing the meaning of the event the victim must attempt to come to terms with several questions: was the incident really a crime? if so, how serious a crime was it? what role, if any, did the victim play in precipitation of his or her victimization? Such questions suggest that there may be considerable variation in the ways in which similar events are understood. In view of this, it is legitimate to ask if particular perceptions of victimization events and of the victim role facilitate or hinder coping processes (Janoff-Bulman and Frieze,1983).

Ferraro and Johnson (1983) argue that, in many instances, battered wives attempt to make an adjustment to their victimization by "rationalizing" the violence directed toward them. The lack of alternatives and the dependency upon the abuser frequently mean that victims of domestic assault deny the physical and emotional harm that the relationship produces. They contend that this process of denial is a significant factor in explaining why women stay with men who victimize them. Similarly, Agnew (1985) and Taylor et al. (1983) suggest that to the extent that crime victims can convince themselves that little harm has been caused by the incident, psychological and emotional stress will be minimized. Agnew also suggests that elderly victims may be less likely than others to neutralize the negative consequences of the victimization experience.

It is not only the perception of the event but also the victim's self-perception that may moderate or exacerbate victimization costs. That the internalization of self-blame for the occurrence of victimization may increase emotional anxiety has long been recognized by criminologists (Elias, 1986; Janoff- Bulman and Frieze, 1983; Karmen, 1984; Miller and Porter, 1983).

Based upon a comprehensive review of available literature, Perloff (1983) maintains that more general perceptions of personal vulnerability may importantly influence the nature of the recovery process. Perloff distinguishes between **unique vulnerability** which involves seeing oneself as highly vulnerable to negative life events while seeing others as much less vulnerable, and **universal vulnerability** which involves seeing oneself and others as equally vulnerable to such negative events. She argues that, prior to victimization, many people see themselves as uniquely invulnerable. In other words, they believe themselves to be much less susceptible than others to criminal danger. While a perception of unique invulnerability may provide some degree of psychological ease, it may undermine the recovery process once a victimization has taken place. This is because the event may create a dramatic discrepancy between pre- and post-victimization perceptions such that those who initially feel safest may be least able to cope with the costs of the victim experience.

What is important in assessing the special problems of elderly victims in this regard, is the nature of the comparison group that is used for making judgments about personal vulnerability. It may be argued that the heightened level of subjective vulnerability characteristic of those older persons who have not been victimized reflects a belief that the "typical" crime victim is someone like themselves (Perloff, 1983; Skogan and Maxfield, 1981). Although we will see in the next chapter that these perceptions may in themselves be problematic, at present it should be noted that if elderly persons see themselves as particularly vulnerable prior to victimization, they may undergo a less drastic change in self-image in the post-victimization phase. As a result, they may be somewhat more immune to the psychological stress which this change in self-image implies.

Financial Security

It is obvious that economic stability may reduce some of the problems that emerge from the victimization experience. Most directly, we have seen that elderly crime victims do not suffer significant losses, in any absolute sense, but that when we take into account the reduced incomes of elderly people, their losses equal or exceed those of other members of the population. This implies that the real financial problems faced by eldery victims have less to do with the nature of their criminal victimization and more to do with the economically subordinate position that they occupy in society. These problems are magnified in those cases in which victims must pay user fees for medical care necessitated by physical injuries sustained in the victimization (Cook et al., 1977). Such findings clearly suggest that the financial impact of elderly victimization may be significantly reduced in those situations in which victims' economic resources are substantial.

Aside from the issue of direct economic loss, it is also true that greater financial stability may facilitate flexibility in responding to the impact of victimization. The elderly victim who is impoverished may reduce his or her level of social activity because the streets and public transportation are seen as unsafe. The victim whose financial situation is less precarious may choose to travel by taxi. Victims whose economic resources are minimal may feel trapped in a high crime rate neighborhood while the victim who is financially more comfortable may elect to move to a building or a neighborhood that affords greater security.

These observations are not meant to suggest that the problems created by elderly victimization are all amenable to some form of economic solution. Still, if economic security rather than insecurity were characteristic of later life, some of these problems would clearly be ameliorated.

SUMMARY

This chapter has examined some of the direct costs of criminal victimization. The data that we have reviewed do not support any overall conclusion that the elderly are most likely to suffer the effects of criminal harm. Admittedly, however, methodological limitations require us to draw such conclusions with caution. With respect to emotional and behavioral domains, for instance, our empirical tools are inadequate. Even in the areas of physical and economic losses, we remain unsure about the subtle and long-term costs that victimization may promote. We also lack sufficient knowledge about a variety of offences (such as medical and health frauds) which are not easily addressed in the context of victimization surveys.

In the next chapter we turn our attention to a consideration of some of the indirect costs of vicimization.

CHAPTER NINE: RECOMMENDED READINGS

Burt, M.R. and B.L. Katz
1985 Rape, Robbery and Burglary: Responses to Actual and Feared Criminal Victimization with Special Focus on Women and the Elderly. Victimology, 10:325-358.

Canada
1984 Canadian Urban Victimization Survey Bulletin 5: Costs to Victims of Crime. Ottawa: Ministry of the Solicitor General.

Cook, F.L., W.G. Skogan, T.D. Cook and G.E. Antunes
1978 Criminal Victimization of the Elderly: The Physical and Economic Consequences. The Gerontologist, 18:338-349.

Fattah, E.
1981 Becoming a Victim: The Victimization Experience and Its Aftermath. Victimology, 4:198-213.

Feinberg, N.
1981 The Emotional and Behavioral Consequences of Violent Crime on Elderly Victims. Victimology, 6:355-357.

Hochstedler, E.
1981 Crimes Against the Elderly in 26 Cities. Washington D.C.: U.S. Department of Justice.

CHAPTER TEN

THE INDIRECT COSTS OF ELDERLY VICTIMIZATION

INTRODUCTION

Even though the elderly may be victimized less frequently than we might expect, this does not necessarily mean that crime does not touch the lives of many older people. If large numbers of the elderly, even though they have not been personally victimized, anticipate that they may become objects of criminal harm, then in a sense, they may be said to experience costs resulting from their knowledge of and emotional response to the criminal victimization of their fellows. Such a conceptualization forces the recognition that feelings of insecurity about person or property may cause mental anguish or constrain people to behave in ways that cheapen the quality of their lives. Thus, those who are vicariously victimized, like those who are directly victimized, may be said to experience costs of criminal danger. According to many writers, it is the fear of crime (as distinct from crime itself) that is the real problem facing the elderly (Baumer, 1978; Main and Johnson, 1978; Cook et al., 1981). Although most elderly, like most non-elderly people, will not be victimized by serious crime, they must nonetheless live with the possibility.

In this chapter we take up the issue of fear of crime with particular reference to the elderly. Drawing upon the available empirical evidence, we will discuss the nature and source of these fears as they relate to the social position of older persons. Moreover, we will examine the social distribution of crime-related anxieties and attempt to determine how demographic, contextual, experiential and psychological factors combine to affect levels of fearfulness.

It will become apparent that the issues that are of concern to us in this chapter are somewhat more abstract and elusive than those discussed in the two previous chapters. This is, in large part, because a fear of crime, unlike a mugging or a theft, does not reference a particular incident that is circumscribed in time and space. Instead, it refers to ways of thinking, feeling and acting that are more pervasive and somewhat more difficult to conceptually delimit. Put simply, we can not count fears of assault as readily as we can count assaults.

Because of this and related methodological problems, the research literature on elderly fear of crime is frequently inconsistent on key issues; and theoretical accounts of elderly fear lack comprehensiveness.

In an even more rudimentary way, these problems may be seen to be rooted in the inconsistencies which characterize the manner in which important concepts are understood and operationalized by those working in this area. It might be advisable, therefore, to begin with a consideration of what the term, fear of crime, means and how it is used in the criminological literature.

WHAT IS FEAR OF CRIME?

The term fear is normally used to describe a physiological and emotional reaction to a stimulus that is both threatening and immediate. Silberman (1978:8) notes:

> From a physiological standpoint, what we call fear is a series of complex changes in the endocrine system that alerts us to danger and makes it possible for us to respond effectively, whether we choose to attack or to flee. The first stage - the one we associate most closely with fear or tension - prepares the entire body for fight or flight: the heart rate and systolic blood pressure go up; blood flow through the brain and skeletal muscles increases by as much as 100 percent; digestion is impaired; and so on. The second stage provides the capacity for rapid aggression or retreat; the third for a slower more sustained response.

In general, fear of crime researchers have shown very little interest in such physiological dimensions of fear and have emphasized instead its emotional character. The attention to the emotional character of fear is clearly evident in the use of questionnaire items that attempt to gauge the extent to which respondents "feel unsafe", "worry about crime" or are "afraid to walk alone in the neighborhood after dark".

For obvious reasons, fear of crime is typically assessed, for reasearch purposes, in contexts quite removed from those in which the fear is actually experienced (Skogan, 1981). Thus, respondents to victimization or crime perception surveys are asked to indicate how much they fear the occurrence of particular crimes or the degree of fear that they associate with particular places, situations or activities. As a result, the data from such studies may be said to speak to questions about "anticipated" rather than "actual" fear (Garofalo, 1981). Responses to such questions are perhaps better conceptualized as "expressed attitudes" than emotional reactions (Skogan and Maxfield, 1981). Empirical operationalizations of the fear of crime concept may be conveniently grouped into three broad categories .

Cognitive Measures

Measures of this type attempt to elicit from respondents their beliefs regarding the extent to which crime threatens them. They might be asked whether or not they perceive local crime levels to be high or whether they think that crime levels have increased in recent years. Alternatively, they may be asked to indicate their chances of victimization within some specified period or to indicate their probable success in preventing their own victimization (Gibbs et al., 1987; Skogan, 1981).

Such cognitive measures are of interest because they imply an external reality with which meaningful comparisons can be made. Thus, subjective probabilities of victimization may be assessed in terms of objective probabilities of victimization and judged to be more or less accurate (Henshel and Silverman, 1975). Similarly, if we define fear as the perception that local crime is increasing, we may be justified in labelling this fear ill-founded if available crime data indicate that levels of local crime are actually decreasing.

On the other hand, it should be recognized that indicators of this type may be inadequate as measures of fear, if by that term is intended something akin to concern or anxiety. Several studies have demonstrated that there is only an imperfect correspondence between cognitive assessments of personal or environmental risk and measures of fear and worry (Baumer, 1985; Clarke, 1984; Giles-Sims, 1984; Miethe and Lee, 1984). Such studies suggest that although people may believe that they face similar dangers, they may express quite different feelings about these dangers. An explicit recognition of this possibility has led some researchers to treat these cognitive measures as causes rather than indicators of fear (Warr and Stafford, 1983; Warr, 1985; Yin, 1980).

Affective Measures

In contrast to more cognitive measures, those which are affective in nature come closest to assessing the emotional content of fear of crime. Items falling into this category would ask respondents directly about how unsafe they feel, how much they worry or the extent to which they are afraid. Such questions are, without doubt, among the most frequently reported in the fear of crime literature.

The most popular items of this type focus on neighborhood safety and involve some variation on the themes: "How safe do you or would you feel walking alone in your neighborhood at night?" or "Is there any place around here where you feel unsafe walking alone at night"? Literally thousand of people have been asked these questions in crime perception and victimization surveys conducted in Canada, the United States and Great Britain. In addition to being used in several smaller scale or regional surveys, the former item is routinely employed in the National Crime Survey and the latter has been used in several studies conducted by the National Opinion Reseach Center (Braungart et al, 1980; DeFronzo, 1979; Eve, 1985; Gibbs et al., 1987). As even a cursory review of the literature would suggest, much of what we know about the causes, correlates and consequences of fear of crime is based upon research which uses these measures.

Despite their popularity, these "global measures" of fear of crime have been criticized by several scholars (Clarke, 1984; Finley, 1983; Miethe and Lee, 1984; Eve, 1984; Gibbs et al., 1987; Maxfield, 1984b; Yin, 1980; Garofalo, 1981). Garofalo (1979) for instance, although making specific reference to the first item mentioned above, raises several issues that are relevant to both measures. First, neither item mentions crime specifically which raises the possibility that respondents may view their neighborhoods as unsafe because of, for example, unsafe or unlit construction sites or unleashed neighborhood dogs. As Garofalo points out, however, the fact that the questions are usually asked after a series of other questions about crime probably minimizes this problem. Second, the term "neighborhood" is given no specific reference and is probably interpreted differently by different respondents. Third, the respondents are asked to think about being alone in the neighborhood but there is no doubt considerable variation in the amount of time that they actually spend on the streets unattended. A more general problem with such global measures, as they are called, is their inability to distinguish levels of fear associated with particular offences (Miethe and Lee, 1984; Gibbs et al., 1987; Yin,1980). If one respondent fears for her personal safety because of a concern about being sexually assaulted while another is unconcerned about sexual assault but anxious about the possibility of being robbed, their responses to the above items would not allow us to detect the difference. With respect to such measures, Gibbs et al. (1987:3) comment:

> The object of fear is vague and open to interpretation. They are limited in their space, time and crime referents which reflects underlying conceptual impoverishment. And it is impossible to measure internal consistency and conduct statistical analysis to examine content validity (i.e., item analysis by means of item-remainder correlations) when the measure of the construct consists of a single item.

In view of these problems, some researchers have attempted to develop indicators which take the multidimensionality of the fear of crime concept into account. Miethe and Lee (1984) for example, operationalized the fear of crime so as to distinguish between fear of personal crime and fear of property crime and found that each involved quite different causal processes. Similarly, Warr (1984; 1985; and Stafford, 1983) in a study of reactions to crime in the state of Washington asked respondents to indicate the level of fear that they associated with a large number of individual crimes.

More generally, it should be noted that affective measures, unlike the cognitive measures discussed above, do not have "objective" empirical referents against which these perceptions may be judged. Thus, while we may conclude that a given cognitive percpetion is inaccurate or incorrect, such a judgment is meaningless when applied to an affective perception such as fear or worry. However, as we discuss below, many commentators have chosen to label levels of anxiety that are not congruent with objective risk as "irrational".

Behavioral Measures

This type of operationalization emphasizes not what people say either about the level of crime or their feelings of safety but what they say they do in response to crime. Respondents may be asked whether they restrict their activities, whether they carry a weapon, whether they lock their doors while at home alone or whether they avoid certain types of people or situations (Hindelang et al., 1978; DuBow et al., 1979; Merry, 1981; Riger et al., 1982). Respondents who answer questions of this type in the affirmative may be regarded as more fearful than those who respond in the negative.

It may be assumed that behavioral measures provide a more rigorous test of fearfulness. Simply because respondents to a survey indicate that they "feel unsafe" we may not be justified in concluding that they behave in ways consistent with these feelings (DuBow et al., 1979; Hartnagel, 1979; Hindelang et al., 1978). Ginsberg (1984-1985) for example, who studied Jewish residents of high crime rate neighborhoods in London and Boston found that although both groups expressed similar fears about crime, their behavior on neighborhood streets was quite different. Whereas the London residents tended to go about their day-to-day business in a way that seemed inconsistent with their expressed fears, the Boston respondents showed much more of a tendency to retreat from public participation. Similarly, Lawton and Yaffe (1980) in their study of elderly public housing tenants found that those who reported being most fearful were least likely to place restrictions upon their mobility. In short, if actions do speak louder than words, behavioral measures may provide more meaningful indicators of public fear than do perceptual indicators.

More critically, it should be noted that behavioral measures employed in surveys do not truly tell us about how people behave but about how they say that they behave. The difference is not a trivial one. As we argued in the previous chapter, many people do not recall patterns of personal action with great accuracy and unless we directly observe their behavior there is reason for cynicism about the magnitude of error regarding self-reported conduct.

Finally, it should be pointed out that many criminologists argue that the behaviors tapped by these indicators are not manifestations of fear but rather consequences of it. This implies a particular causal pattern such that people come to fear crime and then as a result of this fear, to behave in particular ways. The point here is more theoretical than empirical and given that most of our data about fear of crime are derived from cross-sectional surveys, we are unable to make very informed choices between a view of behavior as a form or as an effect of fear.

Conceptualizing Fear: Further Problems

Despite the difficulties that each type of indicator uniquely presents, there are some general comments that can be made regarding the ways in which the fear of crime is measured and investigated.

1. **An Emphasis on Street Crime.** Implicit in most of the global measures of fear of crime and explicit in many crime-specific indicators is an obvious focus upon ordinary street crimes to the exclusion of corporate or white

collar offences (Warr and Stafford, 1983). To be sure, traditional crimes against person and property are a great source of concern to many people but the inattentiveness to more subtle forms of criminal exploitation is an oversight which reflects some rather well known ideological dimensions of contemporary criminology (Johnson and Wasliewski, 1982).

2. **The Conceptualization of Fearfulness as an Enduring Trait.** Much fear of crime research as well as much fear of crime theory tends to encourage a view of such fear as an emotional or psychological property which some people have and others do not. We are thus encouraged to ask; who is fearful and who is not fearful? Such a viewpoint precludes a detailed consideration of the ephemeral, transitory and situational nature of fear.

The problem becomes obvious upon examination of the global measures which figure so prominently in much of the empirical literature. While responses to these items have allowed researchers to categorize sample members as to their levels of fearfulness or to label some social groups as fearful and others as not, it should be emphasized that these questions ask about feelings of fearfulness in relation to rather specific conditions.

This shortcoming becomes apparent if we compare the fear of crime with some other negative emotion such as unhappiness. While there do exist people who are chronically unhappy, most of us are unhappy at some times and happy at others, our moods varying with the social and life circumstances in which we find ourselves. Fear of crime in some of its manifestations may also be more like a mood and less like a stable predisposition, but there is little research that is informed by such an observation (Fischer, 1981; Jeffords, 1983).

3. **A Quantitative Emphasis.** Many limitations characteristic of the fear of crime literature may derive from the fact that research in this area has been limited methodologically. Investigators have almost exclusively employed the quantitative methods of the survey researcher and have thus been willing to treat fear as a finite attitude or behavior rather than as a hazy and problematic social construction (Gibbs et al., 1987).

In addition, there has been relatively little attention paid to questions of process; that is, to the ways in which fears of crime change and develop. In large part, this deficiency results from the cross-sectional nature of survey research designs which do not allow investigators to speak to the dynamic character of fear.

While more qualitative methodologies have been used by some investigators (Merry, 1981; Poveda, 1972), the potential of such approaches has yet to be exploited.

4. **Fear as a Pathology** In the context of most research, fear of crime is regarded as a social problem. In other words, it is implicitly assumed that it is a deleterious condition which is destructive to psychological or social well-being and against which ameliorative action needs to be taken.

Such a conceptualization is obviously limited. We do after all live in a world that poses real risks and to completely ignore those risks would not be prudent. The opposite of fear may not be fearlessness but recklessness.

There is an important empirical and practical distinction between fear and caution (Garofalo, 1981) yet most indicators mitigate against an appreciation of this distinction.

One possible approach to this issue has been provided by Yin (1980). He suggests that respondents should be asked to choose from a list of problems (which would include the "fear of crime" as well as other problems such as income or health) those which are viewed as most troubling. The data yielded by questions of this type, in conjunction with information yielded by more traditional measures would allow the investigator to distinguish those who merely report feeling fearful and those for whom such feelings are subjectively defined as problematic.

FEAR OF CRIME AMONG THE ELDERLY

In this section we turn to a consideration of the research literature which provides us with a description of the intensity and social distribution of eldery fear of crime. We begin by considering the degree to which the fear of crime is a unique problem for the elderly and then proceed to an examination of the more significant factors that affect levels of fearfulness within older populations.

General Patterns of Elderly Fear

In order to make a judgment about the empirical significance of elderly fear of crime, we need to examine three distinct yet related issues. First and most obviously, we must examine the research evidence in order to determine whether, on average, fear levels are higher among the elderly as opposed to the non-elderly segments of the population. Second, we must attempt to assess the relative predictive utility of age by comparing it to other variables that affect variations in fearfulness. Finally, we need to determine the degree to which fear of crime is defined as a personal problem by older persons.

With respect to the first issue, it can be said that most studies report a relationship between age status and fear of crime with the elderly expressing greater fear (Clemente and Kleiman, 1976; Kahana et al., 1977; Main and Johnson, 1978; DeFronzo, 1979; Baumer, 1978; Toseland, 1982; Hindelang et al., 1978; Cook et al., 1981; Canada, 1985b; Cook and Cook, 1976; Eve, 1985; Garofalo, 1981; Skogan and Maxfield, 1981). However, there also exist several studies which suggest that the relationship between age and fear is quite small and in some cases negligible (Colijn, 1981; Yin, 1985; Burt and Ward, 1985; Janson and Ryder, 1983; Lebowitz, 1975; Braungart et al., 1980). A few studies even indicate that the elderly may be less fearful of criminal victimization than more youthful segments of the population (Gomme, 1988; Sacco and Glackman, 1987).

To some extent, these inconsistencies reflect differences in the composition of samples and sampling procedures. The variability in research findings is also influenced by differences in the ways in which the concepts "elderly" and "fear" are operationalized. With respect to the latter concept, for instance, those studies which take into account the multidimensionality of fear of crime indicate that age differentials in fear may vary with the type of offence about

212

which respondents are asked. Skogan (1978) argues that the elderly are not fearful in some indiscriminate fashion but are rather specifically concerned about the threat of personal attack. Similarly, Jeffords (1983) in a study of a sample of Texas elderly found that older respondents were more likely than younger respondents to express anxieties about safety on the street but were more likely to feel safer in their homes. Finally, Warr (1984) who used sample survey data collected in Seattle to examine the fear of sixteen specific crimes found that although a tendency to fearfulness increased with age, the specific nature of the relationship depended upon the crime in question. With respect to rape, the level of fear was greatest among the youngest rather than the oldest group of respondents. However, fear was greatest among the elderly (those aged 66 and above) for eight of the crimes and among the near-elderly (51-65) for the remaining seven.

In general, and despite some important exceptions, the weight of the evidence would seem to support the conclusion that elderly persons are some-what more likely than younger people to express a fear of crime particularly if they are asked about their feelings of personal safety in situations that might involve a violent attack by strangers. It would also appear, however, that age differences in fear are not as strong or as consistent as they are popularly believed to be.

A second approach to the issue would involve an examination of the relative importance of age as a variable that discriminates between fearful and nonfearful segments of the population. As the preceding discussion would suggest, age is not the best predictor of fear of crime. Almost all of the available evidence, including those studies which attribute substantial predictive power to age, would seem to indicate that it is gender rather than age which is most closely related to fear (Baumer, 1978). Those studies which find an effect of age in the context of an analysis that simultaneously takes into account the effects of gender and other social and demographic variables consistently report that the influence of age is considerably smaller than but independent of the influence of gender (DeFronzo, 1979; Toseland, 1982; Hindelang et al., 1978; Lebowitz, 1975; Braungart et al., 1980; Garofalo, 1979; Skogan and Maxfield, 1981).

Earlier reference was made to the fact that studies which only examine the age distribution of fear may be unable to illuminate the ways in which elderly persons uniquely experience fear as a problem (Yin, 1980). There are some studies which employ question formats that allow some judgment to be made regarding the degree to which fear is particularly troublesome for older adults. In general, these studies also suggest that much of the rhetoric which describes the elderly as "prisoners of fear" may tend towards hyperbole. Cook and his colleagues (1981) examined National Crime Survey data in order to investigate the relationship between a concern about crime and a decrease in mobility among the elderly. They found that although crime was the most frequently mentioned reason for staying home, it was not a reason given by a majority of respondents. Yin (1982) used an "open-ended" question to ask elderly Minnesota respondents about the degree to which they defined crime or the fear of crime as a personal problem. He reports that crime was mentioned by only one percent of the sample and that "poor health" and "not enough money" were much more frequently cited as problematic conditions. Similarly

Clarke and Lewis (1982) found among elderly residents of a London borough, crime ranked below "personal health" and "financial worries" as personal concerns. Their analysis also revealed that although almost all of the sample members regarded the local neighborhood as unsafe, only half of them considered fear of crime to be personally important.

Taken together, these studies suggest that with respect to the problem of fear of crime, the elderly may be less affected and somewhat more resilient than popular sterotypes would indicate. However, the elderly are not a homogeneous group and a discussion of the general age distribution of fear of crime leaves unaddressed important variations in the ways in which older persons experience and cope with fear (Clemente and Kleiman, 1976). We need, therefore, to examine those factors which affect fear within the elderly population. Four broad sets of factors are identified and discussed below.

THE CORRELATES OF FEAR OF CRIME

Social Status Variables

By social status variables we mean those major social and demographic categories that designate the dominant social roles that people play and the social experiences to which they are exposed. Two major status variables (in addition to age) have been widely discussed in the research literature.

Gender. As stated, the best predictor of fear of crime is the gender of the respondent. In general, this relationship holds in both elderly and non-elderly samples and for perceptual and behavioral measures of fear (Giles-Sims, 1984; Lawton and Yaffe, 1980; Clemente and Kleiman, 1976; 1977; Finley, 1983; Riger et al., 1978; Baumer, 1978; 1985; Miethe and Lee, 1984; Canada,1985a; Gomme, 1988; Lebowitz, 1975; Clarke and Lewis, 1982; Toseland, 1982; Skogan and Maxfield, 1981; Warr, 1984; 1985). The nature of the relationship is such that females are much more likely than males to express anxiety about the possibility of criminal victimization. The consistency of this finding suggests that the gender distribution of fear of crime is an empirical reality rather than a methodological artifact resulting from a greater willingness on the part of females to admit a fear of criminal harm.

The research also indicates that the effect of gender upon fear may vary between elderly and non-elderly populations. Specifically, among the elderly, the differences between male and female fear levels are smaller than in the case of more youthful people (Lawton and Yaffe, 1980; Clemente and Kleiman, 1976). In other words, sex differences in fear of crime decline with age suggesting that the effect of age is stronger for males than for females (Baumer, 1985). Females are likely to be fearful irrespective of their age whereas males are likely to become fearful as they grow older.

Theoretical discussion of gender differences in fear of crime emphaisze three related themes. The first involves social learning and suggests that the socialization experiences of women encourage the development of a sense of sexual vulnerability that manifests itself in terms of a pervasive anxiety about personal safety (Burt and Estep, 1981; Warr, 1985). A second viewpoint

214

emphasizes the more pragmatic consideration that women are, in general, less physically capable than the young males who pose the modal threat of criminal harm and that their greater fear reflects an awareness of this reality (Riger et al., 1978). Finally, it is argued that women are different than men in that the former, but not the latter, face in addition to all other sources of criminal harm, the unique dangers associated with rape and other forms of sexual assault. Thus, women are more concerned because there is more about which they need to be concerned (Riger et al,1978).

Minority Status. Placement in the stratification system, as measured by racial and economic indicators, is usually a useful predictor of fear of crime although the effects are generally weaker than those associated with gender. Among the elderly and the non-elderly, fear is greater among those who are poorer, those with less education and those who are members of ethnic minority groups (Eve and Eve, 1984; Lee, 1983; Wiltz, 1982; Baumer, 1978; Miethe and Lee, 1984; Braungart et al., 1980; Skogan and Maxfield, 1981). Some researchers have found that the effects of socioeconomic indicators upon fear of crime cease to be significant when other variables are taken into account (Giles-Sims, 1984; Toseland, 1982; Gomme, 1988). Others have suggested that the relationships involving age, minority status and fear of crime are not straightforward. Jeffords (1983), for instance, found income to be an important variable in conditioning the relationship between age and fear such that older persons were more likely to be more fearful only if their incomes were under $15,000.

Explanations of the relationship between economic or racial minority group membership and the fear of crime tend to stress the significance of such membership variables as indicators of personal vulnerability, or of proximity to the threat of criminal danger. In the former sense, it is argued that poorer people have fewer of the economic and social resources that facilitate feelings of safety. They are less able, for instance, to protect themselves or their property or to distance themselves from persons or situations that might arouse crime-related anxieties. Proximity arguments suggest that socioeconomic and racial indicators are proxy measures for residential variables. Put differently, lower status incumbents are more likely to live in neighborhoods with high rates of crime to which personal fear is a rational response.

Contextual Variables

These variables refer not to individuals but rather to the environments in which they live and move. It is assumed that the social context may exert an effect upon behavior and attitudes that is quite independent of those associated with individual- level social or demographic characteristics. Three major types of contextual effects have been indentified in the research literature.

Urbanism. The empirical literature suggests that residents of larger cities are more likely to express fear of crime than are residents of smaller towns or cities (Baumer, 1978; Fischer, 1981; Finley, 1983; Sundeen and Mathieu, 1976; Kennedy and Krahn, 1984; Sacco, 1985a).

Interpretations of the relationship between fear and urbanism tend to stress the fact that bigger cities have higher rates of crime and thus the greater fear is seen as a realistic response to heightened peril (Sacco, 1985a). Other writers have focused analytical attention upon the social pschology of urban life (Fischer, 1981; Merry, 1981). Many public encounters in urban settings, they argue, involve confrontations with others who are strangers in both a personal and a cultural sense; and, such encounters may generate a sense of unease on the part of many people.

With respect to the elderly specifically, several studies have found evidence to support the conclusion that the combined effect of being elderly and being an urban dweller is greater than we would expect based on our knowledge of the individual effects of these two variables (Jeffords, 1983; Ollenburger, 1981; Lebowitz, 1975; Baumer, 1985; Clemente and Kleiman, 1976).

Baumer (1985) suggests that the relationship between age and fear may only be salient under conditions of "moderate threat" such as exists in most of the medium-sized cities in which fear of crime has been investigated. When the level of threat is very low (as may be the case in most small towns and suburbs), neither the young nor the old are particularly fearful. And, under conditions of extreme threat (as in the case of, for instance, cities with very high crime rates) the fear level of the young escalates to a level that resembles the pattern exhibited by older persons.

An alternative interpretation of the interaction between age and urbanism emphasizes the role of community context as a "protective environment" (Gubrium, 1973). Ollenburger (1981), for instance, suggests that in less urban places, residents may define their environment as affording them greater protection from criminal harm and thus to some degree anxieties about personal safety may be diffused. Moreover, Ollenburger argues, given a lack of physical and economic resources, the elderly may be particularly reliant upon the sense of security that the community is thought to provide.

While research generally demonstrates that the burden of fear falls most heavily upon the elderly who reside in more urban places, a more complete understanding of these issues may require a more sophisticated approach to the problem. Researchers have tended to utilize fear of crime indicators which may be somewhat more meaningful in urban as opposed to rural areas. As Lee (1982a) contends, questions which ask about walking alone in the neighborhood at night may be quite inapplicable to the study of residents of rural areas and may thus give a misleading impression of rural-urban differences in fear of crime.

Another limitation of much of the research in this area relates to an implicit assumption that current community of residence is the most salient indicator of community influence. In contrast, Kennedy and Krahn (1984) argue that perceptions of safety may also be affected by the size of the community of origin. In their study of perceptions of crime in a large western Canadian city, Kennedy and Krahn found that elderly persons who had grown up in rural areas were less likely to feel safe in the city than were those elderly who had been socialized in a large urban environment.

Neighborhood. Levels of fear not only vary between cities but within cities as well such that residents of some neighborhoods are more likely to report being concerned about crime than residents of other neighborhoods.

As might be expected, these differences are to some extent explainable in terms of variations in levels of local crime (Lee, 1983; DuBow et al., 1979; Maxfield, 1984; McPherson, 1978; Yin, 1980; Lawton and Yaffe, 1980). Thus, higher rates of neighborhood crime increase the likelihood that neighborhood residents will express anxieties about their safety.

There is, however, evidence which suggests that neighborhood conditions other than the rate of crime influence perceptions of personal danger. In particular, a number of researchers have focused attention upon the role that "signs of incivilities" play in the production of fear (Maxfield, 1984; Smith, 1986; Lewis and Maxfield, 1980; Skogan and Maxfield, 1981; Baumer, 1978; DuBow et al., 1979; Maxfield, 1987). The term, signs of incivilities, is used to refer to those physical and social aspects of neighborhood which might be interpreted by residents as indicators of social disorder. These might include abandoned buildings, loud and boisterous youths, or public drunkenness and panhandling. It is argued that such conditions signal to those who live in the neighborhood that social controls are not operating and that person or property may be in jeopardy (Lewis and Maxfield, 1980). Although they are not serious crimes (and in most cases not crimes at all) the signs of incivility may inspire anxiety on the part of those who routinely confront them.

The research evidence suggests that the presence of incivilities contribute to fear of crime in a way that is independent of and additional to the effects of local crime rates (Maxfield, 1984; Skogan and Maxfield, 1981; Lewis and Maxfield, 1980). The data also indicate that older neighborhood residents may be more sensitive to the presence of uncivil behavior and conditions than younger residents (Baumer, 1985; Clarke, 1984; Maxfield, 1984b; 1987; Kahana et al., 1977). Moroever, Maxfield's comparative analysis of National Crime Survey and British Crime Survey data support a conclusion that older and younger persons may be affected by different types of incivilities. He found that while the elderly were more troubled by the public behavior of teenagers, younger respondents were somewhat more likely to be upset by the presence of idle or drunken men.

Many of the conditions that are conceptualized as incivilities reflect group-supported definitions of what constitutes improper public behavior (Wilson, 1968). A lack of consensus about what will or should be tolerated in public is most problematic in those environments that are socially heterogeneity and lacking in integration. As Maxfield suggests (1987) the members of one generational group may be inclined to define the behavior of another generational group, with which it shares public space, as disreputable and potentially threatening. Similar tensions may characterize the relations between ethnic and racial groups (Merry, 1981).

It may also be argued that in neighborhoods that are characterized by a high degree of social heterogeneity and a low degree of integration, residents may feel more isolated and less able to depend upon others for support (Finley, 1983; Ginsberg, 1984-1985; Kennedy and Silverman, 1984-1985). As a result, residents may be more likely to define themselves as vulnerable and more likely to indicate that they fear criminal victimization.

Housing Type. Anxieties about crime have also been shown to be related to variations in the nature of the residential environment. With respect to the elderly specifically, the data suggest that fear levels are lower in age-segregated housing (Clarke, 1984; Lawton and Yaffe, 1980; Herman et al., 1976; Finley, 1983; Gubrium, 1974; Teaff et al., 1978; Clarke and Lewis, 1982).

The age composition of housing may influence fear levels through effects upon both perceived risk and perceived vulnerability. With respect to the former, the low rates of offending characteristic of the elderly implies that apartment buildings or housing projects populated by older persons will present the average resident with fewer risks than will more integrated settings. Age-segregated building residents may also feel the support of a "protective environment" (Gubrium, 1973) in which contact with neighbors is increased (Clarke, 1984), and in which local leadership and communal norms are in the hands of peers (Teaff et al., 1978). As a result of such processes, feelings of personal vulnerability may be reduced.

In addition to age composition, it has been argued that the demonstration of an active mastery with respect to the immediate residential environment may reduce feelings of fearfulness. Specifically, crime-related anxieties may be alleviated by "territorial" conduct such as the use of property markers, fences or "keep out" or "no trespassing" signs (Taylor et al., 1984). A study in Pennsylvania by Patterson (1978; 1979; Pollock and Patterson, 1980) found that while such territorial behavior was associated with less fear among the elderly, it had no effect upon the fears of younger respondents.

Experiential Variables

These variables refer to those significant encounters, experiences and relationships which magnify or minimize concerns about criminal victimization. We recognize three major types of experiential factors.

Victimization As discussed in the last chapter, victimization surveys indicate that direct experience with crime may result in several emotional and psychological consequences including the fear of crime. Crime perception studies which focus attention more generally upon the determinants of fear support this conclusion (Giles-Sims, 1984; Lawton and Yaffe, 1980; Lee, 1983; Miethe and Lee, 1984; Ollenburger, 1981; Braungart et al., 1980). Although victims are more fearful of crime than non-victims, knowledge of this relationship may do little to explain the level or distribution of fear in the general population. This is beause only a small minority of the population experiences serious victimization and thus the number who are afraid greatly exceeds the number who are victimized (Skogan and Maxfield, 1981). Because the elderly have high levels of fear and low levels of victimization, some commentators have decided that older people (as well as women, whose relationship between fear and victimization is similar) are irrational to be much more afraid than their victimization levels would seem to justify.

It can, of course, be argued that such an interpretation has very ageist overtones (Burt and Katz, 1975). The argument implies that the elderly are somewhat hysterical and that perhaps their fears need not be taken too seriously. This paradox involving low victimization levels and high fear levels has attracted considerable attention in recent years and researchers have been able to offer a number of alternative interpretations of the relationship. In general, these interpretations stress an awareness of the fact that the elderly may be less irrational than earlier conceptualizations may have suggested:

1. As noted above, the fears of older persons are accentuated and diminished by greater and lesser conditions of environmental risk (Jaycox, 1978; Maxfield, 1987; Lee, 1983). This implies that fear is not an unbridled emotion but a rational response to real external threats.

2. As discussed previously, some researchers have argued that the elderly may not in fact have lower rates of victimization when their lower levels of exposure to victimization are taken into account. Thus, to the extent that older persons make the realization that the risk of victimization, when they are exposed, is as high or higher than the rest of the population their fears seem less disproportionate (Stafford and Galle, 1984; Lindquist and Duke, 1982; Skogan, 1980).

3. Some writers have taken this point one step further and suggested that rather than viewing a high level of fear as an irrational response to low levels of victimization, it should be recognized that the high level of fear may be causally prior to the low victimization rate (Rosenfield, 1981; Baumer, 1978; Hindelang et al., 1978). Thus, if older people, because they are afraid of being victimized, stay home at night rather than expose themselves or their property to victimization risk, it would follow that their rate of victimization would be below that experienced by those who are not fearful. When we attempt to examine this issue using cross-sectional data we may be led to the wrong conclusion since we can not adequately clarify the causal order of the variables in question.

   While the argument is an intriguing one, it is not consistently supported by the available empirical evidence (Balkin, 1979; Garofalo, 1981). Moreover, it should be recalled that fear of crime does not appear to be the major factor that keeps people away from potential risk. The elderly are less likely to find themselves in situations in which crimes occur because of their lifestyles and the nature of their role obligations rather than because of paralytic fears.

4. Arguments about the irrational nature of elderly fears assume that it is appropriate to compare fear levels to aggregated levels of crime. While the elderly have low overall levels of victimization, there is evidence to suggest that, with respect to some categories of offences - such as personal theft with contact - their rates are close to those of the general population. If personal theft with contact is the crime that is at the basis of much elderly fear, then we have done little in demonstrating that their rates of other crimes are below those associated with younger persons. The extensive reliance upon global measures of fear has hindered our understanding of exactly what it is that frightens the elderly.

219

5. A final resolution suggests that claims about the existence of a paradox assume that risk rather than vulnerability is the central element of elderly fear. In other words, to argue that elderly fears are excessive, in the presence of risks that are equal to or lower than those faced by other members of the population, presupposes that older persons do not differ in terms of their perceptions of the gravity of the consequences of victimizations which do occur. It might more reasonably be maintained that older persons are more afraid, not because they believe their chances of being victimized are extremely high, but because they believe that they will be able to cope less effectively with the effects of victimization. It may be, therefore, that the higher level of fear expressed by older perons may have less to do with unrealistic perceptions of risks that face them and more to do with realistic perceptions of their own socially and economically disadvantaged position.

Warr (1984) empirically demonstrates the utility of this argument through an anlysis of survey data collected in Seattle, Washington. He was able to show that identical levels of risk did not produce identical levels of fear for all segments of the population surveyed. Instead, age and gender groups showed evidence of what might be termed a "differential sensitivity to risk".

Moreover Warr argues, with respect to certain crimes, high levels of fear may result from the association of that crime in the respondent's mind with what may be termed "perceptually contemporaneous offences". For example, Warr found that with respect to the crime of "begging" there was no relationship between risk and fear among those under 65 years of age although the two variables were related in the elderly sample. This is because:

for elderly respondents the thought of being approached by a beggar entails something more than begging itself. That is elderly respondents may view begging as a prelude to other more serious offenses (e.g. assault or robbery) (Warr,1984: 695).

Thus, the tendency of older persons to express more fear about even relatively minor crimes may not suggest irrationality. A more suitable explanation of the pattern may involve an examination of the greater sensitivity to the risk of harm, characteristic of the more serious crimes with which those minor offences are associated.

Social Support and Social Integration. To the extent that individuals are able to integrate themselves into social networks and derive support from their relationships with others, their fears of criminal victimization may be reduced.

Marital status provides perhaps the most obvious example of the role of social relationships in mitigating fear. Most studies find evidence that the absence or the loss of a spouse or living alone increases anxiety about crime (Finley, 1983; Canada, 1985b; Kennedy and Silverman, 1984-1985; Braungart et al., 1980; DeFronzo, 1979) although some researchers fail to find such a relationship (Giles-Sims, 1984; Lawton and Yaffe, 1980).

Integration into local neighborhood networks may also affect feelings of personal safety (Lee, 1983). A study of elderly residents of London housing projects, for instance, (Clarke, 1984; Clarke and Lewis, 1982) found that while fear of crime was not affected by the total number of social contacts reported by respondents, it was significantly reduced by contact with neighbors.

It may be argued that social isolation is a greater problem for the elderly than for the non-elderly. The majority of older persons live by themselves. The fact that the elderly are more likely to be retired and thus disengaged from occupational or workplace networks, may further contribute to insecurities about personal security (Canada, 1985b). Also, the desire of many elderly people to maintain autonomy from kin may cause them to remain in areas which are undergoing rapid social changes that mitigate against neighborhood integration (Kennedy and Silverman, 1984-1985).

Like other variables that we have discussed, social support probably affects fear of crime through its influence upon vulnerability and risk. A high level of support may make people feel less vulnerable by fostering the perception that others can be relied upon for assistance in the event of a negative life experience such as criminal victimization (Clarke and Lewis, 1982). Such effects may not only reduce fear but also its consequences for personal well-being (Yin, 1980). Social intergration, particularly at the neighborhood level, may also provide residents with a detailed knowledge of the sources and forms of local danger. As a result, they may feel that they face fewer risks and they are better able to manage those risks which do confront them (Merry, 1982; Yin, 1980).

Patterns of Exposure to Crime Information. Popular accounts frequently stress the role of mass media exposure in shaping fear of crime (Friedberg, 1983). Such a position encourages a view of fear of crime as a problem with no strong basis in reality. Instead, its origins are located in the sensationalist and lurid imagery of news and entertainment media.

Upon first analysis, the suggestion that fear of crime is importantly influenced by mass communications is logical and appealing for several reasons (Sacco, 1979). First, it is well known that crime content is a prominent feature of contemporary mass media (Graber, 1980; Dominick, 1978). Second, since most people do not have direct experience with criminal victimization, it would seem that their perceptions must be shaped by vicarious sources of crime information. Third, those groups in society for whom fear is a greater problem (such as the elderly), generally have higher levels of media exposure.

Despite the popularity of this argument, it is open to a number of criticisms:

1. Although some studies report a direct relationship between patterns of mass media exposure and fear of crime, most do not (Gordon and Heath, 1981; Gomme, 1988; Tyler, 1984; Goodstein and Shotland, 1980; Cumberbatch and Beardsworth, 1976; Sacco, 1979; Roshier, 1973 Doob and Macdonald, 1979 Skogan and Maxfield, 1981; Sherizan, 1978).

2. Those studies which do report an effect of media exposure upon fear of crime are frequently unable to demonstrate the hypothesized causal link. Simply showing, for instance, that high levels of fear are related to high levels of media exposure in the context of cross-sectional survey data does not unequivocally show that television viewing causes fear. It could just as

likely be the case that people who are afraid are more likely to stay home and as a result, watch more television.

3. The argument assumes a rather simplistic conceptualization of the audience and it is unlikely that people are as myopic as this position suggests. Most of us do not decide how afraid to be simply by watching television but employ a wide variety of cues, many of which are not mediated by mass communicators (Furstenberg, 1972).

4. How much one watches television is not necessarily an indicator of how much one knows about crime. We do not just absorb mass media content as isolated atomistic individuals but we tell others about what we see and read, and discuss media content with them. This means that even people who do not watch a lot of television or regularly read the newspaper may know about crimes that are reported in the media. Given this, we would not expect the level of media exposure to serve as a useful indicator of who is and who is not afraid.

In general, the evidence would seem to suggest that exposure to mass media may exert little direct impact upon fear of crime. This is not to deny that the media may play a more subtle role in setting the agenda about crime as a social issue or in establishing the ideological boundaries which structure public discourse about "the crime problem" (Sacco, 1979; Smith, 1986).

Although mass communications may have little direct influence upon fear of crime, there is empirical support for the argument that fear develops in response to rumors and gossip about local crimes that circulate within neighborhood networks. An awareness of local crime conditions and familiarity with others who have been victimized has been shown to be related to more intense perceptions of neighborhood danger and personal fear (Clarke, 1984; Clarke and Lewis, 1982; Miethe and Lee, 1984; Skogan and Maxfield, 1981). The stories that move through informal channels may be more salient than those contained in mass media because they tend to emphasize conditions and persons that have relevance to the immediate environment (Goodstein and Shotland, 1980).

While conversations about crime, especially local crime, are characteristic of all age groups, they may have particular relevance for the elderly (Cook et al., 1981; Yin, 1980). As stated, in their study of reactions to crime in three large American cities, Skogan and Maxfield (1981) found that stories about local crime tended to emphasize the violent victimization of older people and women. They suggest that local crime news may be particularly troubling to those who learn that people like themselves are in greatest danger. Moreover, their analysis revealed that older people who personally knew a crime victim were significantly more fearful than younger people with acquaintances who had been victimized.

It was previously argued that involvment in the local neighborhood may bring with it certain benefits in the form of increased social support and reduced isolation. It appears, however, that it may involve some costs as well. To the extent that one learns about one's neighbors and their business, one also learns about local crimes and local victims.

Perceptual Variables

It is, of course, unrealistic to assume that the fear of crime exists in some sort of pscychological vacuum. Instead, the ways in which people think about crime is related to the ways in which they think about other things. It is necessary, therefore, to conceptualize fear of crime in a way that takes account of the larger attitude matrix of which it is a part. Three types of perceptual variables are discussed below.

Beliefs About Crime. Earlier reference was made to the use of cognitive indicators of fear of crime. Such measures are more widely employed by researchers as indicators of beliefs about crime that are conceptualized as being causally prior to fear. This practice has considerable theoretical utility. Warr and Stafford (1983) use the term, "proximate causes" to refer to two types of crime-related percepetions that may be construed as causes of feelings of unsafety. The first is risk or the perceived probability of being victimized. The second is seriousness; that is the perceived gravity of the victimization experience. To be fearful with respect to any particular type of offence, Warr and Stafford argue, people must judge the event as both probable and serious. Using data from their Washington study, they were able to demonstrate the applicability of this model to a wide range of crimes.

Other researchers have also demonstrated the empirical significance of relationships involving measures of fear and of beliefs about risk or vulnerability (Giles-Sims, 1984; Clarke, 1984; Janson and Ryder, 1983; Baumer, 1985). Miethe and Lee (1984) provide evidence to suggest that it is through such variables that non-perceptual factors such as local crime rate, victim experience and the victimization of acquaintances affect fear.

Finally, it should be noted that not only perceptions of the risk or seriousness of vulnerability predict fear of crime but so do perceptions of the efficacy of social control. Put simply, positive perceptions of local police may suppress concerns about personal safety (Baumer, 1985; Baker et al., 1983)

Psychological Malaise. Several investigators have documented empirical relationships involving the fear of crime and a variety of indicators that may be said to tap more general dimensions of an uneasiness about personal or social conditions. Relevant predispositions in this regard include anomia and alienation (Sacco, 1985b; Toseland, 1982), a resentment of social change (Eve and Eve, 1984; Gubrium, 1973; Furstenberg, 1972; Lotz, 1979), pessimism about the future (Toseland, 1982; Eve and Eve, 1984), a perceived lack of control over life circumstances (Sacco and Glackman, 1987; Normoyle and Lavrakas, 1984), a lack of interpersonal trust (Conklin,1975) and dissatisfaction with neighborhood life (Hartnagel, 1979; Conklin, 1975; Hindelang et al., 1978; Yin, 1980).

Again, there are problems relating to the theoretical interpretations of these relationships. While causal arguments are popular (e.g. anomia causes fear) other writers suggest that many of these measures reflect the effects rather than the determinants of fear. Still others maintain that traditional fear of crime measures are themselves indicators of diffuse anxieties about the quality of urban life (Wilson, 1975; Garofalo and Laub, 1978).

Physical Efficacy. Finally several researchers suggest that positive perceptions of physical health reduce anxieties about criminal danger (Giles-Sims, 1984; Eve and Eve, 1984; Braungart et al., 1979; Finley, 1983; Riger et al., 1978).

The most reasonable intepretations of these relationships stress the role of physical efficacy in the reduction of vulnerability. Individuals who feel more healthy may feel more confident in their abilities both to evade criminal danger and to cope with the consequences of negative life events.

FEAR OF CRIME AMONG THE ELDERLY: SOME THEORETICAL ISSUES

The accumulated body of research allows us to provide tentative answers to some of the more important theoretical questions that occupy the attention of those working in this area.

First, assuming that the eldery are more fearful than the non-elderly, how are we to make theoretical sense of this pattern? The simple answer to this question involves a recognition that age-differentials in fear may be understood as a reaction to differentials in the combined influence of perceived risk and perceived vulnerability. The former refers to beliefs about the social and physical environment in which the elderly live whereas the latter involves perceptions of the self.

We have seen that with respect to the elderly there appear to be significant disparities between perceived and actual risk. We have also seen, however, that these disparities cease to be problematic upon closer examination. While actual risks may be lower overall, they are not necessarily lower for selected categories of offences (such as purse snatching or robbery) which may form the basis of much elderly concern about personal safety.

Moreover, the type of information that older persons receive through informal channels of communication may aggravate the sense of risk in that they are likely to hear about the victimization of persons who are much like themselves. In addition, the elderly may have long known what criminologists have only recently discovered - that levels of victimization are low in large part because their levels of exposure to risk are low.

As Warr has argued, even moderate levels of perceived risk among older persons may result in greater fear. Older persons have a heightened sensitivity to risk as a result of their higher levels of perceived vulnerability. We have seen in previous chapters that victimizations involving older persons are more likely to be completed than the victimizations of the non-elderly and that older persons may cope less effectively in the aftermath of victimization. The feelings of elderly vulnerability, which reflect such realities, are conditioned by the social, economic and physical disadvantages which many older persons routinely experience.

As discusssed in Chapters 7 and 8, the concept of lifestyle is of considerable utility in organizing our understanding of patterns of elderly victimization. In a related way, it is possible to suggest that the fear of victimization, like victimization itself, is rooted in distinctive patterns of activity that are characteristic of older populations. Thus, because elderly lifestyles typically involve disengagement from many social networks, they may deny people access to many of the social supports that might reduce anxieties about criminal victimization. Further, to the extent that elderly lifestyles restrict movement in the community, they may encourage people to become increasingly reliant upon the exaggerated and distorted information about crime and criminals that circulates in the form of gossip and rumor. They may rarely seek direct verification of this information and as a result develop an unrealistic sense of the dangers that await them. While neighborhood outings may not bring older residents into contact with offenders, they may increase exposure to "uncivil behavior" particularly on the part of teenagers. The social boundaries which restrict intergenerational communication and understanding and the age- segregated nature of so much social acitivity may accentuate the extent to which such incivilities are regarded as threats to personal safety. The important irony in all of this is that while elderly lifestyles result in lower levels of overall victimization, they simultaneously result in higher levels of fear of victimization.

A second set of theoretical questions relates to the distribution of fear within the elderly population. As we have seen, the elderly are not a homogeneous group and thus fear of crime may be a much more serious problem for some older persons than for others. Those elderly persons, for instance, who are female, poor, recently victimized, disengaged from supportive social networks, pessimistic about the future, informed about local crime, and who reside in large cities, high crime neighborhoods and age-integrated housing are most likely to express anxieties about their safety. Moreover, because the effects of many of these variables are additive, some particular sub-groups of older persons must contend with a condition of "multiple jeopardy" (Toseland, 1982).

In general, it appears that those factors which increase fear of crime in the rest of the population, produce the same effects among the elderly. Importantly, however, it seems to be the case that some of these factors are of even greater causal significance in older populations. As our previous discussion would suggest, these interactions might best be explained in terms of the "unique vulnerability" of older persons.

CONCLUSION

Is elderly fear of crime a major social problem? Answers to this question are, of necessity, normative. To say that something is a "major problem" or a problem at all requires an invocation of personal or social values. Our judgments in this regard depend upon the extent to which we are willing or unwilling to define a condition as tolerable.

One way of determining the extent to which elderly fear of crime is a problem is to compare it to other problems that affect older persons. Thus, we might attempt to assess whether fear of criminal victimization is a greater problem than criminal victimization itself. Our analysis would probably lead us to conclude that it is or is not more problematic depending upon which dimensions of the comparison we wish to emphasize. If we emphasize the relative prevalence of fear and victimization, it is clear that the former affects far more people than does the latter. If, however, we focus upon consequences rather than prevalence, the waters quickly become murky. We would need a metric that could permit the comparison of small numbers of victims suffering the types of physical, social and economic costs that we discussed in Chapter 9 with relatively larger numbers of people experiencing less extreme effects.

Other methods of problem estimation would support the view that the elderly, in general, are not "prisoners of fear" as the mass media sometimes suggest. Comparisons of the fear levels of elderly and non-elderly populations reveal significant but not extreme differentials. Moreover, when given the opportunity to state the problems that trouble them most, the elderly are more likely to cite concerns relating to health and financial insecurity than to crime or the fear of crime; although, as we have seen, these problems may not be truly separable.

The research literature also indicates that it may be a substantial error to dismiss elderly fears as simple paranoia. Instead, these perceptions seem to be sensitive to variations in "objective risk" and to reflect not wholly unrealistic assumptions about the ability of older persons to cope with the occurrence and aftermath of victimization. While it may be fashionable to view fear of crime as an irrational response on the part of the elderly to a world that does not truly threaten them, such a conceptualization is probably not appropriate. Rather than irrationality, elderly fear of crime may represent the exercise of caution by a group in society that frequently lacks the control necessary to manage the risk of criminal harm or to marshall the resources necessary to offset its consequences.

CHAPTER TEN: RECOMMENDED READINGS

Balkin, S.
1979 Victimization Rates, Safety and Fear of Crime.   Social Problems, 26:343-358.

Baumer, T.L.
1978 Research on Fear of Crime in the United States. Victimology, 3:254-264.

Garofalo, J.
1981 The Fear of Crime: Causes and Consequences. The Journal of Criminal Law and Criminology, 72:839-857.

Warr, M.
1984 Fear of Victimization: Why are Women and the Elderly More Afraid? Social Science Quarterly, 65:681-702.

Wilson, J.Q. and G.L. Kelling
1982 Broken Windows: The Police and Neighborhood Safety.   The Atlantic Monthly, March:29-38.

Yin, P.

1980 Fear of Crime Among the Elderly: Some Issues and Suggestions. Social Problems, 27:492-504.

Yin, P.

1982 Fear of Crime as a Problem for the Elderly. Social Problems, 30:240-245.

CHAPTER ELEVEN

THE MISTREATMENT OF THE ELDERLY IN DOMESTIC SETTINGS

INTRODUCTION

Within recent years, criminological images of the elderly have undergone a significant modification. As Gordon (1987:116) notes:

> The image of the elderly as victims of conventional "street" crime is being replaced by a view in which the family and private nursing home settings appear as more hazardous environments.

Accordingly, we turn our attention in this chapter to a consideration of what has popularly come to be known as "elder abuse". Previously, we discussed the ways in which relations between older persons and strangers, in many cases, result in victimization episodes. In the present context, we are interested in an examination of the kinds of maltreatment that result from the actions of family members or others with whom the elderly have more diffuse and more prolonged social relations.

Although we devote a separate chapter to this problem, we do not wish to imply that much of what concerns us in this regard is not criminal, or even that it is "less criminal" or less serious than the types of victimizations that were the focus of previous chapters. To be sure, much of what is conceptualized as elder abuse or neglect is easily covered by conventional definitions of theft or criminal violence. Yet, it is also the case that such definitions exclude much abusive behavior. While, for instance, psychological manipulation or the neglect of emotional needs may not be strictly illegal, they may result in some considerable degree of harm.

Moreover, by giving elder abuse and neglect separate attention, we wish to explicitly recognize two significant aspects of these issues that set them apart from other forms of criminal victimization of the elderly. The first relates to questions of criminological measurement and explanation. As we shall see, the mistreatment of the elderly by those who are supposed to provide care is not as amenable to traditional forms of conceptualization, investigation or theoretical accounting as are the more common forms of victimization that we discussed in previous chapters. As we will discover, the prevalence and social distribution of these forms of victimization are estimated only with great difficulty and our theoretical explanations tend to be eclectic rather than systematic and integrated (Pillemer and Suitor, 1988; Anetzberger, 1987; Phillips, 1986).

A second reason for giving the problem of elder abuse separate attention relates to the distinctiveness of associated policy issues. As will become clear in the next chapter, the attempt to develop and implement programs relevant to the amelioration of this problem may involve strategies quite unlike those that have as their objective the reduction of "garden variety" crimes or the fear of such crimes.

The literature on mistreatment of the elderly by care-providers emphasizes the study of primarily two types of environments within which mistreatment occurs. The first is the institution for the aged such as the extended care hospital or the nursing home. The second is the home. In this chapter we shall emphasize the latter at the expense of the former. As we already know, and contrary to popular impressions, only a very small minority of eldery persons live in institutionalized settings (Hudson, 1986). This implies that to the degree that mistreatment of the elderly is a problem, it is a problem that is more characteristic of domestic than institutional settings.

The discussion in this chapter will follow many of the same steps that guided the analyses in earlier chapters. Specifically, we will attempt to address the empirical dimensions of elder mistreatment in order to develop an understanding of the magnitude and distribution of the problem. Afterwards, we will review and offer a critical assessment of those theoretical explanations which are dominant in the literature. In the next chapter we will turn our attention to a consideration of some relevant policy issues.

THE PROBLEM OF ELDER ABUSE AND NEGLECT

An Emergent Issue

It can be argued that our understanding of elder abuse and neglect is underdeveloped in large part because it is only recently that criminologists and gerontologists have turned their attention to its study. More specifically, it was not until the late 1970s that the problem was "discovered" by the research community (Champlin, 1982; King, 1983; Anetzberger, 1987; Quinn and Tomita, 1986). Moreover, much of what was initially written on the subject was sensationalistic and lacking in empirical substance (Brostoff et al., 1972; Hudson, 1986). In practical terms, therefore, it can be argued that the disciplined examination of familial mistreatment of the eldery is still in its infancy.

This point must not be misunderstood. We are not suggesting that abuse and neglect are themselves new phenomena; only that the recognition of abuse and neglect as victimological problems is a recent innovation. Quinn and Tomita

(1986) maintain that although elder abuse has only recently been defined as a public issue, those who have worked with the elderly have always known of its existence. Consistent with this observation is Stearn's (1986) contention that there exists considerable historical evidence to indicate that violence against the elderly was a pervasive problem during previous centuries.

In view of this apparent contradiction, it is legitimate to ask why social scientists have traditionally appeared reluctant to investigate such issues. In part, of course, this neglect resulted from a more pervasive tendency to ignore the elderly and their problems (Anetzberger, 1987). As we have already noted, it is only in the contemporary period that gerontology has become a "growth industry".

Another, perhaps less obvious reason for this neglect may be related to a more general ideological reluctance on the part of social scientists and the public alike to view the family as a source of discord and harm (Hudson, 1986; Steinmetz, 1978). Our culture, after all, provides us with a highly idealized image of family life and the intensity and pervasiveness of these beliefs mitigate against a willingness to admit that the family may be the site of physical, psychological, emotional or economic violence.

Over the past few decades, however, we have slowly been forced to recognize that much of the harm that we do to each other takes place within the context of familial relationships (Steinmetz, 1977; 1986; Straus et al., 1976; Burston, 1975; Katz, 1980). Although spousal assault, incest and child abuse are presently acknowledged as serious social problems, there was a time not too long ago when they too were largely invisible. To admit the pervasiveness of these problems is to admit the fallacy of idealized belifs about family life and for a long period of time we resisted such admissions. A similar dynamic has obscured our awareness of the abuse of the elderly.

Conceptual Limitations

Unlike many of the forms of victimization discussed in earlier chapters, abuse and neglect signify conceptual rather than legal categories and there is no consensus regarding the most appropriate forms that such conceptualizations should take (O'Malley, et al.,1983; Douglass and Hickey, 1983).

In this respect, several questions lack satisfactory answers. What is the distinction between neglect and abuse (Quinn and Tomita,1986)? How frequent or how intense must mistreatment be before it is to be labelled abuse or neglect (Davidson, 1979; Rathbone-McCuan and Hashimi, 1982; Johnson, 1986; Phillips, 1986)? Should these terms be restricted to physical forms of mistreatment or should they be more liberally applied to include threats of harm or a neglect of emotional needs (Anderson, 1981; Olson, 1981)? Should self-neglect or self-abuse be encompassed by definitions of elder abuse and elder neglect (Anderson, 1981; Johnson, 1986)? If an elderly person behaves in ways that suggest a tolerance of, or adjustment to some form of mistreatment, can it still be considerd abuse (Phillips, 1986)? How relevant is the intention of the perpetrator to our decision to designate some form of mistreatment as abusive (Hickey and Douglass,1981a; Brillon, 1987)?

Hudson (1986) argues that many analysts attempt to avoid difficult problems of conceptualization by developing "extrinsic definitions" which are typological in nature. Thus, the essential conceptual character of the phenomena in question is abandoned in favor of efforts to elaborate the variety of its expression. Such typologies abound in the literature, but there appears to be very little consensus regarding the importance of the distinctions to which they collectively draw our attention (Rathbone-McCuan and Hashimi, 1982).

All of this conceptual ambiguity has serious implications. Comparisons across studies are impeded by the fact that similar empirical phenomena may be differentially categorized while distinctive empirical phenomena may be assigned similar labels (Quinn and Tomita, 1986). Quite obviously, there can be little movement toward the development of meaningful explanatory theory in the absence of a rather precise understanding of what it is that requires explanation (Johnson, 1986). It is also unlikely that effective policy can be formulated or implemeneted when the object of policy attention is vague and unspecified.

A somewhat more complex problem with many contemporary conceptualizations of elder abuse and neglect derives from the tendency on the part of some researchers to utilize these terms in tautological fashion. In other words, abuse is used in ways that describe the actions of the perpetrator of the abuse as well as the harm which these actions produce. By implication, a theoretical relationship is reduced to a circular argument of the form, "elder abuse causes elder abuse".

In response, some writers have suggested the importance of maintaining the distinction between the pain and suffering experienced by older persons and the mechanisms which produce this pain and suffering. Thus, O'Malley et al. (1983) suggest that the term, "unmet needs" should replace the former and the terms "abuse" and "neglect" should be used, in more restricted fashion, to reference the processes which allow needs for physical and emotional support to be increased or ignored. For these writers, then, negelct is a failure on the part of a caregiver to resolve a need of an older person while abuse is an active intervention by which unmet needs are created or sustained. In a somewhat similar fashion, Johnson (1986) focuses upon a definitional process which views abuse and neglect as causes of sustained pain and anguish, unnecessary to the maintenance of the quality of life of an older person.

Definitions of this type are valuable, in part, because they resolve the tautologies of earlier formulations in ways that render meaningful the distinction between causes and consequences. They do so by separating out questions about the intent to harm from questions about how the effects of mistreatment are to be identified. Whether these conceptual advances have a substantial impact upon the development of scholarship will depend upon the degree to which they are accepted as convention by those working in this area.

PATTERNS OF ELDER MISTREATMENT

As discussed in Chapter 7, three methodological approaches dominate the study of elder abuse and neglect (and victimization more generally). The first involves the attempt to access relevant data by examining official agency records or by interviewing health care or social service professionals. The second involves interviews with those who are actual or potential perpetrators of abuse while the third attempts to study elder mistreatment by studying those who are the victims of mistreatment. We also saw in Chapter 7 that each of these strategies has its own characteristic methodological limitations that compromise the quality of the data generated.

While these research strategies are used to estimate the prevalence or social distribution of abusive acts, it may be argued that the manner in which these tallies are constructed may fundamentally misrepresent the nature of the problem. This is because the phenomenon of elder abuse is much less discrete and situational than more traditional forms of victimization. The types of victimization incidents that we discussed in earlier chapters seem to have a relatively precise quality to them. They happen at particular times and in particular places and it makes sense to speak about them as events with a definite beginning and a definite end.

On the other hand, abuse or neglect may not be best conceptualized as phenomena reducible to a number of isolated, independent incidents. Rather, any particular abusive incident is part of a larger overall syndrome of abuse (Rathbone-McCuan and Hashimi, 1982). Further, because such behavior is chronic and long-term (Anetzberger, 1987) a research emphasis upon individual incidents of abuse may create a false reality with respect to situations in which it is truly unclear when one incident ends and another begins.

As we have seen, a further problem common to all three research strategies concerns the fact that both offenders and victims, in a large number of cases, appear to be unwilling to report the abuse to either researchers or health or social service agency personnel. Most obviously, the perpetrator may fear censure if others become aware of his or her actions. Somewhat less obviously, there is evidence to suggest that the perpetrator may be financially dependent upon the victim and may feel threatened by actions with the potential to disrupt the relationship (Pillemer, 1986). The victim may be unwilling to report abuse for a variety of reasons including guilt, embarrassment, or a concern that if others gain knowledge of the situation, the consequence may be an institutional placement (Kosberg, 1988; Davidson, 1979; Anderson, 1981). Additionally, perpetrators and victims may be unlikely to report incidents of abuse either because of psychological impairments which hamper recall or familial traditions that encourage a high tolerance of such conduct (Quinn and Tomita, 1986).

Taken together, these difficulties imply that the link between the "dark figure" of elder abuse and the social reality of such abuse, as revealed by social research, may be tenuous at best.

Estimating Prevalence

One widely quoted source estimates that in the United States, approximately 4% of elders are abused (Block and Sinnott, 1979). According to these writers, the figures suggest that, in the aggregate, elder abuse is somewhat less prevalent than spousal abuse and about as prevalent as child abuse. However, this is only one estimate among many and as Hudson (1986) notes, prevalence estimates range from one to ten percent of the elderly population.

While such general figures make for convenient and effective political rhetoric, they may be telling us very little. As we have seen, there is not much agreement about what it means to be abused, neglected or mistreated and thus claims about the proportion of the population affected may obscure more than they reveal.

The range of behaviors and conditions captured by such estimates is indeed broad since for most analysts, elder mistreatment is best viewed as a multidimensional construct. Some sense of the variety of the conditions which these estimates may or may not include can be illustrated with reference to the major dimensions which many observers would agree require consideration:

Physical Dimensions. This is probably the most obvious and the most extreme form of elder mistreatment. Its consequences include the debilitation of health and in extreme cases, death. Relevant behaviors may include sexual (Tomita, 1982) and non- sexual assault (Pillemer and Finkelhor, 1988), the inappropriate use of medication (Davidson, 1979) or the denial of health- related appliances such as eyeglasses, a hearing aid, or a walker (Quinn and Tomita, 1986). Physical mistreatment may also be linked to various forms of self-abuse. Thus, individuals whose physical needs are not met by others may use alcohol or prescribed medication excessively in order to adjust to their predicament. They may also be less inclined to seek out medical care or to attend to their nutritional requirements (Quinn and Tomita, 1986).

Material Mistreatment. This category references those types of harm which have consequences that are essentially financial. Relevant behaviors may include the systematic and unauthorized withdrawl of savings, the routine diversion of income or the sale of property through fraudulent means (Gordon, 1987; Kosberg, 1985).

Psychological Mistreatment. This may almost be regarded as a residual category which includes a wide range of assaults to the psyche and to the emotional well-being of the elder. At one level, it may reference verbal threats, humiliations, degradation and the creation of fear (Steur and Austin, 1980). Elderly persons may be socially (if not physically) isolated by others in the household in ways that deny basic emotional needs. The consequences of psychological mistreatment may include trembling, disorientation, depression or suicide (Quinn and Tomita, 1986). A final type of psychosocial mistreatment involves the denial of the basic rights of the elderly person. For instance, the individual may be denied visitors or the right to attend church. A denial of rights may also involve the relinquishment of control over one's life situation such that the elder may not even be consulted with respect to important life decisions. The elderly person may be told when to eat, when to sleep and what

233

sorts of activites may or may not be permitted (Kosberg, 1985; Quinn and Tomita, 1986).

An awareness of the diversity that abusive behaviors may take suggests that instead of attempting to generate general estimates of mistreatment, we should perhaps be more concerned with estimates of the relative frequencies of distinctive types of abuse. However, as might be expected, significant variations in methodologies and in the manner in which categories of mistreatment are conceptualized by researchers, mitigate against easy meaningful estimates in this regard as well.

As a result, estimates of relative prevalence found in the research literature lack consistency. While some researchers argue that physical mistreatment occurs with greater relative frequency (Hickey and Douglass, 1981b; Pillemer and Finkelhor, 1988; Anetzberger, 1987) others claim that psychosocial (Block and Sinnott, 1979; Katz, 1980) or financial mistreatment (Shell, 1982; Gordon, 1987) may be more prevalent.

To put the whole matter simply, we do not have access to the types of evidence that permits us to provide firm estimates of either the general prevalence of elder mistreatment or the relative occurrence of its more specific forms. Still, some tentative conclusions may be reached:

1. However elder mistreatment is operationally defined, it occurs with greater frequency than official agency records would suggest.

2. Particularly serious forms of elder mistreatment (especially if they involve physical mistreatment) are probably more likely to come to the attention of authorities than are less serious forms of mistreatment.

3. Those forms of elder mistreatment against which there are less stringent normative prohibitions and which can be more easily rationalized by perpetrators (such as emotional or psychosocial mistreatment) probably occur with greater frequency than do more obvious forms of physical abuse. And, "crimes of omission" probably occur with greater frequency than do "crimes of commission" (Steur and Austin, 1980)

The Correlates of Elder Mistreatment

As with all forms of criminal victimization we would expect, in the case of elder mistreatment, that the probability of being a victim or victimizer is related to prior social and demographic characteristics. In general, the data do support the conclusion that elder mistreatment is not a random occurrence but that it is more likely to be perpetrated by and against some types of people than others. Not unexpectedly, however, we face empirical difficulties in the attempt to determine how elder mistreatmment is socially distributed. Most notably, many studies have not employed random samples or controls which would allow researchers to know with greater certainty whether the factors correlated with abuse in the group studied are likely to be related to abuse in the wider population (Pillemer and Suitor, 1988; Quinn and Tomita, 1986: Salend et al., 1984).

With respect to the social characteristics of the victims of mistreatment, the majority of researchers argue that women are at greater risk than men and that the "old-old" are at greater risk than the "young-old" (Steur and Austin, 1980; Douglass and Hickey, 1983; Steur, 1983; Steinmetz, 1983; Shell, 1982; Anetzberger, 1987; U.S. Department of Health and Human Services, 1980; Brillon, 1987; Quinn and Tomita, 1986; Block and Sinnott, 1979). In a sense, the frequently reported gender imbalance could be deduced from knowledge of the age distribution of the populations typically studied. Since women live longer than men, elderly people are more likely to be female than male; and, the relative proportion of females increases along with the age of the subject population (Alston, 1986; Shell, 1982). It is important to note, however, that not all research supports the conclusion that women are more likely than men to be the victims of mistreatment (Hudson, 1986). In a community survey of over 2000 elderly residents of the Boston area, Pillemer and Finkelhor (1988) found that the rates of abuse for men were twice as high as the rates experienced by women. They suggest that mistreatment of females is more likely to show up in official accounts because women are likely to experience more serious injuries and because women may be less tolerant of abuse.

Most resarchers also contend that the victim of elder mistreatment is typically someone who suffers from a physical or mental impairment (Davidson, 1979; Douglass and Hickey, 1983; Steinmetz, 1983; Anetzberger, 1987; U.S. Department of Health and Human Services, 1980; Brillon, 1987; Quinn and Tomita, 1986; Pillemer and Finkelhor, 1988). Again, however, some recent research disputes the correlational significance of functional disabilities (Hudson, 1986; Wolf, 1986; Pillemer, 1985).

Since most victims are mistreated by people with whom they share a residence (Block and Sinnott, 1979; Anetzberger, 1987; U.S. Department of Health and Human Services, 1980; Brillon, 1987), it appears.that rates of mistreatment are lower for those elderly persons who are willing or able to live alone. In their community survey, Pillemer and Finkelhor (1988) found that the rate of abuse among those living alone was one-fourth the rate of those who lived with someone else.

There is somewhat less consensus regarding the importance of other correlates. It is unclear, for instance, whether rates of elder mistreatment vary significantly across social classes (Alston, 1986; Pillemer and Finkelhor, 1988) although it is frequently reported that the problem is more prevalent among middle and lower income groups (Block and Sinnott, 1979; Quinn and Tomita, 1986). Similarly, the importance of race remains uncertain (Cazenave,1983). While the prevalence of presumably important causal factors such as poverty and multi-generational households is greater in black populations, rates of elder abuse are reportedly lower.

The available evidence also provides us with a rather consistent if threadbare profile of the typical offender. In short, it appears that those who engage in abuse are likely to be related to the elder and to some degree responsible for the provision of care (Hudson, 1986). However, the research is somewhat equivocal regarding the social and demographic characteristics of the perpetrator and the specific nature of the kin relationship. The majority of studies support the conclusion that women are more likely than men to be abusers (Block and Sinnott, 1979; Steinmetz, 1983; Douglass and Hickey, 1983; Steur, 1983). This is consistent with the more general finding that women rather than men are normally expected to assume caregiving roles within the family

(Stone et al., 1987). These data would suggest that in the case of elder mistreatment, women face a situation of "double-jeopardy" (Steinmetz, 1983) in that they appear more likely to be both victims and perpetrators. However, some researchers have found that men rather than women are more likely to mistreat the elderly (Anetzberger, 1987; Shell, 1982; Hudson, 1986).

These differences in findings with respect to the gender composition of abusive populations are reflected in differences regarding the nature of the relationship that links abuser and abused. Some researchers maintain that abusers are most likely to be sons (Shell, 1982; Anetzberger, 1987; Quinn and Tomita, 1986) or daughters (Block and Sinnott, 1979; Douglass and Hickey, 1983; Steinmetz, 1983), while other have found that much elder abuse is really spousal abuse (Pillemer and Finkelhor, 1988; Davidson, 1979).

In part, the resolution of some of these inconsistencies probably involves a consideration of difference among the samples employed by researchers. As Pillmer and Finkelhor (1988) note, the underlying dynamic of elder abuse is that people are mistreated by those with whom they live. In their community study, they found that, in general, elderly people were more likely to reside with spouses than with their children; and, that the rates of abuse were similar in both cases. If, however, a research sample is highly skewed so as to over-represent the very old, a somewhat different picture emerges. This is because as the age of victims increases, the probability that they will have a spouse who is still living and able to provide care decreases. Similarly, as the age of victims increases, the probability that they will be taken care of (and potentially abused by) an adult son also decreases.

In this respect, it is important to emphasize that many studies have shown that those who engage in elder mistreatment are themselves elderly or near-elderly (Pillemer and Finkelhor, 1988; Steinmetz, 1983; Shell, 1982). This once again reflects the general nature of the caregiver population. One national study reports the average age of this population to be 57 (Stone et al., 1987). Thus, whether the mistreated elder resides with a spouse or, with an adult child, it is probable that the abuser is also of advanced age.

Although more complex data on the social and behavioral attributes of those who mistreat the eldery is sketchy, there is the suggestion in the literature that some significant proportion of them abuse drugs or alcohol, (Champlin, 1982; Falcioni, 1982; Steur and Austin, 1980; O'Malley et al., 1983) or suffer from some form of psychopathology (Davidson, 1979; Olson, 1981; Kosberg, 1985). It is also claimed by some that elder mistreatment is more frequent among those who were themselves abused during their formative years (Hickey and Douglass, 1981b).

In general, our knowledge of the social and demographic characteristics of victims and perpetrators lacks specificity and consistency. As a result, we are not able to describe with accuracy, those who are most at-risk of being abused or abusive. Nevertheless, based on the empirical knowledge that we do have, it is possible to theorize about the types of factors and circumstances that make mistreatment more or less likely. We take up that task in the next section.

236

EXPLAINING ELDER MISTREATMENT

The Nature of the Theoretical Problem

Despite the empirical and conceptual ambiguities that characterize the field of elder mistreatment, there has been no shortage of attempts to account for the prevalence and distribution of the problem. Partially as a result of such ambiguities, there has been a tendency on the part of many researchers to attempt to borrow from the theoretical insights that have guided the analyses of related problems.

In particular, theoretical accounts have been influenced by work done in the area of child abuse (Anetzberger, 1987; Steinmetz, 1978). A major assumption of such approaches is that dependency relationships may place children and elders alike in situations in which they are easily mistreated by those to whom their care is entrusted. However, while these theoretical explanations encourage an appreciation of the ways in which elder abuse and child abuse are similar, they may simultaneously obscure an appreciation of the ways in which they are different (Katz, 1980). As Quinn and Tomita (1986) note, for instance, the elderly are more likely than young children to possess economic assets which may increase the probability of financial abuse.

Currently, no single theory of elder abuse may be said to dominate the literature (Shell, 1982). In addition, it is highly unlikely that a single theoretical framework would ever be able to account for the diversity of the phenomena in which researchers are interested (Circelli, 1986; Phillips, 1986).

Although no one theoretical explanation may be sufficient to explain all of the empirical facts of elder mistreatment, each may be of some limited utility. One approach to the problem is to recognize that theoretical questions about elder mistreatment may be phrased in a number of ways and that available theories may be viewed as best suited to answering some of these questions but not others.

Accordingly, we organize our discussion in terms of four distinct, yet related, questions about the nature and social location of elder mistreatment:

1. In the context of domestic situations, why do some people and not others behave towards elders in an abusive or neglectful fashion?

2. How can elder mistreatment be understood as a product of the social relationships that join victim and victimizer?

3. How is elder mistreatment conditioned by the larger social context within which these relationships are situated?

4. How does the content of the social interaction in which the victim and perpetrator are involved stabilize patterns of elder mistreatment?

In the following discussion, we consider contemporary theoretical answers to these questions. Our intention in doing so is not to focus upon the incompatibility of apparently competing views but to emphasize their potentially complementary character.

The Abusive Caregiver

Within some theoretical treatments (as well as within much popular discourse) mistreatment of the elderly is understood with reference to caregiver characteristics which increase the probability that he or she will engage in abusive or neglectful behavior. Put simply, mistreatment occurs because some elders are proximate to or dependent upon those who are likely to be abusive.

Such explanations have important precedents in criminology. Throughout most of the history of the discipline attempts to explain misbehavior have focused upon the characteristics of offenders rather than upon, for instance, the characteristics of victims or victim-offender interactions. The type of argument being examined here represents a recent and specific variant of this more traditional and more general theoretical logic.

We have already made reference to some of the evidence that might be viewed as supportive of this position. As noted, several researchers have reported a tendency toward drug or alcohol abuse on the part of those who mistreat the elderly (Champlin, 1982; Steur and Austin, 1980; King, 1983; Anetzberger, 1987; Quinn and Tomita, 1986; Pillemer, 1986; Falcioni, 1982; Olson, 1981; Pillmer and Suitor, 1988).

Several well known arguments might suggest why substance abuse of the type described in the literature might increase the risk of elder mistreatment. Alcohol abuse might lower inhibitions against violent conduct or allow a caretaker to neutralize the guilt or shame associated with such behavior. Drug or alcohol addiction might result in neglectful conduct if a caregiver is rendered unable or unwilling to fulfill his or her responsibilities. Finally, the elder's financial resources might be channeled off in order to underwrite the cost of an addiction.

A somewhat distinctive set of arguments suggest that elder abuse may emerge out of a normative tendency toward violence and abuse within some families (O'Malley et al., 1983; U.S.Department of Health and Human Services, 1980). In other words, adult children who mistreat their own parents in later life may themselves have been mistreated during their formative years (Hickey and Douglass, 1981b; Falcioni, 1982; Olson, 1981; Shell, 1982). Such arguments provide evidence of the parallels between theories of elder mistreatment and theories of child abuse since it is frequently maintained that parents who were battered as children are more likely to batter their own children. A somewhat different mechanism is required in the attempt to extrapolate this position to the study of elder mistreatment, however, for the simple reason that those who abuse elders are unlikely to have been abused elders themselves (Pillemer and Suitor, 1988; Pillemer, 1986).

At least two such mechanisms are identified in the literature. First, elder abuse may be seen as a form of revenge against a parent who abused the caregiver early in life. Thus, the child who was mistreated in a state of dependency retaliates against a parent when the nature of the dependency relationship shifts (Pillemer and Suitor, 1988; Rathbone-McCuan and Hashimi, 1982). Second, the experience of child abuse may teach the appropriateness of violence as a response to stress or frustration. Thus, children who learn from their parents that physical and emotional abuse are effective and acceptable means of social control may apply these lessons when the situation is conducive to them doing so (Anetzberger, 1987).

In some cases, there is another and more direct way in which a history of family violence may be related to elder abuse. Specifically, what we are calling elder abuse or mistreatment may merely represent a continuity in behavior on the part of victims and perpetrators who have moved into later life. This could be the case, for instance, if adolescents who abused their parents continue to do so into old age (Harbin and Madden, 1979). Similarly, if much elder abuse is really spousal abuse, its origins may be located, not in old age, but much earlier in the life-cycle (Pillemer and Finkelhor, 1988).

In any case, the claim that abusers may behave in violent fashion because they are committed to a belief that violence is under some circumstances an acceptable form of conflict resolution may have important implications for the study of victims as well as for the study of those who victimize them. Familial traditions of violence may cause the victim to view the victimization as legitimate and thus mitigate against regarding even harsh physical treatment as improper (Anderson, 1981).

Elder mistreatment may result from other predispositions acquired during childhood or adolescent socialization (Anetzberger, 1987). Hickey and Douglass (1981b) argue that more general patterns of dysfunctional learning may carry into adulthood and prevent the development of positive relationships. Such individuals may adapt to life problems, such as those relating to elder care, through processes of victim blaming (which could manifest itself in terms of abuse) or evasion (which could result in neglect). Similarly, Circelli (1986) notes that the failure to develop strong parent-child bonds early in life may culminate at a later stage in abusive conduct. These factors may become particularly salient in those situations in which caregiver responsibilities are assumed as a result of guilt or family pressure rather than because of a desire to do so.

Finally, it is possible to argue that the probability of some form of mistreatment may increase if the caregiver is not capable of performing the caregiver role in competent fashion as a result of physical or psychiatric problems (Anetzberger, 1987; Olson, 1981; King, 1983). Thus, caregivers who are themselves elderly may experience poor health or psychological limitations which limit their abilities to provide care (Davidson, 1979).

The apparent importance of a link between various forms of psychopathology and elder abuse suggests an important difference between the abuse of elderly parents and other forms of family violence (Wolf, 1986). Pillemer (1986) argues that adult children who abuse their parents (as opposed to those who abuse spouses or children) do so in the absence of any normative support for their action. While there has existed (and continues to exist) cultural support for - or at least tolerance of - the use of physical force directed against children or wives, this has not traditionally been true in the case of parents. Psychopathologies might therefore provide a better explanation of why some individuals clearly break rules in the case of elder abuse than why other individuals bend rules in the case of spousal or child abuse

In general, theoretical accounts which focus upon the characteristics of those who mistreat the elderly have certain distinct advantages. First, they would appear to be consistent with much empirical evidence. This is particularly true in the case of arguments about psychopathology and substance abuse and somewhat less true in the case of arguments about "cycles of family violence" (Pillemer and Suitor, 1988; Pillemer, 1986). Second, these theories provide an important continuity between our attempts to understand elder mistreatment and our attempts to understand other types of criminal and social victimization. Third, they provide a clear point of policy focus. If the cause of elder abuse is to be located in the physical or psychological characteristics of the abuser, then policy may be conveniently directed toward identifying and modifying those characteristics.

Despite these advantages, explanations of this type are open to logical and ideological criticism. Although they possess a very general utility, to be truly useful, such explanations would require much more rigorous formulation. As they are frequently proposed, they leave several important questions unanswered. What kinds of characteristics result in what kinds of mistreatment? Assuming that the relationship is not a perfect one, under what kinds of conditions is alcoholism or drug abuse likely to result in mistreatment? While psychopathology may explain a general tendency toward mistreatment, how is it related to the occurrence of specific incidents or to variations in the frequency or intensity of mistreatment?

It may also be argued that such theories present a rather narrow picture of elder mistreatment in that they de-emphasize the role played by the victim in abuse and neglect processes. The image of the victim conveyed by such accounts is one of passivity and vulnerability and we are given no understanding of the nature of the relationship that joins victim and victimizer.

Finally, the narrowness of the policy implications that emerge from such theories may be faulted for their failure to foster a critical posture on the problem of elder mistreatment. If the causes of elder mistreatment are thought to be rooted in the malevolence or incompetence of those who reside with the elderly, then we need not concern ourselves with the broader set of structural factors that place elderly persons in such conditions of risk in the first place.

Relational Strain

A second set of theoretical explanations attempts to view mistreatment not as a product of the characteristics of the abuser but as a product of the relationship between victim and victimizer. In general, these arguments suggest that such relationships are likely to engender strain to which adjustments must be made. Theoretical interest centers around the analysis of why these relationships generate strain and how this strain manifests itself as abuse and neglect.

The most general forms of this argument focuses attention upon the ways in which the care required by a mentally or physically disabled elder places an onerous burden upon the caregiver. The lack of congruence between the needs of the elder and family resources may overwhelm the caregiver and promote anger and frustration (Hooyman, 1982).

240

These consequences may be brought about in several ways. First, if the impairments of mind and body are extremely severe, the elder may be in state of almost total dependency and thus in need of constant care and supervision (O'Malley et al., 1983; Luppens and Lau, 1983; King, 1983). Medical advances have made it possible for those with even highly debilitating conditions to remain alive for longer periods of time than was previously the case (Stearns, 1986; Steinmetz, 1983). The caregiver may be forced to go without sleep for extended periods, to forego leisure or cultural opportunities or to pay inadequate attention to his or her own medical needs.

Steinmetz (1983) argues that the psychological and emotional needs of the older person may be an even greater source of stress than those relating to physical disabilities. Advanced age may bring with it unique problems in this respect. What may appear to others as relatively minor matters such as the loss of a pet or the denial of driving privileges may have special significance for the elderly (Brillon, 1987; Quinn and Tomita, 1986). In addition, relatively common afflictions such as dementia or depression may dramatically increase the degree of emotional dependence. The caregiver may lack sufficent insight into the emotional and psychological problems associated with the aging process and assume that the older person is just being difficult (Anetzberger, 1987). Moreover, in an effort to manage the demands of a highly dependent elder, the caregiver may attempt to routinize contacts with the older person and thereby neglect social and emotional needs.

The provision of continuous care to an elderly family member may also be a source of economic strain (King, 1983; Champlin, 1982; Steur and Austin, 1980; Davidson, 1979). In addition to the direct costs associated with these responsibilities, it may be necessary for the principal caregiver to quit work in order to provide care on a full-time basis (Stone et al., 1987).

An important theme in much of the literarture concerns the effects of dependency relationships upon family dynamics and the manner in which the alteration of these dynamics may increase stress and mistreatment. All family members may be affected by the decision to take in an dependent elder. Privacy may be reduced and living conditions may become more crowded. The family's standard of living may require a downward adjustment and household activities and priorities may be reordered.

Steinmetz (1981; 1983) conceptualizes many of these changes in terms of what she calls the "generationally inverse family". The conceptualization is meant to describe the process by which children who were once dependent upon parents assume the alternative role as they become caregivers with respect to an impaired elder parent. As Steinmetz points out, in such cases, it is not just a role that is reversed but a complex set of generationally linked rights, responsibilities and perceptions of self and others (Steinmetz, 1983).

Within the context of generationally inverted families, the caregiver is caught between two generations and two sets of generational priorities and is forced to deal with conflicting expectations (Steinmetz, 1981; 1983). Caregivers who are themselves middle-aged or approaching old age will have recently witnessed or be in the process of witnessing their own dependent children becoming increasingly independent at the same time that an elderly parent becomes more dependent. In particular, female caregivers in this position who may have planned to resume a career or who had planned to return to school, may find that all such plans may have to be indefinitely postponed. It may be necessary to make difficult decisions about whether limited financial resources should be used to pay for a child's wedding or university education or to improve the quality of care for an elderly parent.

These problems may be exacerbated as old unresolved family conflicts become additional sources of strain for family members. Antagonisms which are left over from childhood or early adulthood, and which may have festered over the years, may assume new meaning and new prominence in a situation in which parental roles appear to be reversed (Farrar, 1955; Glasser and Glasser, 1962; Steur and Austin, 1980; Quinn and Tomita, 1986; Steinmetz, 1983). In addition, the elder may be reluctant to relinquish power and may actively deny or subvert the caregiver's authority (Steinmetz, 1983; Quinn and Tomita, 1986). Conflicts regarding who has authority in the home and how household affairs should be managed may become routine.

As well, there are normative dimensions to the problem of relational strain. George (1986) theorizes about the potential for conflict between two dominant types of expectations regarding appropriate caregiver behavior. The first, the norm of reciprocity, requires that parties to a relationship should experience rough equality with respect to losses and gains. The second, the norm of solidarity, demands that family members should be given all possible support and assistance, no matter what the costs. In the context of most enduring relationships, these norms are likely to conflict on occasion. However, George notes, a situation that involves long-term care for a dependent elder will probably cause a permanent normative imbalance. This imbalance may mean that no matter what course of action the caregiver chooses, she is likely to experience feelings of guilt and anxiety. Resentment or anger about the lack of reciprocity can be anxiety-provoking because it violates expectations about solidarity. Similarly, a rigid conformity to the norm of solidarity can result in a neglect of other familial or occupational responsibilities.

There is, moreover, some high degree of normative ambiguity regarding the nature and the extent of grown children's responsibility to provide long-term care to an impaired parent or other elderly relative. While the care of dependent children is a major cultural prescription, there seems to exist somewhat greater ambivalence regarding the dependent elderly (Shell, 1982). Cultural expectations regarding, for instance, which of the grown children should assume the major responsibility, or the role of the extended family in the provision of care are not clearly defined (Katz, 1980; Brillon, 1987). The caregiver may feel forced into the relationship because other options are lacking or because other siblings fail to share the burden (Davidson, 1979; Rathbone-McCuan and Hashimi, 1982).

While the decision to assume the care of an elder family member may provide a rallying point that eventuates in an increase in levels of family solidarity (Davidson, 1979) this is not always the case. Frequently, the decision to take in a dependent elder is made hurriedly and when emotions are running high (Anetzberger, 1987; Davidson, 1979). Family members may be ill-prepared to assume the responsibilities and ignorant of the problems that they are likely to encounter (Quinn and Tomita, 1986).

Theoretical arguments which emphasize relational stress as a cause of elder mistreatment not only have a certain intuitive appeal, but they are also consistent with the more general literature on the etiology of family violence (Phillips, 1986). However like those explanations which focus upon the abusive caregiver, those which emphasize victim-victimizer relationships are problematic in several respects.

One major difficulty relates to the way in which such explanations conceptualize the problem of dependency and its role in the generation of mistreatment. Much of the prevailing wisdom suggests that dependency contributes to abuse by raising stress levels and by placing the elder in a position of powerlessness relative to the abuser. In other words, the dependency relationship both engenders frustration and allows the caregiver to translate this frustration into aggression directed toward the dependent elder. The power differential means that the perpetrator has little to lose by behaving in an abusive fashion (Phillips, 1986).

Yet, this position is open to both logical and empirical criticism. In the former respect, Pillemer (1985) argues that if the power differential is as extreme as many contemporary writers make it out to be, there would be little need to resort to extreme forms of mistreatment. Instead, he suggests, abuse seems more likely when caregivers perceive themselves as lacking power rather than as having power.

Pillemer's (1985; 1986; and Suitor, 1988) analysis of data from three model projects on elder abuse support this analysis of the problem. An examination of data which permitted a comparison of a sample of physically abused elders with a sample of controls revealed that those who were abused were not more likely than the controls to be dependent upon those who abused them; and, that with respect to some measures, they were less dependent. The analysis also indicated that the abused elderly were more likely than the controls to describe their caregivers as dependent upon them for, among other things, housing and financial assistance. Pillemer concludes that in many cases, it is incorrect to describe the abuser as the powerful party in the dependency relationship. Instead, they are frequently offspring who, for one reason or another, are unable to separate from a parent or spouses who suffer from their own mental impairments. It is their dependence and not that of the abused elder's that results in the stress that culminates in abuse. The relationship is allowed to persist, not because the abused elder fears retaliation but because he or she feels a sense of commitment and responsibility to the abuser.

There is also reason to question the general utility of arguments relating to the generationally inverse families. The issue here is less a matter of whether such arguments are correct but rather how widely they can be applied. It will be recalled that in their community survey of elders living in the Boston area, Pillemer and Finkelhor (1988) found that the majority of cases of elder abuse involved spousal rather than parent-child relationships. This would suggest that social dynamics other than those resulting from generational inversion must be given theoretical prominence if the problem of elder abuse is to be comprehensively understood.

Three further limitations of relational stress theories may be identified. First, it is clear that stress is, in itself, an inadequate mechanism for explaining the distribution or intensity of mistreatment. Many more caregivers define their situations as stressful than mistreat their elder charges (Pillmer and Suitor, 1988). What is required in this respect is a more precise articulation of the nature of the linkage between stress and mistreatment.

Second, as was true in the case of theories relating to the characteristics of the abusers, these arguments seem better suited to explaining the general tendency toward mistreatment than the specific manifestations or the timing of episodes of mistreatment.

Finally, the data which are interpreted as supportive of an etiological focus upon relational strain are not unequivocal (Hudson, 1986). Not only is the evidence somewhat inconsistent, it is also open to alternative interpretations. Because a significant proportion of caregivers who engage in mistreatment report that they regard their responsibilities as a source of stress does not imply that the stress is a cause of the mistreatment. It could also be argued that the stress is to some extent, a response to the guilt and anxiety that the mistreatment itself produces in the caregiver. The resolution of this problem, of course requires data that allow investigators to speak to questions about the dynamic character of elder abuse.

Social Structure and Social Change

The relationship between the victim and the perpetrator of elder mistreatment does not exist in a social vacuum but is sensitive to and influenced by more general social, cultural and economic conditions. Theories which emphasize the influence of such conditions adopt a broad rather than a narrow conception of cause. In other words, they do not try to understand the etiology of a particular abusive situation but rather why abuse is widespread.

Stearns (1986) attempts to provide a framework which links changes in levels of elder mistreatment to historical changes in social institutions. Although Stearns contends that the data that would allow us to map these trends are very problematic, he argues that there is considerable evidence to indicate that violence directed against older persons was a prevalent problem during the seventeenth and eighteenth centuries but that it declined over the last century. Current interest in the problem suggests that rates of various forms of elder mistreatment may once again be on the increase. How are the historical variations in levels of elder mistreatment to be understood? Stearns argues that the answer to this question must be located in an analysis of broader social and economic trends which contextualize family relations and thus impact upon levels of family tension and conflict.

High rates of mistreatment of older persons in the preindustrial period, Stearns argues, were in part related to the economics of family relationships. Because during this period, wealth was closely tied to ownership of property, offspring were economically powerless relative to their parents. They may have been unable to marry or to gain economic dependence until parents passed away. These conditions were structurally conducive to the emergence of familial antagonisms which may have resulted in a considerable degree of violent activity on the part of youth directed toward elders.

Stearns notes that industrialization brought with it important social and economic changes which reduced the risk of familial conflict. Specifically, industrialization meant that wealth was less closely tied to property and that increased opportunities for younger generations reduced the economic dependence upon elders. The gradual increase in retirement benefits and the tendency for younger and older generations to occupy separate residences may have also combined to reduce family tensions.

Why then might the rates of elder mistreatment be increasing during the contemporary period? Stearns identifies several factors that might be of significance in this regard. First, changing economic conditions have resulted in the movement of increasing numbers of women into the labor force. This means that in many cases they have been forced to contend with the combined stress of the job and the caretaking situation; or, to make a difficult choice between the two. Second the increase in the number of unskilled, poor and transiently employed persons coupled with the rapid proliferation of tightly regimented white- collar jobs may mean that now more than in the past, the family provides the only significant emotional outlet for stress, anger and frustration. Third, the growth of the elderly population may mean that any one family may be required to assume the resposibility of caring for more than one elder. Fourth, advances in medical science have made it possible to increase substantially the life-expectancy of debilitated persons. Fifth, while the maintenance of separate residences by elderly parents and adult offspring may have initially reduced the potential for conflict, the long term effect of this change may be to isolate older persons and to undermine respect for them. Sixth, there has been an increase in the single-headed (and often strained) households. Finally, the politicization of the elderly and their claims for public attention and public money may increase the likelihood of conflict between older and younger generations.

In a similar fashion, other analysts have emphasized the importance of contextual factors in understanding the problem of elder mistreatment. The role of economic and other external stressors, for instance, have been explored by a number of writers (Champlin, 1982) although the evidence regarding the empirical importance of these stressors remains uncertain (Pillemer, 1986).

Another widely discussed theme relates to the social organization of the family and its relationship to other social institutions. In this respect it has been argued that the pervasive cultural tendency to view the family as sacrosanct may have important etiological implications (Kosberg, 1988; Shell, 1982). One such implication concerns the traditional tendency on the part of legislatures and criminal justice agencies to regard what happens in the home as primarily a private matter. It may be argued that the problem of elder mistreatment, in addition to the problems of spousal assault and child abuse, are aggravated by a long-standing reluctance on the part of public officials to view these issues as something other than private family matters.

The failure of law to effectively penetrate familial relationships may restrict the options available to family members for the resolution of disputes or the amelioration of problems. Black (1983) argues that in the absence of law, the family becomes a locus of informal social control, of which violence may merely be seen as an extreme form.

245

The decline in extended kinship patterns has also been linked to problems of elder mistreatment (Brillon, 1987; Katz, 1980; Davidson, 1979). Thus, if family members do not broadly define the network to which they have responsibilities, the burden of caregiving may fall upon a single family member. Even when caregiving responsibilities are shared by grown children, each of whom has his or her own family, it may be difficult to coordinate care, and conflicts may ensue.

The breakdown of the extended family may also contribute to the isolation (and the sense of isolation) experienced by those involved in abusive relationships (Anetzberger, 1987; Hooyman, 1982; Kosberg, 1988). This high level of social isolation may have two important consequences. First, to the degree that abusers or victims are isolated from the community, they are unlikely to avail themselves of the formal and informal support systems that may assist in the prevention or resolution of the problems confronting family members (King, 1983; Kosberg, 1988; Rathbon-McCuan and Hashimi, 1982). Second, the isolation decreases the likelihood that those who engage in mistreatment will be detected or deterred by formal or informal systems of social control (Pillemer and Suitor, 1988; Pillemer, 1986).

While this logic is compelling, the theoretical status of social isolation is somewhat unclear. As Wolf (1986) notes social isolation may be most appropriately considered a factor that indirectly contributes to, rather than one that directly causes elder mistreatment. The nature of these theoretical relationships is made even more ambiguous by the fact that isolation could quite possibly be interpreted as either a determinant or a consequence of elder mistreatment.

More generally, however, theories that emphasize the study of contextual factors are of considerable value in that they focus our attention upon the social environment within which abuse and neglect occur. In so doing, they not only contribute to a more comprehensive understanding of the problem, but they also point the way to policy alternatives that define community or social development as the appropriate locus of action.

Elder Mistreatment As Interaction

A final type of explanation attempts to understand elder mistreatment as a product of the reciprocal exchange between victim and victimizer. The focus in not so much upon why abuse and neglect occur but upon how they occur. Within this framework, elder mistreatment is not regarded as a thing which emerges full-blown but as a process which develops and escalates (Phillips, 1986; Douglass and Hickey, 1983). Cases of mistreatment may thus be said to involve progress through distinct stages. Interest centers upon the efforts to identify these stages and therefore to explain how abuse and neglect typically change over the career of a relationship. As Phillips notes, such approaches find their more general origins in symbolic interactionist approaches to social behavior. As a result, they conceptualize the relationship between victim and victimizer in terms of, "the image of identity that each holds for the other and that influences the motives, characteristics, and goals that each ascribes to the other" (Phillips, 1986:208).

246

While we do not yet have a fully articulated theory of process, we do have a general, if tentative, understanding of what these processes involve. One major aspect of the process for instance, may relate to the role of socialization in the amplification of elder dependency. Prevailing cultural stereotypes and a lack of knowledge inform caregivers' expectations of the elderly and as a result, there may be an unintentional tendency to force upon the older person rather rigid definitions of who they are, what they feel and what they may or may not do. These expectations may set in motion a process of "infantilization" which denies to the elder many of the rights and privileges of adulthood (Steur and Austin, 1980; Shell, 1982). An adult offspring, for example, may deny the sexuality of an elderly parent or prevent the parent's involvement in basic decisions about his or her own well-being (Beck and Ferguson, 1981; Shell, 1982).

Labelling theories of deviance would lead us to expect that these processes may create a self-fulfilling prophecy which increases elderly dependency and conformity to the caregiver's expectations. Successive losses of power may encourage the elder to accept the caregiver's definition of self and situation. Thus the elder may accept the view that he or she is a burden and, as a result, become more helpless and more obsequious (Quinn and Tomita, 1986; Brillon, 1987). When this happens, the older person's behavior may become increasingly childlike - and from the perspective of the caregiver - increasingly problematic.

Quite possibly, however, the elder may resist the tendency toward infantilization through an obstinate commitment to personal independence (Beck and Ferguson, 1981). The elderly person may react to the caregiver by being verbally combative, by resisting care (Quinn and Tomita, 1986; Steinmetz, 1983) or by attempting to perform household tasks that are defined by the caregiver as beyond the elder's capabilities (Davidson, 1979). While such actions represent an effort to bolster integrity and to deny deviant stigma, they may aggravate the tensions between the caregiver and the elder.

In her study of caregivers, Steinmetz (1983) found that abuse was frequently the culmination of a violent exchange to which both the victim and the offender were parties. In other words, both the caregiver and the elder reacted to the situation, in which they found themselves, with hostility and aggression. In some cases, the problem was exacerbated by the abusive behavior of an aged parent who refused to relinquish his or her control over the adult offspring (Steinmetz, 1981).

The violent exchanges described by Steinmetz involve a complex dynamic. The elder might throw tantrums, or engage in assaultive behavior. They may pout and withdraw or attempt to induce guilt on the part of the caregiver. The caregiver might attempt to talk the problem out but may frequently resort to shouting. As tensions escalate, abuse becomes more likely; although, as Steinmetz notes, it is generally regarded by the caregiver as a "last resort". The tendency reported by Steinmetz for elders to behave aggressively toward caregivers is noteworthy since such observations are obscured by other theoretical positions which forge a clear and obvious distinction between victim and victimizer. In so doing, they fail to recognize how abuse, like other forms of victimization, may be usefully and realistically regarded as a process of social exchange.

Other processes involve those in which the caregiver may activate defense mechanims which deny the gravity of the older person's illness or impairment (Beck and Ferguson, 1981). While the desire to see one's elders as "basically in good health" when they are in reality very ill, or as merely "forgetful" when they suffer from a serious mental impairment is understandable, the consequences may be problematic. The emotional or physical needs of the older person may be unmet if a tendency persists to see expressions of these needs as "whining" and "attention seeking" or as a "natural part of old age" (Anderson, 1981).

Interactionist models suggest that if elderly persons are physically or financially dependent, they may possess few resources that would allow them to alter the course of the interaction (Phillips, 1986). In particular, they may be unable to exert social control upon the caregiver in ways that might stem early and relatively minor instances of abuse. Alternatively, their attempts to exert control may involve the use of methods that the caregiver defines as inapppropriate and in need of a disciplinary response. In either case, mistreatment may become both more frequent and more serious (Anetzberger, 1987).

In general, the value of these interactionist approaches derives from the fact that they conceptualize mistreatment in dynamic terms. Abuse and neglect are not viewed as discrete acts but as processes which unfold and change over time. Moreover, they alert us to the active role that both the victim and the perpetrator of mistreatment may play in these processes.

As stated, however, our understanding of such processes is far from complete. While we have some general understanding of what is likely to occur in the context of abusive relationships, we do not really have detailed knowledge of what consitutes a typical sequence of events. Nor can we say with confidence why these processes are set in motion in the context of some relationships and not others.

Finally, it is worth repeating that processes of elder mistreatment may not in many cases, even represent a unique phenomenon but rather a mere continuation into old age of processes that originate much earlier in the life-cycle. Thus, to the extent that what we choose to call elder mistreatment really represents nothing more than spousal abuse or parental mistreatment among an older cohort, our attempt to define the specific dynamics of elder mistreatment may produce misleading results.

Risk, Vulnerability and Elder Mistreatment

It should be obvious that while each of these theoretical approaches seems to say something of value about the etiology of elder mistreatment, none provides a comprehensive approach to the problem. We have attempted to stress the complementary nature of these perspectives by suggesting that they provide answers to distinctive questions rather than conflicting answers to the same questions.

What do these approaches tell us about the concepts of risk and vulnerability? Like all forms of victimization, elder mistreatment is not a random occurrence but appears more likely to materialize in some relational and familial contexts than others and to involve some types of people and not others. High stress levels, relational inequality, mutual involvment in disputing processes which increase rather than decrease conflict, and proximity to an incompetent or pathological caregiver amplify the potential for mistreatment. Elderly persons who choose to live in such circumstances or who do so because of the lack of alternatives face greater risks of mistreatment.

However, for patterns of mistreatment to stabilize or escalate, victims must perceive themselves and be perceived by those who mistreat them as open to the coercion, manipulation and disregard that such mistreatment implies. Put simply, they must be vulnerable. The theoretical accounts that we have reviewed point to several sources of vulnerability. These include the physical and psychological impairments that prevent effective defense of self and control of the situations that promote mistreatment, the guilt and responsibility that victims may feel toward those who mistreat them and the detachment from the wider social networks that might provide ameliorative resources.

SUMMARY

While we have a vague and general notion of what elder mistreatment is, there is no consensus regarding the manner in which it is most appropriately defined. Operational and conceptual definitions differ markedly and as a result, generalizations about the prevalence of various forms of mistreatment or about the empirical dimensions of its distribution are not easily made.

Research focused upon the problem of elder mistreatment has been limited in scope and style. And unfortunately, much of what we think we know about the problem derives from investigations that lack the rigor normally demanded of social scientific reserarch.

Our theoretical views of the problem have of course been influenced by the unstable conceptual and empirical foundations upon which they are based. The data support a variety of views and theoretical explanations frequently resemble "laundry lists" rather than systematic accounts (Anetzberger, 1987).

While such a state of affairs might promote a cynical view of the efforts of criminologists and social gerontologists, this reaction may not be justified. It is important to remember that the study of elder abuse is scarcely a decade old. Although the demands by politicians, interest groups and policy makers for firm information emerge in sudden and dramatic fashion, research knowledge accumulates at a somewhat slower pace. This gap between our immediate need to know and our inability to know immediately is not a problem unique to the study of elder mistreatment. We have seen that with respect to other forms of elderly victimization, deficiencies and omissions of early research created a void that was filled by inaccuracies, supposition and crisis rhetoric. This suggests a positive prognosis as future theoretical and empirical research into elder mistreatment moves in more sophisticated directions. Having explored the conceptual, theoretical and methodological dimensions of a variety of issues relating to elderly victimization, we are prepared to take up questions relevant to the pragmatic application of this information. The next chapter, therfore, focuses attention upon questions of policy and prevention as they relate to these issues.

CHAPTER ELEVEN: RECOMMENDED READINGS

Block, M.R. and J.D. Sinnott
1979 Methodology and Results. in M.R. Block and J.D. Sinnott (Eds.). The Battered Elder Syndrome. College Park Maryland: University of Maryland Center on Aging. pp. 67-84

Falcioni, D.
1982 Assessing the Abused Elderly. Journal of Gerontological Nursing, 8:208-212.

Hickey, T. and R. Douglass
1981 Mistreatment of the Elderly in Domestic Settings. American Journal of Public Health, 71:500-507.

Kosberg, J.I.
1983 Abuse and Mistreatment of the Elderly: Causes and Interventions. Littleton Mass.: John Wright.

Pillemer, K.A. and D. Finkelhor
1988 The Prevalence of Elder Abuse: A Random Sample Survey. The Gerontologist, 28 (1):51-57.

Quinn, M.J. and S.K. Tomita
1986 Elder Abuse and Neglect: Causes, Diagnosis, and Intervention Strategies. New York: Springer Publishing Co.

Steinmetz, S.K.
1981 Elder Abuse. Aging, 6-10: 215-216.

CHAPTER TWELVE

CRIMES AGAINST THE ELDERLY: POLICY AND PLANNING

INTRODUCTION

For many people, elderly victimization is more a pragmatic than a theoretical concern. Thus, they may be interested in this issue not because of the intellectual puzzles that it presents but because they believe that it is necessary to "do something" about it. In this chapter we focus upon programs, services and strategies intended to ameliorate the social problem of crimes against the elderly.

To a considerable degree, this discussion is grounded in the material presented in earlier chapters. This approach reflects the belief that empirical and theoretical knowledge may usefully inform policy approaches. As a result, we will cover some familiar territory, but with a different purpose in mind.

The claim that crime and victimization policies must be based upon valid empirical principles is almost a truism. Yet, if one theme has been repeated in previous chapters, it is that much of our knowledge about elderly victimization is uncertain. This is more true in some areas of study than others but the point does have some general applicability. This implies that there is not one but rather multiple empirical realities from which policy initiatives may proceed. There does not exist, therefore, a consensus about what needs to be done about crime and the elderly. We will see that the literature supports a variety of viewpoints in this regard and that each has associated costs and benefits.

At a very general level, there is disagreement regarding the relative priority that should be assigned to elderly crime problems. We have seen that older people experience relatively low rates of many forms of victimization and that they do not appear to suffer disproportionately as a result of victimization experiences. Any form of social intervention does, after all, involve the deployment of finite economic and human resources. If we direct many of these resources toward the elderly, we have fewer to commit to other "high risk" groups such as poor, young males who experience much higher victimization rates.

Division thus exists within the criminological and gerontological communities regarding the utility of policy approaches that separate out elderly crime problems for special consideration. Should resources be allocated for the design of programs that prevent elderly crime or should more general crime prevention efforts be undertaken from which it is assumed all members of the population, including the elderly, will benefit? Should funds be set aside to underwrite programs intended to alleviate elderly fear of crime or should more general programs be developed? Should separate legal or social service remedies be implemented to deal with elderly abuse or are initiatives directed against the more general problem of family violence adequate to the task?

These questions point to the distinction between categoric and generic program approaches (Alston, 1986; Crystal, 1986). The former type of response takes as the target of policy attention one particular group - such as the elderly - while the latter is intended to distribute benefits more widely. Each type of approach has its supporters and detractors. It may be argued that with respect to crimes against the elderly, categoric interventions are preferred because they take into account the unique characteristics of elderly populations and the particular types of victimization and other social experiences to which they are exposed. Critics, however, argue that categoric interventions may promote ageist viewpoints by treating the elderly as a special group in need of special protection (Cook et al., 1978). Crystal (1986) suggests that categoric approaches to the problem of elder abuse ignore similarities between this problem and other forms of familial violence. In so doing, he maintains, they create an artificial split in the remedies and systems available to meet similar needs.

Another dimension of this debate concerns the extent to which a narrow emphasis upon crime and victimization is itself the proper target of policy attention. It has been argued that crime problems are not separable from the other social problems that confront older persons (Kosberg, 1985; Crystal, 1986). This would imply that crime problems might be most effectively dealt with not through "crime prevention" or "victim service" programs but through broad structural changes intended to affect the social and economic status of the elderly. While the following discussion is primarily concerned with a somewhat narrower range of policy questions, we will return to a consideration of the role of social development in ameliorating elderly crime problems later in the chapter.

CRIME AND VICTIMIZATION POLICY

Introduction

Since the 1970s numerous communities across Europe and North America have developed programs intended to reduce elderly crime problems (Boston, 1977; Barnes, 1982; Nitzberg, 1982; Persico and Sunderland, 1980). The majority of these programs focus upon the traditional types of criminal offences that occupied our attention in Chapters 8 and 9.

Although these programs differ quite markedly in terms of their philosophies, mandates, priorities and methods of service delivery, they can be categorized according to four major headings: victimization prevention, crime prevention, cost reduction and criminal justice responsiveness. The first two are intended to reduce the prevalence of crimes against the elderly (Canada,1984b; Cohn et al., 1978). Victimization prevention refers to those actions which individuals take to protect themselves from criminal harm. Policies and strategies of this type aim to make individuals more resistant to victimization. They are intended to modify personal habits and practices, rather than the social environment within which crime occurs.

Crime prevention policies, by contrast, seek to prevent the victimization of the individual through a reduction of the environmental sources of crime. Whereas victimization prevention is intended to protect the individual, crime prevention is intended to protect the community.

The third type of strategy, cost reduction, is directed toward the amelioration of the effects of criminal victimization. Victim support services are primarily intended to lessen the physical, economic or psychological impacts of the victim experience.

The final type of policy approach involves attempts to modify the functioning of criminal justice agencies so as to make them more sensitive to the concerns of elderly citizens and more effective in the management of elderly crime problems.

Each type of strategy is considered below.

Victimization Prevention

As stated, the strategy implicit in victimization prevention is the reduction in individual susceptibility to criminal harm. Programs of this type encourage elderly citizens to "harden targets", increase personal vigilance or engage in overt forms of defensive behaviour (Auger and Guarino, 1979, Corrigan, 1981).

The most popular forms of public policy initiative have been police-sponsored seminars or public information campaigns that are intended to provide individuals with information that allows them to reduce personal risk. Such instructional efforts might focus upon:

1.   tips to avoid merchandising fraud

2.   home security techniques

3.   precautions to take while walking in the neighborhood

4.   self-defense techniques

5.   instruction in the use of crime prevention hardware (such as deadbolt locks) or property marking techniques (such as Operation Identification)

Such programs reflect the empirical observation that older persons may be considerably less likely than the rest of the population to engage in a wide range of risk-reducing behaviors (Skogan, 1978).

The information which these programs make available is very specific and very practical. By way of illustration, the following list describes the pragmatic means by which the older person may decrease the risk of purse snatching or robbery without assault - crimes to which the elderly are subjected with relative frequency (Auger and Guarino, 1979:5-6):

1. Think prevention. Do you really have to carry that purse or is it just a habit?

2. If you are going to the grocery store, could you not do as well by taking just the money that you need? Or perhaps a cheque (don't forget to take along proper identification).

3. Do not carry your purse with the strap wound around your wrist or in such a manner as is likely to cause you to be pulled down if someone runs up behind you and snatches your purse.

4. A dangling purse is an invitation to a purse snatcher. A firm grip quite often discourages a criminal act. But if your purse is snatched, release it rather than risk physical injury.

5. Avoid dark places, short cuts, thick trees and shrubs, and sparsely-travelled areas.

6. Do not display cash except in small amounts.

7. Do not leave your purse unattended, such as on the counter, or in a shopping cart while you examine an item.

8. If you are transacting business and have your purse open, do not allow yourself to be distracted.

9. If you're carrying packages or books and your purse, take advantage of the added protection. Put your purse between your body and the packages. A lot of purse snatchers like to strike a loaded down victim.

10. Do not carry openweave or other types of basket purses with bills, wallets, or other valuables lying around in full view, on buses, benches, movie seats or in stores.

11. Never flash large sums of money, credit cards or other valuables. When you carry money, do so inconspicuously on your person.

12. When walking always plan your route and stay alert to your surroundings. When you walk at night, choose busy, well-lit streets and try, when possible, to plan excursions with companions.

The list is a long one and, to prevent other types of victimizations, equally long lists must be consulted. It is reasonable to conclude, however, that observance of these rules probably would result in a decreased risk of purse snatching. As we have noted, the perpetrators of such offenses tend to be young opportunists who select their victims largely on the basis of convenience. Thus as Skogan (1977) observes, behaviors or habits which make the victimization more difficult will likely reduce risk.

Despite the apparent reasonableness of victimization prevention as a crime-fighting strategy, these approaches like all others carry with them particular costs. Two broad issues may be identified in this regard.

First, because such strategies are intended to reduce individual risks of victimization rather than community risks of crime, they create the possibility that victimizations may be merely displaced rather than prevented (DuBow et al., 1979). In other words, in any community there will always be some people who will be less aware or less capable of measures that can reduce victimization risk. If some smaller group did take such measures this could well mean that the burden of victimization will increasingly fall upon the more vulnerable. This displacement demonstrates the dilemma inherent in programs which take the individual but not the community into account.

A second shortcoming of such strategies is that they may tend to increase feelings of fear and isolation on the part of the elderly. The general lesson of many such programs is suspicion. People are warned against trusting strangers and against walking in particular places at particular times. Many situations and many types of persons are seen to pose criminal danger. As a result, the elderly may be increasingly likely to avoid contact with others and to further decrease their mobility and involvement in community life.

Moreover, if victimization programs are to be widely effective, people must be convinced that it is necessary to adopt the behaviors around which the program is organized. If community members are going to seek out and act upon victimization prevention information, they must first define the information as salient. However, attempts on the part of policy managers to use mass media to impress upon the elderly that such information is important, because the crime problem is increasing or because personal risks are high, may exacerbate public fears (Sacco and Silverman, 1982).

Similarly, the transmission of victimization prevention information in the context of the typical "crime prevention seminar" may create an environment that not only increases security consciousness but also fear. An evaluation of one such series of seminars concluded:

> that the mix of seniors, including both victims and nonvictims, with varying degrees of fear of criminal victimization is an important factor in developing fear and security consciousness levels of the seniors involved. When seniors with a low level of fear come to a meeting and meet seniors who have a high level of fear (possibly because of their own victimization or their knowledge of the victimization of a close friend or relative), the interaction between the two groups is likely to promote vicarious victimization in the low-fear elderly, thus increasing their fear. Furthermore, the meetings probably help to promote the discussion of crime with friends, relatives and neighbors which, as we have seen, is associated with a higher level of fear of crime (Norton and Courlander, 1984; 392)

There may of course be exceptions to this pattern. Cohn and her colleagues (1978) evaluated the effects of self-defence training on women's fears of victimization. They found that the general effect of the program that they studied, was to decrease personal anxieties about crime and to increase partic-

255

ipants' sense of personal efficacy. The researchers note, however, that these effects are not typical of victimization prevention measures.

In general, victimization prevention policies work to achieve short-term personal objectives at the expense of longer-term social goals. Although elderly persons involved in such programs may become more resistant to victimization, they risk an increase in fear and isolation. Moreover, from a community standpoint, such programs may have less to do with preventing victimizations than with redistributing them.

Crime Prevention

Whereas victimization prevention views the proper level of intervention to be personal habits and behaviors, crime prevention concentrates attention upon interventions at the community level.

DuBow and Emmons (1981:171) characterize the general principles of the crime prevention strategy as follows:

1. Neighborhood residents can be mobilized by community organizations to participate in collective crime prevention projects.

2. Involvement in these activities creates a stronger community because people will take greater responsibility for their own protection and local problems and, interactions among neighbors will be increased, both formally through the activities of the crime prevention projects, and informally, as by-products of these activities.

3. A stronger sense of community and increased social interaction leads to more effective informal social control.

4. Aside from the direct effects of community crime prevention activities in reducing crime or the fear of crime, these activities may also reduce crime or the fear of crime by rebuilding local social control in the neighborhood.

Thus, in general, crime prevention strategies seek to simultaneously reduce crime and fear by helping to rebuild the sense of local community (Corrigan, 1981). Unlike victimization programs, such initiatives seek to reintegrate community members and thereby reduce the isolation or other negative effects that victimization prevention might promote (Center, 1979; Cohn et al., 1978).

There are many mechanisms which may bring crime prevention programs to realization. In the most obvious and most direct cases, they emerge from deliberate efforts on the part of the police or other formal criminal justice agencies to foster collective crime prevention awareness (Williams and Pate, 1987). Neighborhood Watch and other "block programs" are examples of initiatives that find their origins in formal law enforcement policies. Alternatively, many programs emerge out of other more generic types of community or neighborhood groups such as local rate-payers associations or community service organizations.

How do such organizations impact upon crime problems of the elderly? In one respect, it can be argued that the elderly may be among the most effective members of such groups (Teski, 1981). Because older persons spend much of their time at home, they may be able to effectively monitor neighborhood activities. Further, as long-time residents, they may be more likely to have a sense of the local neighborhood and its problems and to recognize and distinguish between those who do and those who do not belong in the local setting. Since many of the elderly are retired, they may be both able and anxious to acquire the skills and assume the responsibilities necessary for program implementation.

It may also be argued that the elderly may derive personal benefits from involvement in crime prevention organizations. These benefits can include increased interaction with age-peers and local community leaders and thus a reduction in isolation and loneliness (Skogan, 1978). In addition, because such programs treat community residents as active members of a crime reduction effort, rather than as passive consumers of victimization prevention information, they may instill in older persons a sense of personal control (Wiltz, 1982).

Available research, however, suggests that elderly involvement in crime prevention organizations falls somewhat short of this potential. Older persons appear to be less likely than younger people to have heard of crime prevention programs and to belong to such organizations when they have heard of them (Canada, 1985b). Thus, although the elderly may be more likely to be afraid of crime, their fear does not seem to promote crime prevention (Rifai, 1977).

More generally, it appears that despite their popularity, crime prevention initiatives are frequently of questionable effectiveness (DuBow et al., 1979). Skogan and Maxfield (1981) report that effective organizations are likely to prosper in neighborhoods in which there is a high level of social integration and thus a lower level of crime and disorder. In other words, crime prevention organizations develop in the environments that need them least. Further, even in those cases in which organizations do endure, they are likely to involve only a relatively small number of local residents rather than the entire community (DuBow and Emmons, 1981). A further problem facing those social service organizations which attempt to incorporate crime prevention activities into a wider mandate involves the fact that such activities must compete with other priorities for the time and attention of members (DuBow and Emmons, 1981).

Another way to achieve the general objectives of crime prevention is through the modification of the physical environment. The logic underlying "Crime Prevention Through Environmental Design" (CPTED) is straightforward. It suggests that if we design streets and buildings so as to take the problem of crime into account, we should be able to construct community settings in which people feel safer and, in fact, are safer (Newman, 1972; Heinzelman, 1981).

Obvious examples of the CPTED approach involve the increased use of street lights or the removal of hedges or other barriers that might close streets, parks or playgrounds to public view. Public spaces attached to multi-unit dwellings can be designed in ways that permit the intensification of interaction among residents and in so doing, serve more readily to discourage the presence of strangers who might victimize local residents. Streets may be redesigned in ways that reduce casual traffic from outside the neighborhood and thereby help foster a sense of residential identity.

In their most sophisticated forms, such strategies entail formidable costs as well as a high degree of cooperation between crime prevention experts and others, such as architects and private developers (for whom crime prevention may be a relatively low priority). It should also be emphasized that in order to be successful, CPTED initiatives not only require that physical space be designed in particular ways but that it be used in particular ways by residents. Thus, even in those cases in which problems of design may be effectively overcome, there may remain the possibility that residents will not utilize urban designs in ways consistent with the crime prevention goals of policy makers.

Earlier reference was made to age-segregated housing for the elderly which, like CPTED, is intended to reduce crime through the creation of defensible space (Van Buren, 1976). In such environments, the design elements relevant to the reduction of crime and fear among the elderly relate not to physical structures but to the nature of the resident population. Within such settings, residency is restricted to older persons and access to non-residents is controlled. Residents are less likely to feel isolated and as a result, a sense of community and informal policies of mutual assistance and surveillance may develop.

While age-homogeneous housing may provide a supportive environment for elderly residents, there are once again accompanying costs (Skogan, 1977). Most obviously, although such arrangements may reduce crime-related problems, they may also serve to further isolate older persons and thus indirectly contribute to ageism in society.

This breakdown of inter-generational communication is likely to have effects in both directions, however. Older people's fears of those younger than themselves might be exacerbated when interpersonal contacts that might breakdown youthful stereotypes are absent. As we have seen, although residents of age- homogeneous housing may feel safer in their own buildings, they do not necessarily feel safer on neighborhood streets (Antunes et al., 1977).

A final criticism of age-segregated housing policies relates to the ageist assumptions upon which such policies are based. Although women also have a high level of fear of crime and are subjected to particular patterns of criminal exploitation, policy makers do not seriously consider the solution to the problem of crime against women to be gender-segregated housing. As Burt and Katz (1985) point out, the difference in this regard is largely explained in terms of the fact that awareness of sexism is much higher than awareness of ageism both among policy makers and the public at large.

Cost Reduction Strategies

While victimization prevention and crime prevention programs aim to re-duce the probabilities of victimization occurrence, another type of program is directed toward the amelioration of the effects of those victimizations which do occur. One type of service involves the provision of economic, emotional or material support to victims of crime in order to allow them to cope more effectively in the aftermath of the victimization episode. A second type of pro-gram is directed toward the reduction of public fear of crime - a cost experi-enced by those who have not been directly victimized.

Victim Support. Programs of this type emerged in large numbers during the 1970s as victims' issues came to be defined by politicians, policy makers and criminologists as salient issues (Rock, 1986; Elias, 1986). In large part their development reflected the widespread perception that the needs of victims of crime had traditionally been ignored by a criminal justice system primarily con-cerned with processing offenders rather than those against whom they offend (Bard and Sangrey, 1979).

Norquay and Weiler (1981) describe these programs as falling into five major categories:

1. **Services that deal with the crisis of victimization.** This category references those services that assist the victim in his or her attempt to cope with the immediate aftermath of the victim experience. Rape crisis centers, shelters for battered wives and police-victim units are obvious examples.

2. **Services that assist victims and witnesses to participate effectively in the criminal justice system while protecting their rights.** Many jurisdictions have developed courtworker programs which are intended to ensure that victims understand their role in criminal justice processes. In similar fashion, many community service agencies (such as the John Howard Society and the Salvation Army) have initiated programs which endeavour to allow victims to participate more fully in these processes. The nature of the support is quite varied and may include transportation, babysitting or liaison with so-cial service agencies.

3. **Services aimed at compensating the victim for personal damage incurred as a result of crime.** This includes not only private insurance plans but also publicly funded schemes which are intended to offset the financial costs of the victim experience.

4. **Services aimed at achieving restitution, reconciliation or both, between the offender and the victim.** Such programs focus, in reparative fashion, upon the relationship between offender and victim. Restitution has increasingly become a popular court sanction which requires the offender to make cash payments or provide services to the offended party. Reconciliation pro-grams bring offenders and victims together in order to allow them to reach some satisfactory resolution of the conflict which the victimization has cre-ated.

5. **Services that assist the victim to locate and use appropriate existing services.** These programs have been viewed as necessary because many of

the services that victims require are not centralized, and thus needs may be unmet if the various forms of social assistance cannot be effectively accessed.

The movement toward the delivery of such a wide range of services has been heralded as a much needed improvement to a system that has customarily ignored crimes victims' needs. It has, however, been argued by several critics that many of these programs fail to live up to expectations.

Elias (1986) suggests that many such programs - particularly those which operate under the auspices of government agencies - are underfunded and lack commitment on the part of those who manage them. Victims are frequently unaware that such programs even exist and frequently do not meet the criteria that would allow them to be eligible for program benefits (Karmen, 1984). Compensation and restitution programs which are intended to offset the financial losses incurred as a result of victimization normally involve a substantial waiting period and when awards are made, they tend to provide only partial compensation (Shapland, 1986; Elias, 1986).

It is also argued that the needs of elderly victims may be particularly neglected by the current operation of many victim support services. We have seen that when older people are victimized, they tend to experience economic crimes rather than crimes of violence. Most compensation programs, however, define victims of non-violent offenses as ineligible for financial compensation (Elias, 1986). Even when elderly persons are eligible for rewards they are somewhat less likely to know of the existence of the program or to make application for benefits (Ashton, 1981; Hamel, 1979; Forstan, 1974; Alston, 1986; Culp and Calvin, 1977). Elderly victims may be more in need of emergency economic compensation and may therefore be more severely affected by the waiting periods characteristic of most compensation programs. In addition, Ashton argues that the elderly victim may be more likely to be deterred by the complexities of application procedures and less willing to become involved in the bureaucratic entanglements that application implies.

Moreover, while offender restitution sanctions have the potential for reparation to elderly victims, the reality suggests that in the majority of cases they do not achieve this potential (Karmen, 1984). Restitution is only a possibility when an offender has been apprehended and legal action is initiated. Elderly victims, however, tend to be preyed upon by young minority opportunists and by professional con operators and neither group faces particularly high risks of apprehension.

While many victim services fail to meet their ostensible objectives, there are, of course, important differences across programs and across jurisdictions. Elias (1986) argues, for instance, that "grass roots" voluntary associations appear to be more effective in fulfilling their mandates than are state- sponsored agencies. In the latter case, he suggests, victims' needs are too frequently subverted by the professional needs of those who sponsor and manage the programs. He adds that government services to victims are in many respects exercises in "symbolic politics". In other words, they provide the appearance of effective social action in ways that do not require a major investment of organizational resources.

Fear Reduction. Although victimization and crime prevention strategies define the reduction of crime as the primary goal, they are also in many cases directed toward the reduction of fear of victimization. Moreover, there have been policy initiatives specifically directed toward the latter problem (Zion, 1978; Lohman, 1983).

In a comprehensive discussion, Henig and Maxfield (1978) consider many of the available policy options. In general, they distinguish three strategies, each of which implies several specific types of program efforts:

1. **Confidence-Building Strategies.** If fear of crime is rooted in individual anxieties or caused by distorted information which exaggerates actual risk, it may be possible to reduce fear by building the confidence of workers and residents who frequent areas that are considered dangerous. "Tell the truth" campaigns might be undertaken in which mass media are used to provide people with more realistic information about the threat of criminal harm. With respect to our specific interests, the elderly could be given information which would tell them that they are not special targets of crime (Cook et al., 1981). Crime reporting in mass media might be monitored in order to promote a more moderate and less sensationalist picture of crime in the community.

    Confidence may also be built through the effective deployment of "role models" and law enforcement personnel. There is experimental evidence to suggest that feelings of safety may be increased by the presence of uniformed, government employees who are perceived as having ties to the local area. This implies that non-enforcement personnel such as mail carriers or city repair workers could help allay citizen's anxieties if their visibility was increased in high-fear areas (Balkin and Houlden, 1983).

    The use of law enforcement personnel to alleviate public fear of crime may be somewhat more obvious if, for instance, an increased police presence results in lower rates of fear-inducing crimes. But, an increase in enforcement, like other crime prevention efforts, does not necessarily bring with it a reduction in crime; and even when crime is reduced it does not necessarily follow that fear levels will fall correspondingly (Maxfield, 1984a).

    Alternatively, policing resources could be utilized in order to enforce laws against loitering or other forms of uncivil behavior that have been shown to be related to fear of crime (Maxfield, 1987). Wilson and Kelling (1982) argue that only the police have the mandate to maintain order and thus control such incivilities. The police officer who is familiar with local neighborhood values and what those values can tolerate, and who is empowered to "keep the peace" may be in the best position to officially enforce community standards. Their argument suggests that the objective of fear-reduction may be achieved not by extending already strained police resources in new and unfamiliar directions but by a return to traditional order-maintenance activities.

    Finally, an increased police presence may lead to more positive judgements about the police and greater satisfaction with the performance of the police role. Such attitudes, as we have seen, are related to lower levels of fear (Baker et al., 1983; Muir, 1987).

2.   **Community-Building Strategies.** If social interaction builds interpersonal commitments which generate feelings of security, less cohesive communities may benefit from increased levels of interaction among residents (Taylor et al., 1984). To the extent that neighborhoods are able to organize, they can more effectively take action against those types of incivilities (such as abandoned buildings, or noisy neighbors) which realistically lie beyond the purview of criminal justice agencies (Lewis and Maxfield, 1980). More directly, we expect that in organized communities, residents may be better able to deal with local crime problems and to provide the mutual support and assistance which will alleviate concerns about personal safety.

Consistent with themes developed earlier, it is argued that elderly fears may be minimized by residential arrangements which are age-segregated (Lawton and Yaffe, 1980; Skogan, 1978; Kosberg, 1985; Wiltz, 1982; Burt and Katz, 1985; Gubrium, 1974; Teaff et al., 1978; Curtis and Kohn, 1983).

It follows as well, that the limitations that characterize the logic of community crime prevention are equally applicable to these attempts to transform the local environment for purposes of fear-reduction.

3.   **Physical Rebuilding Strategies.** CPTED programming may not only be effective in reducing crime but also the fear of crime. To the extent that environmental design is explicitly directed toward the alleviation of feelings of insecurity, the effort might be made to facilitate the increase or redistribution of pedestrian traffic. The effects of such changes could be to improve the natural surveillance and the general appearance of the neighborhood setting (Toseland, 1982).

Physical redesign may increase the sense of mastery that residents experience with respect to the local environment and thereby ameliorate perceptions of that environment as dangerous (Normoyle and Lavrakas, 1984). An active mastery of the environment can be encouraged through programs which promote territorial behavior with respect to residence and neighborhood. It has been argued that for the elderly specifically, expressions of territoriality in the form of the building of fences or the use of "no trespassing" signs may lead to reductions in crime-related fears (Pollack and Patterson, 1980; Patterson, 1977; 1979).

As in the case of crime prevention and victimization prevention, programs designed to reduce fear levels are not without costs (Henig and Maxfield, 1978; Lohman, 1983). Public policy directed toward the reduction of fear may produce "boomerang effects" such that feelings of insecurity increase rather than decrease. If, for instance, we decide to fight fear by putting more police on the streets as a show of force, we may increase the salience of the crime problem in many people's minds. Elaborate safety measures or hardware that are supposed to make people feel safer may only serve as constant reminders of personal vulnerability (Cook et al., 1981). A similar consequence may ensue if we attempt to use mass media to inform audience members about their "real" chances of criminal risk.

A second problem with fear of crime strategies derives from the fact that, unlike in the case of crime and victimization prevention programs, the objective of such strategies remains somewhat unclear. In other words, while we may argue that the ultimate objective of crime-fighting policies is the eradication of crime, it is less certain that the ultimate objective of fear-fighting policies is the eradication of fear. This is because, to some considerable extent, fear of crime is rooted in the objective dangers that people face. It is only the view of fear as an irrational response to the world, that calls for the elimination of fear of crime as an end in itself. As we have seen, fear is, at least in part, a prudent reaction to a world that threatens us with real risks and it makes little sense to try and reduce those fears when reductions in risk are not commensurate (Maxfield, 1984a).

This implies that unless we understand the empirical relationship between crime and fear, our attempt to manipulate the latter in isolation from the former, may not only be unethical but dangerous. Programs intended to decrease fear may simultaneously decrease caution with respect to potential criminal harm. While such programs may be effective in decreasing fear, they may produce longer term costs by increasing exposure to victimization risk. While it is popular to argue that the resolution of fear of crime problems must involve policy initiatives other than crime control (Lohman, 1983) the control of crime must remain a central feature of any such effort.

Criminal Justice Reactions

Implicit in much of the foregoing is a critique of the criminal justice system. The claim that special action needs to be taken with respect to elderly crime problems suggests that agencies of criminal justice may be faulted for failing to provide adequate levels of service to older persons.

Much of this criticism has focused upon the police. Some observers have noted that there is a need to sensitize law enforcement personnel to the "special needs" and anxieties of the elderly (Arcuri, 1981; Goldstein and Wolf, 1979). This point is said to have relevance not only for victims of crime but also for the larger group of elderly persons who view the police as an all purpose social service agency.

Although there is a tendency among police officers and the public alike to emphasize the "crime fighting" aspects of policing, the empirical data indicate that far more time and attention are centered upon the provision of a broader range of social services (Arcuri, 1981). The police may be asked to assist in medical emergencies, to provide transportation or to settle non-criminal disputes involving neighbors or relatives.

The elderly appear to be somewhat more reliant upon the police for the provision of such services (Sykes, 1976). It is argued, therefore, that the low regard in which the police hold their service function may lead them to take less seriously the complaints and requests for assistance that are initiated by older persons (Arcuri, 1981). The strain inherent in such a relationship may result in an inadequate level of service delivery to the elderly. In response, some police departments have developed more effective systems of referral which are intended to allow police services to be better integrated with those of other community agencies. In this way, elderly concerns which fall beyond the mandate of the police (but for which the police are frequently called) can be dealt with in routine fashion (Ashton, 1981; Arcuri, 1981).

In a related sense it is maintained that special techniques are required in the investigation of elderly victimizations (Goldestein and Wolf, 1979). Older persons may be more unnerved by the victimization experience and more frightened and confused by the procedures and potential consequences of criminal justice processes. Accordingly, some police agencies have developed special programs for elderly victims (Gross, 1979; Morello, 1982). These programs range from the introduction of gerontological training into policing curricula, to the formation of special elderly crime units.

While the introduction of special policing programs directed toward the elderly have some obvious political and public relations advantages, it is unclear whether a large scale investment of resources into such endeavors is warranted. Several studies have shown that older persons, in general, have a very high opinion of the police and report being quite satisfied with the levels of service that they receive (Skogan, 1978; Canada, 1985b; Alston, 1986). When the elderly do complain about police services, their complaints are not significantly different from those of younger persons (Canada, 1985b). Moreover, we have already seen that the elderly are more likely than those younger than themselves to report victimizations to the police; this may suggest that they see themselves as less rather than more alienated from law enforcement. Finally, if the police are ageist in their interactions with older persons, it may in some ways work for, rather than against, the immediate interests of the older person. Sykes' (1976) investigation of police-citizen interaction revealed, for instance, that police officers were more likely to tolerate disrespect directed toward them by elderly persons than they were to tolerate the demonstration of disrespect by younger persons.

Aside from the police, court and victim services have also been criticized for an insensitivity to the needs of the elderly. It has been argued, for instance, that negative views of the elderly discourage active involvement in trial processes and that court systems need to be more proactive in gaining the support of older persons in the investigation and conviction of their offenders (Timm, 1985; Forstan, 1974).

A more proactive approach has also been advocated in the case of victim services (Ashton, 1981; Culp and Calvin, 1977). As we have already discussed, older persons are less likely to know about and use victim services and more likely to be excluded by the eligibility criteria of compensation programs (Hamel, 1979). It has been suggested, therefore, that the eligibility criteria should be relaxed in the case of older persons to allow them to receive compensation for property crime (Hamel, 1979) or on an emergency basis (Ashton, 1981).

Many of these attempts to expand the scope or extend the direction of policy may be faulted for a tendency to treat older persons as passive recipients of programs and services rather than as active participants in the crime problems that confront them. More innovative policies attempt to engage the elderly in the construction and implementation of solutions to the problems of victimization and its effects (Malinchak, 1980; Teski, 1981; Corrigan, 1981; Fattah, 1986; Brillon, 1987). Thus, older persons may be encouraged to assume important leadership roles in victim support, crime prevention or auxiliary law enforcement programs.

The assignment of a significant volunteer role to older persons can achieve some important objectives. First, it may empower older persons by teaching them that they are part of the solution rather than part of the problem (Wiltz, 1982). Second, the delivery of services through informal peer networks, rather than formal state agencies, may result in more effective policy. Third, the active involvement of elderly volunteers allows for the more efficient utilization of strained criminal justice resources.

Finally, we might ask if innovative policies are at all necessary in the attempt to control the crime problems of older persons. Perhaps, the more effective alternative is to strengthen traditional criminal justice functions rather than to dilute resources by fighting the battle on several fronts. Thus, if the police would vigorously pursue those who prey upon the elderly, and if the courts would deal harshly with these offenders, the rate of elderly victimization and accompanying problems would be substantially diminished.

However, based on their analysis of National Crime Survey data, Antunes and his colleagues concluded:

we found that the elderly are disproportionately victimized by young males acting alone who do not threaten with weapons or carry guns. According to some criminologists ...youths of this type should be prime targets for supervision of community-based treatment for the fear is that prolonged contact with the social life of jails may confirm them as criminals and put them beyond "rehabilitation" (Antunes et al., 1977:326).

Thus, a "law and order" policy may be made less effective by virtue of its clash with other criminal justice priorities (Skogan, 1977).

ELDER MISTREATMENT: POLICY AND PROBLEMS

Introduction

Because the criminological and gerontological communities have only recently defined problems of domestic abuse of the elderly as worthy of intensive investigation, we have less well- developed ideas regarding what can be and what should be done. Still, the literature on elder mistreatment identifies several important policy issues. Three of these issues - detection, intervention and prevention - are considered below.

Detection

Quite obviously, the effectiveness of any intervention strategy is ultimately dependent upon the ability to recognize cases of elder mistreatment. However, the detection of such cases is itself a task that is not easily accomplished.

As we have seen, the victims of elder abuse and neglect may be reluctant to report their situations to authorities either because they fear retaliation or removal from the domestic setting or because they feel a sense of obligation to the perpetrator. Moreover, the person playing the caregiver role, who normally would be most likely to identify and seek assistance for physical or emotional problems, has a strong vested interest in keeping such problems hidden.

We might expect, therefore that medical or social service professionals are likely to be the most appropriate agents of discovery. However there are problems in this regard as well. First, such discoveries can be made only when professionals have access to the victims. This is, by definition, unlikely in many cases (Fulmer and Cahill, 1984).

It is also true that although professionals may be well-positioned to discover mistreatment, they lack the specific training that would allow them to do so (Rathbone-McCuan and Voyles, 1982; Anderson, 1981; Kosberg, 1985). This helps to explain why in many cases, elderly mistreatment is reported to official agencies not by health care and social service professionals but by friends, neighbors or family members (Crystal, 1986).

In order to correct this situation, many medical and social facilities have begun to standardize procedures for the identification and referral of cases of elder mistreatment (Quinn and Tomita, 1986). Through the use of such protocols it is intended that emergency room personnel, for instance, will be sensitized to the effects of abuse and neglect or to the attitudinal and behavioral demeanor of the potential abuser or victim (Hooyman, 1982; Kosberg, 1988).

Sengstock and Hwaleck (1987) argue, however, that many of these protocols are inadequate. First, they tend to over-represent physical abuse and to under-represent more subtle forms of emotional or psychological mistreatment. Second, many elder mistreatment identification protocols require highly subjective judgments about the nature of the mistreatment or whether mistreatment has occurred at all. Thus, the emergency room physician or the social worker may be required to employ rather amorphous standards in order to determine whether an elder has been the victim of "verbal assualt" or "inappropriate care".

There are more innovative mechanisms for bringing cases of elder mistreatment to public attention. Some jurisdictions employ telephone "hotlines" which may be used by victims or by those aware of a victimization for the purpose of reporting (Hooyman, 1982; Block et al., 1979). It is also suggested that there are many members of the community who have ready and routine access to abusive situations and whose assistance in case-finding may be solicited. Mail carriers, local merchants, bank tellers, bus drivers, pharmacists, ministers and other members of the "natural helping community" may be asked to play a vigilant role with respect to the ways in which elderly persons are cared for and to report suspicious incidents and circumstances to authorities.

A particulary contentious aspect of the detection issue concerns the appropriateness of mandatory reporting statutes. Laws of this type require medical or other professional groups to document and report cases of mistreatment under penalty of law. Such legislative initiatives, which are modeled after the laws requiring the mandatory reporting of child abuse, have proliferated rapidly over the last several years (Holland et al., 1987; Bisset-Johnson, 1986). Crystal (1987) reports that in the United States, prior to 1980, only 16 states had such laws; but, by 1987 44 states had such laws and several of the remaining six were contemplating the passage of legislation.

These laws, however, have evoked considerable criticism for what are seen as both their pragmatic and ideological limitations (Pillemer and Suitor, 1988; Yin, 1985; O'Malley et al., 1983). In a practical sense, it is argued that, where such legislation exists, it appears to be largely ineffective. Many of these laws employ vague definitions of abuse and neglect and do not specify penalties for non-reporting (Thorbaben and Anderson, 1985; Callaghan, 1982; Salend et al., 1984). In many cases, those who are required by the law to report elder mistreatment are not even aware of the law's existence or feel free to ignore the legislation (Kosberg, 1985). As a result, in many communities cases are more likely to be reported by non-mandated sources than by those to whom the law applies (Crystal, 1986; Faulkner, 1982).

Thus, mandatory reporting laws proceed from the assumption that such legislation is an effective case-finding tool, although the evidence does not suggest that these laws lead us to discover more cases than we would otherwise. (Faulkner, 1982). The popularity of such laws is even more surprising when we consider that neither procedures nor sufficient resources are in place to deal with those cases that are uncovered (Hickey and Douglass, 1981a). The emphasis upon case finding means that both money and human energy are directed toward the detection phase and is thus not available to support the delivery of services to those cases about which we already have knowledge. The vague definitions contained in many laws may result in an even more inefficient use of resources if large numbers of cases are "discovered" which do not properly reflect the spirit of the law (Callaghan, 1982).

This may imply that mandatory reporting laws (like other policy initiatives that we have discussed) may serve symbolic and political, rather than pragmatic ends. Such laws are enacted with much fanfare and little opposition. And, as a way of demonstrating that something is being done about the problem of elder abuse, they involve a far smaller commitment of resources than does the establishment of social service interventions for those cases of mistreatment that are uncovered. It may be somewhat cynically suggested that these laws represent a highly visible, yet low cost means by which politicians may demonstrate their apparent concern for older persons (Crystal, 1986; 1987).

At a more basic level, mandatory reporting laws have been criticized because of their ageist nature. As stated, such laws suggest a legalistic parallel between children and the elderly and in so doing, indicate that older persons may be treated differently than other categories of adults. They imply that persons who are over a certain age and who are the objects of harm at the hands of another, may be denied individual choice with respect to the reporting of the situation in which they find themselves; and perhaps with respect to subsequent action taken by authorities. Members of various professional communities, and not the elders themselves, are defined by such laws as the most appropriate judges of whether mistreatment requires official attention.

The effect of many of these laws is to define being elderly as a disability; and in fact, many pieces of legislation group older persons together with those who are mentally ill or mentally retarded (Cohen, 1978; Crystal, 1987). The laws may demand that the privileged communication between a physician and an elderly patient need not be respected if abuse is suspected (Yin, 1985). They may also require that the older person may be removed from his or her home because others deem the action necessary. By contrast, while we may deplore wife assualt and would encourage women to take steps to remove themselves from abusive situations, we would be disinclined to support legislation that would mandate that such cases be reported and acted upon, irrespective of the feelings or the wishes of the victims (Faulkner, 1982). As Crystal (1987) observes, there is little difference between a 64 year old who is being abused by a spouse and a 65 year old who is being abused by an adult child. Mandatory reporting laws, however, may reify the distinction by requiring the reporting of the latter but not the former situation.

These criticisms may be countered by claiming that the elder victim of mistreatment is reluctant to use existing social and legal resources to ameliorate the situation and thus drastic measures are necessary. However, this itself is an ageist position which infantilizes older persons (Salend et al., 1984). Elderly victims of mistreatment may rationally choose not to report. They may fear realistically that reporting may result in institutionalization or some other undesirable alternative (Katz, 1980; Faulkner, 1982). Moreover, they may wish to avoid the embarrassment and the invasion of privacy that the subsequent investigation would imply. As Crsytal (1987) argues, we must ask whether the state has the right to intervene in a private relationship when it does not seem willing or able to offer anything better.

Intervention

Once cases of elder mistreatment are identified, a next logical step involves intervention in the situation so as to end the mistreatment and to prevent its reoccurrence. Any such intervention, of course, contains within it a working model of how mistreatment is generated. And to a degree, the success of such interventions depends upon the accuracy of the working model. Three broad forms of intervention may be identified.

1. **Treatment.** An obvious approach to the problem of elder abuse involves the employment of treatment and counselling strategies. These interventions are undertaken in an effort to reorient the behaviour and attitudes of family members so as to prevent the occurrence of future abuse.

    Therapeutic interventions frequently take the form of family counselling (Hooyman et al., 1982; Rathbone-McCuan and Hashimi, 1982; Kosberg, 1985). Such approaches emphasize the need to intervene with

268

all family members and not just the victim or the perpetrator of the mistreatment (Rathbone-McCuan et al., 1983; Edinberg, 1986). This approach thus proceeds from the assumption that all family members may be affected by and contribute to the environment within which mistreatment occurs.

Some observers have expressed concern, however, that much of this counselling may be ineffective because it fails to take into account the intergenerational nature of much of the conflict that leads to mistreatment (Hooyman et al., 1982). In other words, there is a tendency to employ therapeutic models that are derived from counselling with abused children or spouses. While there may be some generalizability to such strategies, it is argued that they may be of little utility when applied to situations in which the mistreatment is perpetrated by an adult offspring. It should be recalled, however, that according to Pillemer and Finkelhor (1988) a significant proportion of cases of elder mistreatment do in fact involve spousal abuse. This may imply that counselling and therapeutic models developed to ameliorate problems of spousal abuse may have greater applicability than was once believed.

Treatment strategies may also focus more specifically upon the abuser and the abused. In the former case, alcohol or drug treatment programs may be accessed in order to help the abuser cope with problems of substance dependency. Proceeding from Pillemer's findings that those who abuse the elderly are in many cases economically dependent upon their victims, job training or employment counselling may be utilized in order to allow the individual to gain economic independence (Pillemer, 1985).

Interventions with the victim may focus upon the attempt to provide reassurance and to help the elder cope with the consequences of the mistreatment. The victim may need assistance in dealing with the self-blame that frequently accompanies mistreatment and in resolving the emotional difficulties that mistreatment by an intimate may create. A particularly valuable strategy in this respect may be the use of self-help groups such as those that have been formed to deal with spousal abuse (Pillemer and Suitor, 1988).

While these therapeutic interventions may be directed toward emotional catharsis and reconstruction, they may also have very apparent educational objectives. If mistreatment results because caregivers are unaware of, or misinformed regarding the psychological, social and behavioral correlates of aging, intensive counselling may correct these misperceptions and teach skills that facilitate coping responses (Steinmetz and Amsden, 1983; Hooyman et al., 1982)

2. **Protection.** Protective interventions refer to the delivery of those services which are intended to make secure the physical being or the economic resources of the older person.

The most obvious form of protection, removal of the elder from his or her home, is generally considered the least desirable option and one which should be used only as a last resort (U.S. Department of Health and Human Services, 1980; Kosberg, 1985). The removal of the older person suggests a particularly pernicious form of victim-blaming which attempts to resolve the problem by extending greater social control over the victim rather than over his or her offender. If other family members or friends are unable or unwilling to take the older person in, the consequence may be some form of institutionalization. As we have seen, this is an option which is negatively viewed by many older people (Crystal, 1987; McCuan and Hashimi, 1982).

In those situations which require the removal of the elder because circumstances preclude an alternative, a preferable course of action might involve the use of a temporary "safe house" (Pillemer, 1985; Pillemer and Suitor, 1988). The abused individual would be able to remain in such a shelter until alternative arrangements could be made or until the conditions in the home warrant returning. Shelters of this type are, of course, considered a routine policy option with respect to spousal abuse. In some jurisdictions, rather than remove the elder, the decision is made to move a social service professional or paraprofessional into the home in order to monitor the situation (U.S. Department of Health and Human Services, 1980).

Protection is also potentially achieved through the use of legal interventions directed toward the offender. In the case of serious instances of abuse, existing criminal laws may be able to achieve this purpose. Crystal (1987) notes, however, that several communities have recently enacted special "elder abuse" and "elder neglect" statutes which are intended to criminalize a broader range of mistreatment than normally falls under the purview of the criminal law.

There are several problems with such statutes. First, it is not always clear to whom the laws apply (Crystal, 1987). Neglect, in particular, implies an obligation to provide care but it is sometimes uncertain who is assumed to have such an obligation in the case of an elderly adult. Second, the scope of such laws is frequently so broad that they risk the criminalization of behavior that falls within the normal range of family interaction (Pillemer and Suitor, 1988). Third, their discretionary nature creates the potential for selective prosecution involving particularly newsworthy cases (Crystal, 1987). Fourth, criminal prosecutions under these statutes are only rarely undertaken (Crystal, 1987). Finally, criminal procedures, of which these laws are an example, may be less preferable than civil remedies since a successful action in the former case requires proof "beyond a reasonable doubt" while the latter requires a less rigorous "preponderance of evidence" (Block et al., 1979).

With respect to financial abuse, protective intervention frequently takes the form of procedures which delegate financial authority to a family member or to some agency of the state (Olson, 1981). It has been claimed, however, that these various types of guardianship, trusteeship or conservatorship infantilize older persons and deny their personal liberties (Olson, 1981; Pillemer and Suitor, 1988). Such procedures may also function as a form of victim-blaming which uses the law to control the behavior of the offended party rather than the behavior of the offender.

Gordon (1987) suggests that the popularity of such arrangements arises from the fact they are a low cost means by which state agencies may

270

intervene in large numbers of such cases. Once the estate has been secured, there is little more to do than transfer funds between accounts and pay bills. While the rigorous prosecution, under existing laws, of those who abuse the financial trust of older persons might seem a more just way of dealing with these offences, it would probably produce a less certain payoff.

Increasingly, there has been a movement toward more relaxed standards by which control of financial resources may be transferred to a guardianship or trusteeship arrangement. This is because in many jurisdictions, such processes can only be activated if an elder is declared mentally unfit (Shell, 1982). It is argued, therefore, that there are many older people who, while not mentally incompetent, are functionally impaired and who require assistance with financial matters. Gordon warns, however, that the movement toward tests based upon functional impairment could increase quite dramatically the numbers of older people who will find that they have lost financial control to family members or to government agencies.

3. **Community Support.** The potentially important role of community support has already been alluded to in the above discussions of treatment and protection strategies.

Most generally, community resources may be employed for the purpose of reducing the familial stress which is assumed to precipitate abuse. Elderly day care centers, for instance, may provide respite care which reduces the strain toward mistreatment (Steinmetz and Amsden, 1983). Those with a history of abuse may be encouraged to affiliate with community-based organizations similar to "parents anonymous" groups (which have as their objective the reduction of child abuse). Groups of this type can bring together caregivers who face similar problems so as to provide group-supported definitions of appropriate coping strategies.

Another important dimension of community intervention involves the establishment of procedures which link those involved in abusive situations to community resources (Hooyman et al., 1982; Pillemer and Suitor, 1988). The isolation, which frequently characterizes abuse, implies that both the perpetrator and the victim of mistreatment may be unaware of how they can access information or financial or social assistance. The fact that in many communities relevant sources of support are not centralized but located within specialized government or social service agencies aggravates this problem.

The natural helpers, who were mentioned with reference to the detection of abuse and neglect cases, have relevance here as well. Family, friends and neighbors who have credibility with respect to those involved in abusive situations may be effectively mobilized so as to encourage victims or abusers to seek help. For this to happen, however, the members of these networks have to be educated about the problem of elder mistreatment and the resources that are available. In similar fashion, pharmacists, welfare workers, police officers and others to whom an older person might turn for assistance, need to be informed about reporting procedures and available services.

Treatment, protection and community support should be understood not as mutually exclusive but as complementary strategies. The general problem with all such interventions, however, is their post hoc character. This means that such strategies are intended to address mistreatment only after it has occurred. Thus in the case of elder abuse and neglect, as in the case of other types of elderly victimization, prevention rather than treatment seems to be the preferable option.

Prevention

Strategies of prevention have as their objective the alteration of conditions that are thought to make mistreatment likely. As such, they are more generally directed to the community of elders and their caregivers rather than to the specific cases in which mistreatment is known or suspected to have occurred.

These approaches are addressed to one or some combination of three broad policy questions:

1. How can the placement of elderly persons into situations of potential abuse be prevented?

2. How is it possible to prevent the development of social stress that is assumed to be related to elder mistreatment?

3. How is it possible to prevent the social isolation that creates an environment conducive to the development of mistreatment?

Each of these questions is considered in turn.

Inappropriate Placements. It cannot, of course, be assumed that all family members are equally suited to provide care to an elderly person. As we have seen, there is a strong empirical suggestion that abuse and neglect may result because the caregiver is not economically, physically or psychologically prepared to assume or discharge the responsibilities that such a commitment implies.

This would indicate that those individuals and families who are considering involvement in the caregiving role need to be assessed with respect to relevant capabilities before the responsibility for the care of an elder person is assumed (Kosberg, 1985). Several assessment techniques have been developed and are currently in use.

In addition to such assessments, policy attention may focus upon the need for educational efforts directed toward those who may be willing to assume a caregiving role but ill-prepared to do so. We have noted that in many cases, family members may make the decision to care for an elder in an emotionally-charged context. They may have little understanding of what is involved in such situations, of the aging process or of the problems associated with later life (Steur and Austin, 1980). An effective instructional program can allow family members to make a more informed decision regarding the care of an older person and, to provide a better level of care if an affirmative decision is made.

Part of the problem relating to the placement of elderly persons in inappropriate situations relates to the lack of viable alternatives for those cases in which family members may be incapable of providing adequate care. As Quinn and Tomita (1986) note, we have tended to romanticize the idea of family care and to view it as generally preferable to the narrow range of available institutional options. Family members may frequently feel pressured by predominant cultural values and the lack of alternatives, to assume a caregiving role even when it may be inadvisable to do so.

There is, therefore, a need to support not only those who decide to assume a caregiving role but also those who decide not to do so (Anetzberger, 1987; Kosberg, 1985). The only options to private care need not be hospitilization or nursing home placement. Instead, some have suggested the need to develop non- institutional community alternatives. According to Kosberg (1985:388), such alternatives might include:

> social settings which meet the needs of the elderly such as public housing for the elderly, foster homes, group homes, etc., as well as services that can assist the independence of an older person living in his or her own dwelling. Such community resources can include meals- on-wheels programs, home care and chore services, transportation programs, telephone reassurance and friendly visitor programs and home health care.

As such programs proliferate, the stigma associated with the decision on the part of family members not to assume a caregiver role might be considerably diminished.

Policies that focus upon family assessment and placement alternatives assume that there exists a distinct decision-making point at which such policies become relevant. In some large number of cases, however, as we have seen this may not be true. It will be recalled that Pillemer found that in cases of serious abuse, the elder did reside in her own home with an economically and socially dependent caregiver. Similarly, in those cases of elder abuse which involve aging spouses, questions about family assessment or choice of a caregiver role may never really arise.

Stress Reduction. The view that mistreatment of the elderly is precipitated and sustained by stressful family relationships suggests that programs and mechanisms intended to alleviate stress might reduce the likelihood of abuse and neglect.

Home visit, day-care and related respite programs can alleviate some of the emotional and physical burden associated with the long-term provision of care (O'Malley et al., 1983; Anetzberger, 1987; Hooyman, 1983). Also important in this respect are those services which assist in the performance of instrumental care-related tasks such as shopping, exercise, meal preparation and recreation. The availability of such services must be widely publicized and referrals must be routinized if those who manage these services are to be put into contact with those who need them.

We have noted that economic strains are frequently characterized as among the most severe that family members face in the context of a caregiving situation. If this is true, there is a need for measures which reduce these economic burdens (Kosberg, 1985). Relevant policies may include tax incentives, direct subsidies or cash payments similar to family allowance plans. To be fully effective, programs of this type must be supplemented by monitoring systems which ensure that funds are used in appropriate fashion.

How does the provision of formal services, intended to alleviate caregiver burdens, impact upon the informal performance of and commitment to this role? In this respect, it might be feared that as formal services become increasingly available, informal caregivers may relinquish their responsibilities. The resulting burden on the financial resources of the state might be viewed as prohibitive by some who regard family care arrangements as not only morally correct but fiscally expedient (Anetzberger, 1987). The empirical evidence suggests, however, that the effects of the availability of formal caregiving services upon informal caregiving may not be so extreme. Caro (1986) reports that organized services complement rather than replace informal services; and that even when formal care is widely available, many family members still continue to provide significant levels of informal assistance.

Reducing Isolation. It has been argued that abusive situations develop and escalate in part because the caregiver and the elderly victim become increasingly isolated from the community. While isolation may not directly cause mistreatment, it may be structurally conducive to its development.

Effective prevention might be achieved through informal and formal community supports which reduce this isolation. Again, volunteers, home visit, recreation programs or congregate meal programs might serve this end. Involvement in such activities serves to integrate family members into the wider community while allowing them to derive more direct and tangible benefits (Hooyman et al., 1982).

The attempt to integrate abused and abuser into the wider community may have policy relevance for at least three reasons. First, as we have seen, isolation may directly contribute to stress by reducing service availability and level of emotional support.

Second, a higher degree of social integration serves to empower the older person and to increase awareness of options regarding his or her circumstances. More active involvement in the community may increase self-confidence and reduce feelings of dependency (U.S. Department of Health and Human Services, 1980). These wider networks may offer the older person alternative definitions of the situation, of the caregiver and of him- or herself. In this way, the tendency of caregivers to infantilize or control the elder may be, to some extent, mitigated.

Finally, integration increases the probable success of legal sanctions in deterring mistreatment. Isolation implies that mistreatment remains a low visibility offence. In such circumstances, threats of legal sanction for abuse or neglect will be rendered largely ineffective.

POLITICS AND POLICY: WHAT SHOULD BE DONE?

In this chapter we have discussed several specific issues relevant to the control and the prevention of elderly victimization. It is, however, one thing to detail complex and varied policy options within the context of an academic discussion such as this, and it is quite another to translate these approaches into effective action. While it is reasonable to suggest that the amelioration of elderly crime problems may necessitate a range of diverse services and programs (Jaycox and Center, 1983; Hooyman et al., 1982), political and economic realities are such that "shopping lists" of policy recommendations cannot be implemented en masse. More generally, whether the social problem that concerns us is crime against the elderly, poverty, racism, pollution, mental illness or drug addiction, we are not free to try anything and everything that might work.

The reason is simple. Human and economic resources are limited. The point is obvious but sometimes overlooked in discussions of this type and in the rhetoric of interest groups which defines social problems as crises in need of immediate attention.

It will be noted that in reviewing policy options, we have made no attempt to keep a running account of what all of this would cost. Nevertheless, we would expect the costs to be substantial. We have considered how new programs could be developed and how existing agencies, such as the police, might redefine their mandates. Not only must we recognize large pricetags attached to these policies in an absolute sense, but we must also realize that, to the extent that we direct resources to combat crimes against the elderly, there will be fewer resources available to meet the needs of other groups.

If we are not free to pursue all possible avenues to problem-solving then how are we to decide what to do? There are two answers to this question. The first is political. Those who are critical of the policy process frequently argue that policies tend to reflect interests rather than needs. In other words, political power determines both the priorities for social action and the nature of the action itself. Seen in this way, policy is little more than a cynical expression of interest group politics. This position suggests that policies, even if they are likely to be effective, will not be developed if they run counter to organized and powerful social interests.

The second answer to the question about how we decide what to do in the presence of uncertainty, is empirical rather than political. It suggests that research, particularly research that assesses the impact of different social interventions, is the type of information that most suitably informs choice in this respect.

Too often, however, such evaluations are not undertaken. The evaluation of social programs may itself be a costly undertaking which may draw funds away from program development or implementation and thus displease those who may be more interested in the appearance of doing good than in evidence that their best intentions may be ineffective. When evaluations are undertaken, they lack, in many cases, a sufficient degree of methodological rigor. In such cases, the evaluative data may be equivocal and it becomes impossible to make empirically informed decisions (Rathbone-McCuan and Hashimi, 1982).

275

What then is to be done about the crime problems of the elderly? Our question may obscure two very general but important issues, each of which is relevant to the distinction made earlier between categoric and generic policies. The first issue relates to whether it is necessary to devise or modify social policy so as to define the elderly as a group requiring special attention.

The second issue approaches the generic-categoric distinction from a different angle. Is victimization among the more significant social problems facing older persons? And, to what extent is it separable from other social problems? We consider each of these issues in turn.

Elderly as the Focus of Policy Attention

It would seem that a rather strong case can be made against the large scale development and implementation of programs that focus specifically upon the crime problems of older persons. As we have seen, with respect to most traditional forms of criminal victimization, rates of elderly crime are lower than those experienced by the rest of the population. Even when rates are adjusted for variations in levels of exposure to risk, there do not appear to be extreme differentials in this regard. In addition, older persons appear to be victimized by "less serious" crimes against property rather than by "more serious" crimes of violence. The deployment of police resources toward the control of crimes against the elderly may achieve a reduction but this may not be a wise policy given that the elderly are a "low risk" group (Sykes, 1976). In addition, an increased police presence (like loading older persons down with security hardware or otherwise organizing their paranoia) may diminish rather than increase feelings of personal safety (Cook et al., 1981; Clarke, 1984).

Whether the elderly suffer disproportionately in the aftermath of the victimization experience depends upon the criteria that we employ for making a judgment. On one hand, we have discovered that the elderly do not generally sustain more severe physical injuries. We have also seen that when compared to the rest of the population, they appear to be more likely and not less likely to support legal control. They are somewhat more likely to report crimes to the police and to hold the police in high regard.

On the other hand, it may be argued that the elderly may suffer more severe consequences, particularly of an emotional or economic nature. However, this does not necessarily support the need for specialized programs. The emotional needs created by criminal victimization are probably more likely to be ameliorated by informal social support networks than by formal government policies.

The economic losses resulting from elderly victimization are more serious than those associated with non-elderly victimization, if these losses are adjusted according to income. But, this suggests that older persons suffer not because they are old but because they are more likely to be poor (Cook et al., 1978). Age, therefore, appears to be a somewhat inappropriate criterion for determining who should be proactively encouraged to seek victim compensation, and who should be considered eligible for emergency compensation. Specialized programs fail to take account of the fact that elderly people differ from each other with respect to the resources available to them and that many non-elderly share in common with older persons the conditions that make the economic

276

effects of crime particularly troublesome (Sundeen and Mathieu, 1976). If the eligibility criteria of compensation programs were relaxed so as to include crimes against property and if medical and property insurance schemes were made more accessible to the economically disadvantaged, the unique losses experienced by the poor elderly (and by the poor non-elderly) would be reduced considerably (Cook et al., 1981; Skogan, 1978).

With respect to elderly fear of crime, we again discover that categoric programs may be inappropriate. First, we have seen that contrary to popular belief, most older persons are not paralysed by fear; and that to some extent, the fears which they do express reflect a realistic assessment of the potential consequences of victimization or of the risks that they face if they do expose themselves to potential danger.

Again, fear reduction programs which are directed toward older persons ignore important differences within the elderly population. The neighborhood, rather than any particular demographic group is probably the most appropriate locus of fear programming (Maxfield, 1984b; Lewis and Maxfield, 1980). Those neighborhoods which have crime problems or incivility problems also have fear problems. And, in these neighborhoods, both old and young residents are afraid. Neighborhood interventions intended to control not only fear but also crime and incivility, will benefit the fearful elderly and the fearful non-elderly resident.

Finally, we may ask whether elder abuse and neglect should be seen as posing distinctive policy questions. There is a problem here as well. Some of the recent research which we reviewed in Chapter 11 indicates that a significant proportion of what we may choose to call elder abuse is actually spousal abuse. The mistreatment which occurs between elderly spouses would seem to have more in common with abuse involving non-elderly spouses than with mistreatment that occurs within the context of generationally inverse families. Elder abuse, however, as a master concept which organizes legalistic and social service responses obscures these differences.

In many cases, age-specific policies relating to victimization reflect good intentions. In other cases, they would seem to suggest an attempt to pander to the growing political constituency that the elderly represent. Whatever the motivation behind these initiatives, they would appear in many instances, to reflect ageist assumptions which in the long run undermine the best interests of older persons (Bengston, 1977). As Cook and colleagues note:

> Currently the general consensus separates elderly adults apart as a 'special group' - weaker, frailer, more dependent and quite different from the younger population. If this attitude were to pervade the ranks of the elderly themselves, it would lessen their sense of self-worth and dignity. If it were to pervade the attitudes of those under 65, it could result in stigma being attached to aging. It is ironic that some of the very aging advocates who recommend special programs for the elderly due to their supposed 'special vulnerability to criminals' are just the ones who on other issues (ie mandatory retirement) promulgate the notion that the elderly are as strong and as able as the next person. It is somewhat contradictory to have one set of policies backed by the notion of a special

frailty of the elderly and another backed by the notion of the elderly being no different from other age groups (Cook et al., 1978:348).

Victimization as a Focus of Policy Attention

Policies directed toward elderly crime problems are intended, ostensibly at least, to improve the quality of life of older persons. Yet, it is legitimate to ask how much leverage victimization policies provide in this regard. Are crime and abuse among the most pressing problems confronting older persons? Or, does the attention paid to such problems draw attention away from more significant concerns? Does the amelioration of elderly crime problems lead to more general improvements in the plight of older people? Or, are crime and abuse the result of basic problems that remain untouched by victimization policies?

Crystal (1986) argues, for instance, that large numbers of older persons are affected by problems such as poor financial management or the lack of a caretaker. However, these problems are not as novel nor as dramatic as elder abuse. This is not to deny that elder abuse occurs; only that the public response to it may be disproportionate to its occurrence and at the expense of the mobilization of energy and resources to combat these other problems. In addition, Crystal (1987) maintains that because elder abuse routinely occurs in the context of multi-problem families, its use as an organizing concept for the planning and delivery of services will cause related, and perhaps more basic problems to be ignored.

This point may be generalizable to more traditional forms of criminal victimization. We have discovered in previous chapters that elderly crime problems are intricately related to several other problematic aspects of later life. Victimization and the fear of victimization, we have discovered, are linked to the economic precariousness of older persons, to their exclusion from social networks and community participation, to their sense of powerlessness and their fear of changing social conditions, to their segregation in inner city neighborhoods and to a perception shared both by the elderly and those who would victimize them that they are vulnerable because they are old.

This suggests that an undue emphasis upon crime and victimization as the objects of policy attention will leave unaddressed, and perhaps even mystify, the more basic issues that confront the elderly within the context of contemporary generational arrangements.

CHAPTER TWELVE: RECOMMENDED READINGS

Corrigan, R.S.
1981 Crime Prevention Programs for the Elderly. in D. Lester (Ed.). The Elderly Victim of Crime. Springfield Ill.: Charles C. Thomas. pp. 83-96.

Fattah, E.A.
1986 The Role of Senior Citizens in Crime Prevention. Ageing and Society, 6:471-480.

Faulkner, L.R.
1982 Mandating the Reporting of Suspected Cases of Elder Abuse: An Inappropriate, Ineffective and Ageist Response to the Abuse of Older Adults. Family Law Quarterly, 16:69-91.

Hamel, R.
1979 Assisting Elderly Victims. in A.P. Goldstein, W.J. Hoyer and P.J. Monti (Eds.). Police and the Elderly. New York: Pergamon Press. pp. 67-85.

Hooyman, N.R., E. Rathbone-McCuan and K. Klingbeil
1982 Serving the Vulnerable Elderly: The Detection, Intervention and Prevention of Familial Abuse. Urban and Social Change Review, 15:9-13.

Kosberg, J.I.
1988 Preventing Elder Abuse: Identification of High Risk Factors Prior to Placement Decisions. The Gerontologist, 28:43-50.

BIBLIOGRAPHY: PART II

Agnew, R.S.
1985 Neutralizing the Impact of Crime. Criminal Justice and Behavior, 12:221-239.

Alston, L.T.
1986 Crime and Older Americans. Springfield Ill.: Charles C. Thomas.

Anderson, C.L.
1981 Abuse and Neglect among the Elderly. J. of Gerontological Nursing, 7:77-85.

Anetzberger, G.J.
1987 The Etiology of Elder Abuse by Adult Offspring. Springfield Ill.: Charles C. Thomas.

Ansello, E.F., N.R. King and G. Taler
1986 The Environmental Press Model: A Theoretical Framework for Intervention in Elder Abuse. in K.A. Pillemer and W.S. Wolf (Eds.). Elder Abuse: Conflict in the Family. Dover Mass.: Auburn Publishing Co. pp. 314-330.

Antunes, G.E., F.L. Cook, T.D. Cook and W.G. Skogan
1977 Patterns of Personal Crime against the Elderly: Findings from a National Survey. The Gerontologist, 17:321-327.

Arcuri, A.F.
1981 The Police and the Elderly. in D. Lester (Ed.). The Elderly Victim of Crime. Springfield Ill.: Charles C. Thomas. pp. 106-128.

Ashton, N.
1981a Senior Citizens' Views on Crime and the Criminal Justice System. in D. Lester (Ed.). The Elderly Victim of Crime. Springfield Ill: Charles C. Thomas. pp. 14-26.

Ashton, N.
1981b Victim Compensation and the Elderly. in D. Lester (Ed.). The Elderly Victim of Crime. Springfield Ill: Charles C. Thomas. pp. 97-105.

Auger, J.A. and V. Guarino
1979 Growing Old Safely. Vancouver: Consultation Centre, Solicitor General of Canada.

Baker, M.H., B.C. Nieustedt, R.S. Everett and R. McCleary
1983 The Impact of a Crime Wave: Perceptions, Fear and Confidence in the Police. Law and Society Review, 12:319-335.

Balkin, S.
1979 Victimization Rates, Safety and Fear of Crime. Social Problems, 26:343-358.

Balkin, S. and P. Houlden
1983 Reducing Fear of Crime through Occupational Presence. Criminal Justice and Behavior, 10:13-33.

Bard, M. and D. Sangrey
1979 The Crime Victims Book. New York: Basic Books.

Barnes, N.D.
1982 Crime and the Elderly Victim: A Resource Guide. Chicago Ill.: Council of Planning Librarians.

Baumer, T.L.
1978 Research on Fear of Crime in the United States. Victimology, 3:254-264.

Baumer, T.L.
1985 Testing a General Model of Fear of Crime: Data from a National Sample. J. of Research in Crime and Delinquency, 22:239-256.

Beck, C.M. and D. Ferguson
1981 Aged Abuse. Journal of Gerontological Nursing, 7:77-85.

Becker, H.
1963 Outsiders: Studies in the Sociology of Deviance. New York: The Free Press.

Bengston, V.L.
1977 Comparative Perspectives on the Microsociology of Politics and Aging. in M.A.Y. Rifai (Ed.). Justice and Older Americans. Lexington Mass.: D.C. Heath. pp. 177-186.

Berg, W.E. and R. Johnson
1979 Assessing the Impact of Victimization: Acquisition of the Victim Role among Elderly and Female Victims. in W.E. Parsonage (Ed.). Perspectives on Victimology. Beverly Hills: Sage Publications. pp. 58-71.

Biderman, A.
1981 Sources of Data for Victimology. J. of Criminal Law and Criminology, 72:789-817.

Bishop, J.M. and D.R. Krause
1984 Depictions of Aging and Old Age on Saturday Morning Television. The Gerontologist, 24:91-94.

Bisset-Johnson, A.
1986 Domestic Violence: A Plethora of Problems and Precious Few Solutions. Canadian J. of Family Law, 5:253-276.

281

Black, D.
1970 Production of Crime Rates. American Sociological Review, 35:733-748.

Black, D.
1983 Crime as Social Control. American Sociological Review, 48:34-45.

Block, C.R. and R.L. Block
1984 Crime Definition, Crime Measurement, and Victim Surveys. Journal of Social Issues, 40:137-160.

Block, M.R.
1983 Special Problems and Vulnerability of Elderly Women. in J.I. Kosberg (Ed.). Abuse and Mistreatment of the Elderly: Causes and Interventions. Littleton Mass.: John Wright. pp. 220-233.

Block, M.R. and J.D. Sinnott
1979 Methodology and Results. in M.R. Block and J.D. Sinnott (Eds.). The Battered Elder Syndrome. College Park Maryland: University of Maryland Center on Aging. pp. 67-84.

Block, M.R., J.L. Davidson and J.D. Sinnott
1979 Elder Abuse and Public Policy. in M.R. Block and J.D. Sinnott (Eds.). The Battered Elder Syndrome. College Park Maryland: University of Maryland Center on Aging. pp. 85-95.

Block, R.
1981 Victim-Offender Dynamics in Violent Crime. The J. of Criminal Law and Criminology. 72:743-761.

Blumberg, M.
1979 Injury to Victims of Personal Crime: Nature and Extent. in W.H. Parsonage (Ed.). Perspectives on Victimology. Beverly Hills: Sage Publications. pp. :133-147.

Blumer, H.
1969 Symbolic Interactionism. Englewood Cliffs: Prentice-Hall.

Boston, G.D.
1977 Crimes Against the Elderly: A Selected Bibliography. Washington D.C.: National Institute of Law Enforcement.

Bragg, D.F., L.R. Kimsey and A.R. Tarbox
1981 Abuse of the Elderly: The Hidden Agenda II: Future Research and Recommendations. Journal of the American Geriatrics Society, 29:503-507.

Brannigan, A.
1984 Crimes, Courts and Corrections. Toronto: Holt, Rinehart and Winston.

Braungart, M.M., R.G. Braungart and W.J. Hoyer
1980 Age, Sex and Social Factors in Fear of Crime. Sociological Focus, 13:55-65.

Braungart, M.M., W.J. Hoyer and R.G. Braungart
1979 Fear of Crime and the Elderly. in A.P. Goldstein, W.J. Hoyer and P.J. Monti (Eds.). Police and the Elderly. New York: Pergamon Press. pp. 15-29.

Brillon, Y.
1987 Victimization and Fear of Crime Among the Elderly. Toronto: Butterworths.

Brostoff, P.M.
1976 The Police Connection: A New Way to Get Information and Referral Services to the Elderly. in J. Goldsmith and S.S. Goldsmith (Eds.). Crime and the Elderly. Lexington Mass.: D.C. Heath. pp. 139-151.

Brostoff, P.M., R.B. Brown and R.N. Butler
1972 The Public Interest: Report no. 6: Beating up on the Elderly: Police, Social Work and Crime. Aging and Human Development, 3:319-322.

Buchholz, M., J.E. Bynum
1982 Newspaper Presentation of America's Aged: A Content Analysis of Image and Role. The Gerontologist, 22:83-87.

Burkhardt, J.E. and L. Norton
1977 Crime and the Elderly: Their Perceptions and Reactions. Washington D.C.: U.S. Department of Justice.

Burston, G.R.
1975 Granny Battering. British Medical J. 3:592.

Burt, M.R. and R.S. Estep
1981 Apprehension and Fear: Learning a Sense of Sexual Vulnerability. Sex Roles, 7:511-522.

Burt, M.R. and B.L. Katz
1985 Rape, Robbery, and Burglary: Responses to Actual and Feared Criminal Victimization, with Special Focus on Women and the Elderly. Victimology, 10:325-358.

Callaghan, J.J.Jr.
1982 Elder Abuse Programming: Will It Help the Elderly? Urban and Social Change Review, 15:15-16.

Canada
1983 Canadian-Provincial Task Force Report On Victims of Crime: Highlights. Ottawa: Solicitor General of Canada.

Canada
1983 Canadian Urban Victimization Survey Bulletin 1: Victims of Crime. Ottawa: Ministry of Solicitor General

Canada
1984 Canadian Urban Victimization Survey: Bulletin 2: Reported and Unreported Crimes. Ottawa: Ministry of Solicitor General

Canada
1984 Canadian Urban Victimization Survey Bulletin 3: Crime Prevention Awareness and Practice. Ottawa: Ministry of Solicitor General.

Canada
1984 Canadian Urban Victimization Survey Bulletin 5: Cost to Victims of Crime. Ottawa: Ministry of Solicitor General.

Canada
1985 Canadian Urban Victimization Survey Bulletin 4: Female Victims of Crime. Ottawa: Ministry of Solicitor General.

Canada
1985 Canadian Urban Victimization Survey Bulletin 6: Criminal Victimization of Elderly Canadians. Ottawa: Ministry of Solicitor General

Canada
1986 Canadian Urban Victimization Survey Bulletin 7: Household Property Crime. Ottawa: Ministry of the Solicitor General.

Canada
1987 Canadian Urban Victimization Survey Bulletin 8: Patterns in Violent Crime. Ottawa: Ministry of the Solicitor General.

Caro, F.G.
1986 Relieving Informal Caregiver Burden Through Organized Services. in K.A. Pillemer and W.S. Wolf (Eds.). Elder Abuse: Conflict in the Family. Dover Mass.: Auburn Publishing Co. pp. 282-296.

Cazenave, N.A.
1983 Elder Abuse and Black Americans: Incidence Correlates, Treatment and Prevention. in J.I. Kosberg (Ed.). Abuse and Mistreatment of the Elderly: Causes and Interventions. Littleton Mass.: John Wright. pp. 187-203.

Center, L.J.
1979 Anti-Crime Techniques for Elderly Apartment Dwellers: Organizing Strategies and Legal Remedies. Washington D.C.: National Council of Senior Citizens.

Center, L.J. and J.H. Stein
1979 Anti-Crime Programs for the Elderly. Washington D.C.: National Council of Senior Citizens.

Champlin, L.
1982 The Battered Elderly. Geriatrics, 37:115,116,121.

Chen, P.N., S.L. Bell, D.L. Dolinsky, J.Doyle and McDunn
1981 Elder Abuse in Domestic Settings: A Pilot Study. Journal of Gerontological Social Work, 4:3-17.

Chibnall, S.
1977 Law and Order News. London: Tavistock Publications.

Circelli, V.
1986 The Helping Relationship and Family Neglect in Later Life. in K.A. Pillemer and R.S. Wolf (Eds.). Elder Abuse: Conflict in the Family. Dover Mass.: Auburn House Publishing Co. pp. 49-66.

Clark, M.
1971 Patterns of Aging among the Elderly Poor of the Inner City. The Gerontologist, 11:58-66.

Clarke, A.H.
1984 Perceptions of Crime and Fear of Victimisation among Elderly People. Ageing and Society, 4:327-342.

Clarke, A.H. and M.J. Lewis
1982 Fear of Crime among the Elderly: An Exploratory Study. British J. of Criminology, 22:49-62.

Clemente, F. and M.B. Kleiman
1976 Fear of Crime among the Aged. The Gerontologist, 16:207-210.

Clemente, F. and M.B. Kleiman
1977 Fear of Crime in the United States: A Multivariate Analysis. Social Forces, 56:519-531.

Coakley, D. and E. Woodford-Williams
1979 Effects of Burglary and Vandalism on the Health of Old People. The Lancet, 2:1066-1067.

Cohen, E.S.
1978 Civil Liberties and the Frail Elderly. Society. 15:34-42.

Cohen, L.E. and M. Felson
1979 Social Change and Crime Rate Trends: A Routine Activity Approach. American Sociological Review, 44:588-608.

Cohen, L.E., J.R. Klugel and K.C. Land
1981 Social Inequality and Predatory Criminal Victimization: An Exposition and Test of a Formal Theory. American Sociological Review, 46:503-524.

Cohn, E.S., L.H.Kidder and J. Harvey
1978 Crime Prevention vs. Victimization Prevention: The Psychology of Two Different Reactions. Victimology, 3:285-296.

Colijn, G.J.
1981 Some Aspects of Crime and Aging in the Welfare State: A European Perspective. in D. Lester (Ed.). The Elderly Victim of Crime. Springfield Ill.: Charles C. Thomas. pp. 61-82.

Conklin, J.E.
1975 The Impact of Crime. New York: Macmillan Publishing Company.

Conklin, J.E.
1976 Robbery, the Elderly and Fear: An Urban Problem in Search of a Solution. in J. Goldsmith and S.S. Goldsmith (Eds.). Crime and the Elderly. Lexington Mass.: D.C. Heath. pp. 99-110.

Cook, F.L.
1981 Crime and the Elderly: The Emergence of a Policy Issue. in D.A. Lewis (Ed.). Reactions to Crime. Beverly Hills: Sage Publications. pp. 123-147.

Cook, F.L., and T.D. Cook
1976 Evaluating the Rhetoric of Crisis. Social Service Review, 50:632-646.

Cook, F.L., W.G. Skogan, T.D. Cook and G.E. Antunes
1978 Criminal Victimization of the Elderly: The Physical and Economic Consequences. The Geronotlogist, 18:338-349.

Cook, T.D., J. Fremming and T.R. Tyler
1981 Criminal Victimization of the Elderly: Validating the Policy Assumptions. in G.M. Stephenson and J.M. Davis (Eds.). Progress in Applied Social Psychology. New York: John Wiley and Sons. pp. 223-251.

Corrado, R.R., R. Roesch, W. Glackman, J.L. Evans and G.L. Leger
1980 Life Styles and Personal Victimization: A Test of the Model with Canadian Survey Data. J. of Crime and Justice, 3:189-301.

Corrigan, R.S.
1981 Crime Prevention Programs for the Elderly. in D. Lester (Ed.). The Elderly Victim of Crime. Springfield Ill.: Charles C. Thomas. pp. 83-96.

Croake, J.W., K.M. Myers and A. Singh
1988 The Fears Expressed by Elderly Men and Women: Lifespan Approach. International Journal of Aging and Human Development, 26:139-146.

Crystal, S.
1986 Social Policy and Elder Abuse. in K.A. Pillemer and W.S. Wolf (Eds.). Elder Abuse: Conflict in the Family. Dover Mass.: Auburn Publishing Co. pp. 330-339.

Crystal, S.
1987 Elder Abuse: The Latest "Crisis". The Public Interest, 88:56-66.

Culp, M.W. and M.L. Calvin
1977 Victim Services Programs. in M.A.Y. Rifai (Ed.). Justice and Older Americans. Lexington Mass.: D.C. Heath. pp. 125-134.

Cumberbatch, G. and A. Beardsworth
1976 Victims, Criminals and Mass Communications. in E.C. Viano (Ed.). Victims and Society. Washington D.C.: Visage Press. pp. 72-90.

Cunningham, C.L.
1976 Pattern and Effect of Crime Against the Aging: The Kansas City Study. in J. Goldsmith and S.S. Goldsmith (Eds.). Crime and the Elderly. Lexington Mass.: D.C. Heath. pp. 31-50.

Curtis, L.A. and I.R. Kohn
1983 Policy Responses to Problems Faced by the Elderly in Public Housing. in J.I. Kosberg (Ed.). Abuse and Mistreatment of the Elderly: Causes and Interventions. Littleton Mass.: John Wright. pp. 251-262.

Cutler, S.J.
1980 Safety in the Streets: Cohort Changes in Fear. International J. of Aging and Human Development, 10:373-384.

Davidson, J.L.
1979 Elder Abuse. in M.R. Block and J.D. Sinnott (Eds.). The Battered Elder Syndrome. College Park Maryland: University of Maryland Center on Aging. pp. 49-66.

Davidson, J.L., S. Hennessey and S. Sedge
1979 Additional Factors Related to Elder Abuse. in M.R. Block and J.D. Sinnott (Eds.). The Battered Elder Syndrome. College Park Maryland: University of Maryland Center on Aging. pp. 57-66.

DeFronzo, J.
1979 Marital Status, Sex and Other Factors Affecting the Fear of Crime. Western Sociological Review, 10:28-39.

Dominick, J.R.
1978 Crime and Law Enforcement in Mass Media. in C. Winic (Ed.). Deviance and Mass Media. Beverly Hills: Sage. pp. 105-128.

Doob, A.N. and G.F. Macdonald
1979 Television Viewing and Fear of Victimization: Is the Relationship Causal? Personality and Social Psychology, 37:170-179.

Douglass, R.L. and T. Hickey
1983 Domestic Neglect and Abuse of the Elderly: Research Findings and a Systems perspective for Service Delivery Planning. in J.I. Kosberg (Ed.). Abuse and Mistreatment of the Elderly: Causes and Interventions. Littleton Mass.: John Wright. pp. 115-133.

DuBow, F. and D. Emmons
1981 The Community Hypothesis. in D.A. Lewis (Ed.). Reactions to Crime. Beverly Hills: Sage Publications. pp. 167-181.

DuBow, F., E. McCabe and G. Kaplan
1979 Reactions to Crime: A Critical Review of the Literature. Washington D.C.: U.S. Department of Justice.

Dussich, J.P.
1979 Overview of Elderly Victimization. Paper presented at the Southern Conference on Gerontology, Tampa Florida.

Dussich, J.P.J. and C.J. Eichman
1976 The Elderly Victim: Vulnerability to the Criminal Act. in J. Goldsmith and S.S. Goldsmith (Ed.). Crime and the Elderly. Lexington Mass.: D.C. Heath. pp. 91-98.

Edinberg, M.
1986 Developing and Integrating Family-Oriented Approaches in Care of the Elderly. in K.A. Pillemer and W.S. Wolf (Eds.). Elder Abuse: Conflict in the Family. Dover Mass.: Auburn Publishing Co. pp. 267-282.

Edwards, J.N. and M.B. Brauburger
1973 Exchange and Parent-Youth Conflict. J. of Marriage and the Family, 30:462-466.

Elias, R.
1983 Victims of the System. New Brunswick: Transaction Books.

Elias, R.
1986 The Politics of Victimization. New York: Oxford University Press.

Elmore, E.
1981 Consumer Fraud and the Elderly. in D. Lester (Ed.). The Elderly Victim of Crime.   Sringfield Ill.: Charles C. Thomas. pp. 27-44.

Ermann, M.D. and R.J. Lundman
1982 Corporate Deviance. New York: Holt, Rinehart and Winston.

Ernst, H., H.J. Friedman and P. Freudiger
1978 Perceptual Variance between Elderly Victims and Non- Victims of Crime. Paper presented at the Southwest Social Science Convention, Houston, Texas.

Evans, J. and A. Himelfarb
1987 Counting Crime. in R. Linden (Ed.). Criminology: A Canadian Perspective. Toronto: Holt, Rinehart and Winston. pp. 43-73

Eve, R.A. and S.B. Eve
1984 The Effect of Powerlessness, Fear of Social Change and Social Integration on Fear of Crime Among the Elderly. Victimology, 9:290-295.

Eve, S.B.
1985 Criminal Victimization and Fear of Crime among the Non-Institutionalized Elderly in the United States. Victimology. 10:397-409.

Falcioni, D.
1982 Assessing the Abused Elderly J. of Gerontological Nursing, 8:208-212.

Farrar, M.S.
1955 Mother-Daughter Conflicts Extended into Later Life. Social Casework, 36:202-207.

Fattah, E.A.
1976 The Use of the Victim as an Agent of Self Legitimation: Toward a Dynamic Explanation of Criminal Behavior. in E.C. Viano (Ed.). Victims and Society.. Washington D.C.: Visage Press. pp. 105-129.

Fattah, E.A.
1979 Some Recent Theoretical Developments in Victimology. Victimology, 4:198-213.

Fattah, E.A.
1981 Becoming a Victim: The Victimization Experience and Its Aftermath. Victimology, 6:29-47.

Fattah, E.A.
1984 Victims' Response to Confrontational Victimization: A Neglected Aspect of Victim Research. Crime and Delinquency, 30:75-89.

Fattah, E.A.
1986 The Role of Senior Citizens in Crime Prevention. Aging and Society, 6:471-480.

Faulkner, L.R.
1982 Mandating the Reporting of Suspected cases of Elder Abuse: An Inapporpriate, Ineffective and Ageist Response to the Abuse of Older Adults. Family Law Quarterly, 16:69-91.

Feinberg, N.
1981 The Emotional and Behavioral Consequences of Violent Crime on Elderly Victims. Victimology, 6:355-357.

Ferraro, K.J. and J.M. Johnson
1983 How Women Experience Battering: The Process of Victimization. Social Problems, 30:325-335.

Finley, G.E.
1983 Fear of Crime in the Elderly. in J.I. Kosberg (Ed.). Abuse and Mistreatment of the Elderly: Causes and Interventions. Littleton Mass.: John Wright. pp. 21-39.

Fischer, C.S.
1981 The Private and Public Worlds of City Life. American Sociological Review, 46:306-316.

Fishman, M.
1978 Crime Waves as Ideology. Social Problems, 25:531-543.

Floyd, J.
1984 Collecting Data on Abuse of the Elderly. J. of Gerontological Nursing, 10:11-15.

Forstan, R.
1974 Criminal Victimization of the Aged: Houston Model Neighborhood Area. Denton Texas: North Texas State University, Center for Community Services.

Friedberg, A.
1983 America Afraid. New York: New American Library.

Friedrichs, D.O.
1983 Victimology: A Consideration of the Radical Critique. Crime and Delinquency, 29:283-294.

Fulmer, T.T. and V.M. Cahill
1984 Assessing Elder Abuse: A Study. J. of Gerontological Nursing, 10:16-20.

Furstenberg, F.
1971 Public Reactions to Crime in the Streets. The American Scholar, 40:601-610.

Garofalo, J.
1979 Victimization and the Fear of Crime. J. of Research in Crime and Delinquency, 16:80-97.

Garofalo, J.
1981 The Fear of Crime: Causes and Consequences. The J. of Criminal Law and Criminology. 72:839-857.

Garofalo, J.
1986 Lifestyles and Victimization: An Update. in E.A Fattah (Ed.). From Crime Policy to Victim Policy. London: The Macmillan Press Ltd. pp. 133-155.

Garofalo, J. and J. Laub
1978 The Fear of Crime: Broadening Our Perspective. Victimology, 3:242-253.

Geiger, D.L.
1978 How Future Professionals View the Elderly: A Comparative Analysis of Social Work, Law and Medical Students' Perceptions. The Gerontologist, 18: 591-594.

Geis, G.
1976 Defrauding the Elderly. in J. Goldsmith and   S.S. Goldsmith (Eds.).
Crime and the Elderly. Lexington Mass.: D.C. Heath. pp. 7-19.

Geis, G.
1977 The Terrible Indignity: Crimes Against the Elderly. in M.A.Y. Rifai (Ed.).
Justice and Older Americans. Lexington Mass.: D.C. Heath. pp. 7-11.

George, L.K.
1986 Caregiver Burden: Conflict Between Norms of Reciprocity and Solidarity. in K.A. Pilmer and R.S. Wolf (Eds.). Elder Abuse: Conflict in the
Family. Dover Mass: Auburn House Publishing Co. pp. 67-92.

Gerbner, G. and L. Gross
1975 Living with Television: The Violence Profile. J. of Communication,
26:172-199.

Gibbons, D.C.
1979 The Criminological Enterprise. Englewood Cliffs: Prentice-Hall Inc.

Gibbs, J.J., E.J. Coyle and K.J. Hanrahan
1987 Fear of Crime: A Concept in Need of Clarification. Paper presented at
the Annual Meetings of the American Society of Criminology, Montreal.

Giles-Sims, J.
1984 A Multivariate Analysis of Perceived Likelihood of Victimization and Degree of Worry about Crime among Older People. Victimology, 9:222-233.

Ginsberg, Y.
1984 Fear of Crime among Elderly Jews in Boston and London. International
J. of Aging and Human Development, 20:257-268.

Giordano, H.N. and J.A. Giordano
1984 Elder Abuse: A Review of the Literature. Social Casework, 29:232-236.

Glasser, P.H. and L.N. Glasser
1962 Role Reversal and Conflict between Aged Parents and their Children.
Marriage and the Family, 24:26-51.

Goff, C.H. and C.E. Reasons
1986 Organizational Crimes against Employees, Consumers and the Public. in
B. Maclean (Ed.). The Political Economy of Crime. Scarborough
Ontario: Prentice- Hall. pp. 204-231.

Golant, S.M.
1984 Factors Influencing the Nighttime Activity of Old Persons in their
Community. J. of Gerontology, 39:485-491.

Goldsmith, J.
1976 Why are the Elderly so Vulnerable to Crime - and What is Being Done for
their Protection? Geriatrics, (April):40-42.

291

Goldstein, A.P. and E.L. Wolf
1979 Police Investigation with Elderly Citizens. in A.P. Goldstein, W.J. Hoyer
and P.J. Monti (Eds.). Police and the Elderly. New York: Pergamon
Press. pp. 58-66.

Gomme, I.
1988 The Role of Experience in the Production of the Fear of Crime: A Test
of a Causal Model. Canadian J. of Criminology, 30:67-76.

Goodstein, L. and R.L. Shotland
1980 The Crime Causes Crime Model: A Critical Review of the Relationship
between Fear of Crime, Bystander Surveillence, and Changes in the
Crime Rate. Victimology, 5:133-151.

Gordon, M.T. and L. Heath
1981 The News Business, Crime and Fear. in D.A. Lewis (Ed.). Reactions to
Crime, Beverly Hills: Sage Publications. pp. 227-250.

Gordon, M.T., S. Riger, R.K. LeBailly and L. Heath
1980 Crime, Women, and the Quality of Urban Life. Signs, 5:144-160.

Gordon, R.M.
1987 Financial Abuse of the Elderly and State "Protective Services": Changing
Strategies in the Penal-Welfare Complex in the United States and Canada.
Crime and Social Justice, 26:116-134

Gottfredson, M.R.
1981 On the Etiology of Criminal Victimization. J. of Criminal Law and Criminology, 72:719-726.

Gottfredson, M.R. and D.M. Gottfredson
1980 Decisionmaking in Criminal Justice. Cambridge Mass.: Ballinger Publishing Company.

Gottfredson, M.R. and M.J. Hindelang
1979 A Study of the Behvaior of Law. American Sociological Review, 44:3-18.

Gottfredson, M.R. and M.J. Hindelang
1981 Sociological Aspects of Criminal Victimization. Annual Review of Sociology, 7:107-128.

Graber, D.A.
1980 Crime News and the Public. New York: Praeger.

Grayson, B. and M.I. Stein
1981 Attracting Assault: Victims' Nonverbal Cues. J. of Communication,
(Winter):68-75.

Gross, P.J.
1979 Crime Prevention and the Elderly. in A.P. Goldstein, W.J. Hoyer and
P.J. Monti (Eds.). Police and the Elderly. New York: Pergamon Press.
pp. 38-57.

Gubrium, J.F.
1973 Apprehension of Coping Incompetence and Response to Fear in Old Age. International J. of Aging and Human Development, 4:111-125.

Gubrium, J.F.
1974 Victimization in Old Age: Available Evidence and Three Hypotheses. Crime and Delinquency, 20:245-250.

Hacker, G.A.
1977 Nursing Homes: Social Victimization of the Elderly. in M.A.Y. Rifai (Ed.). Justice and Older Americans. Lexington Mass.: D.C. Heath. pp. 63-70.

Hagan, J.
1984 The Disreputable Pleasures, second edition. Toronto: McGraw-Hill Ryerson

Hahn, P.H.
1976 Crimes against the Elderly: A Study in Victimology. Santa Cruz: Davis Publishing Co.

Hamel, R.
1979 Assisting Elderly Victims in A.P. Goldstein, W.J. Hoyer and P.J. Monti (Eds.). Police and the Elderly. New York: Pergamon Press. pp. 67-85.

Harbin, H.T. and D.J. Madden
1979 Battered Parents: A New Syndrome. American J. of Psychiatry, 136:1288-1291.

Hartnagel, T.
1979 The Perception and Fear of Crime: Implications for Neighborhood Cohesion, Social Activity and Community Affect. Social Forces, 58:176-193.

Heinzelmann, F.
1981 Crime Prevention and the Physical Environment. in D.A. Lewis (Ed.). Reactions to Crime. Beverly Hills: Sage Publications. pp. 87-101.

Heller, K. and W.E. Mansbach
1984 The Multifaceted Nature of Social Support in a Community of Elderly Women. J. of Social Issues. 40:99-112.

Henig, J. and M.M. Maxfield
1978 Reducing Fear of Crime: Strategies for Intervention. Victimology, 3:297-313.

Henshel, R.L. and R.A. Silverman
1975 Perception in Criminology. New York: Columbia University Press.

Herman, E.A., E.S. Newman and A.D. Nelson
1976 Patterns of Age Integration in Public Housing and the Incidence and Fears of Crime Among Elderly Tenants. in J. Goldsmith and S.S. Goldsmith (Eds.). Crime and the Elderly. Lexington Mass.: D.C. Heath. pp. 68-73.

Hickey, T. and R. Douglass
1981 Mistreatment of the Elderly in Domestic Settings. American J. of Public Health, 71:500-507.

Hickey, T. and R. Douglass
1981 Neglect and Abuse of Older Family Members Professional Perspectives and Case Experiences. The Gerontologist, 21:171-176.

Hindelang, M., M.R. Gottfredson and J. Garofalo
1978 Victims of Personal Crime: An Empirical Foundation for a Theory of Personal Victimization. Cambridge Mass.: Ballinger Publishing Company.

Hochstedler, E.
1981 Crimes Against the Elderly in 26 Cities. Washington D.C.: U.S. Department of Justice.

Holland, L.R., K.R. Kasarian and C.A. Leonardelli
1987 Elder Abuse: An Analysis of the Current Problem and Potential Role of the Rehabilitation Professional. Physical and Occupational Therapy in Geriatrics, 7:41 50.

Hooyman, N.R.
1982 Mobilizing Social Networks to Prevent Elder Abuse. Physical and Occupational Therapy in Geriatrics, 2:21-35.

Hooyman, N.R.
1983 Elderly Abuse and Neglect. in J.I. Kosberg (Ed.). Abuse and Mistreatment of the Elderly: Causes and Prevention. Littleton Mass.: John Wright. pp. 376-390.

Hooyman, N.R., E. Rathbone-McCuan and K. Klingbeil
1982 Serving the Vulnerable Elderly: The Detection Intervention and Prevention of Familial Abuse. Urban and Social Change Review, 15:9-13.

Hough, M.
1985 The Impact of Victimisation: Findings from the British Crime Survey. Victimology, 10:488-497.

Hough, M.
1986 Victims of Violent Crime: Findings from the British Crime Survey. in E.A. Fattah (Ed.). From Crime Policy to Victim Policy. London: The Macmillan Press Ltd. pp. 117-134.

Hoyer, W.J.
1979 The Elderly: Who Are They? in A.P. Goldstein, W.J. Hoyer and P.J. Monti (Eds.). Police and the Elderly. New York: Pergamon Press. pp. 1-14.

Hudson, M.F.
1986 Elder Mistreatment: Current Research. in K.A. Pillemer and R.S. Wolf (Eds.). Elder Abuse: Conflict in the Family. Dover Mass.: Auburn Publishing Co. pp. 125-166.

Janoff-Bulman, R.
1985 Criminal vs. Non-Criminal Victimization: Victims Reactions. Victimology, 10:498-511.

Janoff-Bulman, R. and I.H. Frieze
1983 A Theoretical Perspective for Understanding Reactions to Victimization. J. of Social Issues. 39:1-17.

Janson, P. and L.K. Ryder
1983 Crime and the Elderly: The Relationship between Risk and Fear. The Gerontologist, 23:207-212.

Jaycox, V.H.
1978 The Elderly's Fear of Crime: Rational or Irrational? Victimology, 3:329-334.

Jaycox, V.H. and L.J. Center
1983 A Comprehensive Response to Violent Crimes Against Older Persons. in J.I. Kosberg (Ed.). Abuse and Mistreatment of the Elderly: Causes and Interventions. Littleton Mass.: John Wright. pp. 316-334.

Jeffords, C.R.
1983 The Situational Relationship between Age and Fear of Crime. International J. of Aging and Human Development, 17:103-111.

Johnson, K.A. and P.L. Wasielewski
1982 A Commentary on Victimization Research and the Importance of Meaning Structures. Criminology, 20: 205-222.

Johnson, T.
1986 Critical Issues in the Definition of Elder Mistreatment. in K.A. Pillemer and W.S. Wolf (Eds.). Elder Abuse: Conflict in the Family. Dover Mass.: Auburn Publishing Co. pp. 167-196.

Jones, G.M.
1987 Elderly People and Domestic Crime. British J. of Criminology, 27:191-201.

Jones, M.P.
1977 Victimization on Portland's Skid Row. in M.A.Y. Rifai (Ed.). Justice and Older Americans. Lexington Mass.: D.C. Heath. pp. 37-46.

Kahana, E., J. Liang, B. Felton, T. Fairchild and Z. Harel
1977 Perspective of Aged on Victimization, "Ageism" and their Problems in Urban Society. The Gerontologist, 17:121-129.

Karmen, A.
1984 Crime Victims: An Introduction to Victimology. Monterey, Cal.: Brooks/Cole Publishing Co.

Katz, K.D.
1980 Elder Abuse. J. of Family Law, 18:695-722.

Kennedy, L.W. and H. Krahn
1984 Rural-Urban Origin and Fear of Crime: The Case for "Rural Baggage". Rural Sociology, 49:247-260.

Kennedy, L.W. and R.A. Silverman
1984 Significant Others and Fear of Crime among the Elderly. International J. of Aging and Human Development, 20:241-256.

Kennedy, L.W. and R.A. Silverman
1988 "The Elderly Victim of Homicide." Unpublished Manuscript. Edmonton Alberta: The University of Alberta.

Kidd, R.F. and E.F. Chayet
1984 Why Do Victims Fail to Report? The Psychology of Criminal Victimization. J. of Social Issues, 40:39-50.

Kimsey, L.R., A.R. Tarbox and D.F. Bragg
1981 Abuse of the Elderly - The Hidden Agenda I. The Caretakers and Categories of Abuse. J. of the American Geriatrics Society. 29:465-472.

King, N.
1983 Exploitation and Abuse of Older Family Members: An Overview of the Problem. Response, 6:1-2,13-15.

Kosberg, J.I.
1983 The Special Vulnerability of Elderly Parents. in J.I. Kosberg (Ed.). Abuse and Mistreatment of the Elderly: Causes and Interventions. Littleton Mass.: John Wright. pp. 263-275.

Kosberg, J.I.
1985 Victimization of the Elderly: Causation and Prevention. Victimology, 10:376-396.

Kosberg, J.I.
1988 Preventing Elder Abuse: Identification of High Risk Factors Prior to Placement Decisions. The Gerontologist, 28:43-50.

Lau, E.E. and J.I. Kosberg
1979 Abuse of the Elderly by Informal Care Providers. Aging:10-15.

Lawton, M.P. and S. Yaffe
1980 Victimization and Fear of Crime in Elderly Public Housing Tenants. J. of Gerontology, 35:768-779.

Lawton, M.P., L. Nahemow, S. Yaffe and S. Feldman
1976 Psychological Aspects of Crime and Fear of Crime. in J. Goldsmith and S.S. Goldsmith (Eds.). Crime and the Elderly. Lexington Mass.: D.C. Heath. pp. 21-30.

Lebowitz, B.D.
1975 Age and Fearfulness: Personal and Situational Factors. J. of Gerontology. 30:696-700.

Lee, G.R.
1982 Residential Location and Fear of Crime among the Elderly. Rural Sociology, 47:653-669.

Lee, G.R.
1982 Sex Differences in Fear of Crime Among Older People. Research on Aging, 4:284-278.

Lee, G.R.
1983 Social Integration and Fear of Crime among Older Persons. J. of Gerontology, 38:745-750.

Leeds, M.
1977 Residential Security Techniques. in M.A.Y. Rifai (Ed.). Justice and Older Americans. Lexington Mass.: D.C. Heath. pp. 135-148.

Lein, L.
1986 The Changing Role of the Family. in M. Lystad (Ed.). Violence in the Home. New York: Brunner/Mazel Inc. pp. 32-50.

Lejeune, R. and N. Alex
1973 On Being Mugged: The Event and Its Aftermath. Urban Life and Culture, 2:259-285.

Lewis, D.A. and M.G. Maxfield
1980 Fear in the Neighborhoods: An Investigation of the Impact of Crime. J. of Research in Crime and Delinquency, (July):160-171.

Liang, J. and M.C. Sengstock
1981 The Risk of Personal Victimization among the Aged. J. of Gerontology, 36:463-471.

Liang, J. and M.C. Sengstock
1983 Personal Crimes Against the Elderly. in J.I. Kosberg (Ed.). Abuse and Mistreatment of the Elderly: Causes and Interventions. Littleton Mass.: John Wright. pp. 40-67.

Lindquist, J.H. and J.M. Duke
1982 The Elderly Victim at Risk: Explaining the Fear- Victimization Paradox. Criminology, 20:115-126.

Logan, M.M.
1979 Crimes against the Elderly: Cruel and Unusual Punishment. Victimology, 4:129-131.

Lohman, J.
1983 Fear of Crime as a Policy Problem. Victimology, 8:336-343.

Lotz, R.
1979 Public Anxiety about Crime. Pacific Sociological Review, 22:241-254.

Lubomadrou, S.
1987 Congressional Perceptions of the Elderly: The Use of Stereotypes in the Legislative Process The Gerontologist, 27:77-81.

Luckenbill, D.
1977 Criminal Homicide as Situated Transaction. Social Problems, 25:176-186.

Luppens, J. and E.E. Lau
1983 The Mentally and Physically Impaired Elderly Relative: Consequences for Family Care. in J.I. Kosberg (Ed.). Abuse and Mistreatment of the Elderly: Causes and Interventions. Littleton Mass.: John Wright. pp. 204-219.

Maddox, G.
1979 Sociology of Later Life. Annual Review of Sociology, 5:113-135.

Main, B. and A. Johnson
1978 Whole Persons After Sixty: Crime and the Elderly. Washington D.C.: U.S. Department of Health, Education and Welfare.

Malinchak, A.A.
1980 Crime and Gerontology. Englewood Cliffs: Prentice-Hall.

McCall, G.J. and N.M. Shields
1986 Social and Structural Factors in Family Violence. in M. Lystad (Ed.). Violence in the Home. New York: Brunner/Mazel. pp. 98-123.

Mc Ghee, J.R.
1983 The Vulnerability of Elderly Consumers. International J. of Aging and Human Development, 17:223-246.

McPherson, M.
1978 Realities and Perceptions of Crime at the Neighborhood Level. Victimology, 3:319-328.

Maguire, M.
1980 The Impact of Burglary upon Victims. British J. of Criminology, 20:261-278.

Mawby, R.I. and J. Brown
1984 Newspaper Image of the Victim: A British Study. Victimology, 9:82-94.

Maxfield, M.G.
1984 Fear of Crime in England and Wales. London: Her Majesty's Stationery office.

Maxfield, M.G.
1984 The Limits of Vulnerability in Explaining Fear of Crime. Research in Crime and Delinquency, 21:233-250.

Maxfield, M.G.
1987 Incivilities and Fear of Crime in England and Wales, and the United States: A Comparative Analysis. Paper presented at the Annual Meetings of the American Society of Criminology, Montreal.

Mendelsohn, B.
1976 Victimology and Contemporary Society's Trends. in E.C. Viano (Ed.). Victims and Society. Washington, D.C.: Visage Press. pp. 7-27.

Merry, S.E.
1981 Urban Danger: Life in a Neighborhood of Strangers. Philadelphia: Temple University Press.

Merton, R.K
1957 Social Theory and Social Structure. New York: The Free Press.

Miethe, D. and G.R. Lee
1984 Fear of Crime among Older People: A Reassessment of Crime-Related Factors. The Sociological Quarterly, 125:397-415.

Miethe, T.D., M.C. Stafford and J.S. Long
1987 Social Differentiation in Criminal Victimization: A Test of Routine Activities/Lifestyle Theories. American Sociological Review, 52:184-194.

Miller, D.T. and C.A. Porter
1983 Self-Blame in Victims of Violence. J. of Social Issues, 39:139-152.

Morello, F.P.
1982 Juvenile Crimes against the Elderly. Springfield Ill.: Charles C. Thomas.

Muir, R.G.
1987 Fear of Crime: A Community Policing Perspective. Canadian Police College J., 11:170-196.

Nettler, G.
1984 Explaining Crime, third edition. New York: McGraw-Hill Book Company.

Nitzberg, R.
1982 Effective Responses to the Crime Problems of Older Americans. Washington D.C.: National Council of Senior Citizens.

Normoyle, J. and P.J. Lavrakas
1984 Fear of Crime in Elderly Women: Perceptions of Control, Predictability and Territoriality. Personality and Social Psychology Bulletin. 10:191-202.

Norquay, G. and R. Weiler
1981 Services to Victims and Witnesses of Crime in Canada. Ottawa: Ministry of the Solicitor General.

Norton, L. and M. Courlander
1984 Fear of Crime among the Elderly: The Role of Crime Prevention Programs. The Gerontologist, 22:388-393.

O'Brien, R.M.
1985 Crime and Victimization Data. Beverly Hills: Sage Publications.

Ollenburger, J.C.
1981 Criminal Victimization and Fear of Crime. Research on Aging,:101-118.

Olson, P.
1981 Victimization of the Elderly. Paper presented at International Conference on Victim Assistance, Toronto.

O'Malley, T.A., D.E. Everitt and H.C. O'Malley
1983 Identifying and Preventing Family-Mediated Abuse and Neglect of Elderly Persons. Annals of Internal Medicine, 98:998-1005.

Patterson, A.
1977 Territorial Behavior and Fear of Crime of the Elderly. Police Chief.:42-45.

Patterson, A.
1979 Training the Elderly in Mastery of the Environment. in A.P. Goldstein, W.J. Hoyer and P.J. Monti (Eds.). Police and the Elderly. New York: Pergamon Press. pp. 86-94.

Pepper, C.D.
1983 Frauds Against the Elderly. in J.I. Kosberg (Ed.). Abuse and Mistreatment of the Elderly: Causes and Interventions. Littleton Mass.: John Wright. pp. 68-83.

Perloff, L.
1983 Perceptions of Vulnerability to Victimization. J. of Social Issues, 39:41-61.

Persico, J.E. and G. Sunderland
1985 Keeping Out of Crime's Way: The Practical Guide for People over 50. Washington D.C.: American Association of Retired Persons.

Pfohl, S.
1985 Images of Deviance and Social Control. New York: McGraw-Hill Book Company.

Phillips, L.R.
1986 Theoretical Explanations of Elder Abuse: Competing Hypotheses and Unresolved Issues. in K.A. Pillemer and W.S. Wolf (Eds.). Elder Abuse: Conflict in the Family. Dover Mass.: Auburn Publishing Co. pp. 197-217.

Piland, R.
1977 Surviving Old Age: Criminal Justice Response to the Problem. in M.A.Y. Rifai (Ed.). Justice and Older Americans. Lexington Mass.: D.C. Heath. pp. 117-124.

Pillemer, K.A.
1985 The Dangers of Dependency: New Findings on Domestic Violence Against the Elderly. Social Problems, 33:146-158.

Pillemer, K.A.
1986 Risk Factors in Elder Abuse: Results From a Case- Control Study. in K.A. Pillemer and W.S. Wolf (Eds.). Elder Abuse. Conflict in the Family. Dover Mass.: Auburn Publishing Co. pp. 239-263.

Pillemer, K.A. and D. Finkelhor
1988 The Prevalence of Elder Abuse: A Random Sample Survey. The Gerontologist, 28:51-57.

Pillemer, K.A. and J. Suitor
1988 Elder Abuse. in V.B. Hasselt, R.L. Morrison, A.S. Bellack and M. Hersen (Eds.). Handbook of Family Violence. New York: Plenum Press. pp. 247-270.

Pollack, L.M. and A.H. Patterson
1980 Territoriality and Fear of Crime in Elderly and Nonelderly Homeowners. J. of Social Psychology, 111:119-129.

Poveda, T.G.
1972 The Fear of Crime in a Small Town Crime and Delinquency, 18:147-153.

Quay, H., V. Johnson, K. McClelland, P. Perry, M. Faletti
1980 The Economic, Social and Psychological Impact on the Elderly Resulting from Criminal Victimization. Paper presented at the Annual Meeting of the American Society of Criminology, San Francisco.

Quinn, M.J. and S.K. Tomita
1986 Elder Abuse and Neglect: Causes, Diagnosis and Intervention Strategies. New York: Springer Publishing Co.

Quinney, R.
1970 The Social Reality of Crime. Boston: Little, Brown and Co.

Ragan, P.K.
1977 Crimes Against the Elderly: Findings From Interviews with Blacks, Mexican Americans and Whites. in M.A.Y. Rifai (Ed.). Justice and Older Americans. Lexington Mass.: D.C. Heath. pp. 25-36.

Rand, M.R.
1987 Violent Crime Trends. Washington D.C.: U.S. Department of Justice Bureau of Statistics.

Rathbone-McCuan, E.
1980 Elderly Victims of Family Violence and Neglect. Social Casework, 61:296-304.

Rathbone-McCuan, E. and R. Goodstein
1985 Elderly Abuse: Clinical Considerations. Psychiatric Annals, 15:331-339.

Rathbone-McCuan, E. and J. Hashimi
1982 Isolated Elders. Rockville Maryland: Aspen Systems Corporation.

Rathbone-McCuan, E., A. Travis and B. Voyles
1983 Family Intevention: The Task-Centered Approach. in J.I. Kosberg (Ed.). Abuse and Mistreatment of the Elderly: Causes and Interventions. Littleton Mass.: John Wright. pp. 355-375.

Rathbone-McCuan, E. and B. Voyles
1982 Case Detection of Abused Elderly Parents. American J. of Psychiatry, 139:189-192.

Reiman, J.R.
1976 Aging as Victimization: Reflections on the American Way of (Ending) Life. in J. Goldsmith and S.S. Goldsmith (Eds.). Crime and the Elderly. Lexington Mass.: D.C. Heath. pp. 77-82.

Repetto, T.A.
1974 Residential Crime. Cambridge Mass.: Ballinger.

Richardson, J.B.
1976 Purse Snatch: Robbery's Ugly Stepchild. in J. Goldsmith and S.S. Goldsmith (Eds.). Crime and the Elderly. Lexington Mass.: D.C. Heath. pp. 121-126.

Rifai, M.A.Y.
1977 The Response of the Older Adult to Criminal Victimization. Police Chief:48-50.

Rifai, M.A.Y. and S.A. Ames
1977 Social Victimization of Older People: A Process of Social Exchange. in M.A.Y. Rifai (Ed.). Justice and Older Americans. Lexington Mass.: D.C. Heath. pp. 47-62.

Riger, S. and M.T. Gordon
1981 The Fear of Rape: A Study in Social Control. J. of Social Issues, 37:71-92.

Riger, S., M.T. Gordon and R. LeBailly
1978 Women's Fear of Crime: From Blaming to Restricting the Victim. Victimology, 3:274-284.

Riger, S., M.T. Gordon and R.K. LeBailly
1982 Coping with Urban Crime: Women's Use of Precautionary Behaviors. American J. of Community Psychology, 10:369-386.

Rock, P.
1986 Victims and Policy in Canada: The Emergence of the Justice for Victims of Crime Initiative. in E.A. Fattah (Ed.). From Crime Policy to Victim Policy. London: The Macmillan Press Ltd. pp. 261-289.

Rose, V.
1977 Rape as a Social Problem: A Byproduct of the Feminist Movement. Social Problems, 25:75-89.

Rosenfeld, F.H.
1981 Criminal Victimization of the Elderly. in D. Lester (Ed.). The Elderly Victim of Crime. Springfield Ill.: Charles C. Thomas. pp. 3-13.

Roshier, B.
1973 The Selection of Crime News by the Press. in S. Cohen and J, Young (Eds.). The Manufacture of News London: Constable. pp. 28-39.

Ross, M., P. Ross and M. Ross-Carson
1985 Abuse of the Elderly. The Canadian Nurse, 81:36-39.

Ruback, R.B., M.S. Greenberg and D.R. Westcott
1984 Social Influence and Crime-Victim Decision Making. J. of Social Issues, 40:51-76.

Sacco, V.F.
1982 An Exploratory Analysis of the Conceptual Meaning of Perceptions of Crime. Canadian J. of Criminology, 24:295-306.

Sacco, V.F.
1982 The Effects of Mass Media on Perceptions of Crime. Pacific Sociological Review, 25:475-493.

Sacco, V.F.
1985 City Size and Perceptions of Crime. Canadian J. of Sociology, 10:277-293.

Sacco, V.F.
1985 Perceptions of Crime and Anomic Adaptations. Crimcare J., 1:86-108.

Sacco, V.F. and W. Glackman
1987 Vulnerability, Locus of Control and Worry about Crime. Canadian J. of Community Mental Health, 6:99-111.

Sacco, V.F. and R.A. Silverman
1982 Crime Prevention through Mass Media: Prospects and Problems. J. of Criminal Justice, 10:257-269.

Sager, A.
1986 Mobilizing Adequate Home Care resources: A Mutual Aid Response to Stress Within the Family. in K.A. Pillemer and W.S. Wolf (Eds.). Elder Abuse: Conflict in the Family. Dover Mass.: Auburn Publishing Co. pp. 297-313.

Salend, E., R.A. Kane, M. Satz and J. Pynoos
1984 Elderly Abuse Reporting: Limitations of Statutes. The Gerontologist, 24:61-69.

Sales, E., M. Baum and B. Shore
1984 Victim Readjustment Following Assault. J. of Social Issues, 40:117-136.

Sampson, R.J.
1987 Personal Violence by Strangers: An Extension and Test of the Opportunity Model of Predatory Victimization. The J. of Criminal Law and Criminology, 78:327-356.

Scharlach, A.E.
1987 Role Strain and Mother-Daughter Relationships in Later Life. The Gerontologist, 27:627-631.

Scheppele, K.L. and P.B. Bart
1983 Through Women's Eyes: Defining Danger in the Wake of Sexual Assault. J. of Social Issues, 39:63-81.

Schmall, V.L., S.A. Ames, D.A. Weaver and C.A. Holcomb
1977 The Legal Profession and the Older Person: A Shared Responsibility. in M.A.Y. Rifai (Ed.). Justice and Older Americans. Lexington Mass.: D.C. Heath. pp. 81-91.

Schneider, A.L.
1981 Methodological Problems in Victim Surveys and their Implications for Research in Victimology. J. of Criminal Law and Criminology, 72:818-838.

Sedge, S.
1979 Violence in American Society. in M.R. Block and J.D. Sinnott (Eds.). The Battered Elder Syndrome. College Park Maryland: University of Maryland Center on Aging. pp. 5-16.

Sengstock, M.C. and M. Hwalek
1987 A Review and Analysis of Measures for the Identification of Elder Abuse. J. of Gerontological Social Work, 10:21-36.

Sengstock, H.C. and J. Liang
1977 Responses of the Elderly to Criminal Victimization. Washington D.C.: National Retired Teachers Association.

Shapland, J.
1986 Victims and the Criminal Justice System. in E.A. Fattah (Ed.). From Crime Policy to Victim Policy. London: The Macmillan Press Ltd. pp. 210-217.

Shell, D.J.
1982 Protection of the Elderly: A Study of Elder Abuse. Winnipeg: Manitoba Council on Aging.

Sherizan, S.
1978 Social Creation of Crime News: All the News Fitted to Print. in C. Winick (Ed.). Deviance and the Mass Media. Beverly Hills. pp. Sage: 203-224.

Short, J.F. Jr. and R.F. Meier
1981 Criminology and the Study of Deviance. American Behavioral Scientist, 24:462-478.

Silberman, C.
1978 Criminal Violence, Criminal Justice. New York: Random House.

Silverman, R. and J. Teevan
1986 Crime and Canadian Society. Toronto: Butterworths

Skogan, W.
1976 Citizen Reporting of Crime: Some National Panel Data. Criminology, 13:535-549.

Skogan, W.
1977 Policy Problems in Criminal Justice: The Case of the Elderly Victim of Crime. A paper presented at the Annual Meetings of the American Society for Public Administration.

Skogan, W.
1978 The Fear of Crime among the Elderly. in U.S. House of Representatives, Research into Crimes Against the Elderly, PartII. Washington D.C.: U.S. Government Printing Office.

Skogan, W.
1980 "Adjusting Rates of Victimization for Exposure to Risk, to Understand the Crime Problems of the Elderly." Unpublished Manuscript. Evanston Ill.: Northwestern University.

Skogan, W.
1981 On Attitudes and Behavior. in D.A. Lewis (Ed.). Reactions to Crime. Beverly Hills: Sage Publications. pp. 19-45.

Skogan, W.
1986 Methodological Issues in the Study of Victimization. in E.A. Fattah (Ed.). From Crime Policy to Victim Policy. London: The Macmillan Press. pp. 53-79.

Skogan, W.G. and M.G. Maxfield
1981 Coping with Crime. Beverly Hills: Sage Publications.

Smith, D.L.
1976 The Aftermath of Victimization: Fear and Suspicion in E.C. Viano (Ed.). Victims and Society. Washington D.C.: Visage Press. pp. 203-219.

Smith, R.J.
1979 Crimes Against the Elderly: Implications for Policy-Makers and Practitioners. Washington D.C.: The International Federation of Ageing.

Smith, S.J.
1986 Crime, Space and Society. London: Cambridge University Press.

Snider, L.
1988 Commercial Crime. in V.F. Sacco (Ed.). Deviance: Conformity and Control in Canadian Society. Toronto: Prentice-Hall. pp. 231-285.

Solomon, K.
1983 Victimization by Health Professionals and the Psychological Response of the Elderly. in J.I. Kosberg (Ed.). Abuse and Mistreatment of the Elderly: Causes and Interventions. Littleton Mass.: John Wright. pp. 150-171.

Sparks, R.F., H.G. Genn and D.J. Dodd
1977 Surveying Victims. New York: John Wiley and Sons.

Spector, M. and J.I. Kitsuse
1977 Constructing Social Problems. Menlo Park, Cal.: Cummings Publishing Co.

Spitzer, S.
1975 Toward a Marxian Theory of Deviance. Social Problems, 22:638-651.

Stafford, M. and O. R. Galle
1984 Victimization Rates, Exposure to Risk, and Fear of Crime. Criminology, 22:173-185.

Stearns, P.J.
1986 Old Age and Family Conflict: The Perspective of the Past. in K.A. Pillemer and R.S. Wolf (Ed.). Elder Abuse: Conflict in the Family. Dover Mass.: Auburn House Publishing Co. pp. 3-24.

Steinmetz, S.K
1977 Cycle of Violence: Assertive, Aggressive and Abusive Family Interaction. New York: Praeger.

Steinmetz, S.K.
1978 Battered Parents. Society: 54-55.

Steinmetz, S.K.
1981 Elder Abuse. Aging, (Jan/Feb.): 6-10.

Steinmetz, S.K.
1983 Dependency, Stress and Violence Between Middle-Aged Caregivers and their Elderly Parents. in J.I. Kosberg (Ed.). Abuse and Mistreatment of the Elderly: Causes and Interventions. Littleton Mass.: John Wright. pp. 134-149.

Steinmetz, S.K.
1986 The Violent Family. in M. Lystad (Ed.). Violence in the Home. New York: Brunner/Mazel Inc. pp. 51-67.

Steinmetz, S.K and D.J. Amsden
1983 Dependent Elders, Family Stress and Abuse. in T.H. Brubaker (Ed.). Family Relationships in Later Life. Beverly Hills: Sage Publications. pp. 73-192.

Steur, J.
1983 Abuse of the Physically Disabled Person. in J.I. Kosberg (Ed.). Abuse and Mistreatment of the Elderly: Causes and Interventions. Littleton Mass.: John Wright. pp. 234-250.

...ur, J. and E. Austin
...0 Family Abuse of the Elderly. J. of the American Geriatrics Society, 28: 372-376.

...ne, R., G.L. Cafferata and J. Sangal
...7 Caregivers of the Frail Elderly: A National Profile. The Gerontologist, 27:616-626.

...trauss, M.A., R.J. Gelles and S.K. Steinmetz
1976 Violence in the Family: An Assessment of Knowledge and Research Needs. Washington D.C.: American Association for the Advancement of Science.

Sundeen, R.A. and J.T. Mathieu
1976 The Fear of Crime and its Consequences among Elderly in Three Urban Communities. The Gerontologist, 16:211-219.

Sunderland, G.
1978 National Organizations Launch Crime Prevention Programs. Aging:281-282,32-34.

Swift, C.
1986 Preventing Family Violence: Family-Focused Programs. in M. Lystad (Ed.). Violence in the Home. New York: Brunner/Mazel Inc. pp. 219-249.

Sykes, G.W. and K.W. Johnson
1985 The Aftermath of Criminal Victimization. Paper read at the Annual Meetings of the American Society of Criminology, San Diego, California.

Sykes, R.E.
1976 The Urban Police Function in Regard to the Elderly: A Special Case of Police Community Relations. in J. Goldsmith and S.S. Goldsmith (Eds.). Lexington Mass.: D.C. Heath. pp. 127-138.

Taylor, R.B., S.D. Gottfredson and S. Bower
1984 Block Crime and Fear: Defensible Space, Local Social Ties, and Territorial Functioning. J. of Research in Crime and Delinquency, 21:303-331.

Taylor, R.B. and M. Hale
1986 Testing Alternative Models of Fear of Crime. J. of Criminal Law and Criminology. 77:151 189.

Taylor, S.E., J.V. Wood and R.R. Lichtman
1983 It Could be Worse: Selective Evaluation as a Response to Victimization. J. of Social Issues, 39:19-40.

Teaff, D.T., M.P. Lawton, L. Nahemow and D. Carlson
1978 Impact of Age Integration on the Well-Being of Elderly Tenants in Public Housing. J. of Gerontology, 1:126-133.

Teski, M.
1981 Environment, Crime and the Elderly. in D. Lester (Ed.). The Elderly Victim of Crime. Sprigfield Ill: Charles C. Thomas. pp. 45-60.

Thobaben, M. and L. Anderson
1985 Reporting Elder Abuse: It's the Law. American J. of Nursing. 85:371-3.

Timm, H.W.
1985 Eyewitness Recall and Recognition by the Elderly. Victimology. 10:425-440.

Timrots, A.D. and M.R. Rand
1987 Violent Crime by Strangers and Nonstrangers. Washington D.C.: Bureau of Justice Statistics.

Tomita, S.K.
1982 Detection and Treatment of Elderly Abuse and Neglect A Protocol for Health Care Professionals. Physical and Occupational Therapy in Geriatrics. 2:37-51.

Toseland, R.W.
1982 Fear of Crime: Who is Most Vulnerable? J. of Research in Crime and Delinquency, 10:199-209.

Tuchfarber, A. and W. Klecka
1976 Random Digit Dialing: Lowering the Cost of Victimization Surveys. Cincinnati: The Police Foundation.

Tyler, T.R.
1984 Assessing the Risk of Crime Victimization: The Integration of Personal Victimization Experience and Socially Transmitted Information. J. of Social Issues. 40:27-38.

U.S. Department of Health and Human Services
1980 Elder Abuse. Washington D.C.: Administration on Aging.

U.S. Department of Justice
1981 Crime and the Elderly. Washington D.C.: Bureau of Justice Statistics.

U.S. Department of Justice
1987 Criminal Victimization 1986. Washington D,C.: U.S. Department of Justice Bureau of Justic Statistics.

Vaux, A.
1985 Variations in Social Support Associated with Gender, Ethnicity and Age. J. of Social Issues, 41:89-110.

an Buren, D.P.
76 Public Housing Security and the Elderly: Practice Versus Theory. in J. Goldsmith and S.S. Goldsmith (Eds.). Crime and the Elderly. Lexington Mass.: D.C. Heath. pp. 153-158.

ano, E.C.
83 Victimology: An Overview. in J.I. Kosberg (Ed.). Abuse and Mistreatment of the Elderly: Causes and Interventions. Littleton Mass.: John Wright. pp. 1-18.

ineyard, D.
978 The Rediscovery of the Elderly. Society, 15:24-29.

Warr, M.
1982 The Accuracy of Public Beliefs About Crime: Further Evidence. Criminology, 20:185-204.

Warr, M.
1984 Fear of Victimization: Why are Women and Elderly More Afraid? Social Science Quarterly, 65:681-702.

Warr, M.
1985 Fear of Rape among Urban Women. Social Problems, 32:238-250.

Warr, M. and M.C. Stafford
1983 Fear of Victimization: A Look at Proximate Causes. Social Forces, 61:1033-1043.

Weinberg, J.K.
1987 Aging and Dependence: Toward a Redefinition of Autonomy. Social Casework, 68:522-532.

Williams, H. and A.M. Pate
1987 Returning to First Principles: Reducing the Fear of Crime in Newark. Crime and Delinquency, 33:53-70.

Wilson, J.Q.
1975 Thinking about Crime. New York: Basic Books.

Wilson, J.Q. and G.L. Kelling
1982 Broken Windows: The Police and Neighborhood Safety. The Atlantic Monthly, March:29-38.

Wiltz, C.J.
1982 Fear of Crime, Criminal Victimization and Elderly Blacks. Phylon, 43:283-294.

Wolf, R.S.
1986 Major Findings from Three Model Projects on Elder Abuse. in K.A. Pillemer and W.S. Wolf (Eds.). Elder Abuse: Conflict in the Family Dover Mass.: Auburn Publishing Co. pp. 218-238

Wolfgang, M.E.
1958 Patterns in Criminal Homicide. New York: Wiley.

Wortman, C.B.
1983 Coping with Victimization: Conclusions and Implications for Future Research. J. of Social Issues, 39:195-221.

Yin, P.P.
1980 Fear of Crime among the Elderly: Some Issues and Suggestions. Social Problems, 27:492-504.

Yin, P.
1982 Fear of Crime as a Problem for the Elderly. Social Problems, 30:240-245

Yin, P.
1985 Victimization of the Aged. Springfield Ill.: Charles C. Thomas.

Zdorkowski, R.T. and M.W. Galbraith
1985 An Inductive Approach to the Investigation of Elder Abuse. Ageing and Society, 5:413-429.

Zion, R.J.
1978 Reducing Crime and Fear of Crime in Downtown Cleveland. Victimology, 3:34-344.